Prosperity's Predicament

ASIA/PACIFIC/PERSPECTIVES
Series Editor: Mark Selden

Crime, Punishment, and Policing in China edited by Børge Bakken

Woman, Man, Bangkok: Love, Sex, and Popular Culture in Thailand by Scot Barmé

Making the Foreign Serve China: Managing Foreigners in the People's Republic by Anne-Marie Brady

Marketing Dictatorship: Propaganda and Thought Work in China by Anne-Marie Brady

Collaborative Nationalism: The Politics of Friendship on China's Mongolian Frontier by Uradyn E. Bulag

The Mongols at China's Edge: History and the Politics of National Unity by Uradyn E. Bulag

Transforming Asian Socialism: China and Vietnam Compared edited by Anita Chan, Benedict J. Tria Kerkvliet, and Jonathan Unger

Bound to Emancipate: Working Women and Urban Citizenship in Early Twentieth-Century China by Angelina Chin

The Search for the Beautiful Woman: A Cultural History of Japanese and Chinese Beauty by Cho Kyo

China's Great Proletarian Cultural Revolution: Master Narratives and Post-Mao Counternarratives edited by Woei Lien Chong

North China at War: The Social Ecology of Revolution, 1937–1945 edited by Feng Chongyi and David S. G. Goodman

Little Friends: Children's Film and Media Culture in China by Stephanie Hemelryk Donald

Prosperity's Predicament: Identity, Reform, and Resistance in Rural Wartime China by Isabel Brown Crook and Christina Kelley Gilmartin with Yu Xiji, edited by Gail Hershatter and Emily Honig

Beachheads: War, Peace, and Tourism in Postwar Okinawa by Gerald Figal

Gender in Motion: Divisions of Labor and Cultural Change in Late Imperial and Modern China edited by Bryna Goodman and Wendy Larson

Social and Political Change in Revolutionary China: The Taihang Base Area in the War of Resistance to Japan, 1937–1945 by David S. G. Goodman

Rice Wars in Colonial Vietnam: The Great Famine and the Viet Minh Road to Power by Geoffrey C. Gunn

Islands of Discontent: Okinawan Responses to Japanese and American Power edited by Laura Hein and Mark Selden

Masculinities in Chinese History by Bret Hinsch

Women in Early Imperial China, Second Edition by Bret Hinsch

The Rise of Tea Culture in China: The Invention of the Individual by Bret Hinsch

Chinese Civil Justice, Past and Present by Philip C. C. Huang

Local Democracy and Development: The Kerala People's Campaign for Decentralized Planning by T. M. Thomas Isaac with Richard W. Franke

Hidden Treasures: Lives of First-Generation Korean Women in Japan by Jackie J. Kim with Sonia Ryang

North Korea: Beyond Charismatic Politics by Heonik Kwon and Byung-Ho Chung

Postwar Vietnam: Dynamics of a Transforming Society edited by Hy V. Luong

From Silicon Valley to Shenzhen: Global Production and Work in the IT Industry by Boy Lüthje, Stefanie Hürtgen, Peter Pawlicki, and Martina Sproll

Resistant Islands: Okinawa Confronts Japan and the United States by Gavan McCormack and Satoko Oka Norimatsu

The Indonesian Presidency: The Shift from Personal towards Constitutional Rule by Angus McIntyre

Nationalisms of Japan: Managing and Mystifying Identity by Brian J. McVeigh

To the Diamond Mountains: A Hundred-Year Journey through China and Korea by Tessa Morris-Suzuki

To Hell and Back: The Last Train from Hiroshima by Charles Pellegrino

From Underground to Independent: Alternative Film Culture in Contemporary China edited by Paul G. Pickowicz and Yingjin Zhang

Wife or Worker? Asian Women and Migration edited by Nicola Piper and Mina Roces

Social Movements in India: Poverty, Power, and Politics edited by Raka Ray and Mary Fainsod Katzenstein

Pan Asianism: A Documentary History, Volume 1, 1850–1920 edited by Sven Saaler and Christopher W. A. Szpilman

Pan Asianism: A Documentary History, Volume 2, 1920–Present edited by Sven Saaler and Christopher W. A. Szpilman

Biology and Revolution in Twentieth-Century China by Laurence Schneider

Contentious Kwangju: The May 18th Uprising in Korea's Past and Present edited by Gi-Wook Shin and Kyong Moon Hwang

Thought Reform and China's Dangerous Classes: Reeducation, Resistance, and the People by Aminda M. Smith

When the Earth Roars: Lessons from the History of Earthquakes in Japan by Gregory Smits

Subaltern China: Rural Migrants, Media, and Cultural Practices by Wanning Sun

Japan's New Middle Class, Third Edition by Ezra F. Vogel with a chapter by Suzanne Hall Vogel, foreword by William W. Kelly

The Japanese Family in Transition: From the Professional Housewife Ideal to the Dilemmas of Choice by Suzanne Hall Vogel with Steven K. Vogel

The Korean War: An International History by Wada Haruki

The United States and China: A History from the Eighteenth Century to the Present by Dong Wang

The Inside Story of China's High-Tech Industry: Making Silicon Valley in Beijing by Yu Zhou

Prosperity's Predicament

Identity, Reform, and Resistance in Rural Wartime China

Isabel Brown Crook
and Christina Kelley Gilmartin
with Yu Xiji,
compiled and edited by
Gail Hershatter and Emily Honig

ROWMAN & LITTLEFIELD
Lanham • Boulder • New York • Toronto • Plymouth, UK

Published by Rowman & Littlefield
4501 Forbes Boulevard, Suite 200, Lanham, Maryland 20706
www.rowman.com

10 Thornbury Road, Plymouth PL6 7PP, United Kingdom

British Library Cataloguing in Publication Information Available

Library of Congress Cataloging-in-Publication Data

The hard back edition of this book was previously catalogued by the Library of Congress as follows:

Crook, Isabel.
Prosperity's predicament : Identity, reform, and resistance in rural wartime China / Isabel Brown
Crook and Christina Kelley Gilmartin with Yu Xiji ; compiled and edited by Gail Hershatter and
Emily Honig.
p. cm. -- (Asia/Pacific/perspectives)
Includes bibliographical references and index.
1. Daxing Zhen (Chongqing, China)--Social conditions--20th century. 2. Daxing Zhen (Chongqing,
China)--Economic conditions--20th century. I. Gilmartin, Christina K. II. Yu, Xiji, 1914-2006. III.
Hershatter, Gail. IV. Honig, Emily. V. Title. VI. Title: Identity, reform, and resistance in rural
wartime China.
HN740.D383C76 2014
306.0951'38--dc23
2013027919

ISBN 978-1-4422-2574-9 (cloth : alk. paper)
ISBN 978-1-4422-5277-6 (pbk. : alk. paper)
ISBN 978-1-4422-2575-6 (electronic : alk. paper)

Printed in the United States of America

To the people of Prosperity

Contents

Maps

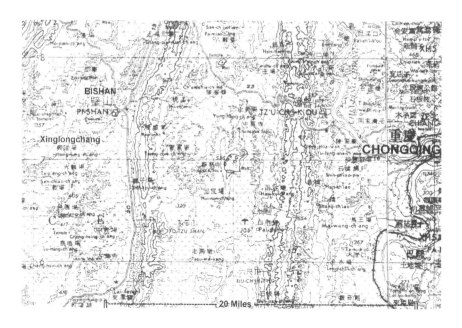

Map 1. Chongqing-Bishan-Xinglongchang (Prosperity). Republican-era map
(public domain) annotated by Michael Crook.

Maps

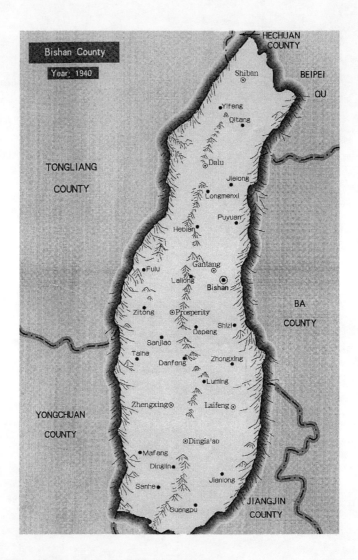

Map 2. Map of Bishan County. Refined by He Xiuyun.

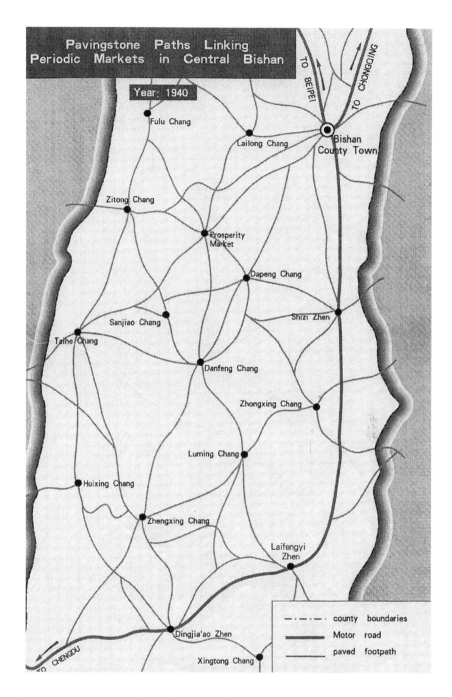

Map 3. Paving-stone paths linking periodic markets in central Bishan. From a drawing by Isabel Crook refined by He Xiuyun.

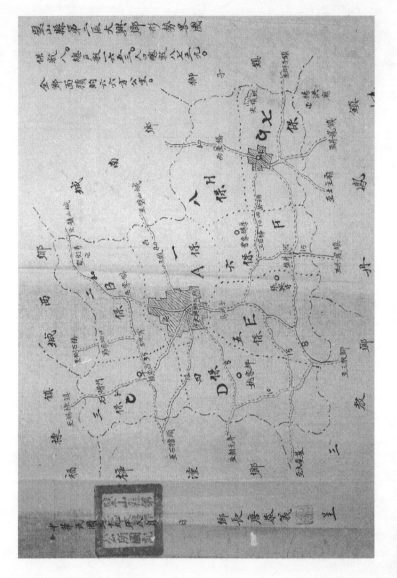

Map 4. Daxing, 1941. Caption top right reads, "Boundaries map of the Rural Township of Bishan County. There are 8 bao, 1,653 families, and a total population of 8,759. Total area: (neighborhood districts) are separated by dotted lines, numbered in Chinese, and also township office in Xinglongchang (Prosperity) is marked with a double triangle. On the Township Office, Rural Township of Daxing, the Second District of Bishan County," superimposed month of the 29th year of the Republic of China" (1941). Below the date, "Submitted by his personal seal.

Preface

Isabel Crook

This book has been long in the making. The path to publication has been more labyrinthine than the street that winds through the market village in Sichuan where I began the research over seventy years ago. A world war, graduate school, other field projects, two revolutions, a number of mass movements, and a thirty-year teaching career went by before I was able to reexamine the field data, revisit the site, and prepare a book manuscript.

It all started soon after I obtained my M.A. degree with a minor in anthropology from the University of Toronto. On my return to China, project director T. H. Sun hired me to join the staff of a rural reconstruction project sponsored by the National Christian Council (NCC) in Sichuan's Prosperity Township. I was to help carry out a major survey of Prosperity's fifteen hundred families. In rural reconstruction circles at that time, attaching a household survey to a project was a new and popular idea, one that T. H. Sun embraced with enthusiasm. The project appealed to me both in its own right and because I was looking for an opportunity to gain more anthropological experience to support an application to a doctoral program. When I arrived in the market village in the fall of 1940, I joined a team of four people—a nurse, a teacher, a sociologist, and T. H. Sun's secretary, the only male member— who had already been engaged in implementing the project for ten months. Before long, I had become good friends with Yu Xiji, the sociologist and medical social worker who, like me, had previously conducted independent field research. Like me, she had also had a Christian upbringing and had been educated in Christian colleges. Together we began the house-to-house survey in the spring of 1941.

The circumstances under which the data for this study was gathered account for both its richness and its gaps. The time was not propitious for conducting a survey. Grain levies, conscription, and press-ganging were causing acute fear and suspicion throughout the countryside. Banditry was endemic. We set out on our household visits armed with stout sticks to beat off the ubiquitous dogs that protected the scattered farm homes from thieves and bandits as well as malevolent spirits. But by this time we were seen by many as familiar, nonthreatening young women, without connections to local authorities, so the dogs were called off and we were welcomed. Even so we proceeded with caution in order not to exacerbate villagers' fears or offend their sensibilities. As well as gathering the necessary information for the survey, we pursued our own research interests, collecting every possible detail for our evolving portrait of the community and its inhabitants. In the evenings, we discussed what we had learned that day, adding each new fact or event to the careful record that ultimately provided the information on which this book is based.

When Xiji and I conducted our survey of Prosperity Township, we did so in the dual roles of researchers and reformers, part of a project whose goal was to improve the material life of local residents. We, and other project staff, did not see ourselves as outside observers but rather as part of the wave of reform and change engulfing Prosperity. Much of the impetus for change came from outside the township—with the exception of some progressive members of the local gentry—and we were both witness to and part of the struggle between outsiders and insiders. It was not uncommon for anthropologists of the time who were employed outside academia—by government or other public agencies, for example—to conduct independent investigations of their own design while carrying out research mandated by their employers. But we did not take up residence in Prosperity to observe and study the community while joining in the daily practice of its life, the usual sense of participant observation. Our work on the project put us in the more unusual situation of being affiliated with an organization that was at the research site for the express purpose of changing conditions, even as we were conducting the research. Rather than trying to fit into existing roles as a participant-observer would do, we brought new roles with us which defined the ways in which we participated in the community. We tried to offer the new services in ways that harmonized with local custom, yet our actions by definition were designed to change life in Prosperity. Hence the staff of our project briefly became minor players in a local power structure we were trying to win over to the cause of rural reconstruction. Much of what we learned about how formal and informal power was exercised in the township resulted from the project's unintentional confrontation with and eventual defeat by that local power structure.

While still in the field, Xiji and I compiled our data, planning to write up our study and submit it for publication to the *Journal of the West China Border Research Society*. In October 1941, with the survey completed, I returned to Chengdu, where I was born and where my father had served as dean of education at West China Union University. Xiji joined me there early in 1942, and together we spent several more months sifting through the materials we had gathered, focusing on extracting the quantitative information from the surveys since they needed to be returned. But before we finished our analysis, circumstances changed dramatically. Conflict in the Pacific arena of World War II intensified, the rural reconstruction project of which we were a part folded, and we had to find other employment. Xiji returned to her professional job as a medical social worker. In my case, my parents had returned to Canada, and my fiancé, David Crook, had gone to England to enlist in the Royal Air Force. I decided to follow David to England, where we were married on July 30, 1942.

During my first year in England, I volunteered for war work in a munitions workshop and joined the Canadian army. Whenever possible, I continued to analyze the Prosperity data. With a project outline in hand, I went to talk to the anthropologists Raymond Firth (then on leave from the London School of Economics to do war work) and Margaret Read of the University of London, who recommended that I submit a proposal to Kegan Paul's Sociology and Social Reconstruction series. After a meeting with Karl Mannheim, the series editor, and the promise of a foreword from Firth, I received a commitment from Routledge and Kegan Paul to publish the Prosperity study. (In his "Plan of the Library" which outlines forthcoming publications, Mannheim lists "*Hsinlung Hsiang—A Field Study in the Red Basin, West China* by Isabel Crook and Yu Hsi-chi," along with *Peasant Life in China* by Fei Hsiao-tung. The listing for our projected study can still be found in early editions of the latter book.)

After the war ended, I entered the London School of Economics Anthropology Department on a veteran's grant to work with Firth. My course work proceeded smoothly until my husband David, newly demobilized from the Royal Air Force, decided to resume his career in journalism by returning to China. I then proposed—and Firth agreed—that, rather than basing my dissertation on the Prosperity material alone, it would be useful to do a study of a second township, perhaps one with a different economic base, to compare with the Prosperity data. I decided to go back to China with David where together we would undertake a study of areas liberated by the Communist Party that party leaders hoped might serve as a sequel to Edgar Snow's 1938 *Red Star over China*.

Going to China in 1947 and visiting the liberated areas marked the beginning of my role as a participant-observer of the Chinese Communist Revolution. In many ways my work under Firth prepared me well for this new endeavor. Firth saw applied anthropology, particularly research that contributed to the formulation of development policies, as a major postwar growth area in a discipline he thought would be increasingly more focused on problems than people:

> There are signs that anthropologists will be asked to take an increasing share
> of work on practical problems, and I think we are all glad that it should be so.
> In providing background studies of social conditions, in helping to diagnose
> causes of friction or of ineffective carrying-out of programmes, in predicting
> what will probably be the results of a given measure, the anthropologist should
> be able to contribute more than he does at present. [1]

Can one be both an activist and a reliable—avoiding the more loaded adjec-
tives "objective" and "impartial"—observer? According to Firth, one could,
and furthermore, he argued, anthropologists have an obligation to contribute
to the societies they study. Commitment, he wrote, should be conducive to
the collection of reliable data because good policy is not founded on bad
research.

Not long after arriving in China, David and I began an eight-month study
of the land reform in Ten Mile Inn. We arrived in the village in November,
and in the months prior to the arrival of the land reform team in February, we
were asked to get to know the villagers so that they would be familiar with us
by the time the team's work began. To do this, we decided to interview
villagers and compile a village history. We did not use a strict set of questions but asked in an informal way about villagers' experiences during the
anti-Japanese war and the first attempt at land reform in the village, and
about our informants' personal lives. Our goal was really only to get to know
the villagers, but in the end, of course, the information we gathered turned
out to be very useful.

A small North China village of around one hundred families, Ten Mile
Inn provided a fascinating comparison with Prosperity. My stays in these two
villages were similar in that they occurred in unusual times—both during
wartime and both during periods of reform. But one reform effort was Nationalist, the other Communist—they were very different in nature. There
were other marked differences between the two villages. Prosperity, much
larger, was strongly affected by its character as a market village. On market
days, it wasn't really a village at all, but had, instead, an urban atmosphere
and liveliness. Ten Mile Inn was a farming village consisting of scattered
households, centered on its land, with only two lineages, which took on great
importance. Prosperity's many lineages contributed to community life with
lineage halls and festivals, but Ten Mile Inn's lineages stood for relationship
and commitment, ensuring that all members had the means to sustain life.
With its mixed economy, Prosperity's population lived in much more varied
financial circumstances. There were outsiders in Prosperity, people without
relatives, as well as people who had been kicked out of a lineage, and those
who had drifted away. There were greater extremes of wealth and poverty—
in Ten Mile Inn we never saw beggars or men in rags. Most of all, though,
my purpose in being in each village was quite different. In Ten Mile Inn,

through observing land reform, David and I hoped to study the revolutionary dynamic of one of the most important revolutions of the twentieth century. By the time we had completed our research, we were caught up in the life of New China, and the notion of doing a comparative study of a Nationalist and a Communist village no longer seemed relevant.

Even the Ten Mile Inn study was not easy to complete, however, because David and I were also asked to teach English at a newly established Foreign Affairs School, where we would help prepare a few dozen students for future diplomatic service. After Liberation, the school moved from Hebei to its permanent location in northwest Beijing, where it became the Beijing Foreign Languages Institute (now Beijing Foreign Studies University). Taking up a faculty post in the English department (David went on to become vice dean of the department), I began a career of teaching which was totally engrossing and included much work on reforming the curriculum, developing appropriate teaching methods for students from rural areas, and defining egalitarian relationships with students, staff, and colleagues. During this time I also continued to participate in mass movements as they came along, the most all-consuming of which, the Cultural Revolution, swept through my campus in the summer of 1966. It was impossible during all these years to take up my previous study; the field data from Prosperity stayed in a drawer until the early 1980s when I stopped teaching.

Retirement presented me with a wonderful opportunity to complete my study of this Sichuan township during the war. As well, during this period, scholarly communications were opening between China and the West in ways that provided a conducive environment for reexamining the material. I felt invigorated by the influx of Western-trained sinologists in the 1980s, some of whom were much interested in my study and provided ideas and substantial encouragement regarding how I might reconnect to work that had lain dormant for so many years. At the same time, Chinese scholarship was also becoming more vibrant, eventually leading to the revival of sociology and anthropology. Yet another motivation for me to return to the study was that I wanted to produce a work that would be useful both to my former students and to those currently enrolled in Chinese universities who were so ignorant about pre-1949 Chinese rural society.

The first step in what became a long road to completing this manuscript was a return visit to Prosperity in 1981 with Xiji, then a professor of child psychology on the faculty of the Teachers' Training College in Beipei, Sichuan.

For the next decade I worked on sifting through my notes and preparing a manuscript, often consulting with Xiji, who had by then retired to Beijing. Along the way Raymond Firth continued to give the project his critical support and encouragement. A 1992 comment of Firth's was particularly significant in view of the book's later evolution. He noted at that time that I hadn't decided whether I was writing an ethnography or a local history. It is clear now that I was writing both an ethnography *and* a local history.

By 1994 I had produced a three-volume ethnography (*Economies*, *Politics*, and *Society*) consisting of twenty-five chapters plus an epilogue, totaling 457,000 words—roughly four times as long as most scholarly monographs. This manuscript was critiqued by a number of China scholars and several editors of China series, all of whom agreed that it deserved publication, but first needed paring down and sharpening. Given the enormity of the task, I asked Chris Gilmartin—a historian whose work I admired and whose perspectives I shared—to work with me to create the new draft.

After much discussion and several trips to Prosperity (in 1997 and 1999), we decided to shift the focus from an ethnography to a historical study, organizing the ethnographic data around the concept of localism and the response to outside pressures for change. To this end, we would focus on the government and the rural reconstruction project's efforts to alter the way of life in Prosperity Township. These issues, especially the projects of our rural reconstruction team, had been more peripheral in the original draft. We also learned in 1999 that a new building was to be built for the Bishan archive and that henceforth its resources would be available to us. While we lamented the destruction of the dilapidated but beautiful old structure that had housed the archive, we realized that such a development would greatly enhance our ability to acquire more information about the government's role in the war years.

We made two more trips to Prosperity in 2001 and 2004 to gather materials and to try to learn more about daily life in the community. In this quest we were greatly aided by the children of Prosperity, for whom we set up an education fund. None of their specific life stories appear in this work, but we are beholden to them for much of what we came to understand about survival strategies of the rural poor in the early twenty-first century—augmenting, in turn, our insight into the earlier period.

Three women share involvement in this story and its telling; it is, in a profound sense, a collaborative effort. Gathering information in Prosperity would not have been possible without Xiji and me cooperating as a team. We complemented each other well. Xiji, an unconventional member of a highly placed family, was also an intensely practical, capable young woman who could turn her hand to anything. In the brief few months she had been in Prosperity prior to my arrival, she had come to know everyone and everything. Her ready acceptance of me, despite my being a foreigner—the only foreigner on the team—was what made my integration into village life possible. To Xiji, I represented a welcome addition to her social life—our other two colleagues' views on subjects of interest being by then all too familiar—as well as someone who could contribute fresh ideas and new dimensions to our work.

In later years, Xiji, who was a superb researcher, could be counted on to discover in the local archive exactly the snippet of information that Chris and I needed desperately. She would present her new data to us with glee, causing great merriment all around. A very modest person, Xiji was initially reluctant to have her name appear as a contributor to this book. In her own view, the worthwhile work she had done in her life was as a medical social worker where, in some instances, she had literally saved lives. Eventually, as she came to recognize her value to us as a researcher, she changed her mind.

As for my collaboration with Chris, it was a source of personal and intellectual delight and stimulation for us both. Chris brought to our partnership her knowledge of Chinese history, her analytical skills, and her understanding of the crucial role of analysis in contemporary scholarship. Learning from her, as she did from me, and debating these ideas so that each person's understanding is enhanced by the other's, seems to me truly the essence of collaboration.

It is a matter of great sadness to me that I am the only surviving member of our group of three collaborators. When Yu Xiji died in 2006 at the age of ninety-two, having lived long and well, it seemed appropriate to celebrate her life rather than to mourn her passing. But I have found it difficult to reconcile myself to the sudden and untimely death of Chris Gilmartin in July 2012. I would have wished her many more years of the rich, productive life she led—as scholar, teacher, colleague, wife, parent, and wonderfully kind and generous friend.

To see the book finished, because we both believed deeply in the usefulness of its content, was vitally important to both of us. On Chris's behalf and my own, I wish to extend heartfelt thanks to Gail Hershatter, Emily Honig, and Mark Selden—noted China historians with long-standing connections to Chris, to me, and to the book—for making this possible. Busy as they all are, I know that taking the time to put the manuscript into a final form so quickly and so well required substantial effort and sacrifice. I am very grateful.

My hope is that this work will serve as a baseline for future researchers. Eventually, I intend to ensure that all of my research materials and my original 1994 manuscript are made accessible to Chinese and other scholars. As a first step in this process, my field notes, translated into Chinese, were published in Beijing this January under the title 兴隆场: 抗战时期四川农民生活调查 *(1940–1942)* [Xinglong Chang: Field Notes of a Village Called Prosperity 1940–1942].

Beijing, February 2013

1. Firth, Raymond. "8. The Future of Social Anthropology." *Man*, Vol. 44 (Jan.–Feb. 1944): 21.

Acknowledgments

Isabel Crook

I would like to acknowledge the contributions made by many people during the research and writing of this book. With Chris not here to jog my memory and add her expressions of appreciation to mine, this is a partial list at best. I hope those who have been left out will attribute the oversight to circumstances and my advanced age.

Looking back over my long life, I feel immensely grateful to my Aunt Hawkesworth, whose generous gift of $500 made possible my return trip to China after my studies in Canada, and my first anthropological endeavors.

I am grateful to the National Christian Council of China for supporting the project on which this book is based and to T. H. Sun for initiating it and for hiring me. Jiang Zhi'ang and James Yen (Yan Yangchu), both well known for their rural reconstruction work at the time, were a source of inspiration. Chris and I later found Jiang Zhi'ang's studies on rural communities very useful; James Yen provided experts from his Rural Reconstruction Institute to advise our project in setting up cooperatives. Peng-Wu shi (Peng Sao), our cook, and a young farmer whose name I cannot now recall contributed to the book through their colorful daily accounts of happenings in the community.

My collaborators, and some other significant contributors, I wrote about and thanked in the preface. Among those I have not yet thanked, I would like to mention in particular Susan Rigdon, an anthropologist from the University of Illinois. Susan worked with Chris and me during our initial years of research and was extraordinarily generous with her thoughts and insights.

In Bishan, we received assistance from county head Ding Hong, as well as Sun Hongying, and we especially valued the helpfulness of the Bishan Archives and Gazetteer Office staff over many years—archives chief Yang Changqian and Gazetteer Office directors Zhang Yongxin and Luo Jun. Gazetteer editors Huang Shichuan and Zhou Qing provided much information and useful introductions to people in the community. Long Jianghou gave us his kind support as township head; he and Wu Zhimin, retired principal of the Daxing Central Primary School, made the arrangements and chose ten excellent participants for the children's education fund. Wu Zhimin also helped us understand various issues, corresponding with us between visits. A local township head in the 1940s, Sun Zhonglu briefed us on the intervening forty years of village history. Cao Hongying was a Bible school girl in 1940; she helped me revisit memories. Wang Anyi, a local Women's Federation cadre, graciously invited us to stay in her home.

Ding Xiaolei, a young Beijing scholar, accompanied us on visits and translated archival materials. Du Juan, a historian from the Yunnan Academy of Social Sciences, visited Xinglongchang and sent an excellent written report on local history and the contemporary situation. Cao Xinyu, a Beijing People's University historian, answered our queries on temple inscriptions and local religions, while Zheng Jiwei provided a list of useful readings on various topics. Pu Yao, a student from Beijing Foreign Studies University, translated difficult archival materials. Huang Wei assisted with research. He Xiuyun improved our maps, showing exactly and beautifully what we wanted portrayed. I am greatly indebted to Yang Lingjuan for her translation of many letters and documents over an extended period. Zachary Scarlett assisted Chris with research and tracked down many references for the final version. Delia Davin, Helen Young, Ellen Judd, Henrietta Harrison, Sabina Brady, and Nancy Jervis made useful comments and suggestions at various times to me or to Chris. Sandra Sachs contributed years of encouragement, discussions with Chris and me, and editing assistance.

In early years, my devoted parents nurtured my self-confidence and firmly backed my plans—even the ones they deemed impractical, such as becoming an anthropologist. My husband David (who died in 2000) and my three sons Carl, Michael, and Paul gave me unfailing love and support and, in recent years, the help with daily life logistics that made my work possible. I also thank Carl for much archival research and Michael for compiling the glossary.

I want to express my gratitude to Chris's family as well—to her husband Peter, her son Benjamin, and her daughter Beth. I was retired, but Chris added collaboration on this book to an already overcrowded schedule. I thank her family for their understanding; I hope and trust they will be pleased with the result.

Introduction

Gail Hershatter and Emily Honig[1]

THE UNUSUAL HISTORY OF *PROSPERITY'S PREDICAMENT*

This book has its origins in two unusual collaborations that between them span more than seven decades. In 1940 Isabel Brown (later Isabel Crook), the daughter of missionary educators who had grown up in west China, graduated from university in Canada and went to the market town of Prosperity, in Sichuan, to work on a township survey sponsored by the National Christian Council (NCC). It was the fourth year of the Japanese occupation of eastern China, and the Nationalist government had retreated to the west, bringing a host of reform projects and new political dynamics with them. Brown teamed up with Yu Xiji, a young Chinese social worker who had been trained at Shanghai University and the Peking Union Medical College before the war, and began a household survey of the village, interviewing members of each household about their livelihood, domestic lives, beliefs, and a host of other topics. At the same time, both young women were drawn into projects to expand schooling for local children, create a health clinic, and sponsor several cooperatives, the most important of which was intended to lower the price of salt for villagers. In the course of their work, they learned a great deal about local power holders, family relations, marketing practices, and a semi-clandestine group known as the Paoge, or Robed Brotherhood. For reasons described in the book, many of the village improvement projects foundered in the face of tensions between the Nationalist government and local power holders. The NCC team was withdrawn from Prosperity. Then Pearl Harbor was bombed, the Pacific War widened, and Isabel married David Crook and relocated to London to do wartime work there.

After the war, Isabel and David returned to China, observed the course of Communist land reform in a North China village, wrote a book about it,

1

raised a family, and taught at what is now Beijing Foreign Studies University until their retirement, weathering the vicissitudes of the Cultural Revolution and other changes. The Prosperity field notes sat in a steel box until Isabel Crook retired in the 1980s. She then used them to write a lengthy manuscript, drawing on the survey to provide a fine-grained portrait of Prosperity in 1940–1941.[2]

In the mid-1990s, at the suggestion of Mark Selden, Isabel Crook undertook a second collaboration, the preparation of a scholarly book based on the Prosperity materials. She chose as her coauthor Christina Gilmartin, a historian of the Chinese revolution and specialist in women's history who had worked for some years in Beijing and was teaching at Northeastern University. Together, they went through the original survey[3] and Crook's manuscript, discussing the significance of the findings, teasing out underlying themes, and bringing the book into conversation with contemporary scholarship on the Chinese countryside. Gilmartin also undertook substantial original research and writing, working closely with Crook in an intense relationship of discussion and debate. Together and separately, the two visited Prosperity seven times between 1981 and 2004, interviewing relatives of some of the original subjects of the village survey and observing transformations and continuities in village life in the half century since the original study. At the time of Gilmartin's death in July 2012, she was at work on final revisions of the manuscript.

The "we" of this book is thus a complex one: it generally refers to Yu Xiji and Isabel Brown in their original role as surveyors and project organizers, but behind this story is another collaboration, that of Isabel Crook and Christina Gilmartin, who together drew on the original village survey and created a multilayered ethnographic history of a rural community. We (Gail Hershatter and Emily Honig), working closely with Mark Selden and with research assistance from Zachary Scarlett, edited and assembled the final version of the manuscript, consulting with Isabel Crook and her family.

This layered nature of *Prosperity's Predicament* provides an opportunity to reflect on the nature of historical explanation more generally. When Yu and Brown conducted their initial survey, their aim was to assess village needs in order to help design programs that could address those needs. In the process, because they were such perceptive observers and because Isabel Brown kept such good records, they collected many stories of broader ethnographic interest. They were not, however, engaged in a deliberate analysis of power relations in the village, nor were they seeking to advance a particular sociological or historical argument about village dynamics. They did not choose the year 1940 for their study because it was a particular turning point in China; that was the year that the NCC sent them to Prosperity, and they just happened to be present to observe some of the difficulties that attended the Guomindang (GMD) expansion into unoccupied China. Many of the questions that animate the present volume emerged only later, because of Isabel (Brown) Crook's subsequent years of work in the People's Republic, her abiding interest in rural issues, and her conversations with Chris Gilmartin, who was herself engaged in scholarly debates about social change and the Chinese revolution. In assembling the final version of this book, we have tried to capture both the richness of the initial investigation and the years of subsequent thought that Crook and Gilmartin gave to this material. *Prosperity's Predicament* is a historical analysis built upon an extraordinary archive of field notes. It is not organized around a single theme, but precisely because of its expansive scope and close attention to individual stories, it powerfully conveys a range of contested issues that were played out in Prosperity and, with important variations, across wartime rural China.

NATIONAL EVENTS AND LOCAL RURAL LIFE

Prosperity's Predicament examines how a rural Sichuanese community responded to the state-building drives of the Nationalist government and the rural reconstruction agendas of Christian and secular reformers at the beginning of the 1940s, when China was at war with Japan and much of the national territory was under occupation by Japanese forces.

At once an ethnography and a microhistory, this study considers the interplay between localism, reform, and resistance in the rural hinterland community of Prosperity (Xinglongchang) in order to explore the material and mental universe of Chinese rural communities situated in what was then called Free China, outside the Communist base areas and Japanese-occupied territory. *Prosperity's Predicament* offers a comprehensive account of village life in a time of Japanese invasion and political dislocation, including the launching and failure of reform initiatives under the aegis of the Guomindang-led national government and the National Christian Council, observations about relationships within families and among neighbors, and portraits of opium smuggling, gambling, health practices, and religious life. Prosperity was a village profoundly dependent upon the market, but its most influential families derived their power from landholding, and the book pays particular attention to how these local power holders responded to, and frequently stymied, state- and reformer-sponsored development schemes. It makes visible the enormous disjuncture between the realities of rural life and state modernizing agendas. It carefully charts the often clumsy and misguided efforts of government and rural reconstruction reformers from the perspective of local residents who ultimately failed to experience much relief from the multitude of painful predicaments plaguing their families and community. Despite the glaring failures of this rural reform effort, from the vantage point of the early twenty-first century, it is evident that this wartime encounter marked an important early step in the reshaping of daily life in rural Sichuan as well as in the integration of this hinterland into the modern Chinese nation-state. Some members of the local elite were attracted to the modernizing agenda of the Guomindang, even as others sought to rework that agenda for their own ends. Initiatives by state and church organizations in education, public health, and marriage reform anticipated the much more comprehensive rural programs undertaken by the Communist Party state as a national priority after 1949. At the same time, the ambivalent and complex response by the local community, particularly its elites, suggests the depth of the challenges that would be faced by the Communists as they sought to establish a presence and lead a revolution in villages such as Prosperity.

Prosperity's Predicament consists of two main parts. The four chapters of part I, "Insiders," provide a detailed account of life in Prosperity. This is not a picture of a static community awaiting outside intervention: the town had long been linked to the wider world in numerous ways. Well before the 1940s this region of Sichuan, just over forty miles from Chongqing, had been settled by successive waves of immigrants, altered by the introduction of New World crops, militarized after the 1911 Revolution, visited by missionaries from the early twentieth century, and incompletely incorporated by the Nationalists, who began to introduce programs in this area in 1935 after a period of warlord control. This first section focuses on internal dynamics and social relations among Prosperity's residents. Chapter 1 centers on what Crook and Gilmartin call "the market way of life,"[4] examining local marketing patterns in the light of other village studies and of G. William Skinner's account of Chinese marketing systems drawing on his own Sichuan research. Prosperity's role as a market town was central to shaping the livelihood of individual households, their relationship to surrounding communities, and the intersection of Prosperity's fate with the wider chaotic politics of Sichuan during the warlord era (1910s–1920s) and the years leading up to the Japanese invasion of 1937.[5] Crook and Gilmartin complement Skinner's work by focusing on the long-term processes of human labor that shaped the market town and its expansion over recent centuries. They offer a particularly rich account of how the market had come to dominate rhythms of community activity—social and religious as well as economic—by the 1940s, even as Prosperity was drawn ever closer into the economic nexus of an expansive Chongqing. Chapter 2, "Living Off the Land: Farm Labor," offers an account of ordinary farming families and the daily practices of farming. Increases in population were met by intensified cultivation until no patch of land was untended by men, women, and children, even as much of the population lived on the brink of food insecurity. Chapter 3, "Not Far Afield: Family Survival Strategies," expands the story of rural livelihood to explore villagers' involvement in the market and how it enabled them to make ends meet, and the effects of this demographic pressure and political chaos on local livelihood.

Women played a particularly prominent role in small-scale market production of all sorts. In the market settlement and its environs, the rich did not always stay rich, and occasionally a poor family moved up a rung or two. But for the most part, farming families were involved in an arduous struggle for survival in a hostile economic environment that witnessed sharp downward mobility for many residents. Chapter 4, "Lineages, Landlords, and the Local Body Politic," turns to the relatively well-off residents of the village, landlords and members of prominent lineages, examining how elite behavior was changing in the aftermath of the warlord years. A key feature of Prosperity's elite was the emergence of retired military men as members of a small coterie of powerful landlords: men who were not much bound by earlier notions of elite propriety, and whose control of an extortionate share of the rice crop positioned them to profit from market manipulations that benefited them while disadvantaging Prosperity's less affluent residents. Chapter 5, "The Paoge and Informal Power," looks at a newer form of local power in which landlords participated: the Paoge, or Robed Brotherhood, through which some elements of the village elite made common cause with less prosperous residents to control opium and other aspects of village economic life. The Paoge were ideally positioned to mediate disputes, profit from transactions of all types, and block reforms that threatened their interests, as part II explores in detail.

The five chapters of part II, "Outsiders," focus on the period following the outbreak of war with Japan and the large influx of "downriver people" into Sichuan and Prosperity. In 1937, Japanese invaders drove the Nationalist government from its capital in Nanjing up the Yangzi River to the hinterland province of Sichuan in China's west, far removed from the coastal areas that had been the primary locus of the Nationalists. The seat of the Chinese government was reestablished in the city of Chongqing, and Prosperity suddenly found itself in the immediate hinterland of China's wartime capital. Chongqing served as the center of the "Great Rear" (*dahoufang*) from which Nationalist authorities directed their war operations against the Japanese. Finding itself in an area that had never been brought completely under central control in the prewar years, the Nationalist government also tried to pacify warlords, suppress banditry, and gain control over the opium trade. The short arm of the government, which had been irrelevant to local concerns when the Nationalists had been based in faraway Nanjing, was now long enough to reach Prosperity.

It was not only the government that was seeking to establish its presence nearby. An estimated fifty million Chinese fled to the interior during the War of Resistance, with the province of Sichuan absorbing the bulk of all refugees. By 1941, the population of Chongqing had more than doubled from what it had been six or seven years earlier. Among these "foreign Chinese" and downriver people were leaders and foot soldiers from some of China's most progressive and reform-minded movements, who brought with them new ideas for promoting economic and government reform, education, and science. They included James Yen (Yan Yangchu), a Sichuan native, founder and head of the Mass Education Movement (MEM); the educator Liang Shuming; the leaders of the industrial cooperative movement; and many foreign and Chinese Christians who had established international reputations building rural reconstruction programs in coastal areas and now transplanted them to inland Sichuan. Among the latter were the leadership of the Shanghai-based National Christian Council, the faculty and student bodies of four Christian colleges, and many other highly educated Chinese Christians employed by church-sponsored agricultural missions and cooperatives. These reformers often worked in collaboration with officials overseeing Nationalist government programs for rural development and governmental reform. Like Yen and Liang, many of the reformers were looking for sites at which to relocate programs they had been operating before the occupation, and for a short period the region from Chengdu to Chongqing became a great laboratory for agricultural and rural reform.

Because of the wartime situation, people who might not normally have cooperated—governmental and nongovernmental reformers—were thrown together under circumstances that virtually compelled them to join forces to modernize rural society, broaden its productive capacity and tax base, and mobilize local people for the war effort. In spite of their efforts, introducing thoroughgoing reform into Prosperity was difficult and ultimately unsuccessful. This section delineates and reflects upon the reasons for this failure. Among them was the contradiction between the state's reform agenda and its imperative to tax and conscript its citizens, hated measures that directly undermined the reforms. Perhaps just as important, many reforms, including those of both the Guomindang and church organizations, challenged local power holders. Even those reforms that did not, such as initiatives in education and health care, were inconsistently implemented by a wartime government under duress that found itself unable to establish a consistent program or a stable presence in rural communities. Chapter 6, "Wartime Reformers," looks at the ways these two reform forces situated themselves in the community, dealt with its local power holders, and initiated their agendas, particularly for educational reform. Some of the state reforms of local governance— rearranging administrative jurisdiction and changing township heads—were met with distaste by Prosperity's residents. Other initiatives, such as the literacy drive, were unfunded mandates designed with no attention to the practical requirements of extending them across the community. Initiatives undertaken by the NCC, particularly in the domain of education, enjoyed limited success when they dovetailed with state initiatives. Chapter 7, "Taking Health Care Public," surveys village health practices and the preliminary attempt of the national government to modify them, then describes how a local clinic established by the NCC made initial steps to transform local health practices. A state inoculation campaign achieved some results, and the NCC's clinic garnered some support, especially among women, but the vast majority of local medical needs continued to be addressed by folk healers, diviners, and shamans. Chapter 8, "Marriage: Reformed and Unreformed," analyzes several state initiatives aimed at transforming gender relations and family roles in rural society, as well as older practices through which villagers negotiated marriage and divorce. The state's Marriage Law, which granted women the right to divorce in a way that foreshadowed the 1950 Marriage Law of the People's Republic, remained a distant abstraction, far less important than local negotiations between families about the marriages of their children. A modern education and other new attributes, however, enhanced the local marriageability of some young people. Meanwhile, the poor practiced their own vernacular form of divorce. Runaway wives simply left an unsatisfactory or abusive marriage and found another spouse, with the family of the new husband paying compensation to the old one in a set of locally recognized transactions that had nothing to do with the state. Chapter 9, "Of Money and Men," turns to two areas of friction between the state and local communities: taxation and conscription. More than any other factors, the state's need to extract revenue and men to support the war alienated the Guomindang from the local population. Here lies perhaps the central contradiction that plagued the Guomindang's reform agenda, which was always subordinate to its goals of strengthening the army and siphoning off resources to the state. Indeed, Brown and Yu were greeted so warmly by villagers precisely because, as young women, they were understood to have absolutely no connection to a state apparatus that people feared and sought to avoid. Chapter 10, "Trial of Strength," analyzes the state's failed efforts to eliminate opium smuggling and gambling, even as local elites who controlled these activities succeeded in shifting culpability to their less powerful dealers and runners. This chapter concludes with a dramatic account of how a state-backed NCC initiative to establish a salt cooperative fell victim to local power machinations orchestrated by a powerful member of the Paoge who feared that it would impinge upon his financial interests.

OUTSIDERS AND PROSPERITY'S PREDICAMENT

The state—and even, to a lesser extent, Christian reformers backed by international missionary organizations—entered Prosperity with far more muscle than a lone shopkeeper or trader. They also presented a different degree of threat to the status quo. Nonlocal merchants might be a threat to trade in a specific commodity or the wealth of a local family, but they did not come to change the rules of the game as Nationalist and Christian reformers did.

Laws on taxation, land rents, the opium and salt trade, and standardization of weights and measures, for example, directly threatened market operations and land ownership practices, as did the producers' and consumers' cooperatives sponsored by both church and state.

Nationalist and Christian reformers entered the locality with different stances toward existing communities. Many Nationalist reformers were committed to weakening the local sensibility that obligations and commitments within the community had to be placed above demands from without. The Nationalist government in the early 1940s was trying to replace local leaders who served as township officials precisely because their primary commitments were not to the state, the war effort, or any of the higher levels of administration that were siphoning off local resources for military and state-building purposes. In the urgency of wartime and in the desperate political struggle to maintain control of the state, the Nationalist government, despite its rhetoric, was more likely to see the competition between the locality and the state as a zero-sum game.

Christian rural workers, in contrast, focused on the positive role that market-demarcated communities could play in winning converts and instituting their reforms. Evangelical work in Prosperity was begun by Annie Wells, an American stationed in Chongqing, in 1908. She was succeeded by another American, Orvia Proctor. But by the time Brown and Yu undertook their survey for the National Christian Council, the emphasis of local missionary activity had shifted almost completely to the "social gospel" of identifying and seeking to fulfill material community needs. Both foreign and Chinese Christians routinely spoke of "natural villages" and of natural communities formed by clusters of villages. Certainly most Christian reformers, including those not sympathetic toward the government, shared the goal of nation building, but their own work concentrated on helping and strengthening the village, the local community, and the home.

Government attempts to introduce change were generally ineffective, not least because the top-down methods favored by the state provoked local resistance. More fundamentally, the Nationalist government had an internally contradictory agenda: to modernize administration and improve the livelihood of peasants on the one hand, and to extract soldiers and taxes from the limited territory they controlled on the other. The NCC, for its part, was full of enthusiastic and dedicated workers, but it lacked resources and had no control over the larger economic, political, and security environment. The NCC was most effective when it could build on initiatives sponsored by the Nationalist government, as it did in attempting to develop schools and clinics.

Both forces, however, were ultimately stymied by local power holders, who proved wily and resourceful in hijacking government and NCC initiatives, blocking efforts to install outsiders as township heads, and sabotaging the formation of a salt cooperative that would have cut into their profits. Prosperity was not an insular community, but it was one that resisted incursions by outsiders. Its predicament was not that of an ancient place that resisted being dragged into the modern world. Rather, it was the predicament of a community coping with a fragile socioeconomic system, now confronted with demands for rapid and deep reform that threatened both the local power structure and its delicate balance of survival strategies. Local men of influence who defended the Prosperity market against the state and other outside interests did not act with the community as a whole in mind, nor did preservation of their own predominance bring any benefits to most residents of the market settlement. But ordinary farmers, as well, had reason to resist the outsiders who proposed to tax their precarious incomes and conscript their sons. Prosperity's people were not averse to change that benefited them, but they had cause to be suspicious of strangers offering something they claimed was better than local social arrangements.

Some changes introduced during this period, such as the promulgation of a Nationalist-sponsored marriage law and reform campaign, prefigured initiatives that would later be taken up more successfully by the government of the People's Republic. *Prosperity's Predicament* provides a look at the difficulties of this pre-1949 process, its limited successes, and the resistance by a local nexus of power that would eventually, after 1949, confront much more determined attempts to transform it. The difficulties of this first close encounter with a nearby national center of state power prefigures the intricacy, and the difficulties, faced by the post-1949 state as it sought to alter local social relationships, decrease precarity, and extract enough surplus from the rural areas to help fund socialist industrialization. *Prosperity's Predicament* also suggests that farmers do not always benefit from reforms undertaken in their name.

ETHNOGRAPHIC HISTORY

Prosperity's Predicament combines rich ethnographic observation with sensitivity to broader historical forces at play in rural Sichuan in the war years. Isabel Brown began the ethnographic data collection used in this study at a remarkable moment in the 1940s. Among the sixty thousand downriver people pouring into the mountainous county of Bishan during the war was an experimental Christian rural reconstruction team under the sponsorship of the NCC and the Methodist Episcopal Church (Church of Christ) that had chosen the market community of Prosperity as its site of operations. The first members of the five-person team arrived in Prosperity in early 1940 at a time when it was already beginning to experience the effects of outsiders in its midst. Military conscription, forced labor, and grain levies were placing a crushing burden on farm families, and within a few months this pressure would be increased with the assault of the Nationalist government on local power structures and its attempt to expand its revenue base. At the same time, the rural reconstruction team quickly introduced social initiatives, including a rural health clinic, a kindergarten, and an embroidery cooperative. The man who inaugurated this project, T. H. Sun, had studied at Cornell University, served as a former secretary of the NCC, and worked with James Yen's Mass Education Movement. He believed that the socioeconomic data collected by his team would facilitate one of the project's most difficult goals—the establishment of a salt cooperative—as well as assist certain medical and educational initiatives already under way. His ultimate objective, however, was to raise the status of the church in Prosperity by tackling the problem of poverty. In his estimation, an accurate picture of rural conditions in Prosperity required that all fifteen hundred of its families living in the township be surveyed.

It was at this time that Isabel Brown teamed up with Yu Xiji and began a house-to-house survey of the village, interviewing members of each of the fifteen hundred households. The fieldwork covered one year, from autumn 1940 to autumn 1941. The core of the research for this book is drawn from the wide range of data collected about the community by Brown and Yu during 1940 and 1941. The copious field notes assembled at that time contain interviews with local informants from throughout the township; records of conversations with marketers, local township leaders, some districtwide administrators of the Methodist Church, and a few local residents who had been employed by the team to provide housekeeping services; and the observations of team members, including two cooperative experts affiliated with James Yen's Rural Reconstruction Institute who were loaned to the Prosperity team for six months. These notes provide a resource on many aspects of daily life, including people's practices and concerns, as well as a chronicle of happenings in Prosperity market village during these two years. A complete write-up of these field notes will be posted at http://www.isabelcrook.com.

The quantitative data collected in this house-to-house survey provide an important account of social structure and material life in Prosperity. This data is the basis for this book's description of the demographic and economic characteristics of Prosperity, including family composition, distribution of men of military age, educational level, land ownership, terms of tenure, mortgage agreements, and principal sideline productions. The class and age structure of the population was also recorded, revealing the uncontestable existence of fairly widespread infanticide and marked social stratification. Statistical data on the size of farms, the amount of land tenancy, sources of farm incomes, and the various types of sideline occupations undertaken by farming families provide valuable insight into the extent of rural poverty and the ways in which ecological pressures stemming from the ratio of population to resources fed the expansion of the nonfarm economy.

This ethnographic data also contains another form of primary source material: translations from inscriptions and records from the locality that are no longer extant. These include inscriptions usually located in Confucian temples about the founding of various periodic markets in Bishan, their origins, and their operations over the last few centuries. Translations from articles in the local Bishan newspaper were also included in these field notes, as were comments on a draft copy of the Nationalist government's census of 1941 that the rural reconstruction team was able to acquire.

By choosing to set up its residences and office in the church compound which was located on the main street, the team was well positioned to observe day-to-day happenings, particularly those connected with the periodic market, when peasants would come in from the outlying areas to sell and buy food and necessary daily items. Over time, the team created solid contacts with many marketers, especially middle-aged women who liked to drop by the project office on market days because there was no other place for them to linger afterward, as it was not considered proper for women to socialize in public. They were glad to have a place where they could sit and rest, drink hot water, and chat. Before long, the office became a type of women's teahouse. By the time the team undertook its survey of the fifteen hundred families in the locality between January and May of 1941, it found that many living in the outlying villages were more receptive to their inquiries, precisely because they had already become well known in the community during the previous year.

The team also chose to begin each interview with a long informal chat in order to establish rapport and a sense of trust before asking for more sensitive statistical information. This approach ultimately yielded much knowledge about people's practices and mentalities. Showing interest in a sick member of the household, for instance, might yield information on concepts of illness and their causes, the nature of the unseen world, and the reputations of various local doctors. These unstructured interviews also prompted discussions about people's sorrows, joys, and hardships as well as the daily dramas of village life with its public quarrels and mediations. Villagers explained to the interviewers their shifting understandings of the power struggles among local power brokers, the illegal and legal exploits of the Paoge, and the local government's efforts to suppress banditry.

Nowhere else in China had women conducted such an ambitious survey, and the fact that they were women helped them gain access to uncensored family dynamics. On the few occasions when Brown and Yu did their interviewing accompanied by men—the former township head and co-op activist Sun Zhonglu, and several young men who were co-op organizers from a neighboring community—they noticed that the men used much more direct and authoritative methods of questioning the villagers, taking little time to establish rapport and maintaining an impersonal demeanor. Villagers, in turn, became somewhat taciturn and guarded. When Brown and Yu called on people in their homes, however, they noticed that the conversations were natural and unforced. Isabel Crook recalls that by the 1940s foreigners were no novelty in Prosperity, and that women had been evangelizing for the church there since 1908. The fact that Brown and Yu were young women was also an advantage; no one regarded them as threatening. Crook recalls that sometimes "we spent more time on gossip than we did on the questions. . . . Also, Xiji was part of the secret. She was remarkable. She was known to be very competent and had assisted villagers with her medical knowledge." While the survey provides part of the basis of this book, much material comes from a journal of day-to-day events in the community as Brown and Yu observed, participated in, or were told about them.

By trekking up to the homesteads in the hills, the rural reconstruction team was able to make contact with segments of the community that might otherwise have remained invisible. They were able to better chart patterns of poverty that might have been missed by researchers who remained in core areas. The poorest in Prosperity lived in mud hovels on upland farms, making themselves as inconspicuous as possible, afraid of running into officials, being press-ganged, or otherwise put upon by those with more power. Some remained elusive in Brown and Yu's survey, particularly those who were engaged in seasonal banditry or part of pauperized families that had already disintegrated. But they might well show up in the data collected on the community as relatives or employees, either domestics or farm laborers.

In some respects the data collected by Brown and Yu compare favorably to the Nationalist government census of 1941, which happened to come into the possession of the rural reconstruction team. When this census document was checked with the results of the NCC house-to-house survey, it was found to be flawed, particularly in areas of concern to local residents. For instance, most families did not want to admit to the existence of members of conscription age, claiming to have only very young or very old males residing at home. The unreliability of Prosperity's township census was so egregious that it was rejected by the Bishan County government and sent back for corrections.

When Christina Gilmartin began to work with Isabel (Brown) Crook in the mid-1990s, they submitted the information assembled by the research team in 1940–1941 to an intensive examination, cross-checking it with local gazetteers and government documents from the Bishan County Archives, the Chongqing Municipal Archives, the Sichuan Provincial Archives, and the No. 2 National Archives in Nanjing. With the help of Susan Rigdon, who also worked on the project for several years, they read extensively in the missionary archives in the United States, particularly at Yale Divinity School and Houghton Library at Harvard University.

Prosperity's Predicament speaks to at least six different ongoing discussions among China historians. The first has to do with rural studies. Writing in the wake of G. William Skinner's work on markets,[6] Prasenjit Duara's on the cultural nexus of power,[7] and important pre-1949 rural surveys and village studies by John Lossing Buck, Fei Xiaotong, Sidney Gamble, Martin Yang, C. K. Yang,[8] and others, it describes the persistent effort and incessant human labor that brought market communities and their many institutions into being. It enumerates conditions that were important to their growth, such as late imperial resettlement policies, but also suggests that the Republican-era operations of state and local power, especially militarized power, increasingly disadvantaged the poor.

Second, looking at the studies of Sichuan by Robert Kapp, Robert Entenmann, Gregory Ruf,[9] Joshua Howard, Danke Li, and others, as well as works on the wartime period in China more generally by Stephen MacKinnon and by Diana Lary,[10] it focuses upon the regional and historical particularities of Sichuan—an area of great change in the Ming–Qing transition, the 1911 Revolution, the warlord period, and the wartime period in which it was the heart of the "Great Rear." This reminds us that China in the twentieth century had many histories and that we cannot project outward from the circumstances of a single coastal city or an interior Communist base area to generalize about the whole.

Third, in the wake of several decades of reassessment of the GMD,[11] the book looks closely at the effectiveness of GMD efforts to enlist the countryside (directly through conscription, military control, and taxes, and more generally through various welfare and uplift projects) in the business of state making and nation building. The Nationalists had an ambitious agenda in the Chinese countryside, but scholarship to date has paid little attention to the actual process of its extension into rural society. *Prosperity's Predicament* allows us a window into the daily difficulties and internal contradictions of this state project.

Fourth, the accounts of secular and church-sponsored reform complement the studies of reformers such as James Yen (by Charles Hayford) and Liang Shuming (by Guy Alitto).[12] *Prosperity's Predicament* is enriched here by firsthand participant observation and by a cooler reappraisal at a distance of some decades from the original events.

Fifth, it suggests that the efforts of the GMD and other reformers to reconfigure the countryside, and the particular shape of rural resistance to those projects, might help us understand what did and did not work for the Communists when they took up some of these many state-building and extractive projects themselves after 1949. In particular, the Communists established an ongoing presence in each village, dismantled local property interests and the Paoge, undertook major mobilizations—and still chose to defer many of their initiatives, such as implementation of the Marriage Law, when they met local resistance. In bringing together ethnographic detail, state policy, and church-sponsored rural reform, this book enables us to see each one differently, and to see daily human activity as the key to whether big initiatives worked or (more often) failed.

And finally, in keeping with Crook's and Yu's 1940s experiences as young women researchers, and with Gilmartin's lifetime of work as a scholar, the book explores how gender was important in social and political life in wartime Sichuan. Women were the majority of hired farm laborers in Prosperity, except during the height of the rice harvest. Their handicraft production for the market kept many families afloat. Landlord wives often managed their estates while the husbands passed their days in teahouses, gambling and making deals. Women were nowhere visible in the ranks of the Paoge, but they did run many of their opium dens. Among the church reformers and local Christians alike, women played a prominent role as purveyors and consumers of literacy training, vocational programs, and clinics. Their individual actions in ending marriages—by unceremoniously leaving—constitute a set of marriage practices that has gone virtually unnoticed in previous accounts of rural China.

Originally, Isabel Crook and Chris Gilmartin planned to write an epilogue providing an overview of developments in Prosperity since the Communist revolution, highlighting how everyday life in the community was reshaped. They wanted to know whether a community coextensive with a market still existed, given the demise of some of its key elements, including the Paoge, the underground economy, and, for a time, the periodic market. They hoped to explain which elements in the old survival strategies became anachronistic, even illegal, and how such changes affected the social dynamic in Prosperity. They wondered whether the politico-administrative unit of the township and the commune and the strictures on rural markets in the collective era had eradicated identity within the market community. And in the subsequent era of commodification, decollectivization, and global marketing, they wanted to investigate what had happened to the primacy of the local market and to the market area as a community of producers, buyers, and sellers. During their visits to Prosperity in the 1990s and early 2000s, they observed the unfolding of a process that had begun in the 1940s: the rise of Chongqing as a major metropolis. Eventually the city and its hinterland, including Prosperity, separated from the province of Sichuan and became a centrally administered municipality, the largest in China—but one whose majority population still lives outside the urban core. Bishan County today is part of the rural support area for Chongqing, affected in major ways by the rise of the city.

In their visits to Prosperity, Crook and Gilmartin reestablished substantial relationships in the community, along the way creating a foundation to help keep local children in school. But the epilogue that they planned to write could not be completed for this book. It remains for others to take up the predicaments of Prosperity's recent history.

NOTES

1. This introduction draws on material initially assembled and analyzed by Isabel Crook and Christina Gilmartin, as well as on research by Susan Rigdon.

2. The manuscript has been published in Chinese as Yi Baisha [Isabel Crook] and Yu Xiji 2012. As noted later in this introduction, the English version will be made available at http://www.isabelcrook.com.

3. The original questionnaires were returned to the NCC offices in Chongqing in 1942. When Yu Xiji tried to locate them in the 1980s, she was told that most likely they had been destroyed in the 1950s as useless pieces of paper.

4. The idea of a way of life associated with a market stems from the works of C. K. Yang (1954) and Skinner (2001) but has also been used effectively by Ralph A. Thaxton Jr. (1996, p. 12).

5. In 1940 the marketing community of Prosperity (Xinglongchang) roughly overlapped with the township of Prosperity (Xinglongxiang). Although Prosperity Market had no fixed boundaries in the way that the township did, it was a distinct entity. In Prosperity, it was the marketing area, not the township, which set community boundaries and gave a sense of place to residents. The market was the center of socioeconomic life, whereas the township was strongly associated with the extractive capacity of the state—military conscription, taxation, and corvée. Township boundaries, while having official status, did not stay fixed: in fact a reorganization of units at the county level and below was under way while the rural reconstruction team was working in Prosperity. New markets did arise over time, when the growth of settlements and population made it impossible for a periodic market to meet demand, but the losses were mainly from the outlying areas and the boundaries of market areas did not change as often as township boundaries. This occurred on the southwestern fringe of the Prosperity marketing environs in 1915 when the periodic market of Sanjiao was established. This development, however, only slightly altered the general marketing area of Prosperity Market that had been functioning since the early nineteenth century. Thus, while we use "locality" to include both the township and the standard market area contained within it, we use "community" to refer to the area served by the market and the way of life supported by it.

6. Skinner (2001). Our description of Prosperity Market lends support to Skinner's observations, made just eight years after the first phase of this research was completed, about how market areas structured space and linked standard periodic markets to one another horizontally, and through a vertical hierarchy to county and provincial market towns. The periodic market ordered time as well, with its big and little market days held in a cycle tied to the agricultural season, which itself can be seen in segments of that other principal organizer of time, the lunar year. Our association of community with marketing area is close to Skinner's conception, but we do not follow his original argument that it was also a discrete culture unit by claiming that the way of life was bounded by and unique to the market area. We are making the more simple observation that the periodic market was the main catalyst for social interaction because, for the majority of Prosperity's people who lived at the edge of subsistence and who were poorly integrated into civil institutions, the market was an essential instrument in their survival strategies. The periodic market was the primary place for the bartering or exchange of goods and services; negotiating loans, land sales, and rentals; mediating disputes; and initiating searches for marriage partners. Community feeling and social relationships outside the family revolved around the commercial life of the market, not around a political or civic identity with the state, of which the township was the nearest representative unit.

7. Duara (1988).

8. Buck (1964); Fei (1945); Gamble (1968); M. Yang (1945); C. K. Yang (1944).

9. Kapp (1973); Entenmann (1982); Ruf (1998).

10. Howard (2004); Li (2010); Barnes (2012); Lary and MacKinnon (2001); MacKinnon (2008); Lary (2010).

11. See, among many others, Kirby (1990); Strauss (1998).

12. Hayford (1990); Alitto (1979).

I

Insiders

Chapter One

The Market Way of Life

On most days, Prosperity's market village, with its small population of eighty-two families, appeared to be a place of little consequence. Lacking much vitality, it seemed to epitomize the monotony of rural life. Usually only a few people could be seen milling around its one narrow paving-stone street, which extended through the village in a twisting fashion around the rising knolls. Even Heling's general store, the most popular shop in the village because it offered a wide variety of goods and services, normally had only a few customers at a time. One young Canadian woman who visited Prosperity in 1941 observed that "you come upon the most repulsive village street imaginable—it's a pigpen and a garbage dump, with pools of ill-smelling stagnant water. Before a church, the village needs a sanitation squad." She was particularly struck by the marked contrast between the market village and the surrounding countryside of "cedar-crested hillocks and staircases of crescent rice paddies" that she had observed on her lovely two-hour walk from Bishan County town.[1]

On market days, however, this lackluster village became a bustling hub filled with the clamor of innumerable business transactions along its thronged street. Soon after sunrise a steady stream of local traders and farmers trekked in from the neighboring hamlets and single farmsteads to offer and consume a wide assortment of goods, agricultural produce, and services. Their ranks were augmented by a few outsiders, peddlers who covered three or four market villages in the valley and itinerant traders who specialized in goods from near and far. Convening every three to four days,[2] at its peak after the rice harvest this periodic market attracted as many as four hundred buyers and sellers who would crowd into the small street, completely overwhelming the village and creating an ongoing hubbub as farming men and women jostled their way through the mob. The people and activities associated with Prosperity's periodic market—especially the deal making, conflict-resolution sessions, and teahouse socializing—transformed the sleepy village into a momentary town or even an ephemeral city.[3]

To someone unfamiliar with rural China in the 1930s and 1940s, these sporadic markets that mushroomed for a few hours every three to five days in many rural communities might have appeared to be disconnected from the main organizations, customs, and patterns of daily life. This first chapter builds upon the pathbreaking study of rural China's periodic markets by G. William Skinner, as well as the local studies by C. K. Yang and Sidney Gamble, to examine the forces that shaped and maintained the marketing community of Prosperity.[4] The chapter uses a local approach to bring out the unique features of Sichuan's "*chang*," which, as commercial villages, were quite distinct from the farming villages (often called *zhuang* or *cun*) that served as sites for small periodic markets in other regions of China.[5] In so doing, the chapter shows the centrality of Prosperity's periodic market activities in fostering strong community structures and sentiments among the almost fifteen hundred families living within its catchment area of some twenty square kilometers.[6] On market day, this street along with its teahouses and restaurants became a public stage where residents interacted in ways that created a powerful sense of entrepreneurial vitality, social intimacy, and local identity.

MAKING PROSPERITY INTO A PLACE

The periodic market in Prosperity that we encountered in 1940 was only a little more than one hundred years old, but our investigations revealed that its origins stretched back almost two hundred years. Although the process of establishing and maintaining grassroots periodic markets like the one in Prosperity was affected by demographic and geographic factors, a close examination of Prosperity's development brings to light the significance of sustained human activity. Creating and sustaining a fixed periodic market required an immense investment of local resources, as well as the deployment of strategies to establish a presence that attracted both buyers and sellers while also stimulating trust. The market community that resulted from these efforts drew scattered rural neighborhoods together into a dense commercial network.[7]

Prosperity emerged as part of a major upsurge of standard periodic markets in Bishan County during the Qing dynasty (1644–1911).[8] The county itself dated back to the Tang dynasty, having been established in 757.[9] It was a rectangular area with mountain ranges on each side, known during the War of Resistance to Japan as the "throat of Chongqing" because it was strategically located where the two highways linking Chongqing and the rest of the province met. One of the smallest counties in China, full of roaming deer, Bishan's population grew slowly, perhaps because it was not traversed by a river. Several times the county was broken up as an administrative unit and wholly or partially adjoined to its more famous neighboring county of Baxian. It was only in the Qing dynasty that Bishan was reconstituted, after the traumatic upheavals of the mid-seventeenth century associated with the demise of the Ming dynasty and the Manchu conquest of southwest China. [10]

In the early Qing, with imperial encouragement and incentives, many new settlers arrived in Bishan from Huguang (the present-day provinces of Hubei and Hunan). This was part of a broader migration in which, as a popular saying had it, "Huguang filled up Sichuan" (*Huguang tian Sichuan*). [11] Compared to stable populations elsewhere in China that could trace their lineages back well over a thousand years, the residents of Bishan County during the wartime era were relative newcomers, having lived there for only ten to twelve generations. As they filled up the county, some settled in a subvalley separated from Bishan County town by the Maolai Hills, which gradually rose to a peak suggesting a dragon with its head reared up, on which stood an ancient temple dedicated to Tuzhu, the Earth God. [12] The terrain then dropped off precipitously into the subvalley, where the market village of Prosperity grew.

The Huguang newcomers who flooded into Bishan rapidly restored previous paddy fields and built new ones. While Bishan's frost-free climate was conducive to rice growing, the hilly terrain and the absence of rivers made this a challenging endeavor. The early Qing newcomers proved much more successful than previous settlers in this county because of the recent introduction of New World crops, particularly corn and sweet potatoes, but also the chili peppers (*lajiao*) that came to characterize Sichuan cuisine. As a result, upper slopes that could not be used for rice could now be cultivated with these high-yielding crops, sustaining a growing population.

Most of the rural marketing system in Bishan County was relatively new. Between 1700 and 1865, the large-scale population growth in this county stimulated an increase in the number of periodic markets from seven to twenty-five. [13] Before this growth spurt, the pioneering farmers who settled in the valley in the late seventeenth century had to trek out of the valley either to the large market in Bishan County town, twelve kilometers to the northeast (approximately two hours each way), or to Danfeng's market seven kilometers to the south. [14] Although the Danfeng market had a long history of operation that stretched back to the Song dynasty (960–1279), it could not compete with Bishan as a seller's market, but offered less expensive prices on its goods for buyers.

The first market established in this subvalley during the Qing dynasty was located some ten kilometers northwest of what would become Prosperity market village. In 1740 Fulu emerged as a periodic market village on the banks of a river that flowed down from the Great Mountains marking the western border of Bishan County and the northern point of this subvalley. Forty years later, the growth in population and economic activity sparked the revitalization of Zitong periodic market, a few kilometers south of Fulu. Originally founded in the Ming dynasty, it went dormant during the devastation in the early seventeenth century, eventually resuming operation in 1780.[15]

As the population increased during succeeding decades, the possibility for sustaining more periodic markets arose. Some 7.6 kilometers east of Zitong and some 10 kilometers southeast of Fulu, a rest stop was created in the first half of the eighteenth century at a fork in the road (*yakou*) where wayfarers paused from their journeys, just before ascending Maolai Hill. Often a fork in the road was chosen as a suitable place for starting a commercial venture in this vast rural landscape, as it could benefit from the convergence of traffic from three directions, which in this case were Zitong market village, Danfeng market village, and Bishan County town. Site selection usually entailed identifying a propitious natural feature, which in this case was a huge banyan tree, a few hundred meters from where a brook fell from a rocky ledge into a sixty-foot cataract. Banyan trees had the dual benefit of providing an expansive canopy blocking the intense Sichuan sun and of possessing auspicious place-making qualities according to the laws of *fengshui*.[16]

Yet another significant reason for this choice was its proximity to the estates of two well-established local farming families living nearby—the Suns and the Zhongs—who were the main financial backers of this development scheme. By donating the land and the labor for the construction of this rest stop, they were well situated to benefit from its commercial development. The gradual transformation of the rest stop into a market village over the next century owed much to the conscious and systematic efforts of these influential families. They accomplished this by developing a commercial center that could serve as a conducive locale for a periodic market, building up a strong clientele for the market among the neighboring rural neighborhoods, and creating transportation links to facilitate vertical trade between this emerging local market and the county town, which maintained strong trade links with other towns and cities, particularly Chongqing.

According to local records, this plan started to take shape in 1750 when a few shops were built near the inn, turning the rest spot into a little trading center (*yaodian*). Farmers in the area traded produce at this site, but the trade did not involve the export or import of grains, meats, or goods.[17] After four decades of operation, the heads of the Sun and Zhong lineages were sufficiently satisfied with the level of business conducted in this place that they decided to finance the construction of five new shops. As the design of both sets of shops included living space in the rear, this type of commercial development promoted a growth in the residential population of this trading center, which was slowly becoming a village.[18]

Local residents also recognized the need to expand the reach of this incipient market in order to facilitate vertical trade, particularly the export of their commercial produce to the towns and cities of Sichuan. In 1790, they funded the construction of a network of paving-stone paths over the hills in order to facilitate transportation between their developing market and Bishan County town. These footpaths encouraged merchants and peddlers to make their way to this market through the undulating clay terrain even in rainy weather by trudging along the cobbled roads up and down innumerable flights of steps, passing through fittingly named places such as Flight of Three Hundred Steps, Foot of Wang Family Cliff, or High Cave. Because of the hills and dales, no wheeled vehicles could traverse this topography, so these stone-paved paths were indispensable for motivating the sellers and buyers to move goods in and out of this new market with baskets, carrying poles, or litters.

To instill confidence in the integrity of this financial undertaking, the small core of market developers, with the Suns taking the lead, contributed land and funds for the construction of a small temple that was built in 1770 under the religious auspices of the well-regarded Caoyuansi, a nearby Buddhist sanctuary.[19] In 1791, the village temple was considerably enlarged with the contribution of three shop fronts from the Suns and two from the Zhongs, evidence of increased prosperity. In addition to serving as a place of worship, this temple housed stone and clay tablets that recorded all the donations contributed by local families for the development of the village. Starting with the first tablet in 1769 that venerated the initial gift of the Suns and the Zhongs, this temple assumed the function of a local historical archive. Clay tablets of a later date commemorated the names of those who had gained merit through support of community projects. When the community was afflicted by certain epidemics in the early nineteenth century, the temple responded by enshrining the relevant deities: a cow deity (Niuwang) after an epidemic of disease among water buffaloes, and a deity of good eyesight (Yanguang Shengmu) after a spate of eye troubles.[20] The temple assumed yet a third role in the village when quarrels erupted in the market over transactions, prompting the village elders to ask the temple's priests to henceforth take charge of all measurements, for which they would receive 1 percent of each transaction. The forging of this connection between religion and commerce proved so successful that the community leaders felt confident in 1830 to proclaim that this trading center was now of the caliber to be considered a full-fledged *chang*, a periodic market, which was given the hopeful name of Prosperity Village Market (Xinglongchang).

The establishment of Prosperity's periodic market required that it be convened on a fixed schedule that was determined by the leading elders in the community.[21] In choosing one of four possible schedules used in this part of Bishan, they needed to consider how Prosperity's timetable would mesh with those of the nearby markets in order to maximize its participation within this well-designed system. Their decision to select the 3,6,9 timetable, meaning that its market met on the third, sixth, ninth, thirteenth, sixteenth, nineteenth, twenty-third, and twenty-sixth days of the lunar month, coordinated well with the schedules of Fulu (a 2,5,8 schedule) and Zitong (a 1,4,7 schedule).[22]

The main reason that it was important to synchronize these periodic market schedules, as William Skinner has argued, was in order to facilitate the import and export trade that flowed between the periodic market villages and the higher-level market towns in the area.[23] Although the periodic market was primarily an occasion for local rural residents to buy and sell products among themselves, it was the itinerant merchants and peddlers who forged the links between the periodic markets in this valley and larger markets in Bishan County town, and to a lesser extent with the two towns south of Prosperity—Dingjia'ao and Laifeng—that were on the main road between Chongqing and Chengdu. When the market in Prosperity's village became standardized, it became part of the economic base that funneled goods into what William Skinner has termed the "district marketing area"—in this case, Bishan County seat—and culminated in the "central marketing area," which for this area of Sichuan Province was primarily the city of Chongqing.[24]

Proclaiming a periodic market in Prosperity in 1830 marked the beginning of a new phase of maintenance that posed difficult challenges. Over the next 110 years, Prosperity's powerful families had to work hard to keep their market village competitive with possible rival upstarts in the vicinity, while also coping with the economic decline and political fragmentation accompanying the demise of the imperial state and the rise of warlordism in Sichuan in the 1910s. The number of periodic markets in Bishan County continued to grow in the last decades of the Qing dynasty, reaching thirty-seven by the 1890s and forty-one by the outbreak of World War II in Asia.[25] Two of these markets began to nibble away part of Prosperity's catchment area, one to the southeast which took the name of Dapeng and one on the southwest corner of this subvalley that assumed the name of Sanjiao.[26] The extent to which Prosperity was able to withstand this competition and preserve the integrity of its market during the difficult warlord era is unclear. However, the floundering and demise of some Sichuanese standard marketplaces during the troubled Republican era suggests that local communities needed to exploit all opportunities to sustain and if possible enhance the drawing power of their markets.[27]

The strength of Prosperity's periodic market to shape its community was to a large extent based on the fact that its rural settlements were dispersed. The hamlets were small, perhaps several dozen in all, and they were clustered together fairly tightly without any main street. Often nestled on hillocks among the paddy fields or hugging the hillsides, these hamlets had pictu-resque names such as Double Pines (*shuangbai*), Water Gully (*shuigou*), Boat Shaped (*chuanxing*), Sacred Lamp (*shengdeng*), Arched Bridge (*gong-qiao*), and Lion (*shizi*). These hamlets each supported a local shrine usually placed on a nearby road. In some places a few dispersed farms would share a shrine that was located on a connecting path in their vicinity. These small shrines, typically a meter high with a curving roof over a small enclosure, were occupied by clay images of the local earth god, his spouse, and numer-ous infants. We counted seventy-nine of these shrines dotting the countryside in Prosperity, an indication of the important unifying force they played in these small neighborhoods. However, these groupings of related families never grew into distinct villages controlled by one lineage and lacked the resources to compete with the periodic market. While the historical records are inadequate for developing a coherent picture of Prosperity's strategies, the ethnographic materials we collected in 1940 reveal much about the type of infrastructure that was built in the village to attract customers on market day.

THE MARKET VILLAGE IN 1940

Our rural reconstruction team first observed Prosperity's market village after making our way from Bishan County town to Prosperity in January of 1940 on foot along flagstone paths that wound between paddy fields. Walking was the only way for anyone to travel to and from Prosperity village, as there was no motor road. During the two-hour hike from Bishan County town, there was often a trickle of traffic of men and women with wicker carrying-baskets on their backs, and porters swinging along under the weight of loads slung from each end of a shoulder pole. This trickle became a stream if we came close to a farmers' market in session. After walking for several kilometers in a southwesterly direction, we began a gradual ascent between terraced paddy fields and dry fields. Finally paddies yielded to unirrigated upland fields, and scattered outcroppings of red sandstone soon introduced a touch of barren-ness that was absent in the lush countryside around Bishan County town. An hour's walk brought us to the crest of Maolai Hill, which presented a broad vista stretching for several kilometers in every direction of Prosperity's shim-mering rice fields, its large estate houses with their watchtowers, some scat-tered hamlets, and its more densely settled market village.

Viewed from Maolai Hill, Prosperity's market village in 1940 appeared as a small jumble of dark gray-tiled roofs surrounded by a dilapidated mud wall and a watchtower that had been built as protection against marauding bandits and soldiers during the unsettled warlord times of the late 1910s. The size of the village had expanded considerably, with seventy-one buildings lining its one narrow, crooked cobbled street of 226 meters.[28] The tile-roofed, lathe-and-plaster-walled long narrow village structures were fronted by wood panels that were shuttered at night and removed in the daytime, opening the insides of these houses to the gaze of passersby. The impressive banyan tree mentioned in the historical records was still alive at one end of the village street, with another banyan located near the other end. The most impressive building was the village temple, which was now called a Confucian temple (Wenmiao), a change that probably occurred during the anti-superstition campaigns of the Republican era in order to be acceptable to the Nationalist government.[29] As in many villages in this era, at the opposite end of the street stood the military temple (Wumiao), dedicated to the martial deity Guan Gong.[30] In contrast to the sense of well-being and dignity conveyed by these two temples and some of the quaint houses and shops, unambiguous indications of poverty were also apparent. Two-thirds of the homes belonged to landless working people: widows who did manual labor or ran street stalls; men who worked as peddlers or casual laborers; and young men who earned their livings as guards in the village militia, as stalwarts in the Robed Brothers (Paoge) described later in this chapter, or through gambling. The poorest residents dwelled in squalid mat-partitioned tenements, and one made her home in a lean-to erected against the temple wall.

The market village, we soon realized, was a safe haven for women at both ends of the economic spectrum.[31] In Prosperity's marketing village, both destitute women and those with some means were able to forge a life without depending on an adult male. One-fifth of the owners of property on the street were widows who had presumably inherited their businesses and residences from their deceased husbands and served as family heads. In addition, the stall keepers on the street were mostly women. With the exception of one tenant couple, they came to the village in straitened circumstances after their families had fragmented. Renting living space in a village tenement, each morning they set up their stalls in front of the premises and packed them up each evening. The elderly widow Hu occupied the lean-to against the temple wall, while other women had dependents who were young or disabled, such as the young widow Xiang-Tian shi[32] whose tenant husband had died in prison, leaving her with two youngsters, or the widow Wang Daniang, aged fifty, whose son was almost blind and unable to do more than peddle chopsticks, spoons, and bowls in the immediate vicinity, or the widow Wu-Cao shi, whose teenage sons were dying of tuberculosis and could only contribute to the family income intermittently by carrying coal. Collectively, these women contributed greatly to the commercial vitality of Prosperity Market Village.

No single landlord or lineage dominated the real estate in Prosperity's market village. Although the Zhongs had invested heavily in the founding of this commercial hub, they did not own even one shop or dwelling on the paving-stone street in 1940. The other founding lineage of Prosperity's village, the Suns, only held a few properties even though their homestead and ancestral hall stood close by. Sun Chuanwu, for instance, owned a pastry shop (No. 16), while the nephew and niece of Sun Zhongyao's mother owned businesses on the street. The fragmentation of lineage corporate holdings was also indicated by the nine properties on the street that were owned by various lineages, some of which were rented out in order to raise funds for the annual ancestral grave-sweeping ritual in the spring.[33] Among the thirty-five families and lineage organizations that owned property in the village, only those surnamed Cao maintained a noticeable presence. Cao Yuexian, the largest landowner in the community, owned the clubhouse, and a distant relative through marriage, Cao-Wei shi, owned the largest teahouse. Cao-Wei shi had been widowed at the age of thirty-five when her husband was killed by bandits in 1930 while he was on a business trip. The teahouse on the street provided sufficient rent to support her and her twelve-year-old son, who lived in the small rooms behind the teahouse. The Cao Lineage Ancestral Worship Society also owned the second-largest teahouse in Prosperity Market Village, using the rent to cover its Ancestor Worship Festival (*Qingming*) activities. Plainly, the richest landlord in the community and his lineage, to say nothing of the other major landlords and lineages in Prosperity, did not see village property as a lucrative investment opportunity.

A distinct feature of Prosperity's market village was its strong commercial orientation. Unlike most periodic market villages in North China, in Prosperity no farmsteads could be found amidst the buildings, more than half of which were used for serving food or drink, while only one-third of its structures were purely residential. The market village had six restaurants, three noodle cafes, six wineshops, five teahouses, and two inns. In addition, refreshment counters had been set up in front of various houses to serve home brew, snacks, or confections to customers who stood about or sat on small stools in the street as they ate. Another indication of Prosperity's commercial character was the existence of eleven retail shops that dealt in medicine, meat, spirits and wine, sugar, salt, or general goods, such as matches, soap, candles, tea, or firecrackers. In addition, four workshops that retailed their own output were located in this commercial hub—two oil presses, a flour mill with a noodle-making annex, and a shop producing funerary objects. (See figure 1.1.)

Some of these enterprises, such as Yang Heling's general store, played a key role in maintaining the economic vitality of this market village. Since moving from Zitong in 1922, Yang Heling had diversified his wares during his successful rise from an apprentice in a funerary shop to the owner of a general store. One of his most popular products was a taffy candy wrapped in red packaging (*hongbao*) that had the name of his shop printed on it. Practically everyone who needed to cement a social relationship by presenting a

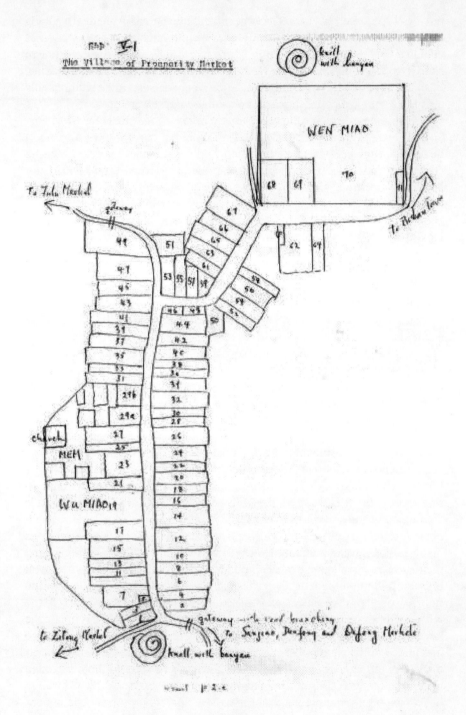

Figure 1.1. Diagram of Prosperity Market Village

gift would stop by his store to pick up a box of this brand-named taffy. Yang Heling scored another coup when he arranged to have his store function as the local post office, for which he was paid eighteen yuan a month. Although almost nobody in the community used these services except Cao Yuexian, who came in to get his newspaper subscription, the post office sign hanging outside of Yang Heling's shop lent it an aura of importance.[34]

The five teahouses and, to a lesser extent, the six restaurants attracted a highly diversified clientele. They provided a public space where people (primarily men) could spend time picking up the local news, pursuing leisure activities, making contacts, negotiating contracts, and arbitrating disputes. Among the teahouses, Wang Mingxuan's was the most popular if you wanted to play a good game of mahjong; catch up on the local village, county, or provincial news; or smoke some opium.[35] If you wanted a good meal, then it was best to stop by Sheng Huaqing's restaurant and inn. The food he served had recently improved dramatically as a result of his marriage to a woman weaver from the well-established Zhong family, which was known for their good cooks. After a wedding, her brothers would come in and cook up a great meal for his customers. While eating, drinking, smoking, or sipping tea, the clientele at these establishments conducted much of the economic and political business of the community.

It soon became apparent to us that Wang's teahouse and another one run by Feng Qingyun had a dual purpose of serving as lodges for two different orders of the Paoge, often translated as the Robed Brothers, a local variant of the better-known Gelaohui society. This society provided protection services to merchants and peddlers, since those engaged in trade and travel, whether prosperous or poor, needed patronage in order to function effectively in an environment of lawlessness and endemic banditry. Having evolved from a clandestine secret society in late imperial China, the Paoge became ubiquitous in urban and rural Sichuan during the warlord era and, as chapter 5 will make clear, often served as an alternative source of local authority to the government. The various lodges established their headquarters in local teahouses which they termed "ports," where they kept themselves well informed on happenings in the community, the county, or even farther afield; served their members; mediated quarrels; promoted their various business ventures; and entertained their guests, including members traveling through the area on business. In so doing, these teahouses added to the commercial vitality of the village and its periodic market. Yet another important function of the Paoge lodges was to protect the market village from bandits, who not that long ago had raided the businesses and residences at will. Whereas the local government was in charge of maintaining security, the Paoge had more effective resources for protecting the market village from lawless elements.

For outsiders, the market village was an entry point for penetrating the community. The American Methodist Episcopal Mission (AMEM), which had begun its proselytizing work in Sichuan at the end of the nineteenth century, quickly realized the strategic importance of basing their rural operations in market villages.[36] The mission that came to Prosperity was able to claim its first Christian convert in 1904. When a few more members joined, the mission rented a shop in the village as a gospel hall, and before long American women missionaries began conducting twice-yearly Bible school sessions for women and girls. After more than twenty years, a sufficiently large number of converts justified the building of a substantial Western-style Methodist church and parsonage in the market village near the Wumiao, on land donated by a local Christian convert. These alien structures were not visible from the street but rather were hidden behind a row of shuttered shops that were part of the church compound. Moreover, no steeple topped with a cross reached for the sky behind these stores on the street, as Methodists disdained such adornment of their places of worship. We were not able to determine whether this inconspicuous placement of the church in 1928 had been by accident or design, but the net result was that the Chinese design of Prosperity's market village was not disrupted by a foreign architectural structure.[37] At the same time, the church and parsonage enhanced the prestige of the market village, especially as no other rural community in this part of Bishan besides Fulu was similarly endowed. Among other activities conducted by the church, its literacy work for girls, directed particularly at the daughters of landlord and merchant families, pleased the members of the local elite.

The last authoritative organization to establish a presence in Prosperity's market village was the provincial government headed by Liu Xiang, which in 1930 declared that the marketing community of Prosperity should henceforth be a township (*zhen*), with its administrative boundaries corresponding to the catchment area of Prosperity's periodic market. Then, in 1935, a local government office was set up on the premises of the Confucian temple. In order to facilitate communication with the county government more than two hours away by foot, a telephone was installed. But when the telephone broke in 1938, no attempt was made to restore service, a subtle indication that the township government, headed by a member of the local elite, was not particularly interested in facilitating the transmission of orders from above. What the community did appreciate about the presence of this local government office was its positive impact on attracting more customers to the periodic market. The establishment of the township government considerably multiplied the services that could be accessed when attending the market. Farmers who needed to pay a specific tax or talk to the township head about a dispute with a neighbor would usually come on market day to make a few purchases or sales in the periodic market on the same trip.

THE MARKETING EXPERIENCE

On market day mornings, the broad array of produce and commodities that were set out along the street and the hundreds of transactions that occurred during the course of the morning demonstrated the economic importance of the periodic market to the members of this community.[38] The market varied in size depending on the season: smaller during the harvest, bigger just prior to the Lunar New Year. Much of the activity involved large-scale traders who came in from outside. The bustle of the marketing day was not limited to a few hours of buying and selling but included a broad range of activities that enhanced the power of Prosperity's market to attract a clientele.

Market day in Prosperity started before dawn and continued until late in the evening. Soon after sunrise local farmers set out for the market, trodding the dirt paths that wound down the hills and alongside the rice paddies and carrying small amounts of agricultural produce—rice, vegetables, eggs, or fowl. Usually they transported just enough to raise the cash for whatever they needed that day: salt, oil, matches, straw sandals, iron tool parts, or the services of a craftsman. Arriving on the narrow crooked street in Prosperity village, they encountered itinerant and local traders, peddlers, merchants, butchers, and barbers who brought with them a wide assortment of goods and produce, including rice, eggs, fresh vegetables, salt, vinegar, matches, and herbal medicines.

At day's start, sales in agricultural produce dominated the scene, for until the farmers had cash in hand they could not make their purchases. Weather-beaten farming men and women in blue gowns and white turbans jostled their way through the mob carrying bamboo woven baskets filled with produce. Here and there some poorly dressed men and a few ragged young lads could be seen lugging around heavy baskets of coal. The size of the crowds coming to this periodic market varied considerably by season. After the autumn harvest, the market experienced its busiest time, with as many as one family in five from within Prosperity sending one of its members. Another peak period occurred after the wheat harvest in late spring. To consolidate business in slack farm seasons (especially in early spring and summer), one market day in every ten was designated as "big," with the result that it attracted enough business to make attendance seem worthwhile to a considerable number of outside merchants and consumers.

Although the overall appearance of this periodic market seemed somewhat chaotic, in fact spatial arrangements in the marketplace were well established and carefully observed by the sellers. On the street the twenty to thirty coal, charcoal, and kindling porters set down their loads of fuel in the open sports ground opposite the Confucian temple. A small vacant lot at a nearby turn in the curving street was reserved for the dozen or so women selling fowl or eggs, with fresh vegetables sold just beyond them. Meat vendors clustered around the local butcher shop, and crockery peddlers congregated near the home of the local potter. The remaining stretch of the market street was occupied by the peddlers of manufactured goods and those offering services, including thirteen barbers, the geomancer and fortune-tellers, and a specialist in removing moles, who was particularly skillful in attracting customers by calling attention to fateful moles on their faces that would bring bad luck to them.

The courtyard of the Confucian temple was reserved for one of the most important financial transactions in the market—the selling and buying of rice. The temple not only supplied a spacious and somewhat secluded area for rice transactions, but it also provided its priests to perform the services agreed upon in 1830 and continued more than a century later. Using a two-step procedure, they measured the grain in order to provide a sense of fairness in rice transactions in this periodic market. After the seller had heaped up the measuring box with grain, the priest used his hand to round it off slightly, with the seller keeping the excess. Then the priest swept his hand across the box a second time to level off the grain. This time he kept the excess, which was expected to amount to one percent of the sale, while the buyer took what was in the box.

The buyers coming to do business in the market were mostly from the farms within an hour's walk of the market village. Unlike in the delta areas of Guangdong and Jiangsu, where producers studied by C. K. Yang and Fei Xiaotong relied on boat agents to vend their goods, in Prosperity farmers represented themselves in the marketplace.[39] Their entrepreneurial skills were on display as they engaged in a horizontal trade that was geared to the minutest transactions in produce, goods, and services, enabling the vast majority of inhabitants to make use of the market's facilities. Those with no money but with some small amount of produce, service, or labor could exchange them for the money required to meet some need. In so doing, they strengthened the economic integration of the community and its links to neighboring rural communities.

An important dimension of this horizontal trade was that some local peddlers and merchants did not just sell in one market but rather took advantage of the interlocking market days of neighboring villages within an hour or so of their homes. In addition to agricultural produce, this trade involved homespun yarn and native cloth, including some that had been dyed blue with indigo, cooking and lighting oil, coal, bricks, tiles, pottery, lime, timber, furniture, farm tools, rain hats, sandals, coffins, and funerary objects.

A second function of Prosperity's periodic market was its import-export trade. Despite being off the beaten path, this periodic market strengthened the economic integration of Prosperity and other rural areas with the towns and cities. This trade was mostly handled by itinerant peddlers and merchants. Depending on their line of wares, some would cover a larger circuit than just the subvalley. This was particularly true if their commodity was town manufactured, as it would be necessary to visit Bishan County town to replenish their stocks two or three times in a ten-day circuit. The most important of the imported items traders brought to Prosperity were salt and sugar. Salt production was a government monopoly, but distribution was left in private hands. Five local men and seven or eight traders from nearby townships peddled salt and sugar each market day. Other products that were imported into Prosperity's periodic market included matches, woks, towels, stockings, machine-spun cotton yarn, peanuts, scissors, tobacco, and some medicinal herbs.

While the import trade was left largely in the hands of peddlers, the export transactions were primarily handled by merchants from the town of Bishan, though a few of Prosperity's well-off merchants also participated in this trade. The main products taken out of Prosperity's periodic market were rice, live pigs to be butchered in Bishan, alcohol, and pig bristles. Bargaining in the rice market was extremely acrimonious, an indication of the importance of this transaction in comparison to other commodities. In this wartime period of rapid inflation, no investment was as profitable as rice. Hence landlords had every incentive to keep their wealth tied up in their rice, and every farmer parted with it reluctantly. There were even cases where people were willing to hold on to their precious grain and risk spoilage by moisture or consumption by the village's omnipresent rats rather than selling before the prices went up. The longer a farmer could hold the rice in good condition, the higher the price. Dealers knew that anyone offering rice before the prices had gone up must be in need of cash, so they drove a hard bargain.

The progression of activities throughout the market day best reveals the ways in which its economic services were closely intertwined with social, cultural, and political life. Most purchases were completed by mid-morning, at which point many of the farming men and most women departed. As those remaining began to pack the open-fronted teahouses, restaurants, noodle cafes, and wineshops, where they gathered to eat, drink, socialize, and conduct business, the next phase of the market day activities began. Market day provided the right atmosphere for raising credit, arranging deals, buying and selling land, negotiating rent, brokering, and consulting a doctor, diviner, or geomancer. It was also a suitable time to resolve a dispute with a neighbor or relative or even an intrafamily quarrel by hashing it out in the street where the crowd could serve as mediators. A more formal business or legal problem could be submitted to arbitration (*jiangli*) in a teahouse, or if it involved an unfair tax assessment or an illegal conscription, it could be taken to the township office.

Entertainment was another feature of this part of the market day. Sometimes amateurs of the Paoge music club performed snatches of popular Sichuan opera. More often a table of mahjong attracted onlookers, especially if the players included a smartly dressed woman from Bishan, strangers speaking in downriver accents and wearing foreign-looking clothes, or secret society guests from important lodges. At this point in the day three groups would still be found in the market: moderately well-off landlords or merchants, idle younger sons of well-off farmers who had money for stakes, and a coterie of personable young men, stalwarts of the Paoge, who lived by their wits and were always available to make up the numbers at the gaming table.

By evening, mahjong had been replaced by *paijiu*, a simple game of chance that was the most popular form of gambling. As evening approached, Commander Cai of the dominant lodge of the Paoge would give the word for the game to begin. Street urchins then hurried along the street hailing gamblers from the restaurants and teahouses to the temple courtyard where tables had been set up by the monks. Here, under the light of flickering torches, gambling went on late into the night. In a single evening, thousands of yuan might be lost or won, especially if one of the county's famous professionals honored Prosperity with a visit and drove up the stakes. Such gambling brought a feverish quality to the market day, at times extending it to dawn. The players were aware of the risks, since in their lifetimes *paijiu* had brought ruin to a fair number of local landowners.

SOCIABILITY, INFORMATION, AND INTIMACY

The market day turned Prosperity's village into a public platform for producing connections, identities, and sentiments among residents living within this twenty-square-kilometer area. The social connectedness that developed through the market day experience did not necessarily engender an emotional closeness, but it did produce an intimate understanding of people's lives. As William Skinner has pointed out, seeing the same people week after week in the marketplace engendered a strong sense of social familiarity.[40] For many, it was the main way to broaden one's social connections beyond relatives and neighbors. People deepened their bonds with acquaintances in the marketplace through repeated exchanges year after year about topics ranging from national news to the personal tragedies afflicting certain families in the community. Market-goers picked up information about the personal details of others' lives by overhearing conversations in the street and by watching what was going on outside and inside the teahouses or the township office. The concept that eavesdropping was intrusive did not exist here, as listening in was a way of life.

As Prosperity in 1940 was a community in which most residents possessed little if any knowledge of the written language, it was the periodic market that functioned as the key site in the community for circulating useful information, a Sichuan pastime that was referred to as *bai longmenzhen*, sometimes glossed as "gossip."[41] Although colorful gossip was certainly a sizable component of *bai longmenzhen*, it also encompassed much more serious matters, including provincial and county politics, market information, corruption, bandit raids, local disputes, people's health issues, and any local occurrence that seemed out of the ordinary. The salient characteristic was that the stories had to be lively, even dramatic, and their telling had to include more than two people. A piece of information about someone's new illness would be spiced up by adding the interpretation that the local diviner had given about its causes. In this process of passing on stories through numerous small-group conversations, people constructed narratives that reaffirmed the shared interests and values of the community.[42] Through repeated attendance, people living in the environs of this market center came to identify as a member of the community and to feel a sense of attachment to the place.

For many in the community, picking up local news mainly occurred in the process of buying and selling produce or goods in the periodic market. The types of news that normally circulated through this information grid included intimate details about family squabbles and health matters as well as news about community affairs such as bandit raids, press-gangings, and corruption. Local merchants and itinerant traders always brought detailed, timely market information from other places in Sichuan and Guizhou as well as news of recent happenings in Bishan County town. Then there were the continuous updates on social and political events in Chongqing and Chengdu, as well as war news. Market news and political information was always highly desired by men as they bought and sold goods in the morning, got their hair cut, gossiped in a leisurely fashion in the teahouses, and perhaps later joined a card game. Married women—unmarried women were socially excluded from attending the periodic market—did their marketing very quickly and then either returned home or looked for relatives or friends so that they could catch up on the latest personal news or listen to a diviner's assessment of someone's health issues. Any passerby might look in at the doctor's open-fronted clinic where he was diagnosing or treating a patient. A mass of information was generated, with everyone who attended returning home with some news and views—true or false, meaningful or trivial, encouraging or disturbing.

The news circulating in the market also drifted back into the outlying hamlets and scattered farmhouses by way of the peddlers on their sales circuits. The day after attending Prosperity's periodic market, rural peddlers set out on either a larger or smaller circuit, depending on their lines of wares. Whether they were heading off to another market village in the subvalley, to Bishan County town to restock, or to vend their wares from farmhouse to farmhouse, these peddlers carried a full repertoire of the latest stories they had picked up in Prosperity Market Village or on their circuits. In addition, those bound for rural destinations were often also willing to take on the responsibility of serving as the eyes and ears of ordinary farmers. A mother who had agreed to have her daughter become a foster fiancée (*tongyangxi*), to be raised by the parents of her future husband, would ask a peddler neighbor to check on how the girl was being treated by her new family. A husband whose wife had run away would ask for help in locating her, either to get her back or to seek compensation from whoever had provided her with a new home.

The information passed around in the market and disseminated by peddlers and itinerant merchants was recast a number of times as it worked its way through the community. As "institutions of sociability," teahouses served as the main locus for shaping the local news.[43] Those sitting around sipping tea would rehash the stories, deciding what aspects should be emphasized and what aspects were insignificant, often skewing them along lines that were acceptable to some influential local notables among the clientele. The end product became the accepted version, as if it had received a public stamp of approval, although there were usually a few people talking among themselves who would point out some inconsistencies with this public account.

This local spin was well illustrated by a sensational account of a bandit raid on the Bishan prison that was being spread in the teahouses. On April 14, 1941, a force of thirty or so bandits from Prosperity and its immediate neighboring townships of Dapeng and Sanjiao were reputed to have made a daring raid on the makeshift county prison to free their comrades. The prison in question was not the regular one, for that had been destroyed by a Japanese bomb in July 1940, which killed some prisoners and enabled others to run away. Those who survived but failed to escape were either released or transferred to this makeshift prison in a family temple outside the city that was guarded by a force of twenty men. According to the teahouse lore, these prison guards were either killed or ran away when a sudden assault was launched on the temple-jail. The bandits then battered holes in the walls, cutting the prisoners' chains with tools they had brought for this purpose, and everyone escaped.

Teahouse sources claimed that the bandits' original plan had been to release their comrades, and then the thirty raiders, having augmented their numbers with the thirty released prisoners, were to raid Prosperity market village and inflict punishment on the township government for being so zealous in cracking down on banditry and to rob the reputedly wealthy downriver Chinese staff of our rural reconstruction project. This planned raid had to be abandoned, however, when the imprisoned robbers were found to be so weak and ill from prison conditions that they had to be carried away.

A few days later the teahouses were buzzing with a new development. On the night of April 18, these bandits had decided to carry out their raid on

Prosperity market village. Leaving Sanjiao at about 10 p.m., they came upon a group of county militiamen as they approached Prosperity. As was their custom, the guards were talking and laughing loudly to make their presence known and avoid any dangerous encounters. The bandits hid in the fields and found an opportunity to ambush them. One militiaman was seriously wounded. The teahouse appraisal of the event credited the county militia with having saved Prosperity, claiming that the encounter had forced the bandits to give up their planned raid.

In evaluating this account, we found a number of embellishments and omissions. Bandits did not raid the prison to free their comrades, but rather the prisoners broke down the doors and escaped after a Japanese bombing raid on Bishan caused the prison guards to panic and flee. The county militia was sent out to round them up without success. By magnifying the prowess of the bandits, portraying them as well organized, intrepid, and ruthless while at the same time casting the militia as courageous and willing to face insuperable odds, the teahouse reports excused the government's failure to deal with the bandits, as well as banditry in general. We heard no speculation or explanation about why none of the escaped prisoners was caught, though they must certainly have been in poor physical condition and unable to travel far or fast without help. Nor did we hear why the township militia was not called upon to assist the county militia in combing the area. These omissions indicated that ordinary people dared not raise such obvious questions because they realized that the escaped men had links, personal or organizational, with local power brokers in the community. Despite these discrepancies, the accepted version of this story that was produced in one of the local teahouses elicited rapt attention whenever it was repeated to other teahouse audiences.

Some of the local stories created in Prosperity's teahouses assumed a social relevance that enabled them to circulate repeatedly. The retelling of these stories both inside and outside of the teahouses served to strengthen a sense of community in Prosperity by creating a compelling narrative of a common past, capturing a traumatic experience, or commemorating the local community's ability to survive a major ordeal.[44] We noted that many local histories recounted at this time focused on the turmoil of Sichuan's warlord period. One particularly horrifying account retold in Prosperity concerned the atrocities inflicted on the civilian population during the eight-month administration of Gu Yusan in the early 1930s. As a junior officer in Liu Xiang's Twenty-First Army, Gu had been sent with his regiment of four hundred soldiers to Fulu market village to administer this bandit-plagued subvalley. One of Gu's first actions was to eliminate his predecessor, a local man from Zitong by the name of Da Shengxian, who reputedly had made himself rich while serving as the township head by acting as a go-between and handing over the ransom to secure the release of people who had been kidnapped by bandits. Gu took the occasion of a Da family birthday celebration to set an ambush. Gu's son, on his father's instructions, was lying in wait and killed Da as he was on his way to the party. Having established himself as a force to be reckoned with, Gu adopted stern measures to eliminate banditry, arresting and beheading all suspects and causing many to flee, especially those who had enemies who might use this opportunity to seek revenge.

This reign of terror was tempered by Gu's mother who traveled all the way from her home in Renshou (near Chengdu) to voice an appeal when she learned of her son's spate of killings. By kneeling down in public and pleading with him to spare the life of a man he was about to execute, she forced him to soften his tactics. Gu's undoing occurred when he succeeded in eliminating the commander of a major bandit troop that had been harassing residents in the subvalley. Unfortunately for Gu, what should have been a major feat turned into a colossal failure, as the warlord Liu Xiang had just succeeded in recruiting this bandit troop into his army. Gu was dismissed in disgrace from his post as township head and was later reported to be pulling a rickshaw on the highway between Chongqing and Chengdu.

Prosperity's four teahouses were not only important places where men would gather to produce an authoritative interpretation of local news or a public memory of a shared history. These places also played a pivotal role in intensifying the magnetic power of the periodic market by providing a public space where men of all social rankings could interact with other members of the community, conduct market-related business, and convene mediation sessions to enforce the customary laws of the community.

Of particular interest to market-goers were the local notables who frequented the market village on market day and hung out in the teahouses. These included some of the wealthiest landlords, the township government leaders, and the teahouse owners. Socially, the long-standing ties of a settled community strengthened the bonds between the leading landlords and ordinary households. Each landlord was a familiar figure with his own personality, style, and connections. His personal life was no secret. He chatted in the teahouse, mediated disputes, perhaps lost some money at gambling, or had a quarrel with his wife, and ordinary people often felt a sense of connection to him.

Teahouse mediations were not the only vehicle for settling disputes on market days. Just as effective was the cultural practice of provoking a noisy public quarrel on the street as a way to deal with a personal problem, particularly a family dispute or a conflict with an authority figure. Noisiness was a necessary attribute since the side with the grievance had to attract attention in order to shame the offender. The public quarrel gave juniors in the hierarchy a way of defending themselves against their seniors. It enabled the weaker party in a dispute to strike the adversary by threatening his concern for "face." The public might listen passively or might intervene to end the quarrel by proposing a compromise in which both parties had to give a little, regardless of right or wrong, thereby avoiding further loss of face to the senior party. Peace rather than justice was their objective.

Typical of rancorous quarrels was one that arose over the ownership of a cat, cats being highly prized creatures in an area plagued by rats and by a cat disease that killed off all but the hardiest. Yang Mengguo had one of these hardy cats, and it gave birth to two kittens, after which it disappeared. Yang soon discovered that the cat was in the home of Yang Desheng, a powerful man in the community. As it was useless to attack a person with this much authority privately, Yang Mengguo contrived to run into him on market day on the crowded village street and in a strident voice demanded the return of his cat. A shouting match ensued. Peace was restored when a man in the crowd of the bystanders proposed that Yang Desheng should return the cat and that in return the owner should present him with one of the kittens.

The noisy public quarrel that gathered a big enough crowd could be effective even in much more serious matters. One involving the military took place on a market day just after the government had announced a fixed low price for rice. A Bishan garrison officer came to Prosperity accompanied by four or five soldiers whom he posted at each end of the village street so that no rice dealers could get away with their supplies. He then proceeded to try to buy up rice at the low fixed price. But the small local dealers all slipped into various village homes and hid their rice. When the officer found no rice in the marketplace, he pressed villagers for the names of local resident rice dealers. Finally, under pressure, someone mentioned the name of the butcher Wang Chang'an, whose miserliness made him unpopular. The officer went to Wang's home demanding rice. Under coercion, Wang agreed to sell two *dou* at the low fixed price.[45] As he was opening the door to his locked storeroom, the officer and his escorts pushed in after him and found a whole *dan*[46] of polished rice which they demanded to buy. Wang adamantly refused, declaring that there was no law prohibiting a family from having a *dan* of rice in their home. The quarrel was loud and fierce, drawing a large crowd whose sympathies were clear. The officer, shouting fearsome threats to preserve his dignity, departed with only two *dou* of rice. Following his departure, the bystanders assessed the incident and decided that the officer must have been paid by Bishan's big rice dealers to buy up stocks cheaply on their behalf. If he had come officially, he would have brought a formal letter from the Bishan County government to the township head and he would have pressed his case to a successful conclusion.

Noisy quarrels were also the required method for handling an insult. This was especially so for a woman, no matter what her social status. Any slur on her character had to be refuted publicly with noisy vituperation; failure to do so amounted to admission of wrongdoing. The result was that gossip and scandals in the community received wide publicity.

Despite its somewhat ramshackle appearance, Prosperity market village continued to attract a relatively large client base on market day. Because of the strength of its infrastructure, Prosperity had been able to meet the challenges it encountered during the turmoil of the warlord era. Prosperity's periodic market was the pivotal institution that shaped the community. Attending the market became deeply ingrained in the way of life of the area, connecting families in many significant ways and generating a strong sense of belonging to the place. Over the course of time, a number of important organizations and institutions came to be established in this market village, including two major temples, the local township government, some lineage associations, and the Paoge.

It was the periodic market, together with the highly productive techniques of intensive mixed farming, that made it possible for Prosperity's nearly fifteen hundred households to support themselves on a mere twenty square kilometers of hilly land. The extra wages and commercial outlets offered by the periodic market provided the land-short households of the community with an effective tool for trying to stave off decline and disintegration. The market's role in Prosperity was not only an economic one; it was a site of shared social life, a place where conflicts were generated and resolved, and the venue where community political struggles became most visible.

NOTES

1. Letter from Julia Brown, younger sister of Isabel Brown (February 2, 1941, after a visit to Prosperity). Julia had been raised in Chengdu, so she was not a newcomer to rural Sichuan.

2. Periodic markets in Bishan met on fixed schedules of three markets in every ten days of the thirty-day month, with three or four days between markets in a regular rotation.

3. The transformative impact of the periodic market on a village was first put forth by C. K. Yang in his study of Zouping County in Shandong (Ching-kun Yang 1944, pp. 1–3).

4. C. K. Yang (1954); Sidney Gamble (1968); G. William Skinner (2001).

5. In the nearby kingdom of Shu in early China, the original meaning of the word *chang* was a market (*shi*). *Hanyu Dazidian* [Enlarged Chinese Character Dictionary], vol. 1, p. 472, quoting the early Qing geographer Liu Xianting's (刘献廷) *Guangyang zaji* (广阳杂记), vol. 2, as follows: "In Sichuan they are called *chang*, in Yunnan they are called *jie*, in Lingnan they are called *wu*, and in Hebei they are called *ji*" (蜀谓之场, 滇谓之街, 岭南谓之务, 河北谓之集). Perhaps the fact that Skinner's initial contact with periodic markets was in Sichuan prompted him to lay more emphasis on the centralizing features of the market in his national study than was the case in other parts of China. In the almost half century since its publication, Skinner's work has sparked numerous discussions, criticisms, refinements, and debates. See, for instance, Duara (1988, p. 17); Wigen (1999, esp. pp. 1184–1185); and Skinner (1977, 721n). While Skinner emphasized the standardized features of this marketing system in order to create a national model, the present study focuses upon local variation as it expressed itself in the daily life of this community.

6. In the summer of 1940, Prosperity had 9 *bao*, 102 *jia*, and 1,497 registered households made up of 7,744 men, women, and children.

7. This historical exploration of the development of a periodic market is unique. Three classic Chinese village studies of the 1940s by Fei Xiaotong for Yunnan, C. K. Yang for Guangdong, and Martin Yang for Taitou, all described farming villages without market functions (Fei Xiaotong and Tse-I Chang 1945; C. K. Yang 1954; Martin Yang 1945). Sidney

Gamble's study of Dingixan County (1968) distinguished three types of farming villages—those with farming only, those with a periodic market as well, and those with both a periodic market and a fair; towns included those with a periodic market and those which also had a fair; and the county town administering the whole. But in much of Sichuan, instead of farming settlements taking on periodic commercial duties, these were carried on by specialized commercial settlements serving the farming community. In 1940 Bishan, there were no farming villages, but only forty small commercial villages with periodic market days, along with two towns with periodic markets and the county seat. As for the farmers, they lived in clusters of farmhouses, which were mostly perched on small hillocks while the surrounding land was terraced into rice paddies. None of these clusters resembled a village, for there were no streets but simply passageways linking the different farm homes. Architecturally, farmhouses and villages were completely different. These farm homes had courtyards, while village houses were long narrow buildings with open fronts onto the street that were boarded up each night.

Earlier studies, including those by Sidney Gamble and G. William Skinner (2001), revealed little about the historical forces that shaped the development of periodic markets outside of large towns. The elites who compiled county gazetteers had little interest in small rural communities outside of the towns. The Qing dynasty county gazetteer of Bishan County published in 1865, for instance, merely lists the twenty-five periodic markets functioning at that time and provides a county map showing their location and distance from the county town (*Bishan xianzhi*, 1992, p. 276). Our understanding of Prosperity's history is derived from carved inscriptions on stone tablets that were kept in the village temple, which among other things served as the local historical archive.

8. Sichuan sheng Bishan xianzhi (1996), p. 71.

9. Sichuan sheng Bishan xianzhi (1996), p. 11. The first people with a recorded history in this area were the Ba people, highlanders who shared Sichuan with the Shu, who occupied the rich Chengdu plain. The Shu were famed as one of the three kingdoms that flourished because of its rich agriculture, its remarkable engineering feat of the Dujiangyan irrigation works, and its extensive trade networks that stretched as far as Burma, Yunnan, and the Yellow River valley (Nylan 2001, p. 311). The Ba were a warrior people from the mountainous area beside the Yangzi River along the Three Gorges and were related to the Tujia peoples living in the mountains of Hunan and Hubei. Even though the Ba people were assimilated by the Song dynasty, some remnants of their culture remained.

10. Many of the previous inhabitants were slaughtered in the upheavals that swept through all of Sichuan at the end of the Ming dynasty. Bishan was reported to have been one of the worst affected by this widespread massacre (Entenmann 1982). On the degree of devastation, which reportedly reduced the population of Sichuan Province from five million to two million, see Van Slyke (1988, p. 64). This annihilation was so extreme that newcomers wanted to change the ideograph in the name of Bishan from "Barrier Mountain" to "Jade Mountain" in order to free themselves from the bad omens of the past and bring good fortune to the county and its people.

11. By 1750, the population of Sichuan had rebounded to nine million, subsequently tripling to twenty-seven million by 1850 (Van Slyke 1988, p. 64).

12. The peak was considered the most auspicious site in the area, and its temple was dedicated to the earth god Tuzhu, who may have been associated with the Ba people. The Tuzhu temple complex was reputed to be the oldest structure in the central part of Bishan County, having been first built on the peak of the Maolai Hills almost one thousand years earlier in the Tang dynasty. According to a local legend, this site was so auspicious that it caused two rival gods, Tuzhu and Erlang (more closely associated with the Shu), to fight over it. They agreed that the one who got there first could take possession. Tuzhu, being the more powerful, won. But Erlang was jealous and determined to destroy the place by dropping great boulders on it. As the boulders were too large for him to carry, he turned them into sheep and drove them up the hill. Since such sheep would automatically be turned back into boulders once dawn broke, the ascent had to be made swiftly. The flock had almost reached the top when Tuzhu, presaging what was happening, imitated a cock crowing, and the whole flock turned back into boulders. In his rage and frustration, Erlang threw down his staff, and this cleaved opened the earth in the ravine, now called Sicaiya, well known to anyone traveling from

Prosperity to Dapeng. The local legend of the contest between Erlang and Tuzhu can be interpreted as a reflection of the historic rivalry between the increasingly Hanicized Shu and the less developed, more ethnically distinct region of Ba, where Prosperity was located. Indeed, the Chengdu area of Sichuan, which had been part of the Shu kingdom, was dotted with Erlang temples, whereas Bishan County only had a few minor temples dedicated to the worship of Erlang. Thus, his defeat on Maolai Peak by Tuzhu arguably symbolizes the triumph of the local ancestral god against the invading god. According to local legend, the resolution of this conflict resulted in the construction of four buildings on Maolai Peak dedicated to Tuzhu rather than Erlang. His domain encompassed not only the entirety of Prosperity Township but also all the surrounding market villages on every side of the peak with their ten to twelve thousand households. Erlang and his place in Sichuan history are discussed in Hinton (2000, pp. 34–58).

Each Lunar New Year at the Dragon Festival, men, women, and children came to the Tuzhu temple with gifts to win the blessing of the god for the coming year. On that day, men and women, young and old, turned out to pray to Tuzhu and his companion deities for their own families' good fortune throughout the coming year. By 8 a.m., solid streams of thousands of men, women, and children could be seen pouring along each of the roads leading up to the temple. Many carried little wicker baskets filled with incense, candles, and cash paper. It was often the women who would pause at the various shrines along the roadways to burn incense to local deities as they passed. But once they approached the temple, the basket was handed to the man of the family to make the formal offerings to Tuzhu and his companion gods.

Since this god presided over the well-being of all the surrounding market villages, perhaps as many as forty thousand people attended the event. Absent were only the poorest farm families in the hills. But even some of these folks ventured forth, for this deity was said to be so potent that even without a gift of firecrackers or incense the visit itself would be enough to ward off evil in the coming year. Unlike ancestor worship, the worship of this senior local god was not lineage oriented or male dominated. Tuzhu was the god of the farming folk, and the farming unit encompassed the whole family, including men and women alike. For more information on Tuzhu, see Zhang Zeheng (2006).

13. The 1865 number was provided by the republished Tongzhi era (1865) Bishan Gazetteer (*Bishan xianzhi*, 1992, p. 276).

14. Danfeng was the site of the oldest market in this area of Bishan, having been established during the Song dynasty under the name of Puzichang (Sichuan sheng Bishan xianzhi, 1996, p. 72).

15. The economy of Zitong was stimulated by its proximity to the same major river that supplied Fulu as well as the lime and coal deposits its residents were able to tap in the Great Mountains. According to the Bishan Gazetteer, Zitong was the site of a periodic market in the Ming dynasty, and as such was the first one to be located in this subvalley. We assume that it must have collapsed in the chaos of the Ming–Qing transition, which explains why a tablet we translated in 1940 gives the date of 1780 for the founding of this market. Zitong was one of seven standard markets established in Bishan County in the Ming dynasty, adding substantially to the four (Laifeng, Danfeng, Puyuanzhen, and Batang) that were founded in the Song era. For a brief account of the establishment of periodic markets in Bishan County during the Song and Ming dynasties, see Sichuan sheng Bishan xianzhi (1996, pp. 59–78, esp. 71–72).

16. Stephan Feuchtwang's essay (2004) alerted us to the significance of trees in place-making processes.

17. See Skinner (2001, pp. 4–5), for a discussion of how these small trading centers constituted a substandard market in his market hierarchy.

18. This process of village creation in Prosperity departed from the more common practice, according to William Skinner, of being founded by a single family or one lineage (Skinner 2001, p. 43).

19. Donations made for the temple's construction were duly recorded on a stone tablet dated 1769.

20. In 1821, the first year of the reign of the Daoguang emperor, an image of the cow deity was installed on the twenty-fourth day of the fourth month, indicating that an epidemic had occurred among local water buffaloes. Leading members of the community fulfilled their obligations by taking measures to deal with this calamity. Similarly, four years later (1825) an

image of Yanguang Shengmu (the holy mother of eyesight) was installed. The previous year, many local people had suffered from persistent eye trouble and had prayed to this deity. Those who believed their ailment was improving had then organized a ceremony of thanksgiving in the goddess's honor, and the following year they installed this image where they could come and worship. In 1940–1941, trachoma and Vitamin A deficiency were still rampant, making blindness a common disability in the region.

21. Spencer (1940, p. 52), as cited by William Skinner (2001, n111).

22. According to the county gazetteer and our findings, the market schedules in use in 1940 Bishan were the 1,4,7; the 2,5,8; the 3,6,9; and the 4,7,10 schedules (Sichuan sheng Bishan xianzhi, 1996, p. 245). The lack of variation compared to what William Skinner found in other places may reflect the fact that Bishan's market system was far flung and underdeveloped until the middle of the Qing dynasty. Other combinations that were used in other areas of China, according to Skinner, included the 1,5,8 schedule; the 2,6,9; the 3,7,10; the 1,4,8; the 2,5,9; and the 3,6,10 timetables (Skinner 2001, p. 16).

23. Skinner (2001), p. 25.

24. Two products did make their way overseas: the pig bristles and *tong* oil produced in rural Sichuan communities.

25. Sichuan sheng Bishan xianzhi (1996), p. 61. By way of comparison, Hechuan County, to the north of Bishan, had sixty-four periodic markets in 1939.

26. As was true for Prosperity's market village, the site where this new commercial center developed was at a fork in the road that catered to travelers making their way between Prosperity and Taihe or between Zitong and Danfeng periodic markets. We have not been able to establish when the periodic market in Dapeng was established, though it clearly was in existence by 1862 when the county gazetteer was published. As the rural research team never visited Dapeng, they never learned about its history. Liu Xianlan, a resident who lives along Dapeng market street, on our behalf determined that the elders of the community believed it came into existence after Prosperity's market commenced operation. It is possible that their opinion is derived from present realities, in which Dapeng has become subordinated to Prosperity. Given Dapeng's placement between the county town and Danfeng on the eastern side of the Maolai Hills, it may have developed at a fork in the road leading to Shizi before Prosperity's market was established, as this eastern section of Bishan County was more commercially developed than the western section (Liu Xianlan, personal communication, 2006).

27. Spencer (1940), pp. 48–58.

28. Sichuan sheng Bishan xianzhi (1996), p. 362.

29. Nedostup (2009), p. 15.

30. Wumiao was built at the beginning of the nineteenth century with an endowment of fifteen *dan* of land, by local people to honor Guan Gong.

31. No major rural studies of this period have noted the ways in which women were able to position themselves in the commercial sector of villages, thereby giving the impression that these communities left little room for women to navigate outside the patriarchal family structure.

32. Here and throughout, the names of married women and widows are given as "XX-YY shi," sometimes rendered in English as "XX née YY."

33. About one-third of the village's eighty-two households belonged to merchants and owners of village businesses. The more prosperous among them maintained their primary homes out in the countryside where, perhaps, a second wife was left in charge.

34. Perhaps as a way to encourage Yang to promote the use of mail in the community, he was allowed to keep all the money he raised from the sale of the minimum allotment of stamps that he was given each month.

35. We counted forty establishments where it was possible to get a smoke of opium in the market village in the spring of 1940.

36. "We selected the hsien city for our mission stations and the market-towns as our pastoral centers" (*West China Missionary News*, May 1929, p. 1). "Market days we stay in the town where we are working and distribute tracts and hold special meetings in the chapel and spend a good deal of time talking with the people" (*West China Missionary News*, February 1937, p. 13).

37. Isabel heard a Swedish scholar put forward a view in a speech in Chengdu in late 1941 about the way in which Christian churches did not blend well into Chinese villages and towns.

38. Because of inflation during this period, it is difficult to estimate what a day's sales might have been worth in the market.

39. Fei Xiaotong (1946); C. K. Yang (1954). In both cases, the agent actually represented everyone in the village. He was very keen to keep the business, so he worked hard to get the best prices he could for the produce.

40. Skinner (2001), pp. 37–42.

41. Two different interpretations exist for the origins of this term *bai longmenzhen*, 摆龙门阵: one is that it emerged from local Sichuan dialect, the second that it emerged from the teahouses of Chengdu. In either case, its literal meaning, that it concerns the laying out of battle strategies, reveals that its origins were connected with the famous literary text *The Romance of the Three Kingdoms*. For further information on its origins, see "Bai longmenzhen shi shenme yisi?" (2007) and "Bai longmenzhen shi shenme yisi?" (2010).

42. For a consideration of the way that gossip serves as a mechanism for maintaining a community, see Nadel-Klein (2009), esp. p. 507; Gluckman (1963); Wickam (1998).

43. The term "traditional institutions of sociability" was used by Qin Shao (1998, p. 1009).

44. As Leo Spitzer (1996) has shown for European refugees, these persistent memories often provided an overarching framework of collective identity.

45. A *dou* is ten liters.

46. A *dan* is a volume measurement for grain, amounting to ten pounds. *Dan* was used as a measurement of land based on the historical yield, that is, the amount of land needed to produce one *dan* of unhusked rice. These amounts were set by the census in the 1940s. As a liquid measurement, a *dan* was one hundred liters.

Chapter Two

Living Off the Land

Farm Labor

Surrounding Prosperity Market Village for several miles in each direction were hamlets where more than 90 percent of the community lived in adobe farm homes, either nestling on the valley knolls among the paddy fields or hugging the hillsides. From nearby Maolai Peak, Prosperity's hills and dales appeared as thousands of tiny islands in a sea of terraced rice paddies that had a green glimmer in spring, gold in autumn, and blue or silver in winter. All that met the eye was human-made scenery. A once shallow, wooded valley flanked by ascending, sometimes craggy, hillsides had been transformed within the previous two to three centuries into irrigated rice paddies and dry upland fields. Prosperity's charming setting was further enhanced by patches of land around the homes that had been turned into garden plots or reserved for picturesque bamboo groves and orchards.

The area's lush appearance belied the fact that life was hard for most farmers in Prosperity, where one-third were just managing to make ends meet and another half were barely able to survive. For these people, engulfed in poverty, the locality's name conjured up a vision that they had no hope of obtaining. Most cultivators in this community grew rice for the market but could not afford to consume it themselves except on rare occasions, living instead on staples such as maize, sweet potatoes, and broad beans. The economic stratification in Prosperity was not as evident as might be supposed. Indeed, to an outsider the community had a surprisingly egalitarian appearance. Both the well-off and ordinary farmers shunned ostentation in day-to-day living, except on ceremonial occasions where extravagance was expected and even praised. The poorest farmers, who lived a life of austerity punctuated with spells of acute deprivation, avoided public places. In short, frugality marked the routines of everyday life in Prosperity. Indications of social stratification were most evident in the survey results collected by us (Isabel Brown and Yu Xiji), which showed an unmistakable trend of downward mobility. For many people, life was hard in the early 1940s and getting worse.

This chapter examines the daily work and yearlong rhythms of farming in Prosperity. The chapter following this one explores the survival strategies, some routine and others extreme, to which households turned when farm income alone was not enough. This was a stratified community: families enjoyed varying access to land and labor, and their housing, clothing, and food exhibited significant disparities. The vast majority either worked their own land or rented land from others. Women as well as men played specific crucial roles in fieldwork; neither youth nor age exempted members of farming families from daily labor. Careful deployment of each family member's efforts, mutual aid, and a lively market in casual farm labor all improved a household's chance of survival. Everyone in the community, however, faced the problem of too many people living on a small amount of land, often in precarious conditions.

DOMESTICATING THE LANDSCAPE:
WOODLANDS TO INTENSIVE AGRICULTURE

The subtropical climate of Prosperity, frost-free twelve months a year with a rainy season usually lasting from April into November, facilitated a long growing season of two crops. But the weather was unpredictable, particularly the arrival of the spring rains, critical to the successful establishment of rice plants. Bishan County sat on a low watershed midway between the Yangzi and Jialing rivers and had only three small rivers, none deep enough for navigation.[1] Prosperity's farmers could only rely on a few small springs and brooks to irrigate their crops. Even more challenging was the terrain, made up almost entirely of hills and dales without any extensive stretches of flatland. These characteristics limited the development of intensive agricultural cultivation in Prosperity until the Qing dynasty.[2] Indeed, Bishan County was described in various dynastic histories as a place of forested mountains and hills where men hunted deer and tigers.[3]

Bishan's transformation into a human-made environment of intense agricultural cultivation was gradual and complex. Key factors fueling this process were the spread of New World crops (maize, sweet potatoes, and red peppers) to Sichuan beginning in the sixteenth century,[4] the commercialization of agriculture in the Chongqing region, a dramatic increase in population, and the introduction of a new variety of rice.[5] The rapid growth in population that occurred in Sichuan in the eighteenth and nineteenth centuries was triggered by the emergence of a strong demand for rice in the Chongqing markets that sparked a rise in prices. Chongqing's vibrant rice markets, in turn, were responding to the needs of communities in the lower Yangzi valley region who began looking to Sichuan in the early eighteenth century as a source for inexpensive rice. As their agents flowed into Chongqing to buy up what they saw as an inexhaustible supply, rural communities in the vicinity of Chongqing converted larger and larger portions of their hilly terrain into terraced rice paddies for commercial agriculture.[6] Farmers undertook both the restoration of old paddies and the expansion of rice paddy fields.[7]

The most successful pioneering farmers were often those adept at terrace construction.[8] With constant care, the clay soil of the Red Basin could hold the terraces without the need for stone embankments. Farmers addressed their water problems by collecting and storing water in some of their terraced fields during the winter.[9] As farmers slowly expanded the amount of land under rice cultivation, they developed three different types of irrigated fields: flood paddies (*goutian*), bordering paddies (*pangtian*), and hill paddies (*shantian*). Located in the few natural watercourses, flood paddies were easy to fill with rainwater and good for storing water. In a dry year they were the most reliable, but in a wet year they flooded easily. Some farmers also complained that fertilizer spread in the water for the rice often drained away and was lost to the neighbor's paddies lower down the watercourse. The prime fields were the bordering paddies that were easy to fill and drain because they bordered the flood paddies. Hill paddies, with far less rainwater draining into them, took a long time to fill and sometimes lost water to seepage. With plentiful rain, the farmer with hill paddies could reap a good harvest, but without it he would have to choose a less lucrative dry crop, thereby suffering a loss, since he still was obligated to pay his rent in rice.

With such innovations it became possible over the course of more than two centuries to convert one-third of Prosperity's undulating hilly terrain into 11,245 *dan* (just under two thousand acres) of terraced paddies.[10] Rice was by far the most lucrative crop, with an annual yield of approximately one hundred thousand bushels, the bulk of it exported to support urban populations, especially in nearby Chongqing. Growing rice so dominated the farm year that the community calendar revolved around it.[11] In Prosperity, rice replaced money as the main medium of exchange: rice was what the state demanded in taxes and its army in levies and what the landlords extracted in rent. It has been estimated that two-thirds of all the rice grown in Sichuan was taken from the producers in taxes, levies, and rents. On average it changed hands seven times during the process of being bought up from farmers, stored, transported, processed, and retailed, with its price rising manyfold before it reached the urban consumer.[12]

One-third of the paddy fields could also be planted with a winter crop. Most valuable was rapeseed, which could be pressed to provide a profitable cooking oil, but winter wheat and broad beans (*candou* or *fudou*[13]) could also bring in some cash. Sowed anytime between mid-October and mid-December, these winter crops gave Prosperity its springtime glory, making the whole valley a checkerboard of blossoming yellow rapeseed and purple broad beans. The beauty of this terrain was enhanced by the glint of the sun on the water being stored in the other two-thirds of the terraced fields, although it also signified that this type of irrigation system prohibited double-cropping in a significant portion of the paddies that were used to store water in the winter.[14]

A similar expansion of farmland occurred higher up on the slopes of these hills. Once covered with trees, they were converted into upland fields. By 1940, some twenty-one thousand *dan* (thirty-five hundred acres) of unirrigated hilly farmland in Prosperity were primarily planted with the coarse staples of maize and sweet potatoes in the summer. Maize demanded little attention and was easy to grow, while harvesting sweet potatoes was the most detested of all field tasks because digging out the tubers from the wet sticky clay soil was so onerous. Other summer crops included sorghum and spring wheat. In the winter these upland fields were planted with broad beans, field peas, and winter wheat. A few of the best dry fields, however, were sown to cash-earning wheat or rapeseed, provided the farmer had plenty of good fertilizer.[15]

Heavily cultivated and subject to erosion, these fields needed fertilizer, most commonly compost made up of dried dung, decayed vegetable matter, and ashes. Preparing adequate compost involved the expenditure of endless hours of light labor. Collecting the dung usually fell to small boys or old men. Equipped with woven scoops and bamboo tongs, they scoured the environs, especially the roadsides, for the droppings of buffaloes, cattle, pigs, goats, dogs, and chickens. Vegetable matter was usually collected by housewives and put in a pile to decay. Ashes were added from the kitchen stove, in which farmers burned roots and stalks of harvested crops. Families well off enough to own a pig constructed a pigsty toilet. This was a cesspool paved with indigenous cement (*sanhetu*), over which suitably spaced planks were laid. A section was fenced off for the family toilet, leaving the rest for the pig or pigs. In this way night soil and pig manure accumulated in the cesspool, to be cleared out at intervals and left to mature. When ready for use, the semi-congealed mixture was diluted and carried in buckets to the vegetable garden or the rapeseed field and there ladled individually onto each plant. Any family with a surplus could sell this fertilizer at a good price.

In 1940s Prosperity, it seemed that an agricultural use was found for almost every spot of land.[16] The border areas between many upland fields and paddy fields were often planted with a row of trees that could be used for building houses or making furniture. Up in the hills there was also a scattering of *tong* oil trees; their valuable sap was tapped in the spring and exported as varnish to Europe and the United States.[17] Two orchards, a peach orchard on the top of Maolai Hill and an orange grove of three hundred trees on its lower slopes, were interspersed with dryland crops. Both belonged to big landowners and were rented out to tenants. When the fruit in either orchard was ripe, the grower would open it to the public to pick what they wanted, paying by weight at the exit. Merchants and peddlers gathered to get their supplies. In this way the grower was spared the trouble of picking, packing, transporting, and marketing the fruit. Clumps of bamboo plants nestled around the clusters of farm homes provided, as the saying had it, clothing, food, housing, and transport (*yi shi zhu xing*). Fibrous sheaves about the stem provided waterproof stiffening for the soles of cloth shoes. New shoots were much appreciated as food. Large strong stems served as bamboo rafters for the roof (in many homes only the ridgepole was timber); smaller stems were split into strips and woven to make the wall of village houses to be plastered over with mud and lime. And finally, tough stems were used for shoulder yokes and for litters. And bamboo had other uses besides. Slender stems were used for hanging out clothes or vegetables to dry, and still smaller ones were used for pipe stems. Cut into strips, bamboo was used for weaving baskets and mats for household use (or cottage industry).

Farmers even found ways to utilize the public lands on the steeper hillsides, covered with scrub and outcroppings of rock, with hill crests often tufted with clumps of pine trees, and the weed-covered sides of the network of pathways linking the clustered farm homes. Every family made use of this "rough land," some for bamboo, trees, or grazing of goats, and all for the gathering of twigs, weeds, roots, and dung. On the hillsides young lads and older men foraged for fuel for their cooking stoves, while the children and the elderly gathered roadside weeds for pig feed. The family pigs and chickens did their own foraging around the homes, supplementing their regular feedings each day. With the expansion of fields and the intensification of agriculture, the farmers in Prosperity transformed a largely natural landscape into a human-made one.

OWNERS AND RENTERS:
THE SOCIAL CONTOURS OF WET RICE CULTIVATORS

The vast majority of residents, about 90 percent, were engaged in farming, but the scale of their agricultural production and their living standards varied greatly. Thirteen percent (111 households) were landlords, another 30 percent (510 households) were owner-cultivators, and the remaining farmers, in 737 households, worked the land as tenants.[18] However, the categories of landlord, owner, and renter were not always the key determinants of socioeconomic status. Many factors combined to make some families more successful than others. Some landlords and owners were struggling to keep afloat, while some tenants ran successful farming businesses.

One significant distinction that affected living standards in Prosperity was ownership of rice land, a status that was enjoyed by 516 families.[19] Those who owned paddy land, even a small plot that was mortgaged, enjoyed a measure of financial security that evaded renters. Land was a precious commodity worth holding on to in hard times, even if the parcel was too small to operate as a viable farm. However, the value of dry land was much inferior to that of rice paddies. The 324 families who only had the resources to acquire these unirrigated upland fields were relegated to a subsistence level of farming, except for the few households with a successful commercial venture such as weaving that provided their main income.[20] Although a segment of the 509 families who were rice land renters were quite affluent, they were always more vulnerable than owners. Their hold on the farmland they tilled could easily be broken, particularly as tenant contracts were only valid for one year. Loss of a rental contract meant losing one's housing as well. (See figure 2.1.)

Among the 516 families who owned rice farms, however, there was a vast range in the quantity and quality of their paddies. At the bottom end of the spectrum, 244 families owned ten *dan* or less of paddy land, scattered in pocket-sized holdings throughout the valley and on the less reliable terraced sections of the hillsides.[21] Of these, twenty-three families clung to a minuscule one *dan* of paddy, requiring them to seek other sources of income in order to make ends meet. The rest of the rice owners (260 households) ran successful farms that ranged in size from eleven to sixty *dan*. At the top of the socioeconomic ladder in Prosperity were twelve very wealthy families who owned the largest farms (sixty-one to three hundred *dan*) comprised of the finest-quality rice paddy land. None of these owners worked in farming but rather lived a life of leisure supported in large part from the rents of their tenants. Some were former members of the military who had built up their estates during the course of the warlord era. Although they themselves might not have had close knowledge of rice farming, the richest were able to hire knowledgeable stewards to supervise their landholdings.

The customary rates of tenure in 1940–1941 were a deposit of from six to ten yuan per *dan* and a rent of 60 to 70 percent of the rice crop (as estimated in the contract). Once the rent was paid in full, the landlord either refunded the tenant's deposit or else retained it and renewed the contract for a further year. For his part, the tenant kept roughly one-third of his rice crop. But while the landlord's share was constant, the tenant's was variable. In a good year he got more, in a poor year less. Profit or loss from his skill as a farmer or the luck of the weather affected him directly. In addition to his third of the

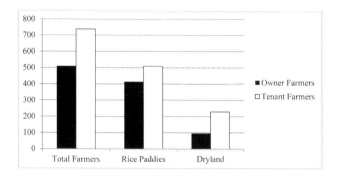

Farm Households:		1,247
Rice land Farmers		923
Owner-farmers	414	
Tenant-farmers	509	
Dryland Farmers		324
Owner-farmers	96	
Tenant-farmers	228	
Landlord Households		111
Other Households (no links to land)		139
GRAND TOTAL		1,497

Figure 2.1. Owners and Renters

rice yield, the tenant kept the whole of the winter crops—rapeseed or broad beans—grown on about one-fourth of his paddy fields. Together with the rice land, the tenant would also have rented some unirrigated fields from his landlord where he would grow sweet potatoes, maize, and beans, chiefly for family consumption.

Contrary to prevailing assumptions that landowners were universally more prosperous than tenants, in Prosperity some 15 percent of the renters were more successful in their businesses, even after paying the customary two-thirds of the harvest in rent, than the 244 paddy land owners at the bottom of the spectrum.[22] A certain economy of scale was the main factor that enabled a small proportion of tenants to prosper. They needed to rent a sizable scattering of paddies that altogether consisted of between twenty-one and forty *dan*, plus have sufficient ready cash to make the required deposits and an extended family with ample labor power.[23] Finding a landlord who would grant a degree of independence, require fewer obligations, and might be willing to issue a simple commercial contract without service encumbrances could also prove significant in these renters' ability to prosper.

In some situations, renters were able to establish leverage over owners. This occurred when a landowner was so desperate for cash that he was forced to lower the rent on his land in return for an increased deposit in cash. If the landowner was unable to refund these funds, then he could not terminate this renter-favorable contract, causing him to eventually either mortgage or sell the paddy land to the tenant.

Most renters, however, did not fare so well. We determined that for the same scale of operations, a tenant received perhaps half the farm income of an owner. This estimate is a rough approximation, taking into account the fact that for the same amount of land the tenant on average kept only one-third of his rice crop but retained all his winter crops and garden produce and a portion of the staples grown in upland fields. Thus half of the tenant farms, according to our data, were viable while 37 percent had trouble getting by or faced desperate circumstances. Those who cultivated land in the fifteen- to twenty-*dan* range tended to be much more successful than those with less, with the ones in the bottom tier holding less than ten *dan*, which brought in an average of 3.5 *dan* of unhusked rice in total after the rent was paid.[24]

The social contours of this community of 1,497 households were highly stratified, rising from a large mass of the poor at the base to a fairly large group of subsistence farmers in the middle and a very small group at the top.[25] (See figure 2.2[26] and table 2.1.) Prosperity's twelve largest landowners, small fry by provincial standards, were rich by local standards. They possessed large landholdings, at least sixty *dan* (roughly ten acres) of rice land, and supported themselves entirely through landlordism; that is to say they lived on rents alone without, to our knowledge, engaging regularly or seriously in any side occupations. Their rice lands were cultivated by tenants only, but on their vegetable plots they sometimes also used hired laborers. These families accounted for less than 1 percent of the total.

Stratum 2 was more complex, comprising three main groups. First were landlords with less than sixty *dan* of rice land who lived partly on rents but augmented their income through professions, local industry, cottage weaving, or political office. Among the best educated in the community, some became traditional doctors or teachers or took clerical jobs—all professions requiring at least six years of schooling. Some used connections within or beyond the township to obtain political office such as township or *bao* head, tax collector, or perhaps, if they had sufficient protection, opium dealing. A second segment of this stratum were merchants who dealt in grain, cotton yarn and cloth, pig bristles and goatskins, oil, wine, and spirits. Some were also involved in opium dealing. Having prospered, they established themselves among the lesser landlords by buying land which they then let out while continuing to derive their main income from trade. A third segment was made up of prosperous working farmers who either had large holdings and well-developed farm sidelines such as pig raising, or a cottage industry such as cotton weaving. These households often hired one or more men or women as farm laborers or weavers. Taken together, these three segments of

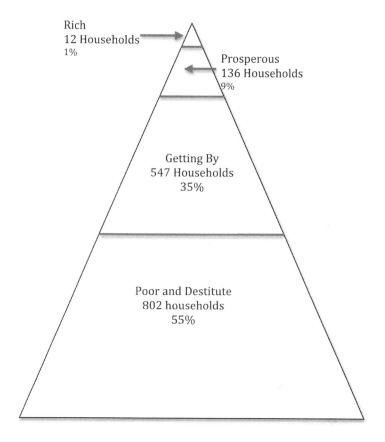

Figure 2.2. Prosperity's Social Strata

stratum 2 comprised less than 10 percent of all households. Although lumped together in this economic classification, these three occupational groups encompassed much more disparity than stratum 1. They were not, for instance, equals in ability to wield political influence: merchants and prosperous farmers rarely competed for power with landlords.

Stratum 3, which accounted for 35 percent of all households, comprised mainly medium to small-scale rice land farmers whose income from farming was not adequate to feed their families. To make ends meet they engaged in small-scale trade or handicraft ventures which required modest amounts of capital. Some were craftsmen who hired out as carpenters, blacksmiths, masons, or tailors. Others were in low-status professions such as herbalist, diviner, or Daoist folk priest. Many men in stratum 3 households had two or three years of schooling, but they often claimed to have forgotten the characters they had learned.

Table 2.1. A Comparison of the Four Strata (1940–1941)

Stratum	Size of Landholding	Households	Percent
1:			
Rich and powerful landlords	61+ *dan*	12	1
2:			
Well-off medium and small landlords and landowning merchants	21–60 *dan*	90	
Prosperous owners	21–60 *dan*	18	
Prosperous tenants	31–60 *dan*	28	
Total		136	9
Upper-Class Total		**148**	**10**
Stratum	Size of Landholding	Households	Percent
3:			
Laboring people and midsize farm owners	6–20 *dan*	25	
Midsize tenants	11–30 *dan*	292	
Total		547	35
4:			
Poor and destitute owner-farmers	up to 5 *dan*	141	
Tenant farmers	up to 10 *dan*	189	
Dryland farmers		324	
Nonowners/noncultivators		148	
Total		802	55
Lower-Class Total		**1,349**	**90**
TOTAL		**1,497**	**100**

Stratum 4 was the largest category, containing 55 percent of all households in the study. These were the landless mini-tenants who eked out their living cultivating poor-quality, high-lying paddy fields or patches of unirrigated land on the more rugged hill slopes. Men sold their labor as farmhands or transport workers; women, as day laborers. Some engaged in petty home industry, such as making incense sticks. Men peddled minute stocks of cheap commodities like straw sandals or offered "lowly" services such as pig gelding or fortune-telling. A few men turned to banditry, but usually only during times of severe food shortage in early spring.

At the lower end of stratum 4 were households in the process of disintegration. Some were the destitute men and women who migrated to the village when they could no longer make a living in the countryside. Their earnings often came from illicit or semi-illicit undertakings: preparing the opium for pipe smoking, theft, prostitution, or serving those at the gambling table. A few young men from disintegrating families were able to use connections to join the militia or do strong-arm work for those in power.[27]

HOUSING

The homes of the elite were usually situated on the best flatland. Spacious and uncluttered, some had a small circular silo situated at the edge of the courtyard. At the base of watchtowers in the courtyards of the wealthiest were padlocked storerooms where these landowners kept ample supplies of grain. Inside these homes, a certain elegance was imparted by the black varnished furniture, often inherited from previous generations. In the guest room, along the wall opposite the door was a long table on which stood the ancestral tablets as well as a number of large porcelain vases, which could be used to hold receipts, feather dusters, or paper flowers. Pushed up against this long table was a square table with carved legs, sometimes inlaid with mother-of-pearl, flanked on either side by a solid, straight-backed carved wooden armchair. On either side of the room stood another pair of similar chairs, each with a tea table in between. The bedrooms were furnished with large wooden beds with carved posts from which hung the ubiquitous curtains. The most impressive bed we saw had a wooden deck along one side on which a chair and small table were fixed, all of which could be encompassed in the privacy of the curtains. It was in fact a small elegant wooden bedroom within the large earthen-floored, rafter-ceilinged room. Bedrooms were also furnished with large solid wooden cabinets and chests for packing away clothing and other possessions.

A special feature in the homes of such families was the presence of a kettle in their kitchens for boiling water. This earthenware pot could be suspended on a hook over the fire hole. Only the elite and prosperous merchant families enjoyed flavorless boiled water for their tea. Although everyone in the community believed unboiled water harmful, the poor drank it because they could not afford fuel, while middle farm families boiled water in their all-purpose wok, which gave it a soupy flavor.

Another special feature of the elite and better-off homes was that they had heat in the damp, penetrating cold of winter. Charcoal was burned in a brass basin, around which the family members and guests would assemble. This burner kept the part of the body nearest the glowing coals warm, but left the rest cold since drafts came in from the open doors and the gaps under the roof. But this ventilation was useful since it swept away the poisonous fumes produced from the addition of fresh pieces of charcoal. Unable to pay for fuel, the poor lived in homes bereft of heat. A saying had it that in summer all suffered from the heat; but in winter it was only the poor who suffered from the cold.

Most conspicuous on the landscape were the homes of the viable middle farm households, as they were typically perched on the hillocks and the lower slopes, half encircled in bamboo. The interiors of their homes were cluttered. Housing already crowded with human beings had also to serve for storage of farm produce, tools, equipment, and raw materials for side occupations, as well as an assortment of other possessions, since nothing could be thrown away that might be of use in the future. Earthenware crocks containing grain or dried legumes stood in corners, boxes were piled against walls, and baskets were hung from the rafters where the contents would be more secure from the hordes of rats. Those fortunate enough to have a buffalo sheltered it in a lean-to or occasionally in a room in the house.

The central room of the main section of the house was used both for entertaining and as a work space. It had a paved or beaten earthen floor and a wide two-paneled wooden door opening onto the courtyard. Its essential furniture included a plain but substantial square table and four backless benches able to seat eight people. The table was ordinarily pushed against the wall opposite the front door and the benches along the side walls. Above the table stood the wooden ancestral tablets, a matter of pride to any family that possessed them. Because of its association with ancestors and gods, this central room was an honored place. One might find a family living in an old straw-thatched central section, while the livestock were sheltered in a newly built, tile-roofed wing, for it would be unseemly to give the place of honor to the livestock.

This central room and the adjoining courtyard were the center of the economic endeavors of the family members when they were not out in the fields. Here they threshed crops, dried grain, preserved vegetables, raised pigs and chickens, constructed and repaired farm implements, and conducted whatever supplementary occupations members of the family engaged in, with all their tackle and gear: the loom of the weaver, the anvil and bellows of the blacksmith, the cauldrons and racks of the soy noodle maker. Precious farm equipment, when not in use, was carefully stored here or under the eaves. And it was in this room, or more likely the courtyard, that social life took place, including our interviews. Provided family members were at home, the doors of the room were left open all day long, winter and summer, to let in light and air. On rare occasions when everyone was away, a large heavy iron padlock secured the door.

Off either side of the central room lay a bedroom lit and ventilated from two high small windows, from the small gap left between the top of the wall and the roof, or indirectly from the guest room. The beds were planks laid on rough trestles with a slender bamboo pole at each of the four corners for hanging the homespun batik bed curtains. In the daytime these curtains were pulled back with big brass hooks. At night they were released to provide the only privacy there was, for the bedroom housed men and women, young and old. Equally important, residents counted on the curtains to keep out mosquitoes in summer and rats the whole year round, as well as the "poisonous" night air. In fact, the curtains kept out ventilation and, in summer, any cooling breeze that might mitigate the stifling humid heat. Cotton-padded quilts, usually well worn, lay folded on the beds in daytime. Other furnishings in the bedroom would include boxes of wood or woven bamboo lathes where clothing and other personal possessions were kept.

Beyond one bedroom was the kitchen, which was entered from the courtyard, though it might also have a small door opening to the back of the house. Dark, damp, and smoky, the kitchen was furnished with a big chimney-less earthen stove. It had one or two fire holes fitted with a cooking pot or wok and a low stool for the person feeding the fire with bits of straw, dried roots, or bought kindling. Just outside the small back door of the kitchen was the pigsty toilet. No thought was given to the health hazard of having the fly-infested toilet next to the kitchen.

More than half of Prosperity's people were poor and vulnerable. The homes of those poorer farm families who farmed a small tract of land might be either a small cottage or a single room in a traditional house turned tenement through overcrowding. These homes, too, were cluttered. The simple furniture could consist of a trestle bed and a small low unvarnished table and one or two low stools, either three-legged wooden ones or, more often, bamboo four-legged ones. In daytime the table and stools were set outside in front of the door. Beds had worn, ragged, and lice-infested quilts.

The vast majority of these families had no ancestral tablets and had to make do with pasting two strips of paper, each with five characters, on the wall opposite the front door. One strip read, "Ruler, Teacher, Father, Heaven and Earth"; the other contained the five characters for the generations of the family to be revered.

We never saw the insides of the mud cottage homes of the very poorest farmers on the upper hill slopes, as we were not invited in when we went around with our questionnaire. We usually sat outside these houses while conducting our interviews. And those living high up in the hills actually fled when they saw us approaching, presumably because they believed we were coming to conscript them. Their houses were all left padlocked. Although we never went inside, we were told that they had no furniture and people slept on straw on the earthen floor.[28]

CLOTHING AND FOOD

The hallmark of Sichuanese Han—men and women alike—was the long blue cotton gown worn over long blue cotton trousers, and the white cotton turban. When the Sichuan farmer was in the fields, or the laborer was transporting coal, or the blacksmith or mason was busy with his trade, he tucked his gown up around his waist. Such clothing reportedly prompted Chiang Kai-shek when he arrived in Sichuan in 1938 to exclaim, "A land of gentlemen!"—for elsewhere only the Han upper classes wore long gowns, while the rest wore short jackets over their trousers.

The ubiquitous turban was considered essential to prevent headaches. Some claimed they were even worn in bed. Turbans were white, the color of mourning, for the loss of Zhuge Liang, a famed strategist of the Three Kingdoms period who had lived more than 1,700 years earlier. His memory had been kept vividly alive in the minds of old and young in Sichuan through the popularization of his exploits in local opera and storytelling.

In Prosperity, the difference in the clothing of the well-off and the poor was less in the style than in the quality and quantity. The better-off families favored machine-made cloth, while the poorer people preferred homespun for its durability. Poor men and women generally had only a single gown and pair of trousers, folded and tied with a broad cloth sash tucked in around the waist. For those who could afford them, padded winter garments were worn beneath the cotton gown in winter. But many owned none and stoically passed the cold, raw winter months wearing an extra cotton garment. Though woolen sweaters had become fashionable in Bishan town, few local people had adopted this innovation.

Among the poor, no attempt was made to hide the fact that most clothes had been patched. The color of the patches rarely matched the garment and might be attached in a convenient rather than a neat way. A poor man without a wife would do his own mending, often in a rough and ready manner. Ragged, unmended clothes were not common except on the worst-treated small runaway foster fiancées.

The clothing of the middle and better-off men and women was made by itinerant tailors who would stay in the home while sewing traditional-styled clothes for the family. In poorer families, it was the women, especially the older women, who made the clothing. Clothes, even those that were ragged or patched, were usually clean. With ample supplies of water near every home, clothing was constantly washed, and we rarely visited a home where garments were not hung out to dry on bamboo sticks. For footwear, men wore straw sandals or black cloth shoes. Women wore cloth shoes, while most children, regardless of the economic standing of their parents, went barefoot, winter and summer.

Some regular rhythms in the eating habits in Prosperity were obvious. For the poor there was the annual rhythm of coarse but adequate fare, punctuated with a period of deprivation. Among the rich and middle farmers and regular hired help there was the even rhythm of a vegetarian diet with an ample meat treat twice a month. There was also the twice-a-year rhythm of meat treats for several days running during the two harvest seasons. In this the poorer farmers shared, provided they were hired as day laborers or took part in mutual aid. Once a year, feasting took place to mark the celebration of the Lunar New Year, for those who were passably off. The best-off entertained many tables of guests. Superimposed on these regular rhythms linked to the farm calendar was an uneven rhythm brought by the occasional bursts of lavish feasting, either as hosts or guests, to mark family ceremonials such as betrothals, weddings, or funerals.

Three meals a day were customary in the countryside among families with sufficient grain. Breakfast was eaten soon after dawn, a midday meal at noon, and an evening meal just after dark. The basic item of diet for those who could afford it was steamed rice at every meal. Thrifty families extended their precious rice supplies in various ways, most commonly by adding broad beans. As time went on and the price of rice rose in the market, the proportion of rice to beans in the pot grew steadily smaller. When wheat was eaten to preserve stores of rice, the flour was mixed into dough and set out along the sides of the cooking pot. Some water was put in the curved bottom of the pot and a lid placed tightly on top. The bun that emerged was baked crisp and hard on the bottom and steamed light and soft on the top. It made a heavy substantial meal. Cornmeal was cooked in the same way.

Middle farm families usually served a small dish of vegetables to be eaten with the steamed rice. The vegetables were either freshly cooked or preserved, for many homes, even those in the village, had a kitchen garden providing small amounts of fresh vegetables the year round. These included beans, peas, cucumbers, squash, root crops, cabbage, stem lettuce, spinach, rape, and chives, along with onions, garlic, ginger, and a great variety of peppers for the highly spiced Sichuan cuisine. At peak seasons, the housewife preserved excess vegetables, drying them or pickling them in brine to make the famous Sichuan spicy pickled vegetable *paocai*. Every "respectable" household had its own pickle crock, a large earthenware vessel, usually a foot to eighteen inches high, with a block of wood serving as a lid. Turnips, beans, green peppers, and onions were cleaned and put into the crock cooked or raw. Roots of fresh ginger, hot red peppers, and Sichuan peppercorns (*huajiao*) were added. Vegetables were constantly being added or taken from the crock for use. The flavor of the pickles derived both from the seasoning and the particular combination of vegetables. Once a pickle crock had been started, it was kept going, for the longer it was in use, the richer and more subtle the flavors. Some housewives won local fame for the excellence of their pickles. A matchmaker would take note of a young girl's skill and include it among the virtues making her a bride to be sought after. In Prosperity these delectable highly seasoned preserved vegetables, for which Sichuan was famous, could not be bought. Each family prepared them for its own use.

Dried vegetables were more mundane. Turnips of several varieties were the most common. They were cleaned, cut in strips, and set out in large drying baskets in the courtyard, or strung together and hung on pegs under the eaves. During the summer and autumn, most farmhouses had festoons of drying vegetables under the curving roofs. The dried tubers, diced and fried in vegetable oil with salt, pepper, or other seasoning, made a tasty relish to go with steamed rice. But cooking oil was expensive, so ordinarily they were boiled. Broad beans made a common dish, boiled and eaten skins and all. When the skins became too tough, the beans were soaked and allowed to sprout slightly before cooking, making them more digestible. (Neighbors criticized our wastefulness when they found we threw away the skins.) Bean curd or bean vermicelli, processed from soybeans, made a popular occasional dish.

In viable farm households, men were served meat twice a month, with an allowance of half a *jin* per person. The meat could be bought fresh on market day at one of the numerous stalls. Women, however, ate little meat, though they could expect to be served chicken and eggs after childbirth.

The menus of better-off families were more varied. Most had supplies of preserved pork hanging from the kitchen rafters, although they were usually kept for guests or ceremonial banquets. However, even in such families most women ate little meat, and a number of older women took Buddhist vows to fast on the first and fifteenth of each month. A few took complete vegetarian vows, bringing honor to themselves and their families.

In poorer farming families, rice (husked and perhaps crudely polished) was an item of diet briefly in the weeks immediately following the harvest, after which it was alternated with coarse cereals and then replaced by them. Coarse cereals or cereal substitutes included maize, sorghum, broad beans, and field peas, with sweet potatoes (boiled or roasted in embers) as the last resort. Poorer farm families also ate vegetables, but boiled in a cereal porridge rather than as a separate dish. Oil was typically lacking from their diet. But it was the shortage of salt—because of its prohibitive price—that they felt most keenly. Meat was only eaten occasionally by the poor, mostly during the two harvest seasons.

The poor endured a longer or shorter period of semi-starvation during February and March prior to the spring harvest, when even supplies of the coarse cereals were dwindling. At all times, men and boys received the bigger share of what little there was. When shortages were worst, it was the young foster fiancées who suffered the most. Severe malnutrition was the lot of many of these girls. Death in poor families was a common occurrence, and these small girls were the most expendable.

At better times, although the poor had no meat treats, they had their small indulgences. Men occasional bought a bowl of cheap and tasty noodles in the market. A familiar sight, too, on market day was the coal carrier swinging along with his two heaped and heavy baskets of coal. On top of one basket lay a small empty cloth bag, and on top of the other a minute bottle. After selling the coal, he would buy a modest measure of rice and a smidgen of oil to take home as a special nonmeat treat for his family on such occasions as a birthday of a father or mother, or to honor a recently deceased grandparent. Even among the poor families treats were important, no matter how small.

FARMING FAMILY MANAGEMENT STRATEGIES

Farming in Prosperity required complex decision making and management of human and material resources. Rural cultivators had to choose what crops to plant and how to allocate their time and efforts in the context of changing weather and environmental conditions. They needed to arrange for time-sensitive extra labor and draft animal inputs, the sale of produce not needed for family consumption, and the marketing of cottage handicrafts or agricultural goods.[29] The family was organized to maximize the labor of its members. In 7 percent of the families, this prompted them to accept additional people into their household, usually indigent relatives, either as a way to expand their labor force[30] or as a form of charity to someone in distress who was able to make some contribution to the household economy.[31] Some families absorbed non-family members to support their labor force. (See figure 2.3 for the number of households and families of various sizes.)

Although the cultural ideal of greatest felicity was to have five generations living in harmony under one roof, more than 90 percent of Prosperity's 1,497 households found this impossible to attain because of insufficient landholdings, poverty, management problems, and low life expectancy. Many prosperous landlord families preferred the nuclear family (husband, wife, and unmarried children) or stem family arrangements (older parent or parents,

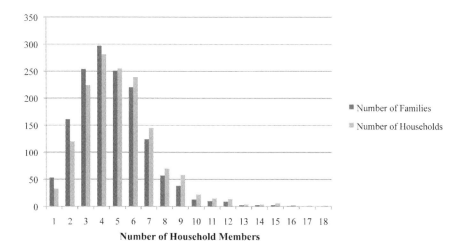

Figure 2.3. Sizes of Families and Households

one of their children, his spouse, and their unmarried offspring), although a few complicated their family composition by taking concubines. For families who combined rice farming with a family business, the extended family pattern facilitated their ability to be successful by making full and profitable use of the labor of all members. In the Dong family, the father worked with his oldest son to run the forty *dan* of rented farmland, while the second adult son managed the family's cloth business.

Among ordinary farm families, the extended family pattern was of brief duration, useful in helping teenage sons start up their families under a supportive parental umbrella, but could not be sustained long term. The vast majority of farm family households found it most efficient to keep their size and composition relatively trim. Almost two-thirds of all families in Prosperity were stem or nuclear families of four to seven members.[32] (See table 2.2.)

Every member of the household—of whatever gender, age, or capacity—was involved in farming. Women worked with the men in the dry paddy fields, hoeing, weeding, pruning, and harvesting secondary crops; they did much of the cultivation of staples in the upland fields and the growing of vegetables; they raised pigs and chickens. Over and above all this farm labor, women were responsible for the household chores—husking rice or other cereals, gathering fuel, doing the cooking, washing clothes, and caring for small children. Women handled vegetables, chickens, and eggs that brought in a regular small flow of cash. In most farming households it was the woman who spent that cash to meet household needs for salt, matches, and other items; and likewise it was typically the woman who provided the family with its little occasional treats—a small measure of rice to break the monotony of broad beans or sweet potatoes, oil to fry a vegetable dish, or potent white liquor to cheer her husband.

Women were helped by the young, the old, and the disabled or ailing members of the household, who took over the lighter chores. Children in farm families learned the daily household and field tasks from an early age. Young boys might tend the buffalo, taking it to water. By the age of ten, boys and girls gathered weeds to feed the pigs, twigs or stalks for the kitchen fire, or cut grass to feed the buffalo. An older girl often worked with a baby brother or sister tied on her back. The elderly, weak, and disabled also contributed to household tasks. The absence of bedridden people in the commu-

Table 2.2. Family Sizes in Prosperity

Family Size	Number of Families	Percentage
1–3	468	31.2
4–7	892	59.7
8–16	137	9.1
Total	1497	100

nity can be attributed to the lack of effective medical care, inadequate nutrition for those suffering from tuberculosis or other common debilitating diseases, and also to the accepted work ethic whereby people simply labored until they dropped.

THE RICE CYCLE

Rice growing placed heavy demands on men, who had to be strong, tough, skillful, and meticulous. The rice-growing cycle started in October with the plowing of all the dry paddy fields after the rice harvest so that they could either hold water or be planted with winter crops. Then in November or December, while the winter crops of rapeseed, broad beans, and field peas were ripening in the dry paddies and upland fields, the farmer, with buffalo and single-bladed iron plow, started preparing his water storage paddies for the spring rice planting. This was strenuous labor for long hours, working knee deep, even thigh deep, in bitterly cold water, for none of it could be drained off since it would be needed to fill the dry paddies later. This second plowing was followed by a third in late March or early April, not long before the transplanting in mid-April.

In early April the farmer chose a paddy field near his home as a seedbed. He plowed it for the third time, harrowed it until the earth and water had been churned into an oozy mixture, drained off any surface water that remained, and then broadcast the rice seeds by hand. During the next few days, while the grains lay on the surface of the mud, a child or an aged member of the household stood guard, shouting shrilly and waving a flag on a long flexible bamboo pole to keep off the flocks of unruly sparrows. Once the seed had taken root, the main task was to regulate the water so that it almost reached the "eye" of the seedling but did not flow over and drown it. The young plants grew at a phenomenal rate, and fifteen days after sowing they were over twenty centimeters high and ready for transplanting.

In the intervening two weeks, the rest of the household had been furiously busy harvesting the crops from double-cropped paddy fields to clear them for the rice. Now the farmer watched the skies for signs of rain, which would facilitate the plowing of the bare, dry, newly harvested fields. Once the rain fell he plowed the land quickly, for newly harvested fields would not hold water until they had been plowed. If he had to rely on borrowing a buffalo, he waited with trepidation lest the fields dry out before his turn came. Once he got the buffalo, he plowed the fields and then broke the clods with foot or hoe. This first plowing of harvested fields was particularly onerous for man and beast, and they could complete only half a *dan* (one-sixth of an acre) in a single day. The second plowing was easier, and they could finish four-fifths of a *dan*. Next, with the help of able-bodied members of the family, the farmer raised water from his storage paddies to fill the fields. Circular-chain wooden pumps that could lift water a foot or more were cranked by hand, while longer ones that could lift it to greater heights required two operators, who cranked them by foot, bicycle fashion. It took hours of strenuous work to fill the dry paddies.

Once the farmer had plowed all his paddy fields and filled them with water, he fertilized them with rapeseed oilcake, at roughly ten *jin* (five kilograms) per *dan* of land. (This involved an unavoidable cash expenditure, for though the farmer grew rape seed, the oil press kept the cake from which the oil had been crushed in part payment for its services.) The farmer broke up the oilcake, mixed it thoroughly with water in a large wooden tub, and floated it around the paddy while he ladled out the fertilizer with a long-handled wooden dipper, distributing it evenly throughout. This ended the ten to fifteen hectic days of heavy male labor required to get the fields ready for the rice transplanting which followed immediately after.

Transplanting was an equally hectic but much shorter task. The farmer gently uprooted the seedlings from their seedbed and bound them together with a straw or fiber into bundles of about thirty-six. He piled these into woven bamboo scoops and, with the help of the family, carried them by shoulder pole to a prepared paddy field where he skillfully tossed just the right number of bundles to each part of the field, then set them out in tiny clumps, each at intervals of about twenty centimeters. Hour after hour, calf deep in water, feet sunk into sticky red clay and bent double from the waist, each man worked transplanting a swath of eight rows or so. An able-bodied man could transplant three *dan* a day. Once all the paddies were transplanted, the whole household could relax after a grueling half month or more.

Thirty days after the transplanting came weeding, which could be done at a leisurely tempo. For this the farmer used his fingers, or preferably his toes, to feel tenderly about the rice and remove weeds, for no farmer would risk injuring the young plants by using an implement. Fifteen days later, the paddy was meticulously weeded a second time.

From the transplanting until the rice bloomed in early August, the farmer carefully regulated the water in each paddy field. Not only should the water level be correct (just below the "eye" of the plant), but the water must not be allowed to stagnate. This too was a meticulous job. As he tended to this, the farmer also worked on the upkeep of the dikes around each field. Only after the rice bloomed could he relax and allow the paddy fields to dry out. Three or four weeks later, in September, the rice was ready for harvesting. At this stage the farmer and his family could lose no time, for the rice had to be threshed, thoroughly dried, and winnowed, ready for storing before the autumn rains started. This was a second rush season, though not so intense as the first.

The man was the linchpin in rice growing, but it also required the coordinated efforts of the whole family. The exacting labor demands of this pattern of rice growing, especially at the critical peak season, affected the scale of farming possible for any particular family.

While many women lacked the strength to handle the buffalo during plowing, they certainly had the agility to handle the work of transplanting rice seedlings. But even though women in Prosperity who found themselves in difficult circumstances were willing to be sole cultivators of an upland farm, they did not step into the rice paddy when it held water. Only men handled the buffalo and worked in the water. It was clearly marked as a male terrain for most of the season, with men bearing sole responsibility for the plowing, transplanting, weeding, and repairing the dikes. Once they allowed the fields to dry out, then the women were allowed to weed and harvest. The importance of rice growing to the state and the identification of men as the rice growers confirmed the traditional view of the superiority of men. This view went unchallenged despite the major role women played in other aspects of farming, without which most farm enterprises could not have continued functioning and many families would have been without food.

BUFFALOES

For most rice cultivators, using a buffalo was at once a must and unaffordable. Paddies could not be plowed without them, as human labor power was not sufficient except perhaps for the most desperate on a very small parcel, yet few could afford to own one. A buffalo cost as much as one *dan* of good rice land, to say nothing of the upkeep, which required the rice straw from twenty *dan*, as well as daily fresh-cut grass, and on heavy workdays a supplement of cereal or broad beans. In order to meet this challenge, most families either agreed to joint ownership or hired the use of a buffalo from a more prosperous farmer. In either scenario, the cooperating families needed to work closely in order to maximize the use of the draft animal while also sharing the burden of supporting it. Joint ownership required careful matchmaking of resources and developing trust. Two neighbors, Zhang and Yang, created a workable relationship in which Zhang, who owned twelve *dan* of rice land, provided all the straw from his land, while Yang, a tenant on twenty *dan*, was able to make up the balance after delivering a sizable quota of his straw to his landlord. The buffalo stayed with Zhang, who had a young son who tended it, taking it to water. Trust initially was based on their kinship link: the grandmother of Zhang was the mother-in-law of Yang.

The majority of small farmers, however, found it difficult to jointly own a buffalo and instead would opt to hire a buffalo from its owner. In such cases, a contract usually was drawn up well in advance, stipulating that the renter would agree to provide the equivalent amount of his own labor to the owner's fields—since buffalo labor was equated to human labor—as well as the buffalo's daily feed. However, setting up an early agreement did not always spare the renter from anxiety, since he had to wait until the owner had finished plowing his own land. When rains for the spring plowing came late, as they did in 1941, renters waited in trepidation. That year we found one farmer in a state of great agitation. Since he farmed 4.5 *dan* of rice land, of which he owned 2 and rented 2.5, he would have to plow his rented land first, since the rent had to be paid in rice. If by then it was too late to plant rice on his own 2 *dan*, he would have to plant another crop, thereby taking a painful loss. Occasionally, we were told, a desperate farmer might rally family members, friends, or neighbors to pull the plow, although we never saw this happen. But nonetheless, it was the five hundred or so small farmers who relied on renting a buffalo who were most at risk from slight vagaries in the weather. Prosperity had some 350 buffaloes, an adequate number for the township's 11,245 *dan*, provided that dozens of small transactions and exchanges worked smoothly and the weather cooperated.

Not only was the water buffalo critical to the success of the rice harvest, but it was also much loved by farming families. The contrast between the care and attention showed to the buffalo and other farm animals, including cats and dogs, was readily apparent. Local people practiced a ban on the slaughter of a buffalo unless it had fallen ill or broken a leg. Hence beef was seldom to be found in the market. It was widely believed that those who violated this ban would subsequently suffer. We came across one young lad currently suffering from an ailment that caused him to chew his bedclothes; this was taken as a sign that he was being punished for this very crime—committed not by himself but by a forebear.

HIRED LABOR

For half of all farm households, selling "bitter" labor (*kuli*) was essential to survival. Both men and women from Prosperity's 654 households of small and dryland farmers hired themselves out, with women making up the majority of casual day laborers. Able-bodied men sold farm labor mainly in the rice-growing season. For the rest of the year they were not tied to the farm and could leave home to seek remunerative employment in a variety of occupations, but especially in transport. Women, in contrast, were tied to the farm not only by tradition but by the dispersed nature of the farm tasks conventionally assigned to them: hoeing, weeding, pruning crops, and gathering fuel, along with the household chores and care of children. Women were available for hire locally throughout the year, making up the bulk of the farm workers hired by the day in non-rush seasons.

Procedures for hiring routine day labor were informal, unlike that for peak season labor. Prosperity was a community of neighborhoods where people knew each other well. If a farmer needed to employ a man, he would count on running into some small farmer he knew on market day and might say, "Come around tomorrow and weed the rapeseed," or "Come on the 10th and hoe the bean field." If the would-be employer was looking for a woman, as was apt to be the case, he would send a word-of-mouth message by a neighbor of hers whom he happened to meet.

The man or woman hired for the day rose before dawn and worked until dark. In the course of the day, the laborer had three meals of plain family fare and at the end of the day got the day's wage in cash calculated at the current price of one *sheng* of rice, roughly a liter, for men, and for women about two-thirds of that amount. (Sustenance for an able-bodied laboring man was officially estimated at fifteen *sheng* of rice a month, and for a woman nine *sheng*, reflecting the accepted attitude on gender equivalence.) Traditionally the laborer was paid in rice, but in 1940 this was commuted into cash, since no employer wished to part with rice when inflation was devaluing the currency so rapidly. Then in April 1941, because the price of rice was soaring ever faster, the day's wage was reduced to the equivalent of half a *sheng* for men. Yet we heard no complaints. Men who were dissatisfied simply chose other employment. Women, on the other hand, were not in a strong bargaining position. There was no shortage of female labor for hire, since the poorest women farmers would neglect their own fields to work as hired laborers.

Those who employed day labor were chiefly the households of medium farmers. As these households could not easily protect their young men from conscription, they sent them off and made up the shortage by hiring women farm laborers on a daily basis, or else, less commonly, they took on a man past his prime as a long-term live-in hired man.

Able-bodied men who sold their labor at the peak of the farm season and women who sold day labor during the rest of the year encountered a wide discrepancy in conditions. The former received what counted as good pay and excellent fare, the latter only modest pay and plain fare. Some of these women were wives of small farmers; others were heads of households bereft of men and left to till upland farms to sustain their families. For the latter, in particular, the slack farm season when there was no demand for hired labor was the most dreaded. These households teetered on the verge of disintegration, and only a steady demand for day labor could keep them afloat.

Peak season labor shortages called for other strategies. Despite the shortage of rice land in the township, farmers in Prosperity still faced acute temporary shortages of manpower. Farm tasks were unevenly spread over the year, with tight bunching in the peak seasons in the spring and autumn, above all in spring. To make matters more difficult, this was wartime, with many men absent, either in the army or evading conscription. Our survey showed that in 45 percent of households there were no men at home of military age (eighteen to forty-two), while in 43 percent there was only one. Only 12 percent had two or more.

To meet the heavy demands at peak seasons, everyone, especially the men, worked under intense pressure and for long hours. Wherever possible, all able-bodied men of the family who were away working secondary jobs came home, and even those who were evading conscription returned despite the risk. (In the autumn of 1941, the central government, fearing a shortfall in rice, declared a moratorium on conscription during the harvest season to encourage men to return.) Families also engaged in mutual aid and labor exchange. Any further shortages were made up by hiring peak season day labor.

At the peak seasons, mutual aid and labor exchange were popular among households of relatives, neighbors, or friends. Each cooperating household contributed labor in proportion to the area of its rice fields. If the family with five *dan* contributed one able-bodied man, the family with ten *dan* had to contribute two. If a family lacked the labor for its required share, it made up the deficiency either by "inviting" a relative (who gave his labor gratis) or by hiring a laborer. If one family had lent a buffalo to another during the plowing, it was repaid at this time with the labor of one able-bodied man for the equivalent number of days. Between cooperating households, no pay changed hands, though some families might pay for hired help in order to make up their due share in the mutual aid. In practice, innumerable adjustments were made in every team of cooperating households, with the aim of making the exchange equitable to each family's satisfaction. One crucial matter was the order in which the fields of the various members would be worked, since those high on the list were less vulnerable to the hazards of the weather. This matter was solved by drawing lots.

Farmers with medium or large farms commonly hired day labor at the peak season, making arrangements well ahead of time with a foreman (*gong-tou*). This man was simply an enterprising small farmer himself who enjoyed the confidence of both those who wished to hire labor and those who wished to sell it. The people he dealt with were his neighbors, relatives, and friends. In the weeks preceding the rush season, the foreman received requests and lined up the number of laborers needed. He found them mostly among small-scale but also medium-scale farmers who could spare labor. Many were young men who were currently working outside the community on transport teams, or in other jobs, who would return especially for the occasion. The foreman then drew up a rotation, fitting each farmer hiring labor into a tight schedule within the limited span of time during which the tasks had to be completed. He received no extra pay for his efforts, but he enjoyed prestige as a man of influence in the neighborhood. Potential employers made a point of being on good terms with him, each hoping to have his turn early on the schedule.

Pay for peak season day labor was the same as that in routine times, but instead of three ample meals of ordinary fare, the laborer enjoyed five, one of them a "meat treat" (*dayaji*, or literally "a sacrifice to the teeth"), which called for half a *jin* of pork per man. In the busy season, hospitality was the order of the day, whether people were brought together through mutual aid, labor exchange, or hiring of labor. The host family whose fields were being worked that particular day was required to provide plenty of steamed rice, liberal quantities of meat, tobacco, and spirits, and one pickled egg for each man to enjoy with his liquor. Hired hands and poor relatives invited to assist shared equally in the food, drink, and festivity. Women came as well as men, even if they were not required in the fields, for there was plenty to do in the kitchen providing five meals each working day, including the meat treat at the noon meal. Women relatives of the family whose fields were being planted often came, some bringing gifts: a jug of liquor, a piece of preserved pork, or confections. Others were poor women relatives with no menfolk. They came because their help would be required at other times of the year, for example, with the thinning of sorghum or maize, weeding, harvesting, and so on. Since only plain fare was provided at other seasons, it was a courtesy to invite such women to "assist" at rice-transplanting time.

Good and plentiful food and drink were provided to sustain the intensity. All this made rush seasons the occasion for family reunions, collective labor, sociability, and feasting. It was a tense, exhausting, but happy time. It was not, however, free of grievances. Since many had few occasions to eat meat, they expected to eat their fill at this time. Any host failing to provide abundantly would be the object of recrimination. In the spring of 1941, there were complaints about a farmer who had served ample quantities of pork but had had his wife undercook it so that the feasters would eat less—or so it was claimed. Another possible source of grievance concerned relatives invited (or not invited) to help. How distant a relative could be expected to work without pay? Some poorer relatives welcomed the chance to cement the relationship with their better-off kinsmen, who might give a helping hand in some other situation, perhaps with a loan in an emergency. And the feasting and jollity was an immediate recompense. The only real bitterness we came across was in the case of women who were not invited to the feasting at rice-transplanting time but were expected to work with neither pay nor banquet at other farm seasons. As one widow complained to us, "They didn't recognize me as a relative at rice-transplanting time. But when the sweet potato harvest came along, they called me. Then, when they paid off the other women, they gave me nothing because I was a relative."

For Prosperity's poorest farmers—men and women, but especially men—the peak season was far happier than the Lunar New Year. The New Year fell in the slack season when poor families could find no employment and many went hungry. But at this time labor was in maximum demand, and the hired help enjoyed the same festival fare as anyone else. The uneven tempo of the agricultural year, whose pivot was rice production, gave farming families a variegated pattern of life marked by rhythms of tension and slackness, of individual toil and collective effort, of sparse living (with hunger for many) and pleasurable feasting and drinking. For many families, however, survival required that they supplement their agricultural income from other sources. It is to those strategies that we turn in the next chapter.

NOTES

1. Bishan's three small rivers are the Binanhe, which runs south along the east side of the county; the Bibei, which runs northeast along the top part of the county; and the Meijiang, which runs south along the west side of the county not far from Prosperity. Sichuan's name ("Four Rivers") is based on the existence within its borders of the Yangzi and three of its tributaries: the Minjiang, Tuojiang, and Jialing. However, its river resources are much more abundant, numbering more than thirteen hundred in all, and also include two other major Yangzi tributaries, the Yalong and Qianjiang. Bishan did not share in the general irrigation potential of the province.

2. From the seventh century, when approximately three thousand households resided in this hilly county, until the early eighteenth century, the population remained relatively low, especially in contrast to the well-irrigated Chengdu plains section of the Sichuan basin. According to the recent Bishan County gazetteer, the population records are incomplete, especially for the Song, Yuan, and Ming dynastic eras, in part because the county's borders were reconfigured several times, so no set of consistent figures was ever gathered for this specific domain over time. However, the slow growth of the market villages in the territory of Bishan from five in the Song to ten at the end of the Ming supports the few records of low population and also stands in marked contrast to the Qing, when twenty-four more market villages were added. In addition, some of the old ones, such as in Meijiang, were reestablished after the turmoil of the late Ming dynasty (Sichuan sheng Bishan xianzhi, 1996, pp. 68–77). The population figures for Bishan come from p. 105.

3. We are indebted to the efforts of Joe Dennis to search through various Taiwan databases available at Harvard University for mention of Bishan in dynastic histories.

4. As Ho Ping-ti argued in his pioneering work on China's population growth, the coming of New World crops to China began in the sixteenth century and permitted a dramatic expansion of cultivated land (Ho Ping-ti 1959, pp. 183–195). Both Laura Murray and James Lee argue that the connections between the introduction of New World crops and the growth of population may be more complicated than originally argued by Ho Ping-ti. In Sichuan, clearly the spread of New World crops was closely linked to the emergence of intense rice cultivation in Bishan and the growth of population (Murray 1985; J. Lee 1982, "Legacy of Immigration").

5. J. Lee (1982), "Food Supply," p. 738.

6. Zelin (1986), esp. pp. 501–504.

7. For a discussion of how this process unfolded in nearby Baxian, see Zelin (1986, p. 501).

8. William Rowe (2007, p. 61) found this to be the case in Hubei.

9. Von Glahn (1987), p. 179.

10. Generally in eastern Sichuan, the amount of land that was devoted to rice paddies in the mid-1930s ranged from 25 to 40 percent. In contrast, on the Chengdu plains, 80 percent of the land was devoted to wet rice cultivation (Cressey 1934, p. 139). In converting *dan* to acres, we have used 7.5 *dan* to the acre for paddy land, and 6 *dan* to the acre for farmland in general—both irrigated and unirrigated. The 7.5 figure is based on John Lossing Buck's (1943, p. 48)

estimate of rice yield in Sichuan in 1941 as averaging seventy-five bushels to the acre. The 6 *dan* figure is from the Chinese Bureau of Statistics, which set the average yield for cereal crops during the 1930s at fifty-five bushels to the acre. It should be noted that the new *dan* as a measure of volume was equivalent to just under six hundred pounds, or ten bushels (sixty pounds to the bushel).

11. In 1938, Sichuan was the largest rice producer in China. In 1941, Sichuan was third largest, behind Hunan and Guangdong (*China Handbook*, 1943, p. 567).

12. John Lossing Buck (1943).

13. *Fudou* is the Sichuanese pronunciation of *hudou*.

14. The China International Famine Relief Commission in Chongqing sent two experts to study possibilities to create a long-term solution to the irrigation problem that would not rely so heavily on rainfall. After surveying the locality, they credited the farmers with having made the fullest and most rational use of all local water resources and judged that no improvement was possible, since Prosperity lacked streams of any size.

15. In Sichuan, approximately 20 to 25 percent of the land at this time was planted with winter wheat, according to Cressey (1934, p. 139).

16. In the opinion of George Cressey (1934, p. 138), who became known through his geographical study of China in the Republican era, no other place in China at this time had "such an extent of slope utilization as the Red Basin."

17. For reasons we were not able to determine, Bishan was not a major producer of *tong* oil varnish. For a discussion of the importance of *tong* oil in China's international export trade, see Yen Chiang-kwoh (1943, esp. pp. 419–420); Hume (1939); and Chetham (2002, pp. 97–98).

18. This rate of 30 percent tenantry was low for Sichuan, which had the highest percentage of tenant farmers in China for the years between 1931 and 1941. In 1938, 50 percent of Sichuan farmers were tenants, while the national average was 30 percent (*China Handbook*, 1943, p. 604).

19. This number appears to include the 414 rice land owner-farmers as well as most of the landlords (Isabel Crook, personal communication, January 26, 2013).

20. Among them, the relatively small group of 96 families who owned their unirrigated fields lived better than the 228 renters.

21. The data for these 244 families, constituting 47 percent of the families who owned rice paddy land, is complete, as is the case for the top tier of 12 landlord families holding sixty-one to three hundred *dan* (3 percent of Prosperity's families). However, of the 516 households owning paddy land, 110 did not respond to this question, but the missing cases were not evenly distributed, with the result that the incomplete data is for the medium (eleven to thirty *dan*) and medium-large (thirty-one to sixty *dan*) families. We only managed to obtain information on this question for 126 medium-sized farms and 14 medium-large farms, suggesting that the bulk of the 110 families who did not provide data for this category were quite sensitive to revealing this specific information.

22. John Lossing Buck's (1943, p. 1) survey in 1941 revealed that this situation was also true for Sichuan as a whole. Of the 509 tenant households in Prosperity, only 323 answered the question in our survey on the size of their holdings.

23. Unfortunately, it is not possible to determine if Richard Gunde's report on deposits in Sichuan, derived from a study by Lü Pingdeng in 1936, are higher or lower than what we found, as his data is calculated on a different basis, suggesting that deposits might have been paid in kind, as they were equal to 60 to 80 percent of the annual rent. But it is worth noting that the percentage of farming households who could pay this deposit without borrowing was 14 percent, quite similar to the percentage in Prosperity who could handle these deposits with a certain amount of ease (Lü Pingdeng 1936, p. 200, cited in Richard Gunde 1976, p. 40).

24. Fields in 1940 Prosperity were one *dan* because they produced one *dan*. A big plot of poor land or a small plot of very good land that produced one *dan* would both be one-*dan* plots. The size was set at a certain time, and it was not changed despite, for example, improvements in irrigation, so a two-*dan* field might be producing three *dan*. At this very time, the government was carrying out a survey because they knew the numbers were wrong and they were losing a lot of grain tax. We hoped they might get to us while we were in Prosperity, but they didn't.

25. We use "wealthy" here in a relative sense. That is to say, some people in Prosperity seemed wealthy in comparison to others in the community. But when looked at in a larger perspective, Prosperity's wealthy did not compare to those on the rich Chengdu plain or even those living in Bishan.

26. This diagram was compiled by analyzing a wide variety of factors presented in the surveys, including amount of land, labor power available, number of elderly people who had to be supported, access to buffalo, and type and profitability of sidelines. For instance, a young couple owning or renting some paddy land, without elderly parents to support, who either sold some of their labor in slack seasons and/or had sidelines, would fall on the viable side, whereas a similar couple who only cultivated dry land, or where the man had just fallen ill, or who had to support elderly parents and very young children, would be categorized among the poor and destitute.

27. In defining our categories, the most difficult distinction to make was that between the third and fourth strata. We shifted the line many times. In the end we set it by referring to the classifications established to implement the 1951 land reform in Prosperity.

28. In 1941 we mentioned our difficulty getting information about these households to Sun Zhonglu, the township head. He said that he knew all about these families and could give us the information for 1940, which he knew by virtue of his position. We could not be sure that other peasants were telling us the truth about their landholdings, but we created a thoroughly non-government context for our survey specifically so that the peasants would be less likely to hide the truth. Xiji even worried that the peasants might feel confident enough to brag and inflate rather than reduce the stated size of their holdings.

29. Netting (1993), p. 7.

30. The reasons for a nuclear, stem, or extended family to accept indigent relatives or laborers into their midst were varied, but when a family dwindled to three members or fewer, the main economic impetus was to create a larger household. Thus, of the fifty-three one-member families, well over a third had taken in additional persons. It was common to find a lone widow who had taken in her long-widowed mother, even though they had different surnames and by Chinese customary family law they were not considered to be of one family. Six percent of the families who found they were short of labor power opted to hire long-term live-in labor to help in agricultural work or with weaving.

31. The family is defined here as the legally recognized immediate kinship group at the core of the registered household. For an anthropological explanation of what constitutes a household and how it is different from the family, see Yanagisako (1979). She expresses criticisms of the work of other scholars who have considered this issue, particularly D. R. Bender (1967, 1971), who has argued that a family is defined by its blood relations while a household is based on common residence. The objections that some anthropologists, such as R. N. H. Bulmer (1960), have raised about the term "household" do not apply to Prosperity's domestic groups, for there was no situation in which households working on one activity were not living together. Further-more, were we conducting this survey today we would not refer to the priests as a household, as their main collective activity was not domestic even though they lived and ate together.

32. Families ranged in size from one to sixteen members, but the mode (most numerous) was four. The mode is more significant than the average, which was five in Prosperity, because the mode was more representative or common than the average. Averages can cover up very important distinctions, for an average would equate one of our sixteen-member families with two of our eight-member families. In Prosperity, the small percentage of families with eight or more members can be taken to represent extended families belonging chiefly to stratum 1 or 2, as only they had sufficient means to sustain the large extended family.

Chapter Three

Not Far Afield

Family Survival Strategies

Prosperity was a crowded place: four hundred persons per square kilometer by the beginning of the war, in our estimation. The density of population put enormous pressure on the land.[1] At peak seasons, as we have seen, agriculture required the availability of large amounts of labor. But even in the absence of major disasters, the available land was not sufficient to maintain the population that was needed for the busy season of rice production. In slack periods, farmers were constantly seeking ways to expand the household economy.

Our visits to almost any farm home in Prosperity in 1940 brought to light the importance of nonfarming occupations to augment the family's income. Prosperity Market provided farmers opportunities to supplement their household income through crafts, services, or commerce. Men and women, old and young, produced goods or provided services for the market, making fuller use of family labor that could not be absorbed in farmwork. Often the niche was so small that it was hardly noticeable, such as washing pig bristles before they were used to make brushes, or collecting and drying herbs that were used to powder the outside of incense sticks. Indeed, this activity in one poor family we visited was so inconspicuous that we had failed to note it until one of the incense-making households drew it to our attention. Market enterprises offered the greatest potential for local landlord investment, as well as a local safety net to cushion farmers from the uncertainties and limitations of farming. Diversification enabled a few to rise and many others to survive. But the early 1940s were a difficult time in Prosperity. When diversifying production was not enough, people turned to other means of survival: casual labor, dispersal of household members, and banditry.

RURAL PROTOINDUSTRIES AND HANDICRAFTS

Farming families in this community developed a broad array of cottage and household industries (see table 3.1).[2] For a few entrepreneurial families, these pursuits brought sufficient wealth to allow them to pull themselves out of the competition for scarce paddy fields, while for others these protoindustrial undertakings provided a significant part of their own subsistence and thereby allowed them to avoid catastrophe.

Aside from a few wealthy landlord families at the pinnacle of the social scale, practically every family in this community, whether affluent or poor, was involved in some moneymaking venture outside of agriculture. In all, we counted almost six hundred rural enterprises, big and small, employing 1,095 people—over 600 of them women (see table 3.2). When we added those

Table 3.1. Rural Protoindustries in Prosperity

Branch of Rural Industry	Number of Enterprises
1. Cloth and Apparel	481
• cotton cloth weaving	450
• tailors	23
• making skullcaps for men	1
• weaving rain hats	3
• weaving straw sandals	3
• batik and other dyeing	1
2. Houses, Furniture, Implements, and Equipment	74
• tile kiln	1
• smithies	10
• carpentry	39
• masonry (stone and tile)	23
• loom construction and repair	1
3. Processing	13
• oil presses	2
• flour mill	1
• wheat noodles	3
• soybean noodles	2
• brewery and distillery	1
• homemade rice hotcakes	1
• homebrewed rice wine	3
4. Sundries	16
• soap (processed in general store)	1
• candles (processed in general store)	1
• cotton tape braiding	1
• cord twisting	1
• basketry	2
• bamboo mats	1
• silver ornaments	4
• ceremonial token money (cash paper)	2
• gilded tokens	1
• incense	2
TOTAL:	**584**

Table 3.2. Economic Status and Secondary Occupations (men and women, 15 years and over)

Economic Status of Household	Number of Households (household breakdown)	Secondary Occupations	
		Men	Women
Stratum 1:	12	No men	No women
	Big landlord		
Stratum 2:	136	310	168
	90 hh medium and home industry with small landlords 28 hh well-off professional tenants 18 hh well-off farmers	236 special plant/80 weaver/66 self-employed/20 civil servant/20 reeler/10 proprietor of service establishment/10 wholesale trade/10 retail trade or broker/4 independent crafts/2 teacher/20 not specified	
Stratum 3:	547	416	422
	255 hh medium farmers 292 hh medium tenants	320 weaver/87 hired weaver/87 independent craftsmen/85 reeler/75 soldier or guard/40 hired labor in agriculture or transportation/35 operator of service establishment/34 professional/30 retail trade or broker/15 proprietor of service establishment/9 skilled employee/6 hired weaver/5 retail trade/3 proprietor of service establishment/3 assistant craftsmen/1 teacher /1 opium/2 semiprofessional	
Stratum 4:	802	367	66
	141 hh small farmers 189 hh small tenants 324 hh dryland farmers 148 hh nonfarming	163 transport and long-term farm labor/100 soldier or guard/58 peddler or broker/43 minor home industry/21 live-in domestic and farm laborer/12 retail trade/11 hired weaver/10 weaver or reeler/12 illicit/2 semiprofessional/1 unknown or absent	
GRAND TOTAL: 1,497 hh		MEN 1,093	WOMEN 656

people involved in services, commerce, and transport, the total number came to approximately 1,700 men and women.[3] In the more prosperous homes, looms clacked, often far into the night. In poorer homes, a disabled man might be found winding pith around carefully trimmed bamboo sticks for candlewicks, or a group of women might be seen lashing palm leaves between two bamboo frames to make rain hats. For the better-off, engaging in a subsidiary occupation in the slack seasons was a means to improving their conditions and perhaps even prospering, while for the vast majority diversifying was a crucial survival tactic.

If the income generated from these diverse secondary occupations was represented on a chart, it would largely match the social pyramid in chapter 2.[4] At the top of the income-generating pyramid were twenty to thirty substantial merchants, with capital of several thousand yuan. Those with moderate resources were able to acquire more advanced equipment or technologies, such as looms, distilleries, dyes, large vats, oil presses, and flour mills, and thus were able to derive a better income. Most of the craftsmen, traders, peddlers, and transport workers were members of poor families with very little capital to invest.

Cotton weaving was by far the most important rural industry in Prosperity and was known as a specialty of Bishan County by the 1930s.[5] Unlike the much wealthier Jiangnan region in East China, where cotton weaving enjoyed a long history extending back to the Song dynasty, Bishan did not develop a significant handicraft textile industry until the end of the Qing dynasty, when suddenly it began to flourish to such a degree that it was commonly said that "everyone spun or wove and there were no idlers in any household." [6] The second era of expansion in Bishan's cotton weaving came in the early years of the Republic, when the outbreak of World War I occupied the attention of the Western nations in Europe and stopped the competition of foreign products with Chinese native cloth production. Bishan textiles experienced a strong upsurge that drew approximately forty thousand men and women into spinning and weaving throughout the county. Yet another rise began in the late 1920s and 1930s when Japan secured a domineering position in the modern cotton mills in Shanghai and undercut the Chinese handicraft cotton industry, which then retreated into the interior provinces, especially Sichuan, Yunnan, and Anhui.[7]

In Prosperity, the textile handicraft industry made up three-quarters of all cottage enterprises. Almost a third of all local families had looms, keeping, at our count, 886 people employed, 587 of them women. Skill in weaving gave women, especially young women in families of strata 2 and 3, considerable standing in their families. It also gave older women in better-off but declining families a way to shore up the family livelihood. Small-scale rural industries gave women, as well as the old and the disabled, an opportunity to help hold together a poverty-stricken family or to keep a solitary self alive.

Weaving was primarily a family affair, with the skills passed on from one generation to the next. Much of the cotton cloth was narrow gauge and produced by foot-treadled looms for local consumption, but some trickled into Bishan County town and Chongqing markets. The typical scene we often came upon was a single native loom set up in the central room, or occasionally outside under the eaves. A resonant clacking of wood on wood would announce well in advance that the loom was in operation, as the weaver—a man or woman—pulled the crossbar forcefully against the frame to make the weave firm and tight, critical for judging the quality of the cloth as well as the price it could fetch. Such a scene represented perhaps 80 percent of the cotton weaving enterprises, belonging typically to households of the lower social strata of this community. But another 20 percent was more advanced and belonged chiefly to households of stratum 2. Once, for instance, we came upon a "factory," with the harsher metallic din of ten wide looms furnished with durable iron parts. The factory turned out to be three separate household enterprises whose families had banded together to rent the spacious ten-section tile-roofed Zeng Family Ancestral Hall for their domestic industry.

The most flourishing enterprise we found was that of Dr. Tao Mingsheng, a prosperous traditional-style doctor and pharmacologist. In addition to twelve *dan* of rice land, Dr. Tao owned five looms and three spinning wheels. His household of fifteen members included eight hired workers, five of them skilled men weavers aged around thirty, and three skilled women spinners and reelers in their thirties or forties. But the vast majority of enterprises relied on family labor only; a small minority supplemented family labor with one hired weaver, while the exceptional household had more than one. Dr. Tao's was the only enterprise relying entirely on a nonfamily workforce.

This busy clatter throughout the countryside was the result of the wartime boom in the cloth market. In the mid-1930s, strong narrow-gauge homespun cloth dominated the local market. But by 1940, both wide-loom and narrow-loom cloth were in demand. The market for local machine-spun cotton cloth had grown rapidly, spurred by the establishment of a government bureau in Bishan town that purchased broad-loom cloth for army uniforms made in its own local factories. However, the rural market for sturdy homespun remained. Although a second bureau in Bishan, the Rural Credit Bureau, purchased quantities of the tougher, narrow-gauge homespun, most families producing homespun sold it themselves in the rural market or to one of the local cloth dealers, while a few others produced it for home use only.

Despite the boom, prosperity was not evenly spread. It was the 15 percent of households with standard looms, and above all those with more than one, that flourished. Those with native looms fared less well. The purchase of yarn was one factor. Ninety-five percent of those with native looms, but only 20 percent of those with standard looms, purchased yarn locally in small quantities at higher prices. Some lacked capital to purchase sufficient quantities to make the time-consuming trip into town worthwhile. Some were women who did not feel comfortable dealing with strangers in town.

The relative state of the two types of enterprise was most sharply revealed in the number of idle looms. Of the 448 native looms, one-quarter were idle; of the 109 standard looms only one-tenth were idle. The major reason for idleness was the loss of the family weaver, usually to conscription, press-ganging, or flight to avoid these, for half the skilled weavers in the community were young men of military service age. This was the sole cause of idleness in the few cases of standard looms and accounted for almost two-thirds of the many cases among native looms. When it came to protecting their sons, better-off families were at an advantage. One of their evasion tactics was for the weaver to leave home (even though this meant leaving the family loom idle) and take employment outside the community as a skilled weaver in a well-off, influential household where he had some protection. Conversely, some of the weavers employed by better-off farmers in Prosperity came from other communities.

The second reason for idleness was lack of capital. This did not bring standard looms to a halt. When they lacked capital, they could obtain an advance of machine-spun cotton yarn from the above-mentioned government bureau in charge of uniform making and receive pay for the finished piece goods according to the quality. The Rural Credit Bureau, on the other hand, did not make advances of yarn for production of the narrow-gauge cloth it bought. Consequently, lack of capital brought idleness to native looms and accounted for one-fifth of all cases.

Although most weavers worked in their own homes, one-sixth worked for wages. These were chiefly young men evading conscription as mentioned above; a mere 2 percent were women. In addition, Prosperity had twenty-five apprenticed weavers (nineteen young men and six girls), who provided the master's family with free labor in return for board, lodging, and initiation into the craft. Hired weavers lived in the homes of their employers, sharing family fare and special meat treats twice a month. They were remunerated in one of two ways: wages or piecework. Those receiving wages were hired by the month or year at fairly good rates, especially if they were skilled in farmwork and agreed to help on the farm when needed. The rates were from 750 to 950 yuan a year. Those paid piecework rates received three to four yuan for each fifteen- or sixteen-meter length of cloth, the amount a fast worker could weave in one long hard day and late into the night.

Both rates counted as good pay, and weavers were considered the elite among hired workers in the community. The advantage of yearlong employment was that it provided the weaver with room and board. The advantage of piecework was that the weaver could tend to farm and household chores. The hiring of spinners or reelers on a long-term basis was rare. This was women's work, and families needing help usually took indigent female relatives into their homes, counting this as providing them with welfare. Among the 315 women whose chief occupation was spinning or reeling, we came across only ten who were paid for their services. Like hired weavers, these ten women also lived in the homes of their employers, sharing family fare but without the meat treats. They were paid either a monthly wage of about fourteen yuan (i.e., 170 yuan a year) or piecework rates at one yuan a bundle of yarn weighing 8.5 *jin* and made up of a skein of twenty to twenty-four strands, depending on the fineness required. As the average spinner could spin three bundles of medium thread in one long day, she was far better off on piecework. Reelers got their board, too, but were paid by the day at sixty *fen*.

The families that profited handsomely from their household industries were those who possessed sufficient capital to invest in necessary equipment or who developed an expertise in an occupation that was connected to urban commerce. As a small landlord, Wang Haizhou had the means to purchase both a flour mill and an oil press, thereby providing necessary services to the community. The outlay needed for a high-ceilinged workshop and heavy-timbered press was beyond the budget of most families in Prosperity, and in Wang's case there was some risk, as another landlord, Wu Wanling, also owned an oil press.[8] Much more driven than his better-educated competitor, Wang operated his press as an owner-proprietor with hired labor, while Wu rented his entire business out to a tenant-proprietor, Liu Haisan, a skilled oil presser, who used family labor and the hired help of two skilled old men.[9] The minimum labor requirement was a pair of operators, one of whom had to be skilled. The labor was so intense that the men could work no more than two or three hours a day, pressing about two hundred *jin* of oil. To keep the press in full operation required more than one team. The press was a large cylinder into which rapeseed was packed and then compressed by percussion, which was provided by two men alternately swinging a heavy beam slung from a high trellis. Heavy blows on the end of the cylinder caused oil to ooze into a vat below. Although there was not enough rapeseed grown in this community to keep both presses in regular operation, in the hot summer months after the harvest, this strenuous work was done entirely at night, often until the small hours of the morning. The orange lamplight, silhouetting the moving men through the open doorway in the otherwise black street, accompanied by the rhythmic thumps pulsating through the village, left an eerie impression.

Wang's two hired press operators were known for their speedy work, regularly squeezing out about two hundred *jin* of oil in a few hours. Thus while Wang's press was widely believed to be doing four hundred yuan worth of business each day of operation, tenant-proprietor Liu was just getting by. Meanwhile, Wang Haizhou added to his income through a subsidiary noodle workshop attached to his flour mill. There two hired laborers operated noodle-making equipment consisting of a wooden form for extruding dough into fine ribbons, and racks for hanging them up to dry in the open air. The dried noodles were cut into standard lengths and packed into one-*jin* bundles ready for marketing. The two laborers, who received board, lodging, and fifteen *fen* per bundle, turned out fifty bundles of noodles a day.

The most prosperous entrepreneur in Prosperity was the bristle merchant, Wei Shuyao, who came from a landlord family in another part of Bishan. His parents had sent him to secondary school and then arranged for him to serve as an apprentice to Wu Yi'an, who monopolized the bristle trade in Prosperity. They may well have selected this profession because of Sichuan's strong role in China's bustling global export trade of pig bristles, which in 1936 amounted to over twenty-five million dollars.[10] Normally this apprenticeship would have resulted in a master like Wu helping his trainee launch a business in his home community while Wu's son inherited the Prosperity enterprise. But Wu's son was not interested in taking over the family business, deciding instead on a career in local politics, where he succeeded in winning an appointment as the township head in the early 1930s. Master Wu was sufficiently impressed by his talented apprentice that he arranged a marriage between his daughter and Wei, and in due course handed over the business, which Wei Shuyao managed very successfully.

Landlords were not the only families in the community who enhanced their wealth through family businesses. During the 1930s, Prosperity's residents witnessed the rise of a fairly poor family through an astute combination of commercial sidelines and agriculture. Farmer Dong Rongfa first started up a commercial venture that required little capital investment—manufacturing firecrackers, for which he earned the nickname Firecracker Dong. He then used his profits to good advantage by renting forty *dan* of prime rice land at a low rate in return for a substantial deposit in silver. Relying on his industrious nine-member family to help cultivate this large tract, Dong was able to produce and market an astonishing yield of fifty *dan* of unhusked rice, while his upland fields produced another two *dan* of coarse cereal for sustenance. In 1933, when his son Dong Taibang turned twenty-two, he decided the family could spare this son's labor from farmwork and provided the startup funds of thirty silver dollars, a significant amount in those days, to launch the son as a cloth dealer.

Building up a successful business from scratch in rural Sichuan during the turbulent 1930s required much more than an initial outlay of capital. Dong Taibang peddled native narrow-gauged cloth in all the nearby periodic markets until he had earned sufficient experience and profits to rent a shop in Prosperity's market village. It was soon clear to him that he needed access to Chongqing banks in order to expand his business further, as they would loan him money far more cheaply than in Prosperity. Even so, since Dong did not own a shop that could serve as security, he had to make a substantial deposit each time he wished to take a one-month loan, the usual term at the time. Thus, to get five hundred yuan, he first had to deposit fifteen hundred, after which the bank gave him two thousand. He also could not travel safely between Prosperity and Chongqing without purchasing protection. To this end, he made a prudent decision to join both the Loom Fairy Society (*Jixian-*

hui), a semi-secret organization of cloth traders, and the local Paoge.[11] On the eve of the war, he had become one of the wealthiest merchants in Prosperity.

The experiences of the Dongs were not typical. Most families lacked the capital and family resources to rise up in these difficult times through engaging in household industries. Rather, they looked for small-scale undertakings in transport, services, and the sale or production of cheap goods. Thus, the twenty-three masons (nine working on tile and fourteen on stone), thirty-five carpenters (of thirty-nine), fourteen master blacksmiths, and twenty-three tailors were all drawn from poorer families in the community. Often these sidelines were linked: the farmer whose side occupation was butchering pigs received the pigskin with its bristles in part payment; he in turn sold these to both the households processing the pigskins and those cleaning and sorting the pig bristles; these in turn were sold to the prosperous local skin and bristles merchant Wei Shuyao, who provided them to a company in Chongqing.

Most of these occupations produced only a small amount of income and were part time at best. During the slack seasons, for instance, two poor families in Prosperity were able to augment their income by making about three thousand incense sticks a day and selling them in the periodic market. In each family, the man's job was to take bamboo from the grove by his house and cut it into sticks of uniform size. The wife's task was to make a thick paste by mixing water with the fine dust left from burning charcoal. With the help of her children, she daubed the sticks with the paste, rolled them to an even thickness, and then sent them on to another household to apply the fragrant herb powder. Both the charcoal and the herbs were purchased locally, augmenting the volume of transactions in the periodic market.[12] When these two families in turn went back to the market to sell their incense sticks, on a good day each one was able to earn an income of 4.5 to 5 yuan.

Candles were used in Prosperity both for lighting and for ceremonial purposes. Their manufacture was a two-step process. The first was the preparation of the wicks, which required little capital outlay and was carried on by members of poor households. Wicks were then sold to the proprietor of a general store, who carried out the second step of dipping them in tallow, a process which increased their value tenfold.

We came upon three separate households engaged in wick making, involving two men and one woman. For raw materials they required only bamboo and pith from reeds, both grown locally. The bamboo they cut into sticks of the required size and then bound them with long strands of pith extracted from the reeds. Candles came in three sizes: ordinary ones for lighting, which required four strands of pith, small ones that required two strands, and ceremonial temple candles, with only one. Wick makers might grow their own reeds and extract the pith themselves, but a semi-invalid we talked with in April 1941 who bought his pith from a grower managed to keep himself alive on his earnings of about three yuan a day.

Another sideline occupation was dyeing. The indigo dye plant was located in a broad-mouthed sandstone cave in one of the many dales around Prosperity. The equipment consisted chiefly of a number of large earthenware vats. Customers brought cloth, usually cotton piece goods from the local cottage weaving industry, to be dyed to order in any chosen shade of blue. In addition, the dyers produced blue and white batik items for sale in the market: door and bed curtains, and large kerchiefs for wrapping and carrying bundles. Batik dyeing involved painting popular local designs in wax on undyed cloth, dipping the cloth in the dye vat, hanging it out to dry, and when thoroughly dry removing the wax.

One occupation that required very little cash outlay was hauling coal from the nearby mountains in the neighboring township of Zitong. Some twenty or thirty coal carriers operating with just enough cash in hand to purchase a load of coal at the mine head would then carry their goods to Prosperity's periodic market to sell the same morning. In this way, they managed along with many other poor people in the town to find a way to eke out a living without resorting to banditry.

Since many families had lost their young able-bodied men to conscription, it was often the women and children, the old, and the ill or disabled left behind who took up many of these petty industry jobs. The weaving of rain hats was carried on by nine housewives in various parts of the township. In one neighborhood we found three women cooperating in the business: a widow, her sister-in-law, and a neighbor. We watched the busy trio lashing bamboo strips into frames for rain hats, then laying waterproof palm leaves on one frame and sandwiching them in with another frame, and lashing the frames together to hold the leaves in place. Unlike the others, these three women belonged to comfortable households and engaged in this as a part-time job for the sake of earning a bit of ready cash. They produced in their spare time an average of one hat a day each, for which they earned fifty *fen* apiece at the end of 1940, but one yuan by the spring of 1941.

Rain hat makers did not market the hats themselves but sold them to a peddler who came around from time to time. This man had succeeded in building up the scale of his operations and could afford to make advance payment to his suppliers. The three women told us that they had persuaded the peddler to advance them twenty yuan for the Lunar New Year celebrations a few weeks before, promising to repay him forty hats at the current rate of fifty *fen* a hat. With cheerful fatalism, they told us that the rate per hat had gone up to one yuan, but because they had agreed to repay the loan with forty hats, they were getting only half what they might have earned.

These vast numbers of small rural industries mainly served local needs rather than trade beyond the confines of the three or four market villages of the subvalley. Most of the technologies used could easily have been two thousand years old. These workshops earned some profits for their proprietors and provided some employment for surplus local labor. But they had saturated the local market. We found few apprentices currently being trained up to expand any of these industries. They had apparently achieved equilibrium.

It was characteristic of some of these petty industries that the marketing was done by small peddlers, who thereby also earned a meager living. Approximately forty men in this community supplemented their income as itinerant peddlers. Carrying their wares—crockery, salt, needles and thread, homespun cloth, gourds, straw sandals, straw hats, and dozens of other daily-use items—they were purveyors of cheap commodities. Mostly from poor rural families, they needed this supplemental income to keep their farms going or they had already lost their farms and were relying on this occupation to stay alive. Depending on their line of wares, these peddlers covered a larger or smaller circuit. Some went to just three or four market villages of the subvalley near Prosperity whose synchronized schedules provided them with a market in session nine days in every ten, while others traveled a larger route. Their capital requirements ranged from the few yuan needed to purchase a stock of bamboo scoops, gourd dippers, chopsticks, or straw sandals, to the fifty yuan or so needed for a reasonable supply of needles and thread, scissors, knives, crockery, matches, or tobacco. Some peddlers acquired their stocks locally, buying up the products of the local minor home industries (rain hats, chopsticks, bamboo scoops, and gourd dippers) or of farm sidelines (chickens, ducks, etc.) to retail in the vicinity. Others went to Bishan and bought products of urban industry—needles, knives, or embroidery thread—or visited centers producing local specialties such as salt, sugar, tobacco, peanuts, and crockery bowls. A peddler with skill and luck might work his way up from selling gourd dippers to selling needles and thread or, with bad luck, might drop back again to gourds, as happened to a peddler we knew whose stock in trade was stolen, forcing him to begin again at the bottom.

"STANDING IN WATER UP TO THEIR NECKS": FARM FAMILIES IN CRISIS

In these ways, under normal conditions, families were able to develop strategies that would enable them to survive. However, any natural or human-made disaster could immediately plunge most farm families, whether well off or poverty stricken, into a serious crisis. For instance, farmers were constantly trying to increase the amount of acreage devoted to wet rice production, causing them to develop terraces higher and higher up on the slopes. When the spring rains came late, these farmers were vulnerable to crop failure, as it was impossible to start a rice crop without rainwater and there were limits on the amounts of water that could be stored. Droughts and flooding were common occurrences. [13] The famine in eastern Sichuan in 1936, which drove massive numbers of farmers into the cities looking for food, was a particularly difficult time for Prosperity's residents as well, although the widespread starvation that occurred elsewhere was averted. [14] Relatively speaking, this community had fared better than most in the region, having suffered only four years of widespread natural calamities in the twenty years preceding our arrival. But farmers remained dependent on the weather, which each year brought disaster to some number of individual families.

Among prosperous and medium-level farming families, overextravagant weddings and funerals could bring sudden decline. Another common cause of misfortune for rich and poor was bankruptcy as a result of a disaster, such as a fire, drought, illness, robbery, business failure, gambling, opium addiction, or perhaps a lawsuit. Approximately half the families of this community lived barely above the hunger line, and they were brought down by relatively minor disasters on a regular basis in Prosperity. The precariousness of their situations was poignantly captured by R. H. Tawney in his observation that the situation of many Chinese farmers of the Republican era was "that of a man standing permanently up to the neck in water, so that even a ripple is sufficient to drown him." [15]

For those living close to the subsistence level, these disasters often caused the family to fragment. The extent of the dispersal of women, children, and the elderly with the disintegration of families can be indicated only obliquely through our statistics. Our survey showed, for instance, that 162 individuals lived in the homes of their relatives, involving 105 host families. Seventy-one host families had taken in one relative, twenty-one had taken in two, ten had taken in three, and three others had taken in more. Relatives most commonly took in a child, a widow, or an elderly person (usually the wife's mother). When they took two it was commonly two children, a mother and baby, or an elderly couple. Our figures on live-in employment add to the picture. One hundred thirty-four individuals stayed in the homes of ninety-one employer families. Fifty-nine of these employees were children fourteen years and under (fifty-three boys and six girls). Finally, figures for self-employed children showed that ten boys aged fourteen and under carried coal.

These figures accounted for only a portion of those left in economic destitution by the breakup of a family; other children were adopted, for they had become members of other families, especially the girls who were taken in as foster fiancées (*tongyangxi*). Some boys from destitute, fragmented, or disintegrated families were also adopted, but most had to fend for themselves. Teenagers might carry coal, while the younger ones tended goats or buffaloes, carried water, or did other domestic chores, receiving no pay but only food and shelter.

Also missing from these figures were poor women who remarried. The community recognized that in the typical nuclear family of the small farmer, a man needed a wife and a woman needed a husband. The Confucian prohibition on the remarriage of a woman in such cases was therefore overlooked. Wang Bingling, a small trader in Prosperity Market, had married his daughter to a poor farmer peddler in the countryside. Three years before our time the young man had gone to Guizhou on business and after a year had still not been heard from. In the meantime, his wife could hardly keep herself and her small children alive. Her own concerned parents arranged for her to come to the village with her children and live with their next-door neighbor, a poor forty-five-year-old rice wine seller named Cao Hanzhou. We heard no criticism of this practical arrangement, even though the required two years had not elapsed since her husband's departure. In the spring of 1941, the new couple had a baby daughter. Following this came news that the husband was not dead but had been press-ganged into the army in Guizhou. But this made no difference to the relationship. If ultimately the husband did come home, the two men would have to come to some settlement. If the woman chose to stay with the wine seller, he would certainly have to pay the soldier husband compensation to enable the latter to afford another marriage. The remarriage of young widows was legitimized by economic necessity. So long as there was no promiscuity and the arrangement was stable, they cast no slur on the woman's character. Yet this did not affect the rigid ban on widow remarriage, which people accepted ideologically and kept in a separate compartment of their consciousness. It lingered on in people's thinking, quite untouched by mundane reality.

As for older people in disintegrating households, so long as they could still make themselves useful, they might find a home with relatives, or live-in employment at reduced rates of pay or in return for food and shelter. On a country road one day we met a weathered sinewy man in his late fifties without a relative left in the world. Although old for his years, he was still able to work. But ahead of him lay the day when he could no longer do so. He did not speak of this nor evince any self-pity but gave us a matter-of-fact account of the personal tragedies which left him the sole survivor in his family. For these solitary older people, the future was bleak; they could expect little charity when they could no longer be useful. Prolonging the life of a person no longer able to make a contribution was not considered a virtue at any level of society. In Prosperity at this time none starved outright, but they easily fell victim to illnesses from which they died because of their weakened condition.

For small farming families, the prime factor in sudden decline was the loss of able-bodied manpower through illness, accidents, and death. Those families who rented a few *dan* of rice land could be brought to ruin by the loss of a man, since tenant families without a strong person to plow and transplant rice automatically lost their tenancy unless they had relatives with a solid economic base. When farmer Fu died, his family had to give up the tenancy and the housing that had been provided by the landlord. Fu's widow hired herself out as a farm laborer and found employment for her ten- and twelve-year-old sons in farm homes where, in return for looking after the buffalo and goats and weeding and carrying water, they were given a place to sleep and the plainest of fare. Sometime later she was introduced to a poor bachelor carpenter in the village and they decided to live as husband and wife. They both continued to support themselves, he as a craftsman and she as a farmhand hired by the day. Three years later, her sons were old enough to give up their nonpaying, live-in farm jobs and began to earn money carrying coal to the market. This income enabled them to rejoin their mother and reestablish the family.

Wives who farmed unirrigated upland fields often were able to cope somewhat more effectively with the loss of a husband, but their sense of crisis was nevertheless quite profound. One vulnerable couple had managed to support a widowed mother and three small sons on the income they generated from their farm and from the husband's goat-butchering business. But even with both able-bodied adults working, they felt compelled to give away a young daughter as a foster fiancée. When the husband suddenly died from tetanus poisoning, his wife, still in her early thirties, was left to support four dependents by taking charge of her family's dryland farm and also hiring herself out as a day laborer during the busy seasons. Five months after her husband's death, we paid a visit to the widow and found her thin and worn, her hair uncombed, sitting on a low bench leaning against the sun-warmed adobe wall of her home. Before her stretched a hillside field of beans, much smaller than those of her neighbors because it had been planted later and not given enough fertilizer. Without any self-pity, she explained that she could not weed the field because she had not eaten for a number of days, as she had to conserve her energy and provisions until day labor jobs were available, which would provide her with both food and money. Significantly, despite the desperation of this family's situation, it could resist fragmentation because it still owned the small dryland farm and held on to some of its resources. In the home were several well-made benches and a decent coffin, which could have been sold, but both the mother-in-law and the widow refused to part with these belongings in case, as the children grew older, their plight became worse.

In such circumstances, a woman often played a major role in arranging for the survival of the dependents as well as herself. Placing children was not difficult. They might be given up for adoption, they might be placed with relatives, or they might find employment. Since infant and child mortality rates were high, there were always families in the community in need of a son. Girls, too, were in demand because poor families with no prospect of affording a traditional-style marriage for a son were eager to secure a bride-to-be by adopting a small girl as a foster fiancée. If, however, the woman had hopes of restoring the family at some future date, she could place a young son temporarily in a farm home where he would do simple chores in return for plain food and a place to sleep until he was old enough to earn money himself. This meant that the son was still hers. As for the elderly, provided they were still able to perform light chores, the woman (or they themselves) would seek a home where their labor was needed and which would provide them with at least the minimum essentials of life. Mostly these homes were those of near or distant relatives, though sometimes the arrangement was simply economic. The woman, after having provided for the young and the old, could now seek work for herself, most commonly casual day labor in the fields or domestic service. The widespread varied market provided other opportunities as well. And she could hope that, as the boys grew old enough to earn some money, the family might be reunited.

While bad luck brought ruin to many families, others succumbed to crippling social vices pervasive in the community. We were struck by the precipitous decline in the fortunes of Xiang Huisheng, a former landowner and township head who gradually lost his property along with his prestige and power because of his gambling and opium addictions. In 1938, at the age of fifty, he had to give up his village home and move to an upland farm where he became completely dependent on his wife, who supported them by cultivating their few remaining unirrigated fields and by her skillful weaving, which brought her renown throughout the community.

The disaster that struck Peng-Wu shi, or Peng Sao (Elder sister-in-law Peng) as she was often known, reveals how suddenly a family could be devastated. She was born into a prosperous family of the Wu clan and was married into a similarly prosperous family of the Peng lineage. This large undivided family augmented its farm income by lending at the customary usurious rates and through the eldest son's trade in cloth. Then came a series of disasters. First, the merchant son was killed by bandits while on a business trip to Guizhou. Soon after, the account book detailing loan agreements was lost or stolen, and the family was unable to collect outstanding debts. The family head, Peng Sao's husband, was a well-known loafer, and his younger brothers and sons followed in his footsteps. Furthermore, both Peng Sao and her husband were opium addicts. When Peng Sao's husband died in 1935, the family lost all its land and she was left destitute with six sons aged three to twenty-two. The family had not been able to afford brides for the older sons, so they remained in the family.

Peng Sao's first step was to move the family to a rented back room in the village and to take odd jobs, sometimes as a domestic servant, a sewing woman, or washerwoman. Sometimes she worked in the fields and at other times vended cheap wares from a street stall. For a while, they lived on her earnings and what the two older boys could make from odd jobs and gambling. Then with the war, the eldest son was conscripted. He escaped but was captured and so severely beaten that when he was returned to the army it would not accept him and the second son went in his place. With these added difficulties, Peng Sao gave up two of the boys for adoption. Her third-born, aged seventeen, went to the proprietor of one of the general stores in the village. The fifth-born, ten, went to a relative of the Peng lineage who had no son. When this proved inadequate, Peng Sao arranged for her youngest and favorite son to go to a government orphanage in a temple elsewhere in the county. She preferred this to adoption since she hoped to be able to retrieve him. However, that was not to be. He died in the orphanage of dysentery.

Eventually Peng Sao lost all but two of her sons. Only the eldest and the fourth-born remained. The former did odd jobs until an elder of Peng Sao's natal Wu family got him accepted into the village militia. The fourth son, eighteen, lived by his wits, mainly through gambling, at which he was singularly lucky and hence in great demand in Paoge circles. Thus, even though Peng Sao experienced the destruction of her family, at least two of her sons managed to survive, and she herself stabilized her livelihood when she got a job as a cook in the market village.

Some impoverished widows preferred not to remarry. They might hire out their labor, sometimes as long-term live-in farm laborers, domestics, or reelers in home industry; they might take in washing or run a stand selling cheap wares, or engage in some minor cottage industry. Among fragmented families, it was not uncommon to find a household of two widows cultivating a few owned or rented fields on the slopes, for women were as skilled as men in dryland farming. The two women could be an elderly mother-in-law and her middle-aged daughter-in-law, in which case relations might be tense, with the former asserting her authority on the grounds of seniority and the latter emphasizing her greater contribution to the joint livelihood.[16] In one particularly bitter case, where two such women owned and shared a small adobe cottage on a dryland farm in the hills, the issue was resolved by dividing the few upland fields between them and each working and eating separately.

Some local destitute men and women from the nearby countryside were able to find service jobs in the village. An older woman might eke out a living as a washerwoman, a servant in an inn, or a vendor running a streetside counter selling homemade cakes or home brew. Destitute men, however, often had greater difficulty than women finding work, as the potential employer could require a guarantor, and only those categorized as "simple and honest folk" (*laoshi ren*) could find one. As difficult as it was for these male insiders, strange men who drifted in from unfamiliar places as far away as Renshou faced an even harder time finding employment. Such people were categorized as "bare sticks" (*guanggun*)[17] and could find no patrons in the community, so they simply drifted from place to place, sometimes finding menial jobs, other times resorting to theft.

BANDITS AND THEIR VICTIMS

Another choice for destitute rural men was to join a bandit gang in the mountains. By 1940, the chaos of the 1920s and 1930s had given way to a more stable situation. Banditry had changed from well-organized gang raids led by ambitious paramilitary men to the endemic banditry of small groups of peasants with little to eat in the two- to three-month period when the grain of the autumn harvest had been consumed but the spring crops were not yet edible. Early spring was the "bandit season." It started with the Lunar New Year holiday, for up to this time many of the precariously poor had been getting through the winter by hiring themselves out as day laborers, but with the holiday came the slack season. To make matters worse, the eve of the New Year was the time for repaying debts, forcing penniless debtors to flee from home. Faced with hunger, some turned temporarily to banditry. Though women did not join bandit gangs, they could and did provide valuable support to their menfolk operating outside the law.

For obvious reasons, it was difficult to gather information about bandits. The poorest of the country poor lived in mud hovels on upland farms. Though they made up perhaps a quarter of rural households, they were the least visible and audible. The men, especially, made themselves as inconspicuous as possible, afraid of running into officials or being press-ganged or otherwise put upon by those with more power. Those who engaged in, or were suspected of engaging in, seasonal banditry for survival were particularly elusive.

The victims of banditry were easier to find. Of the seven or eight robberies that came to our personal attention in the bandit season of spring 1941, the victims were neither big landowners nor poverty-stricken farmers; they were mostly farmers of strata 2 or 3 who went in for profitable side occupations. The farmer who raised pigs and sold them in the market, returning home with cash, or the farmer with a modern loom or two, who had just bought a supply of cotton yarn or who had just finished weaving several bolts of cloth ready for the market—these were the targets.

In late January there was the case of Wu Qingwen, a twenty-five-year-old small owner-farmer who had recently entered the yarn business, buying wholesale in Chongqing and selling retail to neighboring weavers who lacked the capital for bulk purchases. Wu had borrowed the capital from a relative. Late one night, just after the Lunar New Year, when he had returned with a bulk purchase of yarn, and when, as it happened, the man of the household which shared the courtyard was absent, two armed robbers broke in. Wu and his wife made no attempt to stop them, not knowing whether their guns were loaded. They thought they recognized them as men from Sanjiao Market, but having no proof they decided against taking the matter to court and simply suffered the devastating loss.

In mid-March, on one of our visits, we came upon a pale young man, his head bound in a red turban (the traditional cure for a severe headache), a gash on his cheek just healing, and both hands bandaged. He told us he was up out of bed and visiting neighbors for the first time since his encounter with a bandit gang a couple of weeks earlier. The young man, Zhang Shaohua, a farmer-weaver aged about thirty, had bought several hanks of yarn after selling the cloth he had woven. One night soon after, four or five bandits tried to break into his four-room house. Zhang strove to hold the door closed, but they battered it open, slashing his hands in the process so that the top joints of the third and fourth fingers on his right hand were lost, and his left hand was half severed at the wrist. The bandits escaped with three bundles worth several hundred yuan, some bolts of cloth not yet sold, and two new gowns. Zhang reported the robbery to the township office, but without result. After that he dropped the matter since he did not have enough money to take it up to the county court.

In the latter half of March, when we called at the home of a poor farmer, Wu Lingxuan, we found him caring for a young married daughter who had fresh unhealed wounds on her head. The girl had recently married a young weaver and the two lived in a one-room cottage on a winding hillside road. Their sole income came from cultivating a small plot of dry land and weaving cloth on a narrow-gauge wooden loom. Robbers had entered their home in the night and, when the young wife had called out for help, struck her on the head. They got away with five bolts of cloth and enough yarn to weave another fifty feet. To make matters worse, they took two quilts and some ornaments. Father and daughter expressed no hope or expectation that the criminals would be tracked down and the stolen goods returned. They accepted the calamity with the same resignation they would a natural disaster. Their only wish was that they might raise enough capital for yarn so that they could continue to weave.

An Haixiong was the richest farmer we knew who relied solely on farming and farm sidelines. With his family of eighteen, An owned and cultivated forty *dan* of good rice land and another ten *dan* of upland fields. As a sideline, the family raised pigs. On March 16, 1941, An and his sons had driven several fat pigs to market and in the evening returned with about two thousand yuan in cash. That very night, a dozen armed bandits broke in. They shot and killed An's wife and inflicted serious injuries on a grown son and daughter and on An himself. Because An had failed to link himself with the local power holders, he was not among the elite who were off limits to banditry. Instead An was in that group of prosperous and middle farmers who were expected to provide "welfare" to the pauperized small-farmer bandits.

CONCLUSION

In the market village of Prosperity and its meticulously landscaped rural environs, actual prosperity was the privilege of a few, while poverty or near poverty remained the fate of many. Because of the overall shortage of available farming land, it was necessary to identify a need and develop a product in this micro-niche market. Upward social mobility was not unknown in this community, but the flow was quite small in comparison to the steady downward drift, with families at the bottom disintegrating, like a garment fraying at the hem. Such disasters inflicted ruin indiscriminately, affecting both rich and poor. Because so many rural residents lived close to the margin of existence, any stroke of bad luck could spell disaster, and the loss of a household's able-bodied man could produce a dire situation very quickly. Banditry was an interim survival strategy for the poorest men, introducing unpredictable instances of violence into community life.

As perilous as the circumstances of livelihood could be for individual families, the community as a whole appeared stable. As long as the community suffered no major natural or man-made disaster, the opportunities provided by the market, together with the patron-client nature of social organization in the community, provided a safety net rather than a road to prosperity for its members, giving them the barest chance at some security. While the victims might blame fate for their suffering, or express hatred for the individuals they blamed for their plight, the established measures for coping appeared to have brought general acceptance or at least resignation to life's harshness. Carrying the burden of subsistence, the majority of villagers were not active in civic affairs. But, as will be discussed in the next two chapters, the fate of Prosperity's people was not just decided at the household level but was also affected by their connections with those who held formal and informal power at higher levels.

NOTES

1. The population grew throughout the Qing dynasty (1644–1911), reaching 581 people per square mile, which was close to the high density found on the Chengdu plain (Cressey 1934, p. 138; Zelin 1986, p. 501).

2. Some evidence suggests that upland communities of the Red Basin, such as Prosperity, experienced more of this protoindustrial development in the late Qing and Republican era than

the Chengdu plains area. Eyferth (2003, p. 72) came to this conclusion based on his study of Jiajiang County, which includes large areas of plains and uplands.

3. Philip C. C. Huang (1985, p. 3), for instance, has noted this characteristic of Chinese farmers in his study of North China rural society. But when we examine the ethnographic studies of Chinese communities both in the north and the south during the Republican era, Prosperity seems to exhibit a more dynamic entrepreneurial character. In comparison to Daidou in Shandong, for instance, Prosperity had a much more vibrant weaving industry and commercial sector in the 1940s (M. Yang 1945, pp. 23–28). Gaixiangong village, according to Fei Xiaotong (1946), specialized in the silk industry and produced some income from sheep raising, but it did not seem to have the broad array of household industries that were present in Prosperity. C. K. Yang (1954) in his chapter on "Production, Consumption and Income" listed secondary occupations such as carpentry, masonry, and the like but did not reveal the presence of lively household or cottage industries. Isabel and David Crook's work (1979) on Ten Mile Inn in Hebei Province found that the main income during the slack winter season came from "trade and transport" expeditions in which men would take their donkeys and buy in one place and then transport the goods to another place for sale.

4. Among people of means, land was the most desirable investment because of rapid inflation. Anyone with money put it into land. But it was difficult to have the connections to be able to buy land. Merchants immediately put their money into either land or goods because of inflation.

5. Sichuan sheng Bishan xianzhi (1996), p. 214.

6. The quotation about everyone spinning comes from Sichuan sheng Bishan xianzhi (1996, p. 214). See also Myers (1965).

7. The main driving force in the modernization of the Chinese textile industry along the east coast had been foreign, especially British and Japanese (Chin 1937, p. 267).

8. The oil presses in Daidou were also owned by wealthy families (M. Yang 1945, p. 27).

9. Liu gave Wu no down payment but paid an annual rent of twenty-one oil cakes (with a standard weight of ten *jin* each) and all the oil therefrom. (One cake and its oil was worth ten yuan at the end of 1940 but had risen to seventy yuan by May 1941.)

10. As quoted from Department of Overseas Trade, Great Britain, "Report on Economic and Commercial Conditions in China," p. 28, in Shaw (1938, p. 395).

11. This section is based on information provided by Dong Taibang in a 1986 conversation with Yu Xiji.

12. These charcoal pieces were sold in Prosperity's periodic market by some landless households who lived in the mountains above Fulu Market, seven or eight miles distant, and burned charcoal for a living.

13. Sichuan sheng Bishan xianzhi (1996, pp. 98–99) lists all of the floods suffered by Bishan.

14. This famine is discussed in Wright (2000). Even though Prosperity seemed to fare better than other places, drought in the basin's hilly area was worse in the Chongqing area than in the middle of the province (Sichuan sheng difang zhi bian zuan weiyuan hui, 1996, p. 30).

15. Tawney (1966), p. 77.

16. The use of the terms "middle-aged," "old," and "young" in this book is based on the values of that time, which were in turn based on the general physical well-being of people. Life expectancies were quite different, as were marriage ages. A young woman in her late twenties with children would be considered middle-aged.

17. Sommer (2000).

Chapter Four

Lineages, Landlords, and the Local Body Politic

One night Prosperity's largest landowner, Cao Yuexian, was gambling and losing badly in the temple courtyard. His young cousin stood behind him holding his money bag. Cao never placed a bet of under five hundred yuan. As the evening passed and his losses grew to four thousand yuan, someone notified his wife. She awakened two of the tenants and ordered them to carry her by litter to the village. Storming into the temple courtyard around midnight, she wailed shrilly that Cao was ruining the family, that she and her five daughters and one precious newborn son were now threatened with destitution. Since guest gamblers from Danfeng Market were present, the disturbance was an embarrassment to the Paoge. Commander Cai, another powerful landowner and head of a Paoge lodge, urged the couple to fix a date for a mediation to settle the quarrel, forcing Cao to agree. Then his wife quietly returned home, having achieved her goal. The mediation took place a few days later, presided over by Commander Cai and Wang Junliang, Paoge leader. The decision reached was that the deeds for a certain small portion of Cao's three-hundred-*dan* estate were to be put into the hands of the commander for safekeeping.

Cao Yuexian's reckless behavior at the gambling table illustrates both the ongoing economic power of Prosperity's landowners and their shift away from older standards of elite behavior. From its inception as a distinct marketing community, the basis of power, status, and wealth in Prosperity was landownership. Those families who commanded the largest rice-producing estates assumed the socially sanctioned role of gentry, wielding extraordinary power over local governance and the management of resources. Storing their rice until the price was optimal, landlords also acted as big rice merchants; this was where they made their money. Some, as we have seen, invested in other forms of trade as well. Others spent their time relaxing in teahouses, smoking opium, or gambling. But regardless of their daily activities, at the heart of their power was land.

For most of Prosperity's 110 years of existence as a marketing community, these local elites ran their marketing community without formal appointment or much oversight from imperial officials or Republican-era government authorities.[1] This informal arrangement was endorsed by the county officials as a practical measure for maintaining local control over the large stretches of settled territory outside of the county town. As long as they met the state's demands for taxes and maintenance of local order, local elites were left in charge of local governance on an informal basis. Moreover, since Prosperity was a multi-lineage marketing community from its outset, no single kinship group was able to dominate its governance, although the descendants of the Suns and Zhongs, the two landlord families that had founded the market village, by virtue of their continued large investments in its expansion, seemed to have commanded much authority over how it was managed in its early years.

Unlike their counterparts in larger communities, no elite families in Prosperity had ever produced a male heir who succeeded in passing even the lowest rung of the imperial civil service examinations, but such local notables were nonetheless treated by the Bishan County magistrate as gentry (*shenshi*), and they in turn behaved in an upright and dignified manner, upholding the social norms expected of licentiates (*shengyuan*) who had passed the lowest rung of the civil service examination.[2] Indeed, even in 1940, several decades after the 1905 abolition of the civil service examinations, local people still perceived a clear distinction between commoners and gentry, who were recognized as natural superiors by virtue of education and by adherence to a well-established code of moral values.

The perseverance of gentry status well into the twentieth century, however, belied the wrenching social changes that swept through Sichuanese rural communities, fundamentally altering the nature of elite power. After the demise of the Qing dynasty in 1911 and the rise of warlordism, a new type of landlord appeared in local society in Sichuan—an elite group who had risen to power and amassed great wealth through careers in the military or warlord governments. While they could be found in many Sichuan rural communities, such as Guanxian and Dayi, they were especially concentrated in the richer rural areas around Chongqing.[3] The most well known of these new landlords was Liu Wencai, who ultimately controlled an immense estate of eighty-three villages on the Chengdu plain. By the late 1920s, the usual term for gentry (*shenshi*) used throughout China had been changed to *shenliang*, meaning "gentry plus grain," in reference to the new responsibility imposed on them to collect grain for the warlord armies in 1929.[4]

When we arrived in Prosperity in 1940, we wondered what impact the warlord years had had on the social foundations, integrity, and vitality of the rural elite in Prosperity, a not very prosperous community located in a hilly place. Had members of the elite been able to maintain their grip on the community during the torturous years of violent militarism that had plagued Sichuan in the 1910s, 1920s, and most of the 1930s? If so, how? What we found was that even though some degree of "new types of landlordism" had developed there, the impact was not as great as in the richer farming areas. Local elites continued to run Prosperity, as they had historically, deriving their power from lineages and from landownership. Nonetheless, a distinct trend of degeneration was evident in the elite way of life, and the major lineages were showing clear signs of decline. We also found that the Nationalist government had been able to develop the very tentative beginnings of a power base in the community after 1935, when thirty thousand of its troops arrived in the province. But the challenges faced by a largely alien government lacking much of a social base in this province, and the difficulty of sinking roots into a rural community like Prosperity, were immense.

LINEAGE AUTHORITY AND KINSHIP NETWORKS

In 1940, our first impression was that lineage organizations[5] lacked much power or authority over their members, and that whatever social control capacities they possessed in the past had for the most part disappeared. One indication of the weakness of lineage power was the pervasive lack of interest in maintaining ancestral halls (*citang*).[6] The ones that did exist were quite modest in comparison to those on the Chengdu plain or in Anhui. Some ancestral halls, we noticed, were no longer used for lineage ceremonial purposes. The Zengs, for instance, had decided to rent out their spacious ten-section tile-roof hall to three separate households who were operating ten wide looms furnished with durable iron parts on the premises. The lineage head had not even bothered to secure the lineage tablets, with the result that they fell into the hands of an opium-smoking Zeng pauper who sold them to feed his addiction. When the loss was discovered, a noisy public quarrel ensued, but the whereabouts of the tablets remained a secret and they were never recovered by the lineage head. It was widely assumed that one of the better-off Zeng families had connived to gain possession of them.

At the time of the Qingming festival for the worship of the ancestors, only two lineages still gathered their men to celebrate with the customary sweeping of the graves, rebuilding the mound of earth, burning incense and candles, and hanging paper money. Historically, this occasion was central to the organizational vitality of lineages, whose members would end the day by butchering a pig and sitting down to a grand banquet. The inability of most

Qingming associations in Prosperity to rally their lineage members for this important identity ritual suggested a decline in lineage collective spirit, financial resources, and organizational capacity.[7]

Lineages in Prosperity had not always been this weak. While local lineages did not ever command the authority over their members enjoyed by their counterparts in southern Chinese provinces, genealogies and gazetteers provide glimpses of their important role in the early-Qing resettlement of Sichuan. As chapter 1 suggested, the forced resettlement of this section of Bishan began in the late seventeenth and early eighteenth centuries.[8] Lineages provided capacity for the settlers to tackle the difficult challenges of territorial place making, including building rice paddies, constructing homesteads, paving stone paths, producing rice on a large scale, establishing local markets, and maintaining security. Within a relatively short period of time, the founding members of the Sun, Zhong, Huang, Zhang, Yang, and Wu lineages left their homes in Huguang (modern-day Hubei and Hunan), Guangdong, and Guangxi and settled in this central part of Bishan, which was then called Fulili.[9] The families that founded these lineages for the most part were given land grants of unoccupied land to develop. Often two brothers and their wives would settle together in Fulili while other brothers or cousins would settle in a nearby place such as Liutang, Dingjia, or Fulu. The Huang family, for instance, came from Huguang and originally settled in Sacred Lamp Temple (Shengdengsi) on the slopes of the Maolai Hills to the north of the market street, where they built a brick house. There Huang Zuling was able to support a large family of five sons (no daughters were recorded in this genealogy), three of whom moved to Danfeng, some ten kilometers to the south, and started a new branch of the lineage. His third son, Huang Wenkui, stayed at the homestead at Sacred Lamp Temple and was able to develop a strong lineage that counted eleven generations by the early 1940s, numbering forty-three families living in the central section of northwestern Prosperity (*bao* 3 and 6). Along with the Cai, Sun, and Cao surnames, they ultimately came to constitute a middle-sized lineage in this community, overshadowed by the much larger lineages of Wang, Wu, Yang, and Zhang.[10]

An important activity of these early lineages was the construction of ancestral halls and graveyards, and sometimes a family temple. In some lineages the ancestral hall was not a separate structure but rather was incorporated into the homestead, perhaps to economize or as a sign that the hall was not the center of the lineage as a whole but just of the branch in Prosperity.[11] The Sun lineage, for instance, had incorporated its modest ancestral hall into the farm homestead of its founder while the main ancestral hall was built in Liutang. The Wu lineage moved their ancestral hall from Qinggang to Prosperity in the 1940s as part of the process of creating a new center for the lineage.[12] Thus the existence and type of ancestral hall in Prosperity showed how central the community of Prosperity was for each lineage. This caused us to wonder if our original view that most lineages in 1940 did not celebrate the Qingming festival was incorrect; perhaps they had just gone elsewhere for the occasion.[13]

As new communities such as Prosperity were formed, lineages helped to shift the orientation of members from their place of origin to the new locality through place naming. When the Wu lineage, which had first taken up residence in the Zhongxing area of Bishan in 1713 (the fifty-first year of Kangxi), expanded into Prosperity in 1721, it conferred its surname on the territory where new homes were placed, naming it "Wu Family Flat Place" (*Wujiaba*).[14]

Another important place-making function undertaken by the larger lineages was the construction of genealogies, which emphasized patriarchal power. The role of the founding fathers was often described in great detail. These genealogies were not concerned with accuracy, as their records of their particular lineages' patriarchal descent line dropped out any mention of branches that were problematic. They also were willing to construct obvious falsehoods to enhance the grandeur of the lineages as a whole, as can be seen in the Sun genealogy's claim that their Sichuan lineage was connected to Sun Yat-sen. An even more important function of these genealogies was to cultivate a localist orientation among the lineage members. Coming before the creation of Prosperity's village and periodic market, these settlers first reflected a connection with Fulu but then focused on the specific place.[15]

With the development of a market village, every major contribution of a local lineage to its expansion was recorded on tablets placed in the small shrine. This encouraged local lineages to recognize this new market village as a central focus of their economic, political, cultural, and social activities. Some started to spur the market village's expansion by investing in buildings that were deeded to their Qingming associations. In 1940, when these lineages were on the decline, four lineages—those of Sun, Cao, Yang, and Shi— still owned property in the market village that was producing rental income for them.[16] At the same time, those lineages that deeply invested in the development of the market village were forever memorialized, even if their fortunes subsequently declined. The Sun and Zhong lineages ultimately failed to produce large lineage networks and began to see their estates fragment, but were nevertheless honored as important patrons in the community. As members of the most prestigious lineage in the locality, the Suns were descendants of one of the first settlers in this area. Two hundred years earlier the family had owned most of the good wet rice land around the village and had contributed the land and money for the building of Wenmiao temple, contributions duly recorded on a stone tablet dated 1769. One hundred years earlier, their branch of the family held 1,000 *dan* (25 acres), but by their grandfather's day the family's holdings had dwindled to 150 *dan* of top-grade rice land. When he passed away, the land was divided among five sons, ending once and for all the tradition of the Suns being among the large landowners in Prosperity. In 1940 each of the three leading Sun families owned an estate of only thirty-odd *dan*, which considerably weakened their power. But their long-standing gentry roots still conferred much prestige to the leaders of the lineage.

Conflicts within lineages were not unknown. Such an instance occurred in Prosperity when the highly regarded local geomancer Sha Yusu pointed out to gentryman Wang Junliang that his grandmother's grave was a mere eleven or twelve meters away from a far more favorable gravesite up on a promontory facing east and looking down two valleys.[17] Wang Junliang's second cousin, the teahouse proprietor Wang Mingxuan, became apprehensive and angry. The affluence of his branch of the family had declined after the division of the inheritance two generations before, while Junliang's had prospered. Since Mingxuan believed that the success of Junliang's family had caused the deterioration of his own, he was determined to block the move to an even more auspicious gravesite. He protested that the grave land belonged to the Wang clan even though it was registered on Wang Junliang's deed. The confrontation intensified, with each side threatening to take the matter to court in Bishan. Mutual friends, however, counseled a compromise. With their help an agreement was reached, acknowledging that since Junliang's father was an elder cousin of Mingxuan's father, it was appropriate to move the grave, but not to the most auspicious spot—the "pulse" of the dragon. Instead it should be placed just below the pulse. The disinterment and reburial was carried out at midnight, per the instruction of the geomancer, and it was found that the corpse was perfectly preserved after twenty years, proving that the "breath of the earth" at the original site was excellent and that the original geomancer had known his profession.

The lineages began to decline during the early Republican era for a number of reasons. Families often lost young men who were press-ganged into the armies. Even more devastating to well-off families, male infants and some family heads were captured and held for ransom. The turmoil of this time was so extreme that a fence was built around the market village to try to protect it from the lawlessness swirling all around it. The wealthier families of the main eight lineages were subjected to horrific violence by bandits.

At the same time, the Republican government saw lineage assets as the most likely revenue source for funding state projects at the local level. The Republican government's confiscation of lineage temple lands in order to fund public school initiatives significantly eroded the organizational authority of at least one lineage in the community.[18] The Zhang lineage had built up a large lineage charity estate, beginning in 1677 when an elderly widow donated six *dan* of land to build a Buddhist temple, Zhangxinsi, near the Zhang ancestor hall in order to reverse the recent misfortunes that her family had suffered.[19] Over the next hundred years, other members of the Zhang lineage donated another one hundred *dan*. As this temple was located on some of the most productive paddy fields in the community, the Zhang lineage used the rents from the land to support the temple in a very comfortable fashion as well as to cover other lineage expenses. In the late 1920s, mimicking the policy of the Nationalist government, Sichuan warlord Liu Xiang began to seize family temple lands. The Zhang lineage in Prosperity lost one hundred *dan* of the corporate holdings they had donated to Zhangxinsi, and the Buddhist monks associated with the temple began to drift away. Although the lineage was not able to resist this large seizure of temple lands, it was able to stop the government's subsequent effort to swallow the last six *dan* of land in 1935. This time the Zhang lineage took the matter to court and won on the basis that their ancestral hall was located on this last piece of land. In so doing they stopped the government from totally appropriating this temple, but they were not able to find a way to support the priest who tended to it.

Although the power of the lineage organizations in Prosperity had declined during the first three decades of the Republican era, they had not lost all of their financial or political clout. Lineage heads still were respected as informal judges in the teahouses, especially when their members were involved in disputes. A number of Qingming associations continued to function, providing their members with a sense that the blood connections to one another were still supported by an institutional presence in the community. Certain lineages still had a fairly solid financial foundation, as indicated by the fact that the Qingming associations collectively owned 10 percent of the rice paddies in the township. Because lineage members still lived in fairly dense concentrations on pieces of land that had been marked off and imbued with great symbolic meaning by their ancestors, their identities as lineage members were reinforced on a daily basis.[20] Nevertheless, in many cases the Qingming association ownership of the land existed in name only, while in fact the land was in the hands of better-off and more influential families.

LANDLORD SUPREMACY: BIG FROGS IN A SMALL PLACE

Landlords in Prosperity defied easy characterization as a group, although they were considered "small landlords" in government statistics.[21] At the bottom of the spectrum were landowner households who rented out their land from necessity, either because they had lost the vital manpower to farm it themselves (many of these being widows or soldier's wives) or because they urgently needed credit for some family emergency (a marriage, funeral, illness, robbery, natural disaster, or debt incurred through opium or gambling) and obtained this through letting land at a low rent in return for a substantial cash deposit to tide them over. Still others became landlords by renting out land to each of their married sons as a way of resolving bitter tensions in a contentious multigenerational family while still maintaining their legal authority over the property. Some of the medium landlords were engaged in professions such as weaving or geomancy, or were running commercial ventures like distilleries, while smaller landlords, the bottom 10 percent who held five *dan* or less, could not survive on their rents alone. But regardless of whether they were prospering or poor, these landlord families clung tenaciously to their land, for land in this society not only provided the greatest economic security, but it had a strong emotional hold as well.

Medium and small landlords maintained a broad range of relationships with their tenants. Many tenants of medium-sized farms were linked with their landlords in a simple business deal without additional personal obligations. In cases where a landowner's urgent need for cash had forced him to lower the rent on his land in return for an increased deposit, he could not terminate the contract until he was able to refund the deposit. In extreme cases where the landlord was unable to refund the money, he might ultimately have to mortgage or sell his land to the tenant, but such cases were rare.

The holdings of large landlords in Prosperity, while small by provincial standards, comprised at a minimum sixty *dan* (roughly ten acres) and a

Table 4.1. Scales of Landlordism*

Amount of Land Let Out		Number	Percent
Small landlords (1–10 *dan*)		44	39.64
mini to 5 *dan*	12		
small 6–10 *dan*	32		
Medium landlords (11–20 *dan*)		42	37.84
11–15 *dan*	17		
16–20 *dan*	25		
Medium-large landlords (21–60 *dan*)		13	11.71
21–30 *dan*	8		
31–40 *dan*	3		
41–60 *dan*	2		
Large landlords		12	10.81
61–100 *dan*	5		
101–300 *dan*	7		
Total		111	100.0

*Although we surveyed all landowning households (516), we were not able to use data on one-fifth (111) of the questionnaires because it was incomplete. However, none of this incomplete data concerned the largest landowners, as we were able to confirm in a number of ways that there were twelve landlords in the top tier.

maximum of three hundred *dan* (see table 4.1). As was generally true throughout Sichuan, rice production was very lucrative for those fortunate enough to hold large tracts of paddy land, which they rented out to tenant farmers. The income that large landlords enjoyed from renting out this land and from usury was sufficient for them to live lives of leisure. But only 2 percent of the families owning rice land—or 0.8 percent of all the families in Prosperity—fell into this category. The top twelve landlord families in Prosperity maintained a way of life that was distinct from that of lesser landlords or even the prosperous merchants. These landlords were able to be all-powerful on their estates and, for those among them who were so inclined, to command enormous authority in the community, particularly in the domain of customary law and land, grain, and financial transactions. Even though their estates were significantly smaller than those of their counterparts on the Chengdu plain and could not compare with the holdings of their ancestors some two hundred years earlier who had owned large estates of one thousand *dan*, they were in charge of most matters of consequence in Prosperity. Significantly, the major landlords with estates of more than one hundred *dan* all belonged to the larger lineages. Lineage support was important in land transactions, which were very tightly controlled by local notables. Their major challenge was to stave off a further fragmentation of their landholdings and to cope with the residual chaos of the warlord era that had caused so much damage to Sichuan's economy, public security, and governance.

Upward mobility into the ranks of large landowners was rare.[22] Despite the toll taken by changing times, the top elite had been able to maintain a grip on one-sixth of the best paddy fields in Prosperity.[23] They lived on rents alone without, to our knowledge, engaging regularly or seriously in any side occupations. Some of these top landlords may also have owned land in nearby townships and neighboring counties. One-fourth of the paddy lands were owned by absentee landlords, some of whom were reportedly living in the county town.[24]

Although most of these twelve large landowners were not the nouveau riche type—those who had amassed great wealth through military or bureaucratic careers in the warlord governments and then bought large estates—the most powerful patron in Prosperity was precisely this type of landlord. Cai Xunqing, who had originally inherited a meager twelve *dan* of paddy land, was able to build up the fallen family fortunes by pursuing a career in the warlord government's military. By the time he retired in the mid-1930s, he had managed to acquire an estate of one hundred *dan* in Prosperity, perhaps with the help of some insider knowledge about favorable land deals from his kinsmen, who constituted one of the important lineages in Prosperity. While the estate he constructed was not the largest, he was able to appropriate additional power from his wide set of connections and his knowledge of

Sichuan politics, enabling him to succeed in his bid to become the most influential landlord in the community.

Like other landlords, Commander Cai, as he was known in Prosperity, also extended his power by manipulating mortgages—behavior that suggested a darker side of landlord power in Prosperity. In the drought year of 1935, Cai Chuanwu had such a poor harvest that he mortgaged his twenty-*dan* farm for ten years to Commander Cai, his rich relative, to raise 1,330 yuan (66.50 yuan per *dan*). The family continued cultivating the land, paying the commander a twenty-eight-yuan deposit and rent of fifteen *dan*, or 75 percent of the harvest. By April 1941, when we visited Cai Chuanwu's family, six years had elapsed and they had already accumulated enough money to pay off the debt, thanks largely to inflation. But when they tried to do so, the commander had refused, insisting that the mortgage should run for the remaining four years.[25]

The characteristic that united landlords in Prosperity was a lifestyle that featured conspicuous leisure and precluded physical labor. They depended for their livelihood primarily on rents and on interest from loans, mainly in the form of grain. They took two-thirds of the harvest of their tenants without compunction as rent for the land, and were able in some situations to extract a contract agreement requiring the tenant to hold the rice and simply deliver certain quantities on demand, thereby shifting all the storage losses from moisture and rats onto the tenants. There were a number of unwritten clauses to the contract as well. In the case of the bigger landlords, their tenants were expected to perform various unpaid services. These included carrying the landlord, or more often his wife, in a litter when they visited or traveled; repairing buildings; helping with domestic chores and especially with the immense amount of work involved in large-scale entertaining by the house; transporting grain; making small purchases for the "boss"; guarding his home and property from bandits; and even smuggling contraband opium for an addict in the family. Tenants of big landlords served as his clientele or following. They were his personal servitors, his eyes and ears, and his helpers in various schemes and enterprises.

The most important additional obligation on the part of the landlord was the provision of housing to the tenant. The tie between housing and land had important results. First, it produced tenements, for with the parceling of land went the parceling of housing. Second, in the case of larger landowners, the rooms given to the tenants were often part of the cluster of courtyards making up the landlord's own home. Hence his tenants surrounded him and could be called on at any time of the day or night for services and protection. Third, it gave the landlord an additional hold over his tenant, for the tenant who lost his tenure lost his home as well.

Even as they extracted resources and services from their tenants, landlords in Prosperity generally kept to the custom-sanctioned rates and procedures, honoring certain reciprocal obligations, if sometimes reluctantly. Tenants could expect in an emergency to borrow money or grain at less than the exorbitant going rate, or to be given protection from bullying by the authorities or the army, and they could count on receiving a small traditional gift of rice at the Lunar New Year. Reduction of rent in the case of a shortfall brought about by natural causes was accepted in principle, but it did not take place automatically. The tenant would have to call for a mediation in a village teahouse, presided over by an influential and trusted local figure. His landlord would come prepared to argue against any substantial reduction, putting forward his own estimate of the shortfall, for no landlord would permit a tenant to harvest the crop until he had viewed it standing in the field, and perhaps he even stayed to watch it being harvested. The mediator, typically also a landlord with prestige in the community, would propose an adjustment which gave the tenant some relief, although it would not reflect the full extent of his losses. What the mediator sought was a solution that would be acceptable to both parties and at the same time uphold his own reputation for justice. The landlord on his part would find it hard to reject a reduction publicly proposed by mediation, but privately he might drag his feet on implementing the decision. The tenant's only leverage came from public opinion and publicity. When Zhou Yinting was awarded a reduction of rent from six *dan* to four, for instance, his landlord publicly accepted the decision, but afterward in private he put pressure on Zhou to pay him an extra four-tenths of a *dan*. Zhou stalled but wasn't sure he could hold out.

Apart from lowering the rent if the harvest was poor, landlords were expected to loan money or grain to tenants in difficulty, at interest rates perhaps more modest than the going top rates, and to give traditional small gifts of grain at festival times. They went to great lengths to adhere to a code of conduct that was thought of as appropriate to the "gentry" of the imperial era, even though this social category had been officially abolished in the early years of the Republic and was not used in the government census. Gentry status was not just a matter of wealth or connections to ancestors who had passed imperial civil service exams, but was tied to the landlord way of life. For this a man needed an estate worked by tenants, freeing him from physical labor. He could augment his income through professional activity such as becoming a doctor or teacher, but not through commerce. Thus no active merchant in Prosperity could be considered a member of Prosperity's elite group.[26] Men of this rank should be learned, with a minimum of eight years of old-style or modern schooling. They should emulate gentry codes of conduct, exemplifying the traditional virtues of uprightness, benevolence, and filial piety while avoiding rowdy and licentious behavior and manual labor. Such men made the largest contributions to community projects such as repairing a road or bridge. Much social pressure was placed on these affluent elite families to display their wealth by holding extravagant social affairs, such as betrothals, weddings (discussed in chapter 8), birthdays, and funerals, as a way to affirm their high standing in the community.

At the Lunar New Year season, all families who could afford it would entertain friends and relatives, while the prosperous families were expected to entertain the dragon dancers (see chapter 5) as well. Families who had only recently prospered would enhance their social image by expanding the scope of their banqueting. Banquets held in the home were often prepared with the help of a professional cook, especially if more than a few tables of guests were expected. The menu consisted of eight different standard meat dishes, including pork, mutton, and beef (if any was available) along with chicken and fish. These dishes were prepared in advance and kept hot in a vast steamer. For the elite, the standard banquet was made more elegant by serving certain extras, which might include hors d'oeuvres of cold meats, preserved eggs, pickles, nuts, and other delicacies. Following these cold appetizers, it was common to serve a number of stir-fry dishes one at a time. But all this food was merely a prelude to the eight standard banquet dishes. A strong local white spirit was served with the food, and only when the banqueters had eaten and drunk their fill were bowls of rice brought in, completing the meal.

No formal invitations were sent on these occasions. Most guests came because they could trace some relationship to the host family, or they deemed themselves friends, or they had received favors and felt obliged to turn up to pay their respects. Guests were counted by the table, with eight to a table. A banquet of thirty or forty tables was not uncommon among the richest, who might entertain as many as three hundred guests. The number of guests in attendance was an indicator of the host's prestige. The pillars of society tended to spend more than they wished on hosting home banquets, and some gentry landowner hosts, especially those who had lived for any length of time in the city, grumbled about the meaningless extravagance of such grand dinners. But the birthday of any leading figure in the community was always well known, and guests would come to honor him whether he liked it or not.[27]

Another important role that these local notables played was to publicly beseech the heavens to look kindly upon this farming community. In the summer of 1941, when a severe drought threatened the livelihood of Prosperity, some of the local gentlemen of Prosperity, in order to bring rain, donned their formal long black gowns, took the tablet of the Dragon King (*Longwang*) from Wumiao Temple, and paraded it through the highways and byways of the township while the rest of the community looked on. The performance affirmed the authority of the elite and their vital role in maintaining the welfare of the community.[28]

The homes of the handful of elite were usually situated on the best flatland and were encircled by walls. The two biggest landlords, Cao Yuexian and Commander Cai Xunqing, each had a multistoried lookout tower with small windows located in an upward spiral for surveying the surrounding countryside and for gun emplacements. Landlord houses, described in the previous chapter, were uncluttered and featured furniture and amenities unknown in poorer households. These houses were situated in places that were considered to have particularly good *fengshui*, which was expected to benefit its owner. Cao Yuexian, the largest landowner of the community, was widely believed to owe his prosperity to favorable *fengshui*. Located in the flat valley bottom just below Maolai Hill, Cao's house was set on land that was shaped like a boat and was commonly referred to as "the great boat-shaped courtyard" (*chuanxing dayuan*). A flight of paving-stone steps leading from the back of the grounds up to a tenant farmhouse on the slope gave the effect of a rope mooring the ship to the shore. It was this rope which prevented the ship from drifting and was credited with the continuing prosperity of the Cao family over the previous three generations.[29] Not only did this family own the largest estate in the community, but it also reportedly held an additional 150 *dan* elsewhere.

A PROFILE OF PROSPERITY'S LARGEST LANDOWNER: CAO YUEXIAN

Prosperity's largest landowner, Cao Yuexian, took profligate risks at the gambling table, as we have seen. This might well be understood as an isolated quirk, but a broader examination of his activities suggests a deterioration of the moral integrity and legitimacy of Sichuan's local elites during the last decade of the Republican era. Even among modern educated men of this period, a gap developed between the façade of upright moral conduct they were expected to uphold as members of the local gentry and the schemes and behaviors they pursued.

Cao had many advantages at the beginning of his life. This handsome, affable, but somewhat indolent young man had been sent to a good modern secondary school in Bishan County town and had been married to a woman of the Zhang lineage, one of the richest and most powerful in the county. Upon his graduation his father had purchased a leading post for his son in the police force of a small town in western Sichuan, where he worked until his father's death in 1936 gave him a reason to move back to Prosperity to live on his estate.

As a young man of thirty, Cao seemed quite modern compared to other landlords. He did not take a concubine, although he could clearly afford to do so. He kept up with the national news by subscribing to a newspaper, the only person in Prosperity to do so, and maintained his connections with the Chengdu elite by visiting on a regular basis. He also worked hard to establish himself as a personage in Prosperity by joining the Renlongshe, a local Paoge lodge, and assuming an important leadership position as Third Brother (discussed more fully in chapter 5) for a large sum widely believed to have amounted to between two thousand and four thousand yuan.

Although Cao cared greatly about maintaining his prestige, he was not ambitious to acquire extensive political clout in Prosperity, nor was he particularly interested in becoming enmeshed in the day-to-day work of running his estate. Rather, he allowed his strong-minded wife to manage the tenants, which she probably had begun to do when he was away in Chengdu, while he kept up appearances in the market village by frequenting the teahouses. There he often smoked opium with his friends while playing mahjong, attending the meetings and activities of his Paoge lodge, and gambling at the Wenmiao on market day evenings, where he was a consistent loser. These visits provided the occasion to discuss various schemes with some of his closest landlord friends, Commander Cai and Wang Junliang.

When his thirty-first birthday approached in May 1941, Cao Yuexian lamented to his relatives and friends the fact that he could not let the occasion pass unmarked, since the birth date of any leading figure in the community was always well known and guests were bound to turn up. In the event, 190 guests presented themselves to wish him well—40 more than were prepared for. With eight guests per table, this meant a fine conspicuous bustle to set up five extra tables. While men like Cao deplored the banqueting, none dared dispense with it, as it was essential to maintaining an image of power and wealth.

Cao, like members of the other top landowning elite families in Prosperity, was constantly on the lookout for ways to expand his landholdings. Some new-style Sichuan landlords at this time enhanced their holdings through appointment to a government office, by joining the military, or perhaps by winning tax collection rights. Cao Yuexian, however, collaborated with Commander Cai and Wang Junliang, all leading members of the Paoge, to prey upon a middle-aged gentry woman, Zhang-Lei shi,[30] herself the daughter of a landowner and onetime county head. Her husband was no longer competent, fancying himself to be the emperor of China. Zhang-Lei shi, a capable woman, had taken over management of the family's two-hundred-*dan* estate, located elsewhere in Bishan County. The triumvirate concocted a marriage-making strategem with the aim of dispossessing Zhang-Lei shi by disgracing her, gaining guardianship of her schoolboy son, and forging a marriage link between the boy and Wang Junliang's daughter.

Since Cao Yuexian's wife was from the same Zhang lineage as the delusional husband, it was relatively easy for Cao and Wang to devise a scheme that might succeed. They invited Mrs. Cao's handsome sixteen-year-old nephew to their home from his boarding school in the county town and skillfully arranged an "accidental" meeting of the young man and Wang

Junliang's eighteen-year-old daughter Zhengbi in a public place in Prosperity.[31] When the two young people expressed agreement, Wang Junliang immediately arranged a grand engagement party and sent off an elaborate array of gifts to the groom's home. The importance of all this lavish display and the numerous witnesses was to authenticate the betrothal, making it a publicly acknowledged, unchallengeable fact. Soon thereafter Cao Yuexian, as the boy's self-appointed guardian, requested an early marriage. Such haste signified something.

It was at this point that Cao launched a bold move to help Wang and himself get possession of the property. On behalf of his wife and other members of her natal Zhang family, he filed a suit in the Bishan court against Zhang-Lei shi, claiming that she had coerced her husband into signing notes for delivery of the grain rent. At the same time, Commander Cai Xunqing, no doubt with their encouragement, spread the story that Zhang-Lei shi had long since taken a lover and that her eight-year-old daughter was not in fact her husband's.

What they did not count on was the adroit and effective counterattack launched by Zhang-Lei shi, who was able to get support from some important members of the Zhang lineage, including Zhang Yunheng and his family in Prosperity. They insisted that Zhang-Lei shi was a virtuous wife and had not coerced her husband, but rather was justified in cajoling him into putting his seal on the grain note requiring a delivery of rice, since the Zhang tenants stored their landlord's rent grain and delivered it as needed upon the presentation of a note stamped with the owner's seal.

Zhang-Lei shi's natal family, the Leis, also stood firmly behind her. When some of the Zhang relatives in her community took up the attack, forcing her to leave her home, she was able to persuade her natal family to allow her and her daughter to move in. The deranged husband, left on his own, was fed by the tenants, who took pity on him. Then Zhang-Lei shi surprised everyone by returning to her husband's community, collecting her husband, and taking him back to her natal home. Her supporters praised her for her loyalty to her helpless husband, while the Cai clique accused her of kidnapping him.

Nevertheless, this was an unpropitious turn of events for the triumvirate; the sooner the marriage was finalized, the better for them. But Wang Junliang could not let his daughter marry and leave home until he had replaced her with a daughter-in-law to take charge of household affairs. This meant hurriedly carrying out the wedding of his own sixteen-year-old son, still in boarding school in Bishan town. The ceremony, described in chapter 6, took place a scant two weeks after Zhengbi's engagement party, since the boy was already engaged and the girl's family readily agreed.

With the son's young bride installed to take over running the household from the sister, the way was cleared for Zhengbi's wedding with the Zhang heir. But all this effort came to naught, for at this point the dowager grand-mother in the Zhang family died and a large funeral had to be conducted, followed by a suitably long period of mourning, making a wedding impossible for some time to come.

The funeral itself proved a further setback to the Cai clique. Though the Zhang family tried to bar Zhang-Lei shi from the funeral, she not only attended but carried through all the rituals required of a daughter-in-law and did so with distinction. This made it impossible to dispossess her on moral grounds, since mourning for a husband's grandmother was a proof of piety. Her brilliant performance of the rituals was also a public opinion victory for her. Wang, Cao, and Cai had nothing to say. As for the ongoing legal case in the county court charging Zhang-Lei shi with coercing her husband, no ruling had been reached. The feud was at a stalemate.

The final bout in the contest took place after we left. We learned later that as soon as the mourning period was over, Wang Junliang fixed the date for his daughter Zhengbi to marry the Zhang boy, and all was set. But at dawn on the wedding day, Zhang-Lei shi, the groom's mother, arrived at the Wang home, waking the whole neighborhood with her screams and imprecations. As de facto family head, she refused permission for the marriage of her son to Wang's daughter, vowing that she would never give Wang or his daughter any peace. After many hours of this, Wang Junliang capitulated and the marriage was called off.[32]

While many of Prosperity's residents might have concluded that Cao and Wang bungled this affair, an event that caused much more consternation was the blatant disregard Cao and his family showed for customary practices that had been observed by landlords in this community for many decades and which tenants had come to see as their rights. One Lunar New Year, when Cao was away in Chengdu spending time with some friends, his wife failed to issue the customary gift of grain, which was especially needed because of a drought the previous summer. The tenants were indignant, and one of the more militant among them, named Xiang, took matters into his own hands and opened the granary so that the tenants could take what they felt they deserved. Cao's wife sent immediately for her husband, who returned the next day and called a meeting, where he admitted that his tenants had not received their due. While he acknowledged that they had taken no more than was owed them, he stressed that it was wrong to have taken the grain and he asked them to send their leader to him. Xiang and the two others who had helped him complied, believing that the township militia would not cause them any harm if they were called by Cao, but he called in the county militia, who hauled them before the county magistrate. When Xiang and his allies were sent to prison for two years, his wife and children were driven off the Cao property and forced to live in a ramshackle house in the market village, where she ran a small candy stand. After a year, her husband fell into such poor health because of the inadequate food and unsanitary conditions that he was released from prison, but he died before his friends could carry him to his wife's door.

Landlord Cao Yuexian not only was quite willing to destroy the lives of his tenants if they launched challenges to his authority, but he also had little interest in sacrificing potential profits for the public good. When Pastor Xu of the local Christian church approached him with a request to sell some of his rice to the AMEM Shude Girls' School in Bishan County town, which was having great difficulties finding sufficient quantities of rice for its students because of pervasive hoarding, Cao refused outright on the basis that prices were still rising and he wanted to secure the maximum benefit, even though he and his wife had close personal ties with AMEM health workers.

This examination of the activities of Prosperity's biggest landlord suggests a weakening of the moral integrity of the rural elite in Sichuan during the Republican era. Cao lacked much interest in developing his community, but rather devoted his attention to expanding his own personal wealth. He was absorbed with his own power and importance. Meanwhile, the life of leisure that he enjoyed may have facilitated his networking aims, but it was also threatening his health and equilibrium. By indulging in opium smoking in the teahouses for ostensibly social reasons, he was losing his bearings to the extent that he was willing to sacrifice the well-being of his family at the gambling table. While other landlords were willing to intercede to prevent him from causing the utter ruin of his family, no external social or political force existed that was trying to encourage landlord elites of his ilk to play a more beneficial role in their relationships with family, tenants, and communities.

NATIONALIST STATE-MAKING INITIATIVES

At the time of our stay in Prosperity, local government had been in a state of flux for some years.[33] With the fragmentation of the province in the aftermath of the 1911 Revolution, local elites in small marketing communities like Prosperity had been allowed to function in a fairly autonomous manner.[34] During the late 1920s and early 1930s, Liu Xiang's militarist regime had attempted to institute some semblance of civil local administration, but it remained largely a paper organization. The main interaction of the local community with outside authority took the form of onerous extraction of taxes, collected in rice, and occasional bandit-clearing operations.[35]

This relationship changed with the arrival of twenty thousand Nationalist Army troops in Sichuan in 1935 to combat the intrusion of Communist armies under Zhang Guotao that were fleeing the destroyed red base area in Jiangxi. The warlords were so shaken by the various Communist victories that they welcomed Chiang Kai-shek to take charge of the campaign to expel the Communists. Now that he finally had established a foothold in Sichuan, Chiang struck a deal with Liu Xiang, elevating the militarist to the position of governor over all of Sichuan province (Liu Wenhui having been pushed into the neighboring province of Xikang), while the Nationalists would assume control over the counties and below through their newly established inspectorates and *baojia* system.[36] Under the guise of eradicating Communism at the grassroots level, the eighteen inspectorates, of which thirteen were appointed, assumed enormous powers of local control by mandating that households be organized into groups of one hundred, forming a *jia*, with ten *jia* comprising a *bao* and several *bao* grouped together in a district as a *lianbao* (united *bao*).

The *baojia* system the Nationalists devised was not a new creation but rather a historically legitimated system of local control that had been implemented by imperial authorities on a number of occasions, including the end of the Qing dynasty.[37] It had come to be regarded as the best solution for local control problems in late imperial and Republican times.[38] He Guoguang was entrusted with the role of setting up a mobile office in Chongqing to oversee the reforms. The Nationalist government's Military Commission endeavored to create a *baojia* system in Sichuan based on the model that had been set up by the Hubei-Hunan-Anhui Bandit Control and Clearance Headquarters in August of 1932. The plan called for the creation of a new administrative unit, the *lianbao* local government, to be located in the market villages.[39] The *lianbao* system was also intended to stop the penetration of the Communists into the rural localities. In short, the Nationalists were beginning a process of developing local governance along lines they had already used in eastern China, while developing a small core of local cadres who were responsive to their authority.[40]

The new *baojia* system represented an enormous expansion of both the scope and size of the Nationalist organizational structures, involving the appointment of more than nine hundred thousand petty officials at the grassroots level in Sichuan's 152 counties.[41] The first years seem to have been fairly chaotic, but by mid-1936 the provincial government had addressed the major managerial issues through specific training sessions for its new personnel and funding. County heads appointed the township (*lianbao*) heads and expected them to carry out the duties required of them from above, including oversight of the local militia and the collection of taxes. The linchpin of this new local governance system was the identification and recruitment of local personnel. From the very beginning, Chiang's inspectors realized the danger of putting administrative power in the hands of what they called "bullies and evil gentry" (*tuhao lieshen*), but they concluded that there were sufficient "good gentry" to fill these posts.[42] Their aim was to draw the best elements of the local elites into their new system of formal governance. This Nationalist initiative represented more than an expansion of state power into a defiant province, for it also claimed to effect a major shift by promoting democracy and curbing the power of self-interested local elites.

Particularly threatening to local power holders was the Nationalist goal of extending the power of the county head all the way down to the grassroots level through the appointment of *bao* and *jia* heads. In this centralized political system, the *lianbao* head was empowered to appoint a leader for each *bao*, and the *bao* head appointed his *jia* head. A check was put in place on the authority of both the *lianbao* and *bao* heads, as their appointments had to be affirmed by the county head. This appointment system in the rural communities constituted an unprecedented invasion of local autonomy.[43]

In 1935, the gentry in Prosperity began to notice the extension of national state power into their community with the establishment of this revived *bao-jia* local governance system. The government also assumed the right of fixing the formal boundaries of the newly designed territorial political system. This was particularly of concern to the large lineages, which could have their power base fragmented. However, from what we can reconstruct, the government at this time did not gerrymander the *bao* borders in ways that seriously splintered any of the major lineages. Rather, the center of each of the nine *bao* in Prosperity was placed in a natural community, so in the main the reforms formalized the existing situation rather than refiguring it. Furthermore, in spite of the requirement of ten households in a *pai*, ten *pai* in a *jia*, and so forth, the layout of the village and the number of families that actually grouped together made complete uniformity of size unattainable. Some *pai* comprised eight households; others had thirteen. If a *pai* was slightly larger than normal, it was easier to fulfill quotas, but if each *pai* had to produce one conscript, those with ten families began to resent those with fourteen families, for whom the shared burden was lighter.

The results of the new system also varied considerably from one local community to another. In the nearby area of Laifengyi profiled by rural reconstruction activist Jiang Zhi'ang in 1941, the Nationalists chose as the *lianbao* head a mature man who was the popular choice because he was wealthy and thus able to pay up front for public expenditures, which he would then slowly collect from the population. A member of the rich gentry through inheritance, he had a wife, two concubines, and two homes. He was adept at building up connections for the town through lavish entertaining of visiting officials or notables that enabled the town to flourish. Moreover, he dressed like a man of the gentry, wearing a sleeveless jacket (*magua*) over a long gown that had long white-lined silk sleeves that were folded back, quite different in effect from the Nationalist government public servants who wore Sun Yat-sen uniforms.[44] In sharp contrast to Laifengyi's traditional-styled leader, the first *lianbao* head to be appointed in the market village of Xiemachang, just over the Bishan County border,[45] was a twenty-eight-year-old modern businessman who had grown up very poor and had taken up part-time jobs while he was attending a middle school, for which he was eventually suspended. He was obviously an intelligent, energetic, and hardworking man who was said to possess a forceful character. But what made him well known in many circles was his initiative in setting up or joining modern organizations, such as the Association for the Promotion of Local Autonomy (*Zizhi cujinhui*), the National Salvation through Aviation Association (*Hangkong jiuguohui*), and the Auditing Committee for the Eighth County Conference. When he decided to seek a second term as *lianbao* head in Xiemachang, a group of influential gentry opposed him, charging him with embezzlement and nepotism. Their stand stirred up a lot of opposition from the militia, who laid charges of corruption in the county, but whatever the truth of the matter, he was vindicated, no doubt aided by his good connections and strong support from the county head, and was able to continue in office.[46]

Unlike these two communities studied by Jiang Zhi'ang, Prosperity was located off the main highways and was cut off from modern transport. Laifengyi was by far the largest of the three communities: a key storage center for rice grown in the county, a rich rice-producing area, and a place that traded heavily in cloth, opium, and tobacco.[47] As one of the three towns in the county, it was dominated by large landowners who considered themselves to be gentry and made a great deal of their money in selling rice when the prices were high. As a result, they aimed to keep their control over the local administration with the introduction of the *lianbao* system. Xiemachang was a periodic market village more similar in scope to Prosperity, but because it was located on the highway, it was linked to the large metropolitan center of Chongqing as well as the fast-developing district of Beipei on the Jialing River. Starting in the 1920s, Beipei had been developed as a modern center by Lu Zuofu, a Sichuan farmer who made his fortune building the Minsheng Corporation, a shipping company that moved goods up and down the Yangzi River. Lu used his profits to gradually turn Beipei from a bandit-infested place into "a miracle in the desert" and "the most progressive single rural area in China" by building a town hall, a hospital, a sewer system, a comprehensive school system, a clean modern hotel, and a museum of natural history.[48] The Beipei district (county) government and forward-thinking members of the community found this leader who was capable of promoting a more modern local administration most suitable for their purposes and were willing to back him unwaveringly through the sharp local factional struggle mounted against him.

The choice of *lianbao* heads in Prosperity reveals the importance of educational background, membership in a prominent lineage, and a claim to "modern gentry" status. The first *lianbao* leader appointed in Prosperity was twenty-eight-year-old Wu Huanyun, the adopted son of a prosperous pig bristle merchant, who had graduated from the Bishan secondary school and become well known in the community for his zealous participation in the Nationalist Party's anti-superstition campaign. On one occasion, he berated a diviner for preying on the superstitions of the poor, and when she paid him no heed, he struck her, causing her death. This unfortunate incident, which caused an outcry at the time and forced him to leave Prosperity for a while, did not disqualify him from being appointed as the first *lianbao* head in the community. We do not know as much about his replacement, except that he had a modern secondary school education in the county town and came from the highly respected Sun lineage that had founded the market village. In 1939 this second man was followed as township head by a younger cousin, Sun Zhonglu, also in his late twenties.

Sun Zhonglu, a personable young man in his late twenties, was of medium height and slender build. His years spent at the leading government-run secondary school in Bishan gave him the air of a well-educated man, capable of handling any situation that might arise in his community. He drew support from his cousin, Sun Zhongyao, who held the important post of the principal of the village primary school. The prestige of these two Sun cousins rested on four factors: gentry origins, modern education, connections with the educated elite in Bishan, and ethical performance in public and private life. Perhaps more than any other important personage in Prosperity at this time, these two cousins commanded a great deal of respect despite their young ages because of their gentry ancestry. Indeed, in the eyes of Bishan's big landowning gentry, the Suns were the only true gentry in Prosperity.[49] And yet, while the Suns were clearly part of the core landlord group in Prosperity, they would have been classified as small landlords, as they owned less than fifty *mu* of land.[50]

The accession to power of the younger Suns was greatly aided by the decision to send them to Bishan County town to attend a modern secondary school, where they established connections with the new Westernized elite that was being produced through this school system. It was these cousins who set up the first branch of the Nationalist Party in Prosperity in 1938, reportedly attracting 110 members, most of whom were not active. Sun Zhonglu and Sun Zhongyao also each did a stint at a Nationalist Party training school.[51] Sun Zhonglu recruited all twelve members of his Paoge lodge into the Nationalist Party.

An important aspect of Sun Zhonglu's appointment was that he had the backing of one of the three main gentry factions contending for a share of power in the county town, the modernizing He lineage faction. One of its leading members was He Zhengsheng, who had been principal of the Bishan secondary school when Sun Zhonglu was a student. At this time He Zhengsheng was concurrently in charge of the Bishan Three People's Principles Youth League (*Sanmin zhuyi qingnian tuan*). He's strong endorsement of Sun Zhonglu as *lianbao* head was a critical factor in this appointment, showing that by 1939 the Nationalists had been able to implement their policy of assuming a dominant role in the selection process.

As in Xiemachang, Prosperity experienced continual resistance to this new system of government appointment from above. Wu Huanyun found himself the target of attack within a few months of having assumed the *lianbao* head position in Prosperity, when he was charged with misappropriating public funds by Yang Huanzhang, the litigator for the Sun faction in Prosperity.[52] The case was bitterly fought in the Bishan County court for more than a year. In the end, unlike what occurred in Xiemachang a few years later when the inspectorates were watching these court cases more carefully, Wu was dismissed from office and ordered to refund the government one thousand yuan. While no rival was able to dislodge the Sun faction in the next few years, Sun Zhonglu was subjected to continual harassment and court cases challenging his authority. These types of challenges reveal that local power holders perceived this new system of governance as a threat to the traditional patron-client basis of authority. The appointment of younger middle school graduates with a modern education may have been seen as an even bigger threat, as they held a different outlook on society and envisioned a different type of world from their elders.

The *lianbao* head supervised a small staff that reported to work in the government's simply furnished office, overseeing conscription, taxation, education, and public security. An important new function of the *lianbao* government was to establish a local legal procedure that served as an alternative authority to the teahouse justice system. People without much standing in the community—especially the poor, outsiders, and women—were the main beneficiaries of this new system, as the cases were decided on their merits rather than on the status of the plaintiff and defendant. It was also free, compared to the teahouse mediations, which required the loser to pay for the tea. Poor people without patrons could now take their disputes to the *lianbao* head, who was vested with the power to adjudicate such issues as unacceptable conduct, theft, assault, and divorce. When the *lianbao* head had a modern education, as was the case with all three of Prosperity's appointees, their decisions would be based on a modern interpretation of customary law with some understanding of the codified law practices. Interestingly, these *lianbao* heads did not stop their patron-client mediation role in the teahouses, which was still socially necessary. Sun Zhonglu often heard such cases in the teahouses. This new local legal system was not seen as a threat to the establishment, but rather was regarded as supplementary and as primarily serving a different clientele.

One of the earliest cases that came before Sun Zhonglu was brought by a man who worked as a petty official in Bishan County town. Having discovered a love letter written to his teenage daughter, he demanded that a local tailor be punished for his son's misbehavior. The *lianbao* head heard the case and fined the tailor twenty yuan, a sum large enough to pay for the simple set of furniture for the township office which was still in use in our day.

The county magistrate preferred not to get involved in disputes within the rural communities since most were either tied with community power and factional struggles or were family quarrels. When disputes escalated up to the county court, they were often sent back to the community for solution. One such case involved a well-off landowning farmer named Sun who had three sons. The two older brothers believed that their third brother Haiyun was pilfering from them. This led to never-ending quarrels. To restore tranquility in the home, the father gave Haiyun his share of the inheritance, and the young man with his wife and children legally became a separate family. Then in 1939 Haiyun was press-ganged. Unable to cultivate the rice land herself, the wife leased the fields to a tenant. The father now greatly regretted his premature division of the property and, with the help and encouragement of the litigator Wu Huanyun, disowned the daughter-in-law, accusing her of infidelity to her absent husband (the usual way of stripping a woman of her property). In the father's name, Wu then wrote a note to the tenant forbidding him to pay the rent to the woman and demanding it be paid to the father. The tenant did as he was told. When he refused to pay the woman the rent, she took the matter for adjudication to the township head. Sun Zhonglu, a member of her husband's lineage, nevertheless ruled in favor of the woman. Undeterred, Wu Huanyun took the matter up to the county court. But Sun too went to the county and pleaded on the woman's behalf. She won the case and kept the property—and in refusing to act in favor of his fellow lineage member, Sun Zhonglu gained a certain amount of respect for his display of uprightness in public and private life. Sun's integrity was further measured by the fact that he did not add a single *dan* to his modest landholdings during his term of office.

The Nationalist Party's decision to select the younger members of the Sun lineage as the core members of its local political initiative seemed quite enlightened. Compared to other lineages at this time, the Suns seemed the most likely to be able to command the respect of the local community while also being committed to the goals of the Nationalist party-state.[53] The big unknown at this time was whether they could cope with the Paoge, which had dropped its secret society status long ago and functioned like a patron-client organization for men who had to transport goods outside of the community. Wu Huanyun, ousted from office in 1935, had been closely connected to and supportive of the Paoge. The question that remained to be seen was whether the Suns would be able to develop local governance in Prosperity that would be acceptable to lineages, landlords, and the Paoge, which had the potential to function either as a supporter of law and order or a countervailing force. It is to the Paoge as a locus of power that we now turn.

NOTES

1. For a discussion of the relationship of local elites to government authority in late imperial and Republican times, see Ch'ien (1970, esp. p. 45) and Duara (1988, pp. 1–2, 159–160).

2. According to G. William Skinner, local elites living in small marketing communities rarely had passed the imperial civil service examination. See Skinner (1978). An examination of the Bishan Gazetteer published in 1862 (second year of the Tongzhi reign) clearly shows that the degree holders in this county came from the towns, especially the county town, not the small market communities. Significantly, Chang Chung-li (1967, pp. 142–143) shows that the quotas for civil *shengyuan* degree holders were lower in Sichuan than in the wealthier provinces. In the pre-Taiping period, Zhejiang had a quota of 8 percent whereas Sichuan was limited to 5.4 percent.

3. In Chongqing, 90 percent of the landlords were of the new variety, of which half were from the military and 26 percent from the bureaucracy. Interestingly, those from the military were able to acquire much larger estates, averaging twenty-five hundred *mu*, while those from government backgrounds only held on average a five-hundred-*mu* estate. In Dayi County, almost all of the landlords were considered "new," while in Guangxian, three-quarters of the landlords were of the new vintage while one-quarter were of the old type (Sichuan sheng difang zhi bian zuan weiyuan hui, vol. 1, 1996, p. 53).

4. Jiang Zhi'ang (1941), p. 25. We originally thought when we heard the term *shenliang* that the *liang* meant "good gentry" to distinguish them from the term *tuhao liesheng*, or "evil gentry," that was quite prevalent in political discourse during the Republican era.

5. We follow James Watson's definition of a lineage (as cited by Evelyn Rawski): "a corporate group which celebrates ritual unity and is based on demonstrated descent from a common ancestor" (Watson 1982, p. 594, as cited in Rawski 1986, p. 245). For an overview of the scholarly literature on kinship from the 1950s until 1986, see James L. Watson (1986).

6. In the Republican era, fourteen ancestral halls could be found in Bishan County town, and fairly large-scale ceremonies were held in the ancestral halls of Zhengxin (two), in Dingling (two), in Dingjia (two), and in Dalu (three) (Sichuan sheng Bishan xianzhi, 1996, p. 726).

7. Ruf (1998, pp. 53–55) gives no indication of similar atrophy in his study of Baimapu in Meishan county, Sichuan. Instead, Ruf notes that at least one family member was always expected to attend the rites and feasts of each Qingminghui, or the association would be considered inactive. He also notes that some families, especially the larger and more prosperous ones, maintained membership in multiple Qingminghui. During the actual Qingming festival some men would make appearances at several banquets throughout the day before settling at the major banquet of the family's principal Qingminghui.

8. For a full discussion of the resettlement of Sichuan during the early Qing dynasty, see Robert Entenmann (1982).

9. Some came directly, some settled briefly in other provinces like Guizhou, and some settled in other places in Bishan before moving to the Prosperity area.

10. According to Wu Zhimin's discussions with us in 2007, there were eighty-three surnames in Prosperity in 1983.

11. Ruf (1998, p. 173 n24) reports that this type of ancestral hall was also common in his community on the Chengdu plain.

12. Wu Zhimin (2007) explained the reason for this shift because of construction in Qinggang, which was located on the main road between Chengdu and Chongqing.

13. Ruf (1998) also makes this point. Although we never verified this suspicion, we now realize that the Yangs may well have gone to Fulu for their Qingming rituals, as this was the center of their lineage, according to Wu Zhimin (2007).

14. Our understanding of the Wu lineage history has been greatly aided by Wu Zhimin, who first gave us an overview of the family history in a letter on April 12, 2004. Subsequently he lent us a copy of the recently reconstructed Wu genealogy, which had been revised with the aid of materials from the Fujian branch of the Wu lineage. Then on March 6, 2008, he sent materials concerning the Wu lineage's Hakka origins and their development in Fujian's Ninghua County at the foot of the Wuyi Mountains, including a 2000 news report published in

the Wuxi City newspaper: Yin Ling, "Hakka (Wu Lineage jiapu) Discovered in Rongchen (Chengdu)," (February 28, 2000) and "The First Wu Lineage Cultural Festival Carried out in Ninghua" (from *Sanmin ribao*, October 9, 2007, Xinhua Network, Fujian Channel).

15. As Emily Ahern (1976) saw in her study of Taiwan genealogies, more attention is devoted in these texts to creating ties with the new homeland than to fully documenting the patriarchal descent line.

16. The Shis were no longer a significant lineage in the community, and their property in the market village was mortgaged, probably by the man who had been renting it since 1920.

17. The promontory was thought to represent a dragon's head, while the view represented broad, bright prospects for the Wang descendants.

18. We did not look into the impact of this ordinance on the landholdings of Caoyuansi, an old rural temple that predated the two village temples and was probably established by the oldest lineage in the area, the Cao lineage.

19. Jerry Dennerline (1986) has shown that charity estates in Wushi were often set up by widows and that they often could protect them against property disputes.

20. At least some of these larger lineages in Prosperity may still have possessed the capacity to respond to major threats to their well-being. A contemporary sociological study by Jiang Zhi'ang in two nearby communities revealed the capacity of lineages to mobilize their members to combat challenges to their authority. Jiang reported that one lineage was sufficiently disturbed by the audacity of certain women proposing to attend its Qingming festivities that it posted an announcement which read, "Women are forbidden to attend. If this rule is broken, there will be public criticism" (Jiang 1941, p. 12). Jiang was also impressed by the actions of another nearby lineage when it discovered that its ancestors' graves had been robbed. He noted that the members quickly held several meetings to decide how to handle the problem, which in his estimation showed that in this locality "blood relations had considerable strength" (Jiang 1941, p. 43). While Jiang did not specify the county, it is clear from his references that this township was located in either Beipei or Baxian.

21. Small landlords were defined as those holding less than fifty *mu* of land, according to the *Minguo zhengfu zhujichu tongjiqu* (1936), cited by Gunde (1976, pp. 494–495).

22. The vast majority of Prosperity's landowners—over four-fifths—had acquired their holdings through inheritance and had not been able to augment them. Only one-fifth—eighty-four families—had entered the ranks of new landowners within the lifetime of the current family head through purchasing land or gradually gaining full ownership of it by loaning money to an owner who had pledged his land as security.

23. We recorded the names of the eight largest landlords, noting that they came from some of the more prestigious Cao, Cai, Wang, and Zhang lineages. They were as follows: Cao Yuexian, Cai Xunqing (Commander Cai), Wang Junliang, Wang Junzhao, Sun Wengzhou, Zhang Jizhi, Zhang Jiheng, and Zhang Shaoyun.

24. Some were originally local merchants or landlords who had prospered and moved to Bishan town to better pursue their business interests. Absentee landlords were not included in the survey that we (Crook and Yu) conducted. There were also some nonresident institutions which functioned as absentee landlords. One example was the Fujian School Club of Bishan which owned some twenty to thirty *dan* of Prosperity's poor, hilly paddy fields, the rent from which helped support a school for children from Fujian province who were residing in Bishan County.

25. During our survey we recorded only eleven mortgages, because initially we had failed to distinguish them from ordinary tenure. We assume that in addition to these eleven, some or most of the tenants recorded as having occupied their land for their lifetime (numbering thirty-four) as well as some of those in occupancy for over ten years (numbering thirty-two) were in fact owners who had mortgaged the land and were currently cultivating it as tenants.

26. Jiang Zhi'ang (1941, p. 26) found in Laifeng that some of the elite there that were considered gentry were involved in commercial ventures, with one of them having invested in a distillery that proved very lucrative.

27. For the guests, too, these celebrations could be a burden. Each guest was expected to bring a standard gift (*chabao*), usually of confections, which was supposed to be worth roughly

the same as the hospitality he received. Poorer people often feared the banquets of their more prosperous relatives, neighbors, and friends.

28. As Prasenjit Duara (1988, p. 246) points out, "The prestige-laden and emotive power of symbols, such as those of Longwang and Guandi, which were at the same time sufficiently vague (or multivocal) to accommodate different interests, were the key to the generation of authority in the cultural nexus."

29. We were never able to ascertain if Cao Yuexian was a descendant of Cao Kunting, who we learned from Sun Zhonglu belonged to one of the few families in the area who had survived the turmoil of the late Ming.

30. Here as elsewhere in this book, this is a Chinese form of address for married women, where Zhang is the name of her husband and Lei the name of her father.

31. This "accidental" meeting is discussed in chapter 7.

32. From one angle, this could be seen as a trial of strength between three influential landowning male marauders and their prey—a woman—in which she was the victor. It showed that while a woman was particularly vulnerable to allegations of infidelity, at the same time there were weapons available to her. The first was the adroit use of rituals to affirm her Confucian moral rectitude and hence her unalienable position in her husband's family. Her second weapon was the unremitting noisy quarrel, a nuisance tactic that was lowly but could be effective. Seen from another angle, this was a struggle between two families or groups of families. In this case the husband's immediate kin allied themselves with the Prosperity triumvirate against her, but she had the support of influential men of her powerful natal family and their allies. A record of the proceedings in the county court case would have revealed who these individuals were, but we had no access to the documents. A married woman was not an isolated, helpless individual in her husband's patriarchal family. Though she could be slighted, scolded, and beaten, she could not easily be deprived of her status or driven out of the family. This would have brought loss of prestige to her natal family.

33. For further details on this period, see Kapp (1973).

34. Before its arrival in Sichuan, the Nationalist Party regarded the province as a repository of "resurgent localism" (Kapp 1973, pp. 2–3).

35. Much of this activity was carried out by military under garrisons and the *tuanzong* or local militias. Kapp (1973, p. 11) states that in the early Republican years there was a vast buildup of local militias in Sichuan. By the early 1930s, some estimated that these militias counted more than half a million members. They exercised considerable control over bureaucratic institutions and supported local civic projects such as waterworks, a cement plant, and machine shops (Kapp 1973, pp. 39, 58). He notes (1973, p. 45) that following the collapse of the Qing and the militarization of Sichuan it became too dangerous for peasants to personally deliver their tax payments to local collection centers. Instead the army or local militias were often dispatched to collect this money. Kapp (1973, p. 55) also discusses bandits specifically and mentions that local militias were often left with the problem of clearing bandits.

36. Kapp (1973), pp. 109–112. For the contention that GMD military entry into Sichuan helped weaken Liu Xiang's military power, see Shen Songqiao (1989).

37. Much scholarly attention has been devoted to the Nationalist local control system (*baojia*) during the Nanjing Decade. Our work is most informed by the works of Duara (1988), Xiao (1960), R. Lee (1949), Ts'ai (1993), and W. Wei (1985).

38. Scholars disagree about whether the Nationalists primarily emulated the Qing model or made substantial alterations, but as with many Nationalist initiatives, they recognize that it was implemented unevenly, in large part because of inadequate financial resources or administrative expertise. As Lane Harris usefully discusses in his unpublished paper (n.d.), this system was much more important in Nationalist discourse than as a subcounty administrative system. Scholars best represented by William Wei (1985) tend to present this system as adopted wholesale, while Kristin Stapleton (1997) and Shen Songqiao (1989) argue that the Nationalists used this system as a basis for reconfiguring state-societal relations.

39. Ran (1999).

40. Ran (1999).

41. Sichuan by early 1937 had a total of 4,621 *lianbao* heads, 57,556 *bao* heads, and 873,562 *jia* heads (Ran 1999, p. 74).

42. Kapp (1973, p. 111), quoting Sichuan sheng zhengfu mishuqu (1935, p. 80).

43. On the very local level, the *bao* head was nominally concerned with security, although local people also kept their guns (Huang Tianhua 2007, p. 97).

44. Here we are drawing upon the research of Jiang Zhi'ang (1941). We know that Jiang Zhi'ang's township B was Laifengyi in Bishan County because he noted that the last character in the place name was "yi," meaning a highway post where horses are changed. This was the only changing post within his research area.

45. Jiang Zhi'ang (1941). Based on its description, we are fairly certain that this place (called township A in the study) is Xiemachang in Beipei, the site of Jiang Zhi'ang's Rural Reconstruction Institute. Therefore, we hereafter refer to it as Xiemachang in our text.

46. Jiang Zhi'ang (1941), p. 28.

47. Jiang Zhi'ang (1941), p. 4.

48. Hayford (1990, p. 192). The second quotation comes from Hugh Hubbard (1947). In 1936 Beipei (now pronounced "Beibei") was established as a Jialing River Small Three Gorges Rural Reconstruction Experimental District (Jialingjiang xiaosanxia xiangcun jianshe shiyanqu) (Sichuan baike quanshu, 1997, p. 264).

49. In 1983, Zhang Xiru, leading member of the county gentry, said of the Sun family, "They were members of Prosperity's upper class and belonged to the biggest-name group. All the brothers and cousins were well-educated. They had a lot of influence and can be considered the main feudal force there." Mr. Zhang apparently considered the others upstarts of the warlord period.

50. See note 21 (Gunde 1976) on the definition of small landlords. Their decline in wealth mostly occurred as a result of the lack of primogeniture over the preceding two hundred years. The founder of the lineage had held one thousand *dan* of land in the middle of the eighteenth century, and the lineage easily could contribute the land for the building of a shrine in the market village in 1769. But by the end of the nineteenth century the lineage head's landholdings had dwindled to only 150 *dan*, and by 1940 his grandsons each held farms of around 30 *dan*.

51. In 1983, we were told that they attended a Nationalist military-run school that trained spies located in Enshi, Hubei.

52. Yang Huanzhang, the tenant of an influential landlord Li Jusheng, was able to sublet his land, leaving him the free time to take on the role of a full-time litigator for the gentry who shared his political perspectives. Having effective skills, contacts, and knowledge of how to function in the county court was a very useful political tool in this era.

53. On similar characteristics of the ideal local bureaucrat in the late imperial period, see Ira Lapidus (1975, p. 27).

Chapter Five

The Paoge and Informal Power

Despite the attempts by provincial warlord governments of the Republican era to extend their political control down into rural communities, a powerful source of authority in Prosperity in 1940 was the sworn brotherhood known as the Paoge, sometimes rendered in English as the Robed Brothers. In its evolution from a clandestine secret society during the late imperial era, the Paoge had overcome many weaknesses as it transformed itself into a territorially based organization.[1] After the Republican government was established in 1911, the Paoge evolved from an urban militant organization to a rural patron-client network of peasants, laboring people, and gentry who wanted protection services in very unsettled times. By the wartime era it constituted a daunting force in this locality. Dominated by local landlords, the Paoge was also attractive enough to merchants that they bought protection and safety by obtaining high honorary ranking in the organization. Its lodges were more effective in exerting power, regulating social control, mediating conflicts, and enriching the cultural life of the community than the formal township government, lineage networks, or religious institutions, and at times it overlapped with all of these. Yet its activities in rural communities such as Prosperity have been largely unrecorded.[2]

This chapter explores the nature of Paoge power in Prosperity in the early years of the Sino-Japanese War: its history, visible economic activities, leadership, cultural functions, and ties to a murky underground economy. It begins with the historical roots of the Paoge in Sichuan and its infiltration into the market villages during the late nineteenth-century years of Qing dynasty decline. It focuses on the Paoge's chief patron, Commander Cai; the organization's institutional behavior and tenacity; and its cultural strategies for gaining wide social acceptance. In Prosperity, the Paoge was an integrating force that provided a host of valuable services to its local members while reaping financial benefit from illicit practices including its promotion of gambling, racketeering, and smuggling. The Paoge was capable of exercising considerable political power, alternately utilizing, bypassing, and challenging the local government. It resisted the penetration of the state with some measure of success, and many of Prosperity's residents regarded it as a more responsive and authoritative political organization than the local government.

ORIGINS AND DEVELOPMENT OF THE PAOGE

The origin of the Paoge is somewhat blurry, part of a more general rise of banditry and secret societies in the last years of the Qing dynasty. It is believed to have developed from roving bands inspired by the White Lotus movement and possibly the bands of poor men known as Guolu that operated in Eastern Sichuan and along the borders with Hunan and Shaanxi.[3] Scholars hold different views on the complex relationship between the Paoge society and the more widely known Elder Brother Society (Gelaohui), with the latter employing a more intricate initiation procedure and organizational structure, but for our purposes they can be considered closely related, if not identical.[4]

The breakdown of the Qing imperial state provided a stimulus for the growth of the sworn brotherhoods. Like many clandestine secret societies of the late imperial era, the Paoge constructed an egalitarian association of itinerants (fortune-tellers, stall keepers, scribes, alchemists, singers, begging Buddhist monks and Daoist folk priests, actors, and martial and circus performers) who aimed to overthrow the alien Manchu dynasty. To emphasize their right to be gentlemen, they adopted the long robe (*pao*) as their required garb, hence the name Paoge, or "Robed Brothers."[5] In the last few decades of the Qing dynasty, officials began to be alarmed by the rapid numerical and territorial expansion of secret societies. In 1883, Ding Baochen, who was then serving as governor-general of Sichuan, wrote to the magistrate in Baxian County, "Sichuan province is a vast area with bandit types [*feilei*] as ubiquitous as grass. The Guofei [*Gulu hui*], brotherhoods [*Huifei*], religious sects [*jiaofei*] and salt bandits are everywhere. They rob the people on the roads during the day and break into homes during the night."[6] Despite his warning, the Qing authorities were not able to curb the growth of these secret societies, and by the late nineteenth century a French priest reported that the sworn brotherhoods had managed to infiltrate "all of the municipalities" in Sichuan.[7] The growth of the brotherhoods in the Chongqing region was also stimulated by the establishment of Chongqing as a treaty port in 1891 and the resulting commercial development.[8] The Qing government was not able to muster the resources to stop their growth; in 1909, the governor-general of the province failed to convince the newly formed provincial assembly to develop a plan for curbing the power of the Elder Brother Society and other related organizations. By that time, the Paoge was no longer just an organization of lower-class men but had managed to penetrate all strata of Sichuan society, including the landed elite and well-off merchants, many of whom joined the secret society in order to broaden their connections and gain use of Paoge protection services.[9]

The 1911 Revolution greatly enhanced the legitimacy and power of the Paoge in Sichuan, accelerating its transformation from mobile mutual-protection bands of men to territorially based organizations.[10] In the buildup to the revolution in Sichuan, Sun Yat-sen's Revolutionary Alliance had drawn on the anti-Manchu nature of the Paoge to win its support for the Republican forces. The alliance had recruited some leading Paoge members into the Republican army and infiltrated the Paoge with its own members.[11] Secret society participation in the Republican-led anti-Manchu railway agitation in 1910 and 1911 in Sichuan was later acknowledged by Sun Yat-sen as preparing the ground for the successful Wuchang revolutionary uprising that overthrew the Qing.[12]

A crucial engagement in the revolution was the capture of Chengdu, which Yin Changheng, the Revolutionary Alliance commander, accomplished with the help of the Paoge. When the rebellious poor and disenfranchised laboring people turned out in the tens of thousands, the city fell and Yin Changheng became the Republican governor of the province. Yin decided to rely on the Paoge and even made himself the top Rudder Man (*duobazi*), or high-ranking official, of the society, dubbing his Republican government a Paoge government.[13] Yin was reported to have paraded around the streets of the capital wearing red robes as a sign of his enthusiasm for the Paoge. As a result, the Paoge acquired high status, prompting members of the gentry and landlords to see it as representative of the new power that could provide them with protection in chaotic times.[14]

This Paoge government, however, did not last long, because the Republican provinces of Guizhou and Yunnan refused to recognize it, invading Sichuan with the intent to "deliver it from Gelaohui control."[15] Furthermore, Yin Changheng found the Paoge organization far too loose to be politically effective. The individual local "ports" (*matou*) that comprised the Paoge were often well organized but overall were not well coordinated with other "ports." (The terminology was apparently derived from the fact that the Paoge and similar organizations had come up the Yangzi River.) As a result, Yin abandoned the Paoge as a major component of his power base and encouraged their departure from the government.[16] By February 1912, the Chengdu and Chongqing municipal governments had begun to suppress the Paoge.

In subsequent years, however, Paoge influence in the countryside continued, as the organization evolved from a fraternal mutual-aid organization of the oppressed and exploited to a patron-client network embracing the gentry and landlords on the one hand and the peasants and laboring people on the other. It was also at this time that Sichuanese began to classify the Paoge associations into "clear water" (*qingshui*) lodges whose members were accepted as legitimate leaders who threw their weight around but defended community interests, and "murky water" (*hunshui*) lodges made up of bandits who preyed upon farming and urban communities.

During this period, the Paoge came to incorporate two distinctly different types of members: professionals (*zhiye Paoge*) and semiprofessionals (*ban zhiye Paoge*). The professionals ran the society's territorially based orders and lodges. Their daily life involved sitting around in the teahouse that served as the Paoge "office," where they conducted business, entertained guests, and enjoyed recreation, including gambling. The semiprofessionals joined the Paoge to facilitate their own economic and social activities. Semiprofessional members included famous commercial and industrial figures as well as leaders in the fields of education[17] and politics, and above all, members of the military.

If the new Republican order had succeeded, these rural Paoge lodges might have gradually disappeared. But the Republic crumbled in Sichuan and nationwide, and in its wake regional warlordism emerged, providing fertile ground for Paoge growth. The warlord era, which began in the middle of the 1910s and continued in Sichuan until 1935, involved almost constant contention among five or six warlords, with an estimated 467 conflicts between 1911 and 1932.[18] Skirmishes and battles were almost a constant way of life, and Chongqing changed hands frequently until the early 1930s, when Liu Xiang succeeded in establishing a relatively stable warlord administration there. The ongoing conflict gave rise to a pressing demand for weapons, acquired from Shanghai and paid for in opium drawn from Sichuan, Xikang, Guizhou, and even Yunnan. This two-way trade was in the hands of the Paoge. Secret societies were able to develop a thriving business in guns, opium, and salt smuggling, which ultimately drew many men into the underground economy.[19]

The deterioration of social cohesion in rural localities, many of which were plagued by both intermittent warlord skirmishes and bandits, provided an opportunity for the Paoge. It became an informal political authority that maintained a semblance of law and order while providing protection services to those willing to pay. At the same time, it was able to extract a great deal of money from running gambling tables in the local teahouses, storing grain and opium, and collecting membership and homage fees.[20] The rise of warlordism in Sichuan created fertile ground for a dramatic expansion of the Paoge society in rural communities.[21]

THE PAOGE'S GRIP ON PROSPERITY

Little is known about the arrival of the Paoge in Prosperity. The temple in this market village did not record the date or circumstances connected with its coming, nor did any county document note its arrival in any of Bishan's other market villages. [22] In contrast to their great interest in the history of *The Three Kingdoms* and the various personalities and battles of the warlord era, Prosperity's residents knew little about the actual development of the Paoge in their community. Indeed, the one piece of its history that our informants did relate to us—that the organization had been formed at the end of the Ming with the express purpose of overthrowing the "foreign" Manchu conquerors—proved to be inaccurate. [23] No doubt the Paoge's grip on the community was facilitated by the inability of the government and the local elites to provide minimum public security, the militarization of society in the warlord years, and the patron-client and protection services that Paoge lodges were able to provide to its members.

Like other Sichuan communities in the 1910s, Prosperity was beleaguered both by warlords and by predatory bandits. It became so unsafe in the late 1910s that roaming bands dared to come down from the hills right into the village to rob residents. One well-off family was almost ruined financially by the high ransoms; they were forced to pay for the return of their kidnapped sons, who ultimately were both returned dead. [24] A prosperous farmer, Cai Zhangyun, fared better when bandits kidnapped his only son around 1920. Once he was able to raise the hefty ransom of several hundred yuan, the teenager was returned alive. But even though the youth recovered enough from his ordeal to develop a useful skill as a stone mason and start a family of four children, he suffered from mental illness in midlife that was blamed on his earlier trauma. The agony of this very violent period in the late 1910s and early 1920s left long-term scars on the community.

It is easy to imagine that the local gentry, large landlords, and strong lineage heads in Prosperity would have welcomed some "clear" upright Paoge lodges in those years. The Paoge was able to offer a measure of protection and found ways to negotiate with the "murky" bandit types. It was not until the early 1930s that Liu Xiang, the warlord of the Chongqing area of Sichuan, launched a major effort to suppress these emboldened bandits. [25] The reduction of bandits in this area, however, did not spark a lessening of public support for the Paoge in the market villages. Just when the security needs that justified their local support became less pressing, the weakening of warlordism in Sichuan province in the mid-1930s and the arrival of twenty thousand troops of the Nationalist government motivated many warlord military officers to retire and return home. [26] Many quickly assumed leadership positions in the local Paoge lodges, using their expertise and connections to build the authority of the Paoge at the grassroots level.

PROSPERITY'S UNOFFICIAL CHIEF

In Prosperity the most notable returning warlord officer was Brigade Commander Cai Xunqing, who retired from the Twenty-Ninth Army after it was defeated by Liu Xiang in 1935. Cai came home a much wealthier man than when he had set off to join the warlord armies a decade or two earlier. Although the Cai lineage in Prosperity was one of the five largest in the community, his family's economic status had been on the decline in the early twentieth century, and he had only inherited a relatively small landholding of twelve *dan* upon the death of his father. His parents had succeeded in arranging his marriage at an early age, perhaps before their economic woes were apparent, to the daughter of one of the county's rich Zhang families, providing him with assets and contacts that proved useful when he decided to embark on a military career. As he rose in one of the Sichuan warlord armies, he slowly accumulated resources that enabled him to expand his landholdings in Prosperity to over one hundred *dan*. His wealth was prominently displayed in the renovation of his home, which was adorned with a wall and a watchtower, and by the addition of a second wife and then a concubine, as well as the acquisition of some maids (*yatou*) to wait upon his household.[27]

The extent to which Cai was able to use Paoge connections to boost his financial circumstances while he was in the military remains unclear, but most leaders in the warlord armies at that time maintained strong connections with the Paoge.[28] One indication of his contacts with the society was the marriage of his son in the early 1930s to the daughter of Cao Xianghui of Zhengxin, an important Paoge figure in Bishan County who owned a six-hundred-*dan* rice land estate, and whose brother reportedly owned one thousand *dan*. By all accounts this wedding was a dazzling affair. To accompany his son's bride to her new home, Commander Cai sent two platoons of soldiers, one armed with rifles, the other with pistols. Landowner Cao, for his part, wined and dined them for three days, along with all the other guests who came to honor the family on this occasion. Poor and landless kinsmen, tenants, and neighbors of both families not only were allowed to enter and partake of the meal, but also gathered up leftovers from the tables to take home.

After his retirement from the army in the mid-1930s, Cai became an eminent local personage in Prosperity. Choosing to enter politics in the informal sphere centered in the teahouse rather than taking a post in local township or county government, he launched a bid to become head of the leading Renlongshe lodge in the nearby Chengnan Market. Then he brought it to Prosperity, where he challenged the local Renlongshe lodge in which Sun Zhonglu held a key executive post as Fifth Brother. Ultimately, Cai's lodge was able to eclipse the Sun lodge, giving rise to a strong rivalry between Commander Cai and the Suns.

Cai's success in this endeavor was greatly facilitated by his vast network of connections, constructed outside Prosperity during his time of service as a commander in a warlord army. Most important, he had forged close links with two of the Paoge's most powerful county chiefs. One was the formidable Chen Xueqiao, head of the Bishan General Association of the Paoge (*Bishan zongshe*), who controlled all five orders throughout the county. The other was Zhang Ming'an, secret society chief in the important town of Dingjia'ao, who was a sworn brother of the Communist Eighth Route Army commander Liu Bocheng.[29] With these connections, it became possible for Commander Cai to orchestrate the departure of the two Sun cousins who were his most capable adversaries in Prosperity—Sun Zhonglu and Sun Zhongyao. As a result of his maneuverings, they were invited to participate in a special training program of the Nationalist Party that was difficult for them to refuse, as it represented an unusual opportunity to escape the limitations of rural life and develop their careers in the large urban center of Chongqing.[30] This left the control of Paoge activities in Prosperity to Commander Cai.

When our team arrived in Prosperity in 1940, it was made eminently clear to us that Commander Cai, a well-built man of medium height in his early fifties, was the most powerful personage in the community: more influential than the recently appointed head of the township government, Sun Zhonglu; more powerful than Cao Yuexian, Prosperity's biggest landowner with his three-hundred-*dan* estate; more authoritative than any of the various local religious leaders; and more domineering than the patriarchs of the three largest lineages (the Wu, Yang, and Zhang lineages) in the community. Although Commander Cai's hundred-*dan* estate made him a powerful landlord, the crucial factor underpinning his powerful position in the community was his role as the Elder Brother (*daye*) of the dynamic and expanding Renlongshe lodge.

Commander Cai's military bearing was quite suitable for an Elder Brother in these unsettled times, a man who had to take charge of difficult situations and stand tough. He sometimes was called upon to use forceful means to settle disputes and to challenge decisions of the township head that threatened to infringe upon the power of the Paoge in the community. He was obliged to protect his members and sometimes his entire community against the bullying tactics of the soldiers of the Twenty-Ninth Army, who might suddenly swoop into Prosperity and try to commandeer a litter, demand the use of a local mill to husk their rice, or billet their soldiers in the town. At the same time, Commander Cai also had to exhibit qualities that would engender respect from his own membership, community leaders, and the government leaders in Bishan County town. In his public role as a distinguished local notable, he aimed to embody the Confucian virtues of benevolence, filial piety, and uprightness. Eight years of old-style education made the commander an educated man in the eyes of the community and enhanced his image as a member of the gentry.

Commander Cai's lodge benefited from his ability to successfully draw in members of the local gentry, the most significant of whom were Cao Yuexian and Wang Junliang. Their wealth and status in the community as leading landowners and habitués of the teahouses on market days lent more respectability to the local organization. Another influential person whom Cai brought into his faction was Wu Huanyun, the leading member of the large Wu lineage in Prosperity and a former township head. Wu on several occasions served as his main litigation master. Commander Cai also realized the value of acquiring allies who had large stores of liquid assets. He enticed Wei Shuyao, the leather and pig bristle merchant, to make a sizable contribution to the Renlongshe lodge in return for a high honorary rank that safeguarded the goods he transported for his business.[31] Wei also underwrote the entertainment costs for Commander Cai when he wined and dined the lodge's important guests.

Commander Cai selected bright and able young stalwarts for his lodge—men who could entertain guests and do well at the gambling tables in the lodge's teahouse. Some stalwarts were sons of deceased better-off members of the Paoge who had fallen on hard times, typically through gambling or opium, and the Paoge was perhaps discharging felt obligations while at the same time profiting from the young men's services. These stalwarts were always on hand to make up a table of mahjong players or entertain the society's guests. A recommendation from Commander Cai could win people whom he favored a job in the local militia, a post that still left plenty of time for gambling and carrying out the services expected by leading members of the lodge, while adding to their income and providing them with a bit of clout. Among the most successful in the Renlongshe lodge were two brothers, sons of a local schoolteacher who had died twenty years earlier, leaving his widow penniless and with four small sons to support. The mother had adopted out two sons but managed to raise the other two by selling home-brewed rice wine at a street-side counter. These boys grew up skilled at living by their wits. One of them in 1940 had just succeeded in gaining admission to the county armed militia. The second boy was picked by Commander Cai to serve as a member of the four-man committee that ran the Paoge recreation club in the market town. For a period he had also run an opium den. He turned out to be a particular favorite of the commander, who often called him to make up an extra hand at mahjong.

A successful leader of a sworn brotherhood lodge in the Republican era needed to exercise superb mediation skills to protect the interests of the members of his lodge.[32] Commander Cai fit this bill perfectly. He was a formidable person who knew how to use his temper effectively in support of even the most humble members of his lodge. He also was adept at resolving complicated problems faced by members of his fraternal order. He had to make himself available to intervene in conflicts that might suddenly erupt and to muster all of his resources to prevail. These characteristics were well displayed in a bitter fight that broke out between a coal porter and a coal miner working in a mountain pit near Zitong. The miner had started the dispute by complaining about the carriers' practice of slowly picking through the coal piles in search of the best lumps rather than just hauling off a load straightaway. Some miners were beaten in the ensuing row, prompting the owner of the mine to demand that the porters show remorse for their deeds by treating their victims to a meal that included some meat dishes. For Peng Guanghui, a sixteen-year-old coal porter from Prosperity, this demand could have spelled disaster. With no savings to draw upon and hardly any family resources at his disposal—his father had died and his mother had moved in with a widower-carpenter in Prosperity Market Village—he needed all his daily earnings from hauling coal to pay for his room and board. With some foresight, Peng had joined one of the local Paoge lodges a few months earlier. Like many young men who had to venture outside of Prosperity to make a living, he realized the value of swearing allegiance to an organization that could provide some measure of protection. Luckily for Peng, his lodge was headed by Commander Cai, who quickly ordered some of his tenants to carry him in a litter over to the neighboring township of Zitong, where he contacted the elder of the local Paoge lodge. Before long, this elder and Commander Cai managed to force the pit owner to drop his demand that the coal carriers treat the miners to a meal.[33]

Commander Cai's informal power ultimately was much greater than the formal power commanded by the township government head, Sun Zhonglu. To be sure, Cai did not seek conflicts with the township government but rather tried to give the appearance that he worked in harmony with Sun. Theoretically the township head had the authority to appoint the *bao* heads, but the Paoge often could overrule him. One telling instance occurred when Sun Zhonglu evinced strong reluctance to reappoint Yang Desheng, one of Cai's henchmen, to the position of head of *bao* No. 1, which was the most important district, as it encompassed the market village itself. Everyone knew that Yang reaped great financial benefits from his position as *bao* head. But he was also suspected of having committed more outrageous acts. One instance cited by local residents was the dubious circumstances surrounding the death of Mr. Da, Yang's own son-in-law, who was killed as he tried to fend off fourteen bandits who had broken into his home one evening. Although no conclusive proof linked Yang Desheng to Mr. Da's death, he was widely suspected of having instigated this murder. One reason often cited by local people was that changing circumstances had eroded the value of this kinship relationship for Yang. He had originally been very keen on arranging the marriage for his daughter because Mr. Da's older brother, Da Shengxian, had served as a district government head in the early 1930s. But the appeal of this contact vanished suddenly when Da Shengxian was killed while leading a bandit suppression drive. Another reason for public concern about Yang's involvement in this affair was that he directly benefited from his son-in-law's demise when his widowed daughter moved back into his home, putting the management of Da's estate, which had been bequeathed to her two young sons, into Yang's hands.

Commander Cai's relationship with Yang Desheng went back several decades and was cemented by their common histories, as both had sought upward social mobility through careers in the warlord armies. Some local residents suspected that Cai had helped Yang in his efforts to win the freedom of those accused of committing the murder of Mr. Da. Yang's daughter pursued the matter with determination and managed to have the culprits arrested at great personal expense—two thousand yuan in court fees. But in the end, four of the six she had accused were allowed to go free, at least one of whom was known to have had close personal ties with Commander Cai. Despite the murkiness of Cai's role in this affair, it was quite clear to all in the market town that Sun Zhonglu only agreed to Yang's reappointment as *bao* head because Commander Cai insisted on it.

Although Cai was clearly more powerful than township head Sun, he routinely harassed the incumbent by raising claims of bribery, embezzlement, or graft against him in an attempt to have him removed from office. Typical of this harassment was a case that riveted Prosperity off and on for eighteen months. Early in 1940, Sun Zhonglu was taken to court in Bishan by Wu Huanyun of the Cai faction on a charge of misappropriating public property, namely three machine guns from the township armory. In his own defense, Sun argued that the township had purchased the guns when banditry was rife. Now, with the restoration of relative peace, they were rusting, so he had scrapped them. In fact, in a nod to lineage loyalty, he had given them to a cousin to smelt down and use for the construction of iron looms for his household weaving industry. County head Wang Shidi took no action, recognizing this as a ploy in the ongoing local factional rivalry. But the plaintiffs did not let the matter drop. In October, when the head of the district (*qu*) came on a tour of inspection, Commander Cai himself took the opportunity to press the ongoing charge of corruption. The inspector attempted to mediate a solution by proposing that Sun settle the matter by paying three hundred yuan into the township treasury. He dropped his efforts, however, and proceeded on his inspection tour when Commander Cai demanded Sun pay one thousand yuan. The issue of the guns smoldered for another six months, and then Commander Cai sent Wu Huanyun to the county court to press the case anew. This time the county head referred the matter back to the township. But by this time Sun Zhonglu was no longer in power (a story explored more fully in chapter 6). The new township head, being an outsider and fresh to the job, was not eager to get embroiled in a local feud. He put the matter in the hands of the manager of the township office, who happened to be a member of the Sun faction. When Wu Huanyun discovered this, he came to the village office to vent his rage. For one long evening he could be heard the length and breadth of the village reviling the Suns. But that was the last we heard of the machine guns.

In time, Commander Cai became much more than the senior patron of his lodge; he became the chief patron of Prosperity, one who acted as the father figure for the community. Even though the members of his lodge only represented a portion of the Paoge membership in the community, in his public persona he behaved and was widely accepted as the senior public leader of the entire community rather than as a factional leader. Cai fulfilled this role when the skies over Prosperity were unexpectedly filled with Japanese bombers heading for Chongqing and Chinese bombers trying to intercept them. Soon the planes of some of the inexperienced young Chinese airmen plunged down into a field, causing great consternation. Although it was clear that the airmen needed to be taken to the hospital in the county town for medical attention, no one was willing to take any action until someone with authority assumed responsibility for handling the situation. It was Commander Cai—rather than the township head—who was brought to the scene. He immediately took charge of the situation and arranged for the wounded airmen to be carried to Bishan County town, two hours away by foot, paying the cost of the litters and the hospital fees out of his own pocket.

Another example of the magnanimous way in which Commander Cai used his wealth to confirm his benevolent role as the informal leader of Prosperity occurred in April of 1941 when Liang Taiyun, a member of the Bishan local militia who was a resident of Chengnan township, was wounded while taking part in a mopping-up operation against the bandits. After he was shot in the hip, the bandits dispersed and his fellow militia members carried Liang into Prosperity's market village. They arrived at the deserted township office at midnight, but Commander Cai, who was gambling with Wang Junliang at house No. 28, took charge. When it was ascertained that the wound was serious and required the attention of medical authorities in Bishan County town, Commander Cai called a litter, paying ten yuan to the carriers and two yuan for the registration fee at the hospital. In so doing, the commander was well aware that this act of generosity and benevolence would be the topic of discussion in the teahouses for days to come, providing an endorsement of his role as the paramount person in command of Prosperity.

THE PAOGE AS A COMMUNITY ORGANIZATION

In early 1940, the Paoge was a well-established and visible local organization in the market village, where it ran two teahouses and a clubhouse. At first we thought that the teahouse run by Wang Mingxuan was the liveliest place in the market village because of his convivial and outgoing personality and impressive singing abilities. Over time, we realized that large numbers of men frequented his establishment because it served as the hub for one of the local lodges of the Paoge. Referred to as a "port" (*matou*), this teahouse was the meeting place for the members of the Renlongshe lodge. The chief patrons congregated here on market day so they could easily be seen and found by their clients and the general public. Here they performed their roles as judges of customary law by mediating disputes and validating various financial transactions. At the same time, they also cultivated ties with notables from other communities and in the county town by entertaining them in the teahouses.

This "port" also played host to outsiders coming and going on business of one sort or another. Any stranger able to identify himself as a Paoge brother could be put into direct contact with an executive member of the lodge and receive hospitality, help, or protection, as needed. Another form for affirming their status was officiating at special ceremonies, especially during the Lunar New Year festivals. The close connection between the market village and the Paoge was also underscored by Prosperity's use as the site for the convening of biannual membership meetings for four Paoge lodges. [34]

Although the Paoge was secretive about certain of its undertakings, much of its business was carried on openly in the market village, and people had no hesitation in freely describing its orders, lodges, [35] ranks, membership, and rules. From the public events of the Paoge, it was obvious that the organization was able to appeal to a broad spectrum of the community. Indeed, no other corporate body in Prosperity was as large or drew its membership from as many strata. Every man in Prosperity, we were told, belonged to one or another of the township's six local lodges, for if he did not, "his position in society would be unclear (*shenjia bu ming*) and he would have no one to vouch for him."

How Prosperity's residents picked a lodge to join was supposedly based on their rank as determined by a traditional Confucian social hierarchy. Of the four lodges that were headquartered in the market town, the two that belonged to the Benevolence (*Ren*) Order—the Renlongshe being more prestigious than the Renluoshe—were at the top of this social hierarchy, as they theoretically drew their members from the gentry. Next in importance were two lodges affiliated with the Righteousness (*Yi*) Order, which was said to be composed of well-off farmers who cultivated their own land. [36] We saw no sign of the two lodges based out in the countryside, but we were told that they were affiliated with the lower two orders—the Rites (*Li*) Order, purportedly made up of landless cultivators and other laboring people, and the Wisdom (*Zhi*) Order, for merchants, innkeepers, and peddlers. It quickly became apparent to us that the social strata definition of the lodges we were familiar with—those affiliated with the Ren and Yi orders—could not have applied to their current membership, who were drawn fairly broadly from laborers, merchants, professionals, and gentry. Local people claimed that joining a lodge of the top order was simply a matter of greater cost and stricter ethical standards. Our observations confirmed that it was money, factional considerations, personal connections, and personality that determined the order and specific lodge a man joined. As for the claim that no one whose family had a bad reputation would be admitted to a lodge of the top order, this was patently untrue. Two key members of two of the leading lodges openly flouted taboos: Feng Qingyun for wife stealing (a story told in chapter 8) and Wang Mingxuan for sleeping with his daughter-in-law.

What was most notable about the Paoge was that its lodges were led by large landowners and other local notables. Practically anyone with ambition to be somebody in the community seemed to feel that it was important to join the Paoge and become one of its patrons. In return for a pledge of loyalty, as the lodges' leaders they vouched for members, mediated quarrels of the rank and file, and came to their rescue when they were bullied or clashed with outsiders. Patron-client ties were highly personalized. Favors were not bought and sold but were requested and agreed to in the course of a social engagement, often at a dinner in one of the village restaurants. These ties were reaffirmed at festival time when the patron gave a banquet in his home and all those beholden to him were expected to come, thereby enhancing his prestige. Although other corporate bodies in the township—the large lineages and the landlords—also invoked patron-client ties, the Paoge, with its powerful bonds of solidarity between men, was the only cohesive patron-client structure in Prosperity.

Within each lodge, whether of a higher or lower order, members were ranked in a hierarchy of older and younger brothers. Sixth Brother was the highest rank an ordinary member could reach. At the bottom came the Ninth and Tenth Brothers, who made up the bulk of the membership.[37] Some of the most prestigious members of Prosperity assumed leading roles in one of Prosperity's market village lodges, including large landlords, rich merchants, and township officials. In the case of the more affluent members, sizable contributions were expected at the time of entry and promotion. Our informants recalled the rather steep sums paid by the community's biggest landlord, Cao Yuexian, when he returned home in 1936 after resigning his post as police chief in a small town. Upon being admitted into the Renlongshe lodge as Third Brother, he made a contribution which some claimed was two thousand yuan, while others believed it amounted to four thousand yuan. The position of Third Brother gave him an enormous amount of influence in the organization, enabling him to take a direct part in the councils that oversaw operations of the lodge, which wielded significant informal power in Prosperity.

Well-off merchants who joined or were recruited into the Paoge were known to make sizable contributions as well. Those who bought high honorary ranks received both protection and benefits of various types. With its network of connections, the society could help merchants evade surcharges as they transported their goods. The pig bristle agent Wei Shuyao never regretted the large sums he paid for his honorary membership, telling us that for any merchant, membership was indispensable; with the right connections he had the ability to transport the bundles of processed bristles to Chongqing without having to pay tolls at any point along the way. This was thanks to Commander Cai's close ties with the powerful head of the leading lodge in Bishan County town. Another aspiring trader, Dong Taibang, decided that he preferred the services offered by the Robed Brotherhood over the Loom Fairy Society (*Jixianghui*) and at considerable expense upgraded his membership in this secret society by buying an honorary rank of Third Brother in 1941 after he had prospered by selling machine-spun cloth to downriver people. Merchants with smaller businesses than Wei's cultivated their Paoge standing by paying for promotions whenever they could. Two local farmers, who became itinerant cloth dealers in 1938 when the market began to expand after the outbreak of war, each joined the Paoge society. Both flourished, and in 1940 one bought promotion to the rank of Third Brother. The other went up from Ninth to Sixth Brother in the spring ceremonials and from there up to Fifth Brother in the winter, despite the rule that members should spend at least one year in any rank.

In the rice trade especially, it was important to have local support against outsiders. Although the central government legislated the rice prices at levels far below market value, it did not set up an apparatus to enforce them in local markets. This opened the way for town merchants to solicit local protection to squeeze rice holdings from local dealers at the legislated cheap prices. Cornering the market in a particular commodity in a market village could be highly profitable, but it required clout. The ultimate example was opium, but traders in commodities as ordinary as salt and pig bristles also used connections to advance their trade. The informal power holders looked on the leading merchants as allies or potential allies, people who could provide them with cash in return for political services.

The vast majority of the members of the Paoge in all the lodges were not gentry members, prosperous farmers, or merchants, but farm laborers or those who sallied forth on their modest ventures as peddlers, porters, itinerant barbers, tailors, fortune-tellers, or mole removers. Membership was essential for anyone whose work took them into rural areas where strangers were distrusted and might be thrown into a village lockup by local authorities for a few days while a check was done to see if they had committed any crimes in the locality. Such troubles could be avoided, or at least minimized, by joining a Paoge lodge and securing patronage. In Prosperity, peddlers and coal carriers who paid for admittance as rank-and-file members of a local lodge had patrons to protect them from bullying when they traveled to neighboring townships. Traders able to purchase ranks in the society at levels corresponding to the value of their stock could count on some security from bandit raids and exemption from numerous local tolls on the highways to Chengdu and Chongqing.

Membership for laborers was not an inexpensive proposition. Indeed, given the costs that had to be incurred when joining the Paoge, the veracity of the common belief that every man in the community belonged seems doubtful. Certainly some of the poorer farmers who derived little benefit from this society would hesitate to pay the fees and associated expenses. To join a lodge, an ordinary laboring man had to find three members to sponsor him, fete them at a banquet, pay an admission fee, and go through the ritual initiation at one of the twice-yearly ceremonials. In 1941 scraping together the admission fee for the top lodge of three yuan was in itself a burden. Managing the cost of entertaining three sponsors—or six sponsors if the applicant's family was not deemed upright and needed a waiver—was onerous. For instance, Peng Guanghui, the sixteen-year-old coal porter described earlier, had been obliged to entertain six sponsors at a feast in order to join because his widowed mother was cohabiting with a widower-carpenter in Prosperity Market and was no longer considered a virtuous woman. The cost to Peng was at least double the amount of the admission fee, though it paid off when Commander Cai came to his rescue after the coal mine brawl a few months later.

Members like Peng did not involve themselves in the day-to-day activities of the lodges. Few of them took part in the gambling that was the most conspicuous activity of the society. They were rarely seen at the twice-yearly ceremonials of the society; they could not readily spare the money for the feast and apparently they did not feel it imperative to worship their patron deity. Impoverished members did not seek promotion, even though the fee for an ordinary promotion was only two yuan in 1941; their concern was to secure a strong patron to help in an emergency. Membership was their insurance policy. In return they would pledge full loyalty and obedience to their lodge's patrons.

This web of patron-client ties gave the local executive members, especially the Elder Brother (*daye*) of the six Paoge lodges in Prosperity, a firm power base in the community. Though this network was informal, in many ways it rivaled that of the formal political governance of the township government. It was reinforced by Paoge regulations compelling respect for the lodge elders, including "Do not deceive the Eldest Brother on pain of death," "Never fail to obey orders of an older sworn brother on pain of having to drink water used for washing feet," and "Do not plot to betray or kill an Eldest Brother on pain of death."[38]

In an effort to distance itself from its "murky" roots, the Paoge represent- ed itself in public as being "clear." To this end, it put out three sets of regulations for its members: the Ten Rules, the Ten Points of Etiquette, and the Twelve Prohibitions (see boxes 5.1–5.3). These were a mixture of Confu- cian strictures (obey one's elders and be filial to one's parents); guidelines about conduct (walk properly, do not sit with both feet on a table, do not be quarrelsome, and do not be arrogant); and codes to protect the organization (do not commit adultery with the wife of a sworn brother and do not cause the society loss of face). They were also sprinkled with a dose of supersti- tious worries—no breaking anything in a teahouse because it was seen as an ill omen portending that one would kill another person in an accident. These ideas were inculcated in a variety of ways, including through local operas and singing groups.[39]

While it was generally thought that the ethical rules of the Paoge were not strictly enforced, nonetheless we found that they still had some clout. One of the best examples we observed involved the traditional doctor and herbalist, Zeng Deyuan, who had a quarrel over a money matter on market day with a man from Zitong market village. In the heat of the argument, Zeng tore his opponent's gown. Onlookers separated the two men and persuaded them to settle the matter by mediation. Zhang Xiongqin, the Elder Brother of the

---

Box 5.1. The Ten Rules

    1. Be loyal to the country.*

    2. Be filial to one's parents.

    3. Obey one's elders—in age or rank.

    4. Preserve distinction between high and low, large and small, old and young.

    5. Be friendly to neighbors—especially to those in other orders.

    6. Be impartial and unbiased in one's dealings.

    7. Do not quarrel within the family.

    8. Do not provoke quarrels between two parties by reporting bad things to each side.

    9. Do not tell outsiders the rules of the society.

    10. Observe the ten ranks of the society.

    *Our informant had perhaps unwittingly replaced "the ruler" with the contemporary concept of "the country."

Box 5.2. The Ten Points of Etiquette
 1. Show respect for the Eldest Brother.
 2. Dress neatly.
 3. Walk properly.
 4. Do not break cups in a teahouse.*
 5. Do not sit with both feet on a table or chair.
 6. Do not cheat or rob others.
 7. In the case of an Eldest Brother, never refer to oneself as such.
 8. Do not be arrogant.
 9. Do not oppress the weak or poor.
 10. Do not curse others or use bad language.
 *Breaking a cup in a teahouse was an ill omen, portending that one would kill another by accident.

Yixingshe lodge where Zeng was a member, adjudicated the dispute. The money matter was soon settled, but Zhang then took the occasion to censure Zeng for rowdy behavior incompatible with the society's code and stipulated that he replace the torn gown. Though Zeng agreed at the time, he did not keep his promise. After some time, Zeng's opponent reported this to the senior man of his own lodge in Zitong, and the latter sent a note to Zhang. The humiliated lodge head castigated Zeng and declared that he would be suspended unless he replaced the gown. Again Zeng promised but again failed to do anything. When the head of his lodge received a second note from the head of the Zitong lodge, he summoned Zeng to tell him that he was suspended. Unrepentant, Zeng said he would resign. The infuriated Zhang said, "I expel you!" Since expulsion from one lodge meant no other lodge could accept him, Zeng capitulated, agreeing to accept suspension until he had fulfilled his obligation.

The Paoge were sponsors of Prosperity's most visible rituals and entertainment. Much of this activity centered on Guan Gong, a hero from the period of the Three Kingdoms who was deified in folk Buddhism and was portrayed both as the red-faced god of war and the patron god of business. Guan Gong was a symbol of loyalty and courage.[40] In imperial times Guan Gong's image could be found throughout the country in Wumiao temples of the state religion. These temples to the military authority, which were paired up with Wenmiao temples to the civil authority, were to be found in every town as well as many market villages like Prosperity. With the establishment of the Republic in 1911, state religion was abolished, but the Paoge continued to embrace Guan Gong as their patron figure. The local lodges in Pros-

Box 5.3. The Twelve Prohibitions

   1. Do not commit adultery with the wife of a sworn brother, on pain of death.

   2. Do not plot to betray or kill the Eldest Brother, on pain of death.

   3. Do not deceive the Eldest Brother, on pain of death.

   4. Do not spy for a hostile group, on pain of banishment.

   5. Do not start rumors, on pain of banishment three thousand *li* from one's native place.

   6. Do not reveal society secrets, on pain of three years' imprisonment.

   7. Do not cause the society loss of face, on pain of death.

   8. For messengers, do not lose letters one is entrusted with, on pain of death.

   9. Do not become angry with a sworn brother whose rank is senior to one's own, on pain of death.

   10. Never fail to obey orders of an elder sworn brother, nor to help a younger sworn brother, on pain of having to drink water used for washing feet.

   11. Do not prefer women to one's sworn brothers, nor be unfilial to one's parents, on pain of expulsion.

   12. Do not be quarrelsome, on pain of having one's tongue cut off.

perity worshipped him, albeit in a somewhat perfunctory way, at their twice-yearly public ceremonials.

One of these occasions was the Festival to Welcome the Lunar New Year (*zhongnian shenghui*), which took place on the tenth of the twelfth month of the old year. A number of days previous to this, a steward from each of four of the Brotherhood lodges posted a large red paper notice on the gate of Wumiao temple inviting members to a banquet and giving the time, place, and cost (which was two yuan). A flurry of firecrackers announced the beginning of the worship of the patron god. Those seated in the teahouses did not bestir themselves, leaving the worship to the stewards of each lodge and any rank-and-file members who cared to attend.

In the temple, each steward lighted incense, burned cash paper, and then placed three dishes of food on the altar. The handful of worshippers kowtowed first to Guan Gong, then to the other gods flanking him. After these obeisances, each steward, with his small following of rank-and-file members, returned, bringing with him the three untouched dishes of food. These he placed on a table which had been set out in the street in front of the particular restaurant where his lodge was to banquet. Incense and candles were lighted, and the three dishes were now offered to the spirits of those sworn brothers of the lodge who had died.

After these rituals the proceedings livened up with feasting and drinking of the potent local white spirit. But the stewards still had tasks to perform. Each now led the members who during the secret proceedings of the previous night had been admitted to membership or promoted in rank on a tour of all the banqueting tables of each of the other three lodges. In his hand the steward held a large sheet of red paper on which was inscribed the name of each new member, his introducer, his guarantor, and the Eldest Brother who had sanctioned his admission. When the steward had read the list aloud, the members of the brother lodge chorused, "Thank you," while the newcomers knelt to make one kowtow to the members of the brother lodge who rose to accept the obeisance. The little delegation then passed on to the next restaurant where another lodge was banqueting and so on to all the brother lodges in a small introduction ceremony.

The second festival of the Robed Brothers was the *dandao hui* held on the tenth of the fifth month to commemorate the bravery of Guan Gong.[41] Again business was transacted and Guan Gong was worshipped. This time a table draped with a red cloth was placed before the god's image in Wumiao temple, and a small lamp was lit and hung before it. The ceremony itself was scarcely more elaborate than the previous and just as poorly attended.

These gatherings promoted the values and stature of the brotherhood and provided the occasion for admission of new members, promotions, demotions, suspensions, and even expulsions, as well as for feasting and socializing. As the majority of members could not afford the fee for the inevitable banquet required on such occasions, however, the turnout was scarcely a hundred for all four lodges combined.

The Paoge teahouses and music club provided a form of cultural entertainment that was unrivaled in the community. In these years entertainment of any sort was very limited in Prosperity's market village. The local government seemed unable to serve this function, and it was the Paoge that provided entertainment. They sponsored a music club in a village building lent free of charge by Cao Yuexian. Here amateur singers under the guidance of a paid music master practiced, and on market day afternoons they performed in the open-fronted clubhouse while the guests gambled and passersby might pause to enjoy a favorite aria. The repertoire consisted of items from Sichuan opera based on stories from *The Three Kingdoms*, highlighting the exploits of the master strategist Zhuge Liang, Sichuan's most beloved hero.[42]

To provide entertainment at New Year's, the Paoge established the Full Moon Committee (*shang yue hui*), a secular ad hoc committee made up of leading members of the local lodges. In 1941, the two heads of the Full Moon Committee were Cao Yuexian, Prosperity's biggest landlord, and Wang Junliang, one of the top eight, both executive members of Commander Cai's lodge. A third member was Wu Huanyun, the leading political activist of Cai's power faction. While the top lodge dominated, members of other lodges were also represented, including Yang Rongting, who was head of a *bao* and of the lowest Yi lodge.

In 1941 the expenses for the New Year's festival came to about two thousand yuan, at a time when a bushel of rice cost about forty yuan. About one thousand yuan were needed in cash for the construction of the dragon; for the cash paper, incense, and candles lighted in its honor and in honor of the earth god; for firecrackers; and for fireworks on the final evening. Another one thousand yuan were needed to provide a banquet for the performers each day—sometimes twice or even three times a day—to reward them for their efforts. The Full Moon Committee raised the cash and found the hosts. Money was raised in three ways: through a standard levy of two yuan on village shops and homes, through special contributions from households who paid to have the dragon perform outside their home, and through a contribution from the secret society's recreational club of its profits from the previous two months of gambling.

The procedures for collecting the funds were simple and direct. In the last ten days of the old year, an advertisement appeared on the wall of Wumiao temple inviting people to sign up for a "drum." For a "big drum," costing six yuan, the dragon and its band would perform outside one's house for ten minutes, and for a "small drum," costing four yuan, they would do so for five minutes. Such performances would bring the family special good luck in the coming year.

Nominally voluntary, levies to support the dragon dancers were in effect a community obligation. When Wang Haizhao, a miller who had prospered so conspicuously in the preceding year that he was able to build an extension to his home, refused to donate the basic two-yuan surcharge, he was publicly rebuked. The first reproach occurred when the dragon stopped in front of his house to collect the two-yuan levy. Sharp words were exchanged between the dragon dancers and Mrs. Wang, who came out to pay the fee. When the Wangs were mocked for having refused to host the dragon, Mrs. Wang hotly justified their actions with the comment, "We only entertain those who bring *zabao* [a formal gift, which theoretically covered the guest's share for the costs of the hospitality], but the dragon brings no *zabao*." Such a statement was seen as an act of open defiance of the community's norms, for no one else expected a *zabao* from the dragon dancers, who were being thanked through such meals for the blessings they brought the community. In this exchange the Wangs not only dared to resist the social pressure put on them but afterward even voiced disbelief in the auspicious powers of the dragon.

The dragon dancers did not limit their public display of disdain toward the Wangs to this one exchange but found another opportunity on the last day of the festival. As the dragon set forth from the market village for its cremation, casting its final blessing on all the homes that it passed, it made an ostentatious detour in front of miller Wang's home, climbing through a shed into a backyard, then squeezing through a gap in the tumbledown village wall, and skirting the village before getting back onto the path leading to its cremation site. The dancers explained that the northern end of village street where miller Wang's home was located had to be avoided because it was inhabited by "unclean" (evil) spirits. These public humiliations ultimately bore fruit. When some of miller Wang's pigs died several months later, it was widely reputed that this sad event had occurred because he had lost the protection of the dragon. He decided to redeem himself by donating liberally to the North Star Ceremony in the eighth lunar month, which ended up costing him far more than the contribution expected of him for the dragon.

One other occasional source of funds could be a gift of one hundred yuan—the estimated cost of constructing a dragon—required from any family to whom a son was born as the result of the theft of a dragon's eye the previous year, but such a circumstance had not occurred in Prosperity for twenty years. (Because they were thought to guarantee the birth of a son, dragon eyes were valuable and could also be snatched at other times of the year.) When Prosperity's dragon arrived back in the village from its pilgrimage to Tuzhu temple in 1941, people were startled to find that its eyes had disappeared. This was four days too early, for normally it was only after the completion of the dancing on the night of the nineteenth that snatching and grabbing of the amulets was permissible, and even then the dancers were expected to remain alert to protect the dragon. Even though the amulets had been snatched earlier than was permissible, no fuss was made because it was obvious that the star dancer, Wei Shuyao's seventh brother, had stolen them (with the consent of his fellow dancers) for his sister-in-law, who after seven years of marriage had borne no children. And everyone knew that the merchant Wei Shuyao was one of the most generous funders of the festival and a leading member of Commander Cai's lodge of the Paoge.

As for hosting the dragon dancers, the committee had to find several dozen families willing to take this on. The cost of treating the minimum of three tables of guests to a lavish meal came to a minimum of forty-five yuan (at fifteen yuan per table). But such hospitality enhanced the host's public image. In 1941, twenty-two families volunteered readily or otherwise. The hosts of the dancers were the chief landlords, most *bao* heads, and prospering merchants or shopkeepers in the village. But they also included two guards who could hardly have been expected to afford the expense unless they had recently had good luck at the gambling table or earned a substantial sum for special services performed. All who hosted the dragon were publicly honored and invited to the grand farewell-to-the-dragon banquet hosted by the Paoge festival.

At the close of the festivities, the Full Moon Committee posted up the detailed accounts on the temple wall. They noted, "Amounts collected from the sixth to the nineteenth of the first month: (in cash) 566.00 yuan; (in rice) 90 *sheng* (at current prices worth four hundred yuan); two piles of cash paper; several pairs of candles; and a belated additional six yuan." The committee also posted a public thank-you note naming all those who had hosted the dragon, along with those who had made other special contributions. With this the committee had completed its duties and was dissolved, to be reconstituted a year later in time for the following lunar festival.

This open and honest handling of finances stood in stark contrast to the subterfuge and corruption that characterized the handling of business wherever any major profiteering was possible, either in legal government dealings or smuggling. The functioning of the Full Moon Committee showed that there existed a minor tradition of open democratic procedures that operated when there was little at stake and no need to account to a higher level, and when publicity and honor were to be gained from public service.

THE UNDERGROUND ECONOMY

Paoge lodges were able to exploit both legal and illegal economic opportunities, particularly gambling, opium smuggling, and protection rackets.[43] Gambling went on in one or another of the village teahouses every day, but mostly on market day afternoons and evenings. Professional gamblers, some of them from outside Prosperity, dominated the action when the stakes were large. Though only a small proportion of the population in Prosperity was actively involved, gambling was a significant and pervasive phenomenon. Young men without property who lived by their wits could be found gambling day after day. These were the stalwarts who were always available to help with the entertainment of the Paoge guests. Gambling was their occupation and the source of their livelihood. Other single men drawn to the tables were hired laborers and weavers, restless for some change and excitement after long hours of work. On their one day off a month, some of them gathered at Cai Yunqing's "poor man's" teahouse to gamble for low stakes. In contrast, men of poor farm families on the whole avoided gambling, though they might pause at a teahouse to watch a game in progress, and occasionally, if the stakes were low, to place a bet.

Men from big landowning families also were drawn to the gambling tables, often out of boredom. But the leading men of Prosperity used gambling as an opportunity to make, consolidate, or deploy connections essential for their various schemes. While they were considered men of leisure, they were only idle in the sense that they did not engage in physical labor and that their timetable was flexible. They might spend hours on banqueting and drinking with guests, and much of the night gambling, but this was essential work. The socializing entailed in gambling was closely tied up with maneuvers for power and wealth. Among these men, some, like Commander Cai, who as host gambled incessantly, seemed neither to gain nor lose much, while others, like landlord Cao Yuexian, who was discussed in chapter 4, might lose heavily.

Apart from the profits, gambling was also important to the local lodges of the Paoge because it enabled their "ports," located in an off-the-main-highway market village, to attract crowds. The comings and goings of people, many of whom circulated in a large radius taking in Chongqing, kept the community's leading figures closely tied to the vast brotherhood network. For some, gambling was a way of cementing their relations with influential men who could be of use to them. Feng Qingyun habitually went to Bishan County town, where he played mahjong with various key people there, deliberately losing sizable sums. The relationship between winner and loser was subtly preferable to that between briber and bribed.

The gambling games were mahjong and *paijiu*. Mahjong, a game of skill, was played at any or all hours of the day as a way of passing the time pleasurably, of entertaining guests, and especially of cultivating and using the web of "connections." For serious gambling the game was *paijiu*, a swift game of chance requiring no skill, at which large sums of money could be lost or won in just a few brief moments. Thirty-two cards were dealt out among four players, four to a player in a first round and another four in the second. One player served as the banker. After the first round was dealt, onlookers examined the various hands and placed their bets on the hand they guessed would win. The second round was dealt, and the players laid down their hands. The banker then swept in all the stakes and paid the winner. The game itself was vacuous, but when enough onlookers had gathered to lay bets, the atmosphere was tense; when stakes were high it became electric. *Paijiu* gambling started off each market day afternoon in the various teahouses. As evening approached and crowds became too big for a teahouse, half a dozen youngsters of the Paoge bustled around preparing the Wumiao temple courtyard. After borrowing benches, obtaining candles or torches, and arranging the seating, they summoned the gamblers to the temple, where gambling would go on until midnight. Throughout the evening the urchins ran errands for the gamblers, brought them tea or hot wet towels, and received tips in return.

If word went out that visiting professional card sharks had arrived and were playing for high stakes, the courtyard would become packed, and the session might go on all night and even continue into the next day. On one such occasion a well-known professional arrived in Prosperity from Danfeng Market. The gambler's father, the rich and influential proprietor of the general store there, had recently died, leaving his wealth to his two sons. Both had become professional gamblers, touring the market villages of the county. Though it was still early afternoon, gamblers at once assembled. By mid-afternoon the visitor had lost over one thousand yuan. Gambling went on the rest of the day and night, with elated local people winning steadily. By the following morning, however, the tide turned. Local people began to lose. By mid-afternoon the professional had made considerable gains, and toward evening when the two-day nonstop session closed, he had won a small fortune and departed, carried away in a litter.

Sometimes the locals could prevail at the gambling tables. One night we were awakened at 2 a.m. by wild cries. Seeing the flickering light of flames, we thought the temple was on fire. But it was only the torches lighting the temple courtyard, where the shouting was inspired by the size of the sums changing hands. In the morning we learned that a visitor had lost over nine hundred yuan in a single round as banker. He had promptly sold one *dan* of rice for 570 yuan, but he had no way of paying the remaining balance of his debt without parting with some of his land.

Much of the Paoge's income came from the gambling tables. With mahjong, the proprietor of the teahouse collected ten to fifty *fen* per round, depending on the size of the stakes. With *paijiu*, the rate was 10 percent of the winnings each round. Wang Mingxuan's teahouse, which served as the port for Commander Cai's lodge, collected around fifty yuan an evening throughout January 1941, though on the night of January 3, when stakes were unusually high, it took in over one hundred yuan. At *paijiu* sessions in the temple courtyard, where the turnover was far bigger, the society could make several times that amount. On one particular evening in November 1941 when we kept track, the sums collected amounted to over five hundred yuan.

In Prosperity, Commander Cai would not countenance any form of cheating. Even petty theft at the gambling tables was not tolerated. Once the commander felt he had lost face when a homeless youth named Hai'er, who had moved out of Prosperity with his prostitute mother after his father was locked up, returned on a market day and managed to make a few small thefts by hanging around the gambling tables. On the following market day when Hai'er returned, hoping for more plunder, the commander literally kicked the wretched lad out of the village.

More profitable than gambling was the income derived from opium. Unlike gambling, opium operations were largely covert, as the distribution and sale of opium had become illegal with the establishment of the Nationalist government in Chongqing in 1938. Nationalist government prohibitions caused some decline of the opium trade, particularly in the cities and large towns, but they were not able to change the popular attitudes and habits in this rural community. In fact, in early 1940 there was no sign that these prohibitions had made much of a dent in the Paoge's opium business. There were three chief opium dealers in Prosperity. Two were members of Cai's lodge: Wang Mingxuan, proprietor of the teahouse serving as this lodge's port, and Zhang Guangquan, a bankrupt landlord who was the brother-in-law of Wang Junliang. The third dealer was Feng Qingyun, a member of Prosperity's largest lodge, the Yixingshe, and a proprietor of the lodge's teahouse. Anyone interested in smoking some opium could easily procure some in these teahouses.

Commander Cai often joined his guests in smoking opium, though compared to many others in the township, his habit was not excessive. He was, however, linked through marriage to a major dealing family in the county. Aside from these lodge and family links, he may well have maintained some ties to the opium trade through his army connections. It was a well-known fact that his and other warlord armies were deeply involved in the production and sale of opium in the 1920s and 1930s in order to pay for the purchase of arms.[44] An indication of the continuing vibrancy of these links between warlord army officers and opium trafficking in Bishan County was the prominent role played by a nephew of Lan Wenbin, the onetime division commander in Liu Xiang's Twenty-First Army, in the local opium trade. Chen Kaidi of Taihe Market used his uncle's ties to become one of the main opium dealers in the county and was reputed to convey this illicit drug in a fleet of trucks protected by armed guards. Chen and other county dealers delivered opium, which mostly was grown in the neighboring province of Xikang, to Prosperity, as it was not available locally.

There was no censure of those who made profits from opium, nor of those who smoked it and became addicts, although everyone knew that addiction took its toll on many families. The Paoge, with its vested interest in drug smuggling, continued to be successful in promoting the social acceptability of opium smoking. The impact of the opium traffic on Prosperity's residents was noticeable. Based on county statistics that were gathered at that time, we estimated that Prosperity had only about one hundred addicts, slightly more than 2 percent of the adult population and about 9 percent of the male adults.[45] Rarely did working farmers in the community smoke opium. Rather, it was the transport workers among the laboring people who were the most vulnerable. When youth or health gave way, a porter could find himself forced to take a puff of opium to enable him to complete his journey. Gradually he could find himself more and more dependent on the drug. It is most likely for this reason that government statistics showed a sharp rise in addiction among adults in the thirty to fifty age range.[46]

Also vulnerable to addiction were those involved in the opium trade itself; they were in constant contact with smokers and in some cases were paid in opium rather than cash. People both rich and poor also took opium as medicine either to suppress symptoms of dysentery and other ailments or as a painkiller. This further added to the number of smokers. Some idle landlords also took up the habit, including Prosperity's largest landowner, Cao Yuexian. Some of the better-off owned their own paraphernalia and smoked at home with their wives and aged parents. It was not considered seemly for women or the elderly in such families to smoke in public places. But land-lords and prosperous merchants smoked both in private and public. Sharing an opium pipe was looked upon as a gracious way of extending hospitality and promoting good relations.

The Paoge society was also thought to make a considerable amount of money on its protection racket, although these dealings were even more covert than the opium smuggling. Even in times when banditry was rife, gamblers were never attacked when they left the Paoge teahouses with large amounts of money. The Paoge saw the gamblers as their guests, and as hosts they took responsibility for their safety. At the same time, their opium deal-ers did not suffer from bandit attacks, nor did the merchants in Prosperity who purchased honorary executive memberships in the lodges. Unlike the local government, the Paoge had the means of providing the necessary secur-ity.

The Paoge was central to life in 1940s Prosperity. It might even be said that the Paoge provided the sociopolitical structure of the community, pro-viding a patron-client matrix that dominated Prosperity and gave boundaries to its identity. The Paoge operated the market on behalf of the community, helping the village flourish in competition with other market villages. It provided entertainment—the music club, gambling, and opium—from which it made money. It provided services: notarizing, mediating disputes, and disseminating news and information while adding its own spin. And it kept up a religious function by organizing and funding the Lunar New Year wor-ship of the local god Tuzhu.

But perhaps the most important thing the Paoge did was to provide secur-ity at the marketplace and on the routes to and from the market. No traders on the roads were robbed, no shop was robbed, and even a small theft by the pauper boy Hai'er, as we have seen, resulted in expulsion from the village by Commander Cai. The community needed security for this market, on which their livelihood depended, and the government did not and perhaps could not provide it. Although the village militia under the township head had scarcely a dozen unarmed men, many guns were in the hand of the farmers, who provided security on the roads. The Paoge kept order in the village on market days, which was key to the local economy. Commander Cai was a powerful and popular leader. Overall, the sentiments of the local people were with the Paoge.

Nevertheless, the organization was far from entirely benign—not only because of its involvement with opium and gambling, but also because it was the location of factional splits, struggles, and sometimes violence. The Paoge was not a centralized organization but rather a federation of factions that pulled together on issues that concerned the whole community, even while leading individuals within it jousted for power and wealth. During our year in Prosperity, we observed jousting for power between Commander Cai as the aspiring traditional gentry, Sun Zhonglu as the modernizing Guomindang member, and Feng Qingyun as an out-and-out adventurer of the kind later glossed by the Communists as "local bullies and evil gentry" (*tuhao lie-sheng*). This story is told more fully in chapter 10.

As the de facto local informal government, in the early 1940s Paoge members played a crucial role in resisting reforms at the township and village level initiated by the Nationalist government and other reformers, a subject explored in part II of this book. Those drafting the county reform policy apparently thought they could solve the problem of rooting out corrupt individuals such as Feng Qingyun by sending in trained outsiders as township heads while calling on the upright gentry to give full support. And yet, if the Robed Brothers Society in Prosperity was typical of rural Sichuan community-based brotherhoods, then the distinction between "clear water" and "murky water" societies was an ambiguous one. Had reformers fully recognized the nature of this multifaceted Paoge "enterprise," which controlled the market, perhaps they could have devised a more successful policy for dealing with the Paoge.

NOTES

1. For a discussion of the origins and early development of the Paoge (Gelaohui), see Cai Shaoqing (1984); Jacobson (1993); Liu Cheng-yun (1983); and Tang Shaowu et al. (1986).

2. Scholars such as William Skinner and various missionaries who frequented rural Sichuan have mentioned the power of this organization in rural market villages in late imperial and Republican times. More recent studies such as by Kristin Stapleton and Mary Lee McIsaac have delved into the urban operations of the Paoge in Sichuan during the late imperial and Republican eras (McIsaac 1994, pp. 175–188). Kristin Stapleton (1996, pp. 29–30) observes that "despite the prevalence of the organizations, detailed community-based studies of them are practically non-existent." She comments that this might be so because the Paoge and similar organizations "were so common in Sichuan before 1949 that many commentators have taken [their power] for granted."

3. Stapleton (1996), pp. 30–32. On the origins of the Guolu, see Qin Baoqi and Meng Chao (2000).

4. McIsaac (1994), pp. 112–113. She cites Tang Shaowu et al. (1986) for the view that the Paoge are akin to the Elder Brother Society, and Zhao Qing (1990) for the position that the Paoge should be seen as different. Xiong Zhuoyun and Wu Shaobo (1989) argue that in Sichuan the terms are essentially interchangeable. Isabel Crook recalls that when she was growing up in Chengdu, "Gelaohui" was the common term used to refer to the main sworn brotherhood. She did not hear the name "Paoge" until she went to Prosperity, where she assumed that they were one and the same.

5. Wang Chunwu (1993), pp. 23–24.

6. Wyman (1997, p. 91) quotes a document from the Sichuan Provincial Archives, Baxian collection (Junshi 3001 #4 Governor-general Ding Baochen to Baxian magistrate on January 26, 1883).

7. Wyman (1993), p. 99.

8. Wyman (1993), pp. 90–93.

9. Wang Chunwu (1993), pp. 26–27.

10. This point was strongly emphasized by Zhang Tongxin, professor emeritus at Renmin University, in an interview in Beijing in the spring of 2005.

11. Tang Shaowu et al. (1986).

12. For a full discussion of Sun Yat-sen's cultivation of the Sichuan Paoge as allies of the Revolutionary Alliance as early as 1909, see Wang Chunwu (1993, chap. 6). Sun is reported to have said that if it had not been for the Paoge's participation in the antigovernment Railway League and the rank and file of the Qing army, the final rebellion against the Qing would have been delayed by six months to a year (Wang Chunwu 1993, p. 103).

13. A *duobazi* (rudderman) was a higher position than a *Daye* (Elder Brother), who was in charge of a single lodge.

14. This material is from the memoirs of Fan Shaozeng (1982). Fan Shaozeng could be considered the head of the Chongqing-region Paoge. He controlled the opium trade with Shanghai, where he had linked himself with Du Yuesheng of the Green Gang. Further details of their relationship can be found in Shen Zui (1992).

15. Stapleton (1996), p. 38.

16. According to Xiong Kewu, a prestigious Sichuan Revolutionary Alliance member, the Chengdu government debated at length about whether it should reform or outlaw the Paoge before Yin expressed his exasperation with the organization; "Shudan shigao" [Draft History of the Party in Sichuan], in *Xinhai geming shi congkan* [Collected Works on the History of the 1911 Revolution] (1980, pp.167–182), as cited in Kristin Stapleton (1996, p. 56, n60).

17. Tang Shaowu et al. (1986), pp. 158–159.

18. You Xin (1932, p. 4), cited in Richard Gunde (1976, p. 24).

19. Stapleton (1996), p. 29.

20. Fan Shaozeng (1982), pp. 235–256.

21. Mary Lee McIsaac (1994, p. 177) shows how this also happened in the urban districts of Chongqing during the warlord period. She argues that warlord conflicts in the 1910s and 1920s spurred an increase in Robed Brotherhood memberships in Chongqing. She writes, "The destruction wrought on Sichuan's rural areas by their armies swelled the ranks of poor and landless peasants, and created a steady stream of poverty-stricken peasants and unemployed laborers flowing into the cities such as Chongqing. In the unfamiliar and hostile environment they faced there, the Robed Elders was one of the few entities offering necessary assistance and protection."

22. No documents were found in the Bishan archives confirming the existence of the Paoge in Prosperity before the war, and our informants did not reveal much historical knowledge of this organization's development in this locality.

Interestingly, the Bishan Gazetteer (Sichuan sheng Bishan xianzhi, 1996) has very little of value about the Paoge in the county or its various townships before 1949. We also noticed that many of the Sichuan histories that were published in the 1980s and early 1990s did not pursue this topic in much detail and that the official biographies of well-known Bishan Communists who originally were active in the Paoge omit this fact. A case in point would be the biography of Ye Chenyi (1896–1972). See *Bishan xianzhi* (1992, pp. 760–761).

23. Interview with Superintendent Liu, 1941.

24. Interview with Cao Hongying about the plight of her parents and two of her siblings in the late 1910s and early 1920s on February 2, 2005.

25. He appointed Regimental Commander Gu Yusan to wipe out the bandits, and Gu, as discussed in chapter 1, used harsh measures that took the lives of numerous innocent people.

26. Under the influence of the Nationalist government in Nanjing, the Sichuan provincial government began to reduce its bloated armies (Kapp 1973, p. 107).

27. While we did not have an opportunity to talk with his maids (*yatou*) in the 1940s, we did interview one of them in 1983. She no longer lived in Prosperity, having married a PLA soldier from Guangdong in 1950 and later moved there, but she had returned to her native place on this occasion to visit her father. That transcript is included in our raw data, but we have not drawn from it because it seemed overly influenced by the political atmosphere of the revolutionary era.

28. For instance, Liu Xiang, who was the most powerful militarist in Sichuan in the mid-1930s, maintained close ties with the Paoge. See Kristin Stapleton (1996, p. 43), where she draws upon Xiong Zhuoyun (1984).

29. In the late 1920s Liu Bocheng led an uprising at Fuxun, but he was defeated and wounded in one eye. After receiving treatment in Chongqing he convalesced in Bishan, during which period he became close friends with the influential secret society head Zhang Ming'an (interview with Huang Shiqian, head of the Bishan County Office, 1983).

30. Isabel Crook, interview with Sun Zhongyao in 1983.

31. As a Third Brother of the dominant lodge of the Paoge, Wei paid no taxes in Prosperity, and when he passed through Bishan he notified the powerful Eldest Brother there and again paid nothing. From the county he took a small road to Chongqing, knowing that the bandits would not rob him because of his Brotherhood connections, and thereby avoided certain transit taxes.

32. Stapleton (1996, pp. 41–42).

33. We were told of this incident in 1983 by Peng himself.

34. The four lodges that were located in the market town were of the top two orders: Benevolence (*Ren*) and Righteousness (*Yi*). Out in the surrounding countryside there were two other lodges, one of the Rites (*Li*) Order and one of the Wisdom (*Zhi*) Order. According to the customary ranking of these orders, *Ren* was first, *Yi* second, *Li* third, and *Zhi* fourth. Lodges of the fifth order, Trustworthiness (*Xin*), did not exist in Prosperity in the wartime era.

35. The Paoge consisted of several orders. Each order might have lodges in more than one location.

36. Prosperity's largest lodge was Yixingshe, of the second order, traditionally for farmer-owners. Its acting head was Zhang Xiongqin, a farmer who had prospered through the cloth trade. The nominal head was Liao Zhibing of Bishan. We never met either of these men, but ranking as Third Brother was Sun Zhonglu who was township head in the summer of 1940. Another important member was Feng Qingyun, opium dealer and teahouse proprietor at No. 14, an ambitious man of untiring activity and obvious acumen, well versed in the inner workings of the power network. A split-off from this lodge was Yiheshe, which some said was headed by Cao Daihui, a farmer and Daoist folk priest, and others said by Yang Rongting, a prosperous farmer and head of *bao* 6.

37. Though ranks numbered from one to ten, there were actually only six with Eldest Brother and Third and Fifth Brothers making up the executive ranks, and Sixth, Ninth, and Tenth making up the rank and file. Elaborate reasons from history and legend accounted for the omission of the other four ranks. Second Brother (*erye*) was banned in deference to the hero-god Guan Gong, for he himself was second brother of the trio (in which Liu Bei, ruler of the Kingdom of Shu, was eldest, and Zhang Fei was third). Locally there was a second reason. Bandits were called *bang laoer*, *lao-er* being a more intimate way of saying *erye*. Fourth Brother (*siye*) was banned because originally there had been a fourth brother, but he was never close to the others and was thought of by some as an intruder. Seventh and Eighth Brothers were missing because of the betrayal by the seventh and eighth brothers in the band of 108 heroes in the fictional tale of *Water Margin* (*Shuihu zhuan*).

In addition to the Brothers there were boys, as young as ten or twelve, called Youngsters (*yaomen*), who served as errand runners. Most of them served openly, but one or two were secret messengers (*an yaomen*, as opposed to *ming yaomen*), known only to the Eldest Brother and serving him alone.

38. Taken from "The Twelve Prohibitions," which was given to us by Liu Zhiquan, the district superintendent for Bishan for the American Methodist Episcopal Mission. The full list of these prohibitions is given in box 5.3. Our informant commented, "During the Qing dynasty, these prohibitions were actually enforced. The Eldest Brothers were all-powerful and had the support of legend. Now things are different, though some of the prohibitions still hold good."

39. For instance, the notion that members of the Paoge should be loyal to one another regardless of the obstacles was reinforced through the often-told story of Yang Jue'ai and Zuo Bodao. In the Warring States period, the story went, Zhu Kingdom had a very good king, and many learned scholars congregated at his court to help him. Two of these scholars, Yang and Zuo, were good friends who decided to go to this court. So they set out from their hometown to

help the king. Both were very poor, and their food and clothing were inadequate. On the road a snowstorm blew up and both were in danger of freezing to death. So Zuo said to Yang, "I am not as learned as you. Since we both can't go on without food or clothing, I will give you mine and you can go ahead." Yang, of course, refused. So Zuo pretended he needed to relieve himself. Yang waited for him, but he did not come back. So Yang went to find him. He found Zuo's food and clothes by the roadside. Zuo had taken off all of his clothes and climbed into the hollow of an old tree where he had died. Yang buried him and took the clothes and food and went to Zhu, where he became rich and famous. Later, he went back along the road where he had buried Zuo and made offerings and moved his remains to a grand gravesite. The new grave was near that of a famous general who was angered at having a new neighbor. He tried to drive Zuo's spirit out of the territory. One night in a dream Zuo came to Yang, crying and begging to have his body moved elsewhere so he would not be disturbed in his tomb. Yang wrote letters of appeal to the god of the place, but the general was too powerful. So Yang decided that if the god could not fight the general, he would. He committed suicide beside Zuo's grave and the next morning the people found the grave of the general destroyed and the bones of the general scattered around.

40. For a discussion of the role of Guan Gong in another part of China, see C. K. Yang (1961, pp. 159–161).

41. *Dandao hui* was a famous opera related to a story in the *Romance of the Three Kingdoms* where Guan Gong attended a banquet offered by Lu Su, who was plotting to recover the city of Jingzhou. Guan Gong realized that it was a trick and foiled the plot with courage and wit.

42. The club came to a sudden end when a quarrel broke out between the two leading officers. The music master had asked for a raise in pay because of inflation. Feng Qingyun not only opposed this but pressed for the abandonment of the club, arguing that whereas the gambling winnings were currently divided between the four lodges in the village, if gambling took place in the teahouses serving as Paoge ports, each could keep its own gains.

43. From what we could discern, the Paoge in Prosperity in the war era did not exert as complete control over the financial dealings of the periodic market as was the case in the late 1940s in the markets observed by William Skinner. They were blocked from weighing produce, as this was under the control of the priests. See Skinner (2001, p. 44).

44. Kapp (1973), p. 56.

45. This figure is based on a report issued by the Bishan County Bureau for Curing Opium Addicts in September 1938 which estimated 4,706 addicts in the county, based on the numbers of those caught. Assuming addiction was as prevalent in the countryside as in towns and along the highways, Prosperity would have had about a hundred addicts. As a percentage of the total adult population of 4,205 (eighteen years and over), this would be 2.29 percent; as a percentage of total male adults (1,158), it would be 8.9 percent. However, in our view addiction rates in rural market communities in Bishan were not as high as in the large towns. This roughly correlates with the finding that approximately 10 percent of the Chinese population was addicted to opium in the late nineteenth century (Spence 1975, p. 154).

46. Table 5.1 provides information on the ages of addicts.

Table 5.1. Statistics on Opium Addiction in Bishan County*

By Age:		By "Grade of Certificate"	
under 20	62	grade 1:	18
21–30	816	grade 2:	78
31–40	1,667	grade 3:	1,010
41–50	1,380	"very poor"	3,600
51–60	599		
over 60	182		
TOTAL:	**4,706**	**TOTAL:**	**4,706**

* No definition of addiction was given; the four-grade economic scale was also undefined.

Paddy fields of Prosperity with newly planted mulberry trees on the dikes. Hu Xiping, Prosperity, 1983.

Approach to Prosperity Market, with poplar-lined highway and western Great Mountains in the distance. Hu Xiping, Prosperity, 1983.

Plowing one paddy field while harvesting the one above, tying the sheaves, and threshing, using a box with tall bamboo mats. Hu Xiping, Prosperity, 1983.

Plowing with buffalo. Hu Xiping, Prosperity, 1983.

Reaping and threshing rice in a field below a house. Hu Xiping, Prosperity, 1983.

Drying and winnowing rice in the courtyard of a whitewashed house, with vines hanging out to dry under the eaves and straw stacked below.
Hu Xiping, Prosperity, 1983.

Looking down on the Prosperity Market street with Maolai Shan in the distance. Hu Xiping, Prosperity, 1983.

Middle section of the Prosperity Market street. Hu Xiping, Prosperity, 1983.

One of the few old looms still in operation—used to weave homespun cotton cloth for the Guizhou Miao people. Hu Xiping, Prosperity, 1983.

Old-style loom. Hu Xiping, Prosperity, 1983.

Next four photos: Dragon Dancing at the Lunar New Year in Bishan. Hu Xiping, 1983.

Left to right: Zhou Mingzhi, Daxing Commune vice head of women's work; Yang Yuzhen; Isabel Crook; Cao Hongyin; and Yu Xiji. Yang and Cao were former Bible school girls we knew well in 1940/1941. Hu Xiping, Prosperity, 1983.

Left to right: Isabel Crook, former slave girl Yang Shufang, and Yu Xiji. Hu Xiping, Prosperity, 1983.

Isabel Crook with County Head Xiang Taihua. Hu Xiping, 1983.

Isabel Brown (Crook) in 1940.

Left: Yu Xiji in about 1940. Photo courtesy of her family. Right: Chris Gilmartin, Beijing. Photo by Bekki Tippens.

Chris Gilmartin, Yu Xiji, and Isabel Crook. Beijing, 2004.

II

Outsiders

Chapter Six

Wartime Reformers

When Japanese invaders seized most of China in 1937 and 1938, the Nationalist government transferred its capital from the relatively prosperous and commercialized eastern coastal area of Jiangnan to the hinterland city of Chongqing in Sichuan Province. Prior to that time, the Nationalist government had little influence in this part of China, which had been wracked by internecine struggles of warlords for control of its rich resources. From the mid-1920s onward, seven warlords fought one another intermittently to expand and protect their territories. Warlord administration was carried out through the "garrison area" system: the major warlords staked out their territory, assigning portions of it to lesser officers who received no pay for themselves or their troops but were given the freedom to raise taxes, recruit troops, and maintain security by whatever means they could. This system ravaged the rural areas, banditry became endemic, and the merciless attempts to crush it added to the insecurity and violence.

The invasion of Japan sparked a very different war from the one that had gripped Sichuan in the preceding decades. Sichuan was suddenly the destination point for a large migration, as the transfer of the capital to the deep interior of the country brought with it a flood of institutions, including many industries and universities, as well as "downriver" people from the occupied areas of the coastal provinces, among them secular and religious reformers. By 1940, recurrent Japanese aerial bombings of the Nationalist capital city of Chongqing, less than forty miles away, prompted many downriver refugees to seek the safety of remote rural areas such as Prosperity.[1] This downriver influx included professionals, students, and secular and religious reformers, such as the educator Liang Shuming, the sociologist Jiang Zhi'ang, and the well-known James Yen (Yan Yangchu), who had headed the Mass Education

Movement in Dingxian, Hebei Province, before the war and now chose to relocate his new projects in the neighboring community of Xiemachang.

Meanwhile, the Nationalist government was attempting to implement changes in Sichuan, aiming both to modernize rural areas and to cultivate patriotic citizens who would support the war effort. In 1938, the year after arriving in Chongqing, the central government passed the War of Resistance and National Rehabilitation Act, which put on an equal footing—by making them interdependent—the efforts to build the country's economy and the apparatus of state. With political fragmentation and the competition for scarce resources threatening the war effort, the government set out to mobilize the population for the war effort and to disable its rivals for political allegiance and control over the country's economic resources. This meant an attack on warlords and bandits, the opium trade, the gentry's hold on local government, and above all on the Gelaohui (of which the Paoge in Prosperity was a version) and its ties to all of these.

It was in 1940, then, that these two sets of outsiders—those representing the state-building enterprise of the Nationalist government and those who belonged to the burgeoning rural reconstruction movement composed of numerous religious and secular organizations—launched reform agendas in Prosperity with the aim of transforming institutions and practices. During the late 1920s and 1930s, many tensions had hampered relations between the government and these rural reconstruction reformers, sometimes becoming antagonistic. However, with the Japanese occupation of north and central China, the governmental and nongovernmental forces fleeing into the interior were compelled to work together.

This chapter examines the nature of the two programs—one official and the other nonofficial—implemented in Prosperity in the early 1940s, paying particular attention to their different goals, resources, and approaches. In the case of the Nationalists, this endeavor involved a complex array of political and economic reforms that were imposed in a top-down fashion and placed a significant focus on increasing bureaucratic central authority at a local level, but also included some attention to improving education and health care (discussed in chapter 7) and to a lesser extent women's status (the subject of chapter 8). The rural reconstruction initiative was undertaken in Prosperity by the National Christian Council (NCC), an ecumenical organization representing Protestant churches in China, which sent in a team to focus on a bottom-up reform approach to improve the quality of rural life, hoping in the process to enhance the influence of the local church in the community.

The striking differences between these two groups mask important common features that facilitated many positive interactions. Both recognized the strategic importance of the market village as the center of their operations and created an effective presence there to push their reforms. They both also understood the importance of establishing relations with the local elite. Finally, both saw the need to create a systematic body of knowledge about the community through statistical surveys.

When the Nationalist government and the NCC rural reconstruction team inaugurated their reform packages in Prosperity in 1940, they sought to do so in a bold style that would create a durable impression on the community. Although the specific fashion in which they presented their initiatives to the community differed, they both announced their presence dramatically. For the Nationalist government, this meant proposing a set of reforms that asserted central control over township governance. Nationalist reformers attempted to alter the relationship between the community and the upper levels of government. For the NCC, declaring its arrival entailed establishing an ostentatious presence in the community and obtaining the endorsement of important personages in order to indicate the power of their operation, which promised to take significant steps toward poverty alleviation while also providing support for certain state-building programs at a local level.

ADMINISTRATIVE REFORM

The government began its bold approach to local reform on July 1, 1940, by announcing that Prosperity would be merged with the neighboring township of Dapeng and that its name would be changed from Prosperity Township (Xinglong lianbao) to Daxing Xiang.[2] This merger was based on a program that had been promulgated in 1939 to reform local governance. Echoing Sun Yat-sen's earlier pronouncements that county governments should serve as the "basis" of the nation and should become "autonomous units," the Nationalist government sought to circumvent the provincial government and develop stronger links between itself and the counties in unoccupied China.[3] In the case of Prosperity, it cited bureaucratic reasons for the change in administration. The modernization of the postal system made it necessary to eliminate duplicate names in every province, and Sichuan had two townships named Prosperity (Xinglong). The decision to merge Prosperity with the neighboring township of Dapeng was also a good occasion to change the name by taking one character from each—the "Da" from Dapeng and the "Xing" from Xinglong. The meaning of the new name was quite similar to the old one, as clearly indicated by the English translation, "Greater Prosperity Township." However, by completely altering the resonance of the name, the government had made its point: the power to determine the name of a place did not belong to the community but rather was the prerogative of provincial and central government authorities. The name that the community had once picked for itself disappeared from official maps, which henceforth referred to the locality as Greater Prosperity—Daxing.[4]

Prosperity was not the only locality targeted for reconfiguration in this county. In all, ten townships in Bishan were amalgamated, reducing the total number from forty to thirty-five.[5] The guideline for determining which communities would be amalgamated was size: any township with less than one thousand households would lose its administrative status.

The Nationalists claimed that a major benefit of the reforms was that they would streamline government expenditures, but they clearly also provided a convenient opportunity to reduce the power of the *bao* heads. Thus, at this time of readjustment, it was announced that Prosperity's nine *bao* would be condensed to six, and six *bao* taken from Dapeng were condensed to two, making a total of eight in the enlarged township of Greater Prosperity. As a result, three *bao* heads were out of a job, and the remaining six would find that their power bases were reduced, as they could no longer count on a loyal constituency, often from the same lineage.

Another significant feature of the 1940 government reform of Prosperity was that the local elite would no longer retain the right to have one of its members fill the position of township head. Rather, the county head would implement the "law of avoidance" and appoint outsiders to run the township government, thereby assuring that his directives would not be ignored, circumvented, or significantly altered at the behest of local notables. While installing outsiders in the provincial and county governments had been a well-established practice under imperial regimes, it had never been used at a grassroots level in Sichuan before. The Nationalists had good reason to expect resistance to their rule at a local level. The current township head was one of the younger members of the Sun lineage (see chapters 3 and 4), Sun Zhonglu. He was reputed to have been a capable and loyal township head as well as one of the leading party members in the locality. Thus it would be difficult for an outside-appointed official to outshine him.

At the same time, steps were supposed to be taken to build up the Nationalist Party apparatus in this rural community. One course of action was to effect an increase in local party membership and inject some vitality into the dormant local party branch (No. 58) that had been set up in Prosperity in 1938 by Sun Zhonglu. An important group to be targeted was principals of the newly established public schools, as they would be expected to play an important role in promoting patriotism and discipline. The civil county officials were also instructed to hold short-term training courses for all township and *bao* officials, including captains of township militias.

The approach of the Nationalists in challenging critical aspects of Prosperity's political authority initially seemed to have been somewhat effective, particularly in creating the larger township, bolstering party membership, and streamlining township government. However, as we shall see, there was resistance to the other aspects of political reform, and internal conflicts also hampered the reform effort. Popular acceptance of the merger of Prosperity and Dapeng into one township proved to be problematic. This proposal was undoubtedly damaging to the future development prospects of the periodic market in Dapeng and thus constituted a downgrading of its status. Without a government office in its market village, many farmers living on the outskirts of this community would often choose to do their marketing elsewhere. More important, this community no longer had a local political force that could represent its interests at the district (*qu*) or county level. Clearly Prosperity's government would be more inclined to channel resources into its own market village rather than that of Dapeng.

The tensions produced by Dapeng's loss of status because of this merger were manifested in the Lunar New Year's celebrations in 1941. It was the custom at the Lunar New Year for Dragon Lantern dancers of each market village to pay courtesy calls on its neighbors to shed blessings on them. Each village had its own distinctive dragons, the number and types reflecting its relative wealth. Dapeng, at this time, was the only village in the subvalley with the most prestigious straw dragon (as opposed to the cloth and stiff-backed dragons); moreover, Dapeng had four dragons while Prosperity had only one. The type of dragon, the skill of the dancers, and the timing of its visit all signified the degree of respect expressed by one village to its neighbors. In Prosperity, two Paoge activists, reputed to be the best dancers in the community, were responsible for the dragon and its performances.[6]

The celebration in 1941 initially appeared to be routine. On the first day of the courtesy visits, Dapeng's dragon appeared in Prosperity to honor and bless the village and to perform. The reception was noticeably restrained, with only the minimum number of firecrackers set off in its honor. Commander Cai hosted a banquet for the dancers; this was his duty as the head of the local Paoge lodge in the township and would be reciprocated by his counterpart in Dapeng when Prosperity's dancers made a return visit. Prosperity's dragon, however, was not dispatched to Dapeng until it had visited every other market village in the area. Furthermore, Prosperity did not send its best dancers. Nonetheless, when its young novices appeared in Dapeng on the afternoon of the last day of dancing, they were given a seemingly warm reception. In fact, so lavishly were the dancers wined and dined that most were unable to rise from the table to dance their thanks and make their way home. This would have brought widely publicized humiliation to Prosperity and its leading figures. But someone managed to run the two and a half miles back to Prosperity to alert the festival organizing committee, and Prosperity's best dancers were sent immediately. As the thank-you dancing belatedly got under way, Dapeng honored Prosperity's dragon with a shower of molten iron, the indigenous substitute for fireworks produced by the local blacksmiths who had assembled along the market street. Each one tossed balls of molten iron into the air, which his apprentice would strike with a bat. They created such a shower of fiery droplets that the clothes and skin of the seasoned dancers were riddled with burns; one had his hand so severely burned that he went to the NCC's medical clinic for treatment.[7]

If this incident is any indication of the attitude of locals to the merger with Dapeng, it is not surprising that they rejected the new name, Greater Prosperity (Daxing). Although "Daxing" was used in all government documents, villagers continued to use the old name of Prosperity (Xinglong). The Paoge also refused to recognize the new name but rather continued to register its local lodges and members by the old place names,[8] reflecting a popular perception of the government as "them" versus "us" people.

From the beginning it was clear that the most difficult political reform to enact was the new system of appointing outsiders to serve as township heads. The Nationalists were not sufficiently prepared to implement these reforms and often had to improvise. The choice of Tang Gongyi as the first outsider to hold the township head post in Prosperity was clearly a temporary expedient, for although he was a secondary school graduate, he had not attended a Nationalist training program on government administration practices. Furthermore, he was not a true "outsider" as he was a member of the elite of the neighboring township of Zitong, where a number of the larger lineages from Prosperity also resided, having spread across marketing community lines over the preceding several hundred years. Thus he had significant insider knowledge of the internal political dynamics in Prosperity, as well as very strong personal ties with Sun Zhonglu, the former township head. What remained to be seen was whether he could negotiate the insider-outsider status successfully enough to gain the respect of both the local power holders and the general populace in the community.

A major dispute that occurred between a resident of Prosperity and the army provided Tang an opportunity to prove his worth to the community. The conflict erupted when the army requisitioned the use of a local mill to husk its rice. When the mill's owner, Sun Bingchen, refused to comply, the soldiers beat him up and knocked him unconscious. Sun Zhonglu, as the most powerful member of this mill owner's lineage, was immediately called to the scene and quarreled loudly with the captain. The matter was then turned over to the township head for mediation. At the mediation the irate captain justified his action by accusing Sun Bingchen of having stolen military rice. Members of the Sun lineage insisted that the soldiers had framed Sun because of his unwillingness to lend his mill and threatened to file a lawsuit. Since no agreement was reached between the angry parties, Tang realized there was no easy solution, so he instructed the two sides to submit a report stating both positions that would then be submitted to the county government. With this decision, the captain and his remaining soldiers were willing to return to Bishan with the rice.

The next morning Tang Gongyi was able to secure the help of a clerk in the civilian branch of the county government who traveled to Prosperity to hear the township head's account of the incident. Tang also summoned the influential men of the community to present the facts. The county clerk listened sympathetically, even expressing indignation that country people should be so roughly treated. But trying to remain impartial, he also asked if there might have been some reason why Sun Bingchen in particular had been singled out for such treatment. Relatives conceded that the man had a temper but insisted that if he was at fault the captain should have taken him to court rather than have his soldiers beat him up. The clerk agreed and promised that the captain would be duly dealt with. The session closed with local people in high spirits, assured that they had the backing of the civilian authorities.

At this point, the clerk learned that a punitive expedition of twenty armed soldiers of the Bishan garrison had set out for Prosperity under the command of a captain, though not the same one as the previous day. The county clerk set out to avert a conflict and was able to get the captain to halt his detachment long enough to hear the clerk's explanation of how matters stood. After convincing the captain that this dispute needed to be resolved, the clerk proposed that the two of them call on the injured man to ask after his health and to present him with ten yuan to cover the cost of medicine. When the captain agreed, members of the Sun lineage were pacified and agreed to drop their threat of legal action.

Although Tang adeptly demonstrated his ability to defend the community, it was unfortunate that the dispute involved the Sun lineage, as he was widely perceived as their agent in the locality. His troubles stemmed in large part from the fact that upon assuming this position, he essentially kept the administrators who had worked under the previous township head, Sun Zhonglu. Most important, Tang had retained the previous vice head of the township, Sun Bingling, a member of the Sun lineage, and all of Sun Zhonglu's *bao* heads. Although he did throw out the map Sun Zhonglu had drawn up with his proposals for how the *bao* should be reconfigured and designed his own plan for reducing and merging Prosperity's nine *bao* with Dapeng's four *bao*, this action was not sufficient to convince other power holders in the locality of his independence. As a result, Tang was continually harassed over alleged unfair rice and straw levies by Commander Cai, who took the matter to the county court. At this point, Tang was abruptly transferred back to his native Zitong as township head, replacing the outsider incumbent there, who like Tang was being charged with unfairness in the collection of levies of military rice.

The overall evaluation of Tang's administration varied considerably in the community. While his ability to work with local elites to deal with the conflict with the army was appreciated, as an outsider he had not proven to be more honest than an insider. In fact, the finances of the township were found to be in complete disarray after his departure, and he refused to return to straighten out the mess. Thus it was generally agreed that his seven months in office had not resulted in any significant changes and his removal from office was not regretted. Some people credited the Cai faction with Tang's ouster. Others credited Tang with success in his efforts to regain control in his own community by having his supporters lay charges against the outsider incumbent there.

After Tang Gongyi's departure, a new township head was appointed. A native of the city of Yunchuan, sixty kilometers from Prosperity, Tang You-tan had graduated from a modern urban secondary school. But unlike his predecessors Tang and Sun, he had taken a special six-week training course for local government officials, designed to improve the quality of local ad-ministrators. Tang's vice head was Shao Guoxie, another graduate of the training course. Tang brought with him four teachers from his hometown for support, displacing all but two of the local teachers in the central primary school.

Tang's service as township head was made difficult by government de-mands to decrease administrative personnel, as well as by challenges to his power by the local gentry and military. In 1941, the Nationalist government issued a series of instructions to streamline local government. This meant doubling up the duties of township officials: the militia captain was directed to serve as secretary of the Office of Security, and the village teachers, being public employees, were to serve as unpaid secretaries to the other three departments in addition to their regular paid schoolwork. Soon after, a re-vised instruction called for the four offices to be merged into two, with the vice township head taking charge of the Combined Offices of People's Af-fairs and Security, and a second official heading up the Combined Offices of Economics and Culture. And not long after this directive came yet another call for a "three-in-one system." This required a township head to serve concurrently as head of local government, principal of the central primary school, and director of the military training program for men in the reserve (everyone aged thirty-seven to forty-two). Similarly, each *bao* head was also to act as principal of the *bao* school and as assistant guards officer of the township. Before long this directive was replaced by another, called the "four-in-one system," whereby the township head was to take on the further duties of economic development director.

Meanwhile, Tang had to contend with a series of challenges by local gentry. Their first criticism of Tang was that he lacked strength in dealing with banditry. Local gentry cited the increase in the number of violent rob-beries since he took office, failing to acknowledge that this increase was typical of the early spring beginning of "bandit season." Nonetheless, Tang called a meeting of all the *bao* heads to discuss measures to strengthen security.

The most serious charge against Tang culminated in a petition instigated by the Cai faction and signed by seventy-three local residents, charging him with complicity in a bribery case. The case involved two hundred yuan allegedly paid to the guard Cao Guoliang by a certain family to allow their conscripted son to escape from custody. The father of the escaped conscript, for reasons that remain unclear, had then filed a charge of corruption against Cao that the township head had apparently not forwarded to the county as he should have. This was cited as evidence that Tang failed to deal with corruption among the guards. But the petition lost much of its force when Tang had the guard arrested. Still, the alleged two-hundred-yuan bribe provided a popular topic for gossip, with local women teachers speculating that the township head had pocketed the money to finance his affair with the attractive young Jiang Yunbi. Others claimed that the guard Cao had kept it, sharing part with fellow guards and spending the rest on Xiang Yaoniang's young daughter, with whom he was having an affair. The charge had to be dropped when Tang was called to Bishan and publicly cleared of misconduct.

In addition to having to negotiate difficult relations with the local elite, Tang also had to contend with the military. The complexity of entanglements in which he became embroiled is exemplified by an incident that occurred in March 1941, when Tang disciplined two soldiers for beating up a local man and breaking his wrist. The man, Wu Yunsheng, was a fifty-year-old laborer from the village who teamed up with his farmer son to carry a litter. In this instance, a platoon officer escorting his soldiers back to Bishan with their loads of military rice demanded that Wu carry them. A disagreement ensued, and the officer ordered two of his soldiers to "teach Wu a lesson." The fight was immediately reported to township head Tang, who arrested the two soldiers, removed their badges, and locked them up for the night. Suspecting that the irate officer would retaliate, Tang then called on each *bao* to request that members owning guns stand by the following day. And so the next morning, armed men from all over the township gathered in clusters in the fields and hills of the village. Tang's worries were not unfounded, as twenty soldiers from the county units, commanded by a captain, arrived at midmorning. Unfortunately, the guards protecting the township office fled in fear, and so the Bishan soldiers were able to walk in, seize Tang, bind him, and take back the confiscated badges. When Commander Cai arrived on the scene, Tang was released.

However, this was not the end of the problem. Tang took the injured Wu to Bishan to consult a locally famous bone doctor, expecting the expense to be assumed by the army. He then went to the county government office to file charges against the platoon commander. The military branch of the county government challenged Tang's charges, and the case was then submitted to the Chongqing-Beipei garrison headquarters, a department under the central government in Chongqing. When the case was heard, the platoon commander charged that Tang had mobilized armed civilians to attack the army. For this alleged crime, Tang was put into a military prison in the capital. The Bishan civilian authorities quickly raised the two-thousand-yuan bail from shops in the town and secured Tang's release pending trial. Tang returned briefly to Prosperity, collected some possessions, along with the one thousand yuan of government money that was supposed to be used to pay the schoolteachers, and fled to an unknown destination. Eventually the Bishan County government received Tang's resignation pleading ill health. The county, however, refused to accept the resignation.

Given that Tang was not in Prosperity, the government had to appoint another township head. Guo Ankang was a twenty-seven-year-old native of Taihe, a thriving market town about fifteen kilometers from Prosperity. He had graduated from the Bishan Vocational Secondary School and, like the second Tang, had completed a training course for township heads given in the city of Yunchuan. Upon graduation he had been appointed head of a city ward. And, again like Tang, he had come into conflict with the military. The county's solution was to remove him from harm's way by transferring him to Prosperity Township. To bolster himself in his new posting, Guo had brought his brother to head up the Office of Economic Affairs, which controlled taxation, his wife to serve as manager of the township office, and two guards to join the local militia.

Unlike his predecessor, who had been a complete novice, Guo had already held office once and approached his new posting with more circumspection. On arrival, Guo went directly to the teahouse "port" for the top lodge of the local Paoge and announced that he had been instructed to convey the county head's regards to Commander Cai. When Guo had been in office little more than a month, he made use of traditional forms of cultivating personal relations by giving a small banquet, entertaining three tables of guests—two of men and one of women. The men included leading members of the two chief factions of the local elite (one represented by Cai Xunqing, Wang Junliang, and Feng Qingyun, and the other by the two Sun cousins) and two men from the NCC cooperative project. The women guests, hosted by Mrs. Guo, included four women from the NCC project, Feng Qingyun's mother and concubine, and the wife of one of Prosperity's leading landlords. Although the township's tight budget did not allow for entertaining, Guo went to this expense to cultivate local personages of influence.

In spite of these efforts, Guo faced a number of difficulties, the most serious of which concerned the return of his predecessor, Tang Youtan, who waged a local campaign to regain his position of township head, claiming that his resignation had never been officially approved. Both issued accusations and appeals to the county authorities, as well as letters, each requesting confirmation of his appointment. There was no reply for six weeks, during which time Prosperity had two acting heads. In the end, Guo was confirmed in office. At the same time, Tang was given a new posting as head of Chengnan Township in the suburbs of Bishan, where his presence was unlikely to be noticed by the military men he had offended in Prosperity.

Although Guo managed to stay in power longer than the previous township heads, he was ultimately unable to effect significant change. As we shall see in subsequent chapters, in order to remain in office, he had to compromise with the local informal power holders. Therefore, his efforts to stop gambling, ban opium, and remove corruption in taxation and conscription were less than successful.

EDUCATION

Political reform was not the only intervention of the Nationalist government in Prosperity. In wartime China, the Nationalist government also drew up plans both to expand public schools into rural localities and to promote adult literacy, with the expectation that these educational initiatives would also inculcate nationalist sentiment and create a stronger sense of civic responsibility. The process of instituting these educational reforms in Prosperity during 1940 and 1941 helped to shape the evolving relationship between the state and local society as well as to reveal the limits of central authority.

Reforming education had been on the agenda of the Nationalist government ever since it assumed power in 1927.[9] At the First National Education Conference in May 1928, education was designated as a vehicle for conveying Sun Yat-sen's Three People's Principles to the masses of Chinese people with the expectation that such instruction would produce nationally conscious citizens who would evince a stronger connection to the nation-state than to their families or lineages. The Provisional Constitution of 1931 asserted the rights of every citizen to enjoy public education (*yiwu jiaoyu*), and subsequent legislation stipulated the percentage of budgetary allocations that the central, provincial, and county governments had to contribute to this construction.[10] These educational provisions were much easier to enact than to enforce, particularly in the multitude of villages and county towns. According to one study, the Nationalist state was successful in wresting control over the content of textbook materials from the localities, a struggle that had been going on since 1914.[11] Moreover, in its first seven years of rule, the Nationalist government reportedly more than doubled the elementary student population and increased the number of elementary schools by almost 50 percent.[12] It had therefore supplanted the dominance of Christian-run schools as the main purveyor of free education in rural communities.

In 1935, the Nationalist government ordered all provinces to institute public education, and Sichuan attempted to comply by passing an ordinance for one year of public schooling.[13] However, it appears that not much progress was made in Sichuan until after the installation of the Nationalist government in Chongqing. In 1939 the Education Department of Sichuan passed a long-term plan to improve education in the province by setting new requirements at all levels of education, increasing the funds available for this purpose, adding educational supervisors, and restructuring the administrative system.[14] The Nationalist government issued a major directive on education in April 1940, which was intended to induce local governments to confront these kinds of problems as part of a general effort to upgrade education. It stipulated that each township should have one six-year higher (*gaoxiao*) primary school, and each district (*bao*) should establish a four-year lower (*chuxiao*) primary school. Moreover, it called for the expansion and improvement of the facilities, which were to be paid for out of local resources (see table 6.1).

Government initiatives did have some impact in Prosperity. In the decade leading up to 1940, state-funded public schools had been established not only in the village but in each of the hundred-household *bao*. By 1940, Prosperity Township had one main six-grade primary school and nine *bao* four-grade primary schools, one for each hundred-household unit. The total enrollment in these schools was 680 pupils, 669 of them between five and fourteen, and the remaining 11, fifteen years or older. There were another eleven students attending secondary school in town.[15] Teachers' pay was provided by the county, while the local government was required to supplement this by pro-

Table 6.1. Central Directive Regarding the Financing of Schools*

Process to be Financed	Main Township School (lower and upper primary)	*Bao* School (lower primary)
Setting up school	250 to 500 yuan for each class; paid by the county from its "public fund" and "property"	County authorized to make grant from 200 to 400 yuan per class (*bao* expected to raise necessary funds)
Conversion of old-style school	Grants made only for purposes of enlargement (costs of improvement met locally)	Grants made only for purposes of enlargement (costs of improvement met locally)
School salaries and expenses	Min. monthly pay for principal = 30 yuan Min. monthly pay for teacher = 20 yuan Expense allowance per class = 72 yuan	Min. monthly pay for principal = 20 yuan Min. monthly pay for teacher = 18 yuan Expense allowance per class = 60 yuan
Special circumstances	Schools may apply for grants from a special fund, putting forward reasons for grant. Each application will be considered on its merits.	Same as main township school

* "How to Collect Money for Central and *Bao* Primary Schools," *Central Government Publication*, April 1940.

viding a monthly grain allowance, accommodation, cooking facilities, and other amenities. In Prosperity, the teachers were allocated rooms in the Wenmiao temple and were provided with a cook and two domestics to wash clothes and clean the rooms.

Even if an unprecedented number of county children were receiving some schooling, the need for further reforms was self-evident. The physical atmosphere of the main primary school was not conducive to learning. It was housed in the Wenmiao temple, which functioned concurrently as temple, market, and school—not to mention that it already housed the local government office, as well as the military barracks and jail. Maintenance of the buildings had been neglected, and students of Prosperity's primary school faced the deplorable uncleanliness of the crowded marketplace, where every third day the babble of the grain market at best impeded students' concentration, and at worst prevented the teachers from being heard altogether. Moreover, students faced the intrusion of open, odorous, and unhygienic latrines in the courtyard for the convenience of the surrounding marketeers. Finally, the main primary school lacked sufficient equipment, such as chairs, desks, benches, and blackboards.

The 1940 government directive sparked no immediate response in Prosperity because the township head, whose responsibility it was to raise and procure local funding, was busy defending himself against a charge of corruption. In June, when still nothing had been done, members of the NCC project proposed a meeting of influential figures in the community to discuss the state of education. At the meeting, local notables readily expressed willingness to help finance the following improvements: transferring the grain market from the Wenmiao to the Wumiao temple, removal of open latrines, repair of buildings, and construction of more desks, chairs, benches, and blackboards.

However, it was up to the incumbent township head, Sun Zhonglu, to secure the funds. Fortunately, Sun Zhonglu was an "intellectual," a graduate of a secondary school in Bishan, with close connections to Bishan's educated elite, including those in the county seat. Sun Zhonglu was a critical leader of the modernization-minded elite, strongly endorsing a shift away from traditional Confucianism, exploration of more Western ideas, and a more modern curriculum. Working with his cousin, Sun Zhongyao, principal of the primary school, Sun Zhonglu was able to secure promises for eight hundred yuan in only a few weeks. The money bought timber and other supplies, as well as securing the services of a contractor from Chongqing to make the necessary furniture and building repairs. But these promising developments were compromised by an unexpected ousting of Sun Zhonglu and the appointment of the outsider, Tang Gongyi, as township head. As one of his first actions in office, as mentioned earlier, Tang fired four of the local teachers to make openings for his own appointees. Unsure if Tang was trustworthy, the wealthy people who had pledged money to Sun Zhonglu for the cost of the school improvements withdrew their promises and tied their purse strings. With no money to pay the contractor, work came to a standstill. In fact, for the entire autumn term, the students endured a shortage of desks, benches, and blackboards, while the unused timber remained stacked in the courtyard.

After Tang Gongyi failed to procure the necessary funds for these improvements, the township sought the help of the Bishan County finance committee. By this time, the Nationalist government had recognized the precarious nature of local funding and instructed its county-level offices to implement a system to raise funds for educational improvements. Therefore, the Bishan Finance Committee was authorized to allow township governments to farm out the right to collect a 1 percent commission on rice and cotton sales to the highest bidder, who was to hand over one-third of the amount collected to the schools. However, the money realized from the sales tax did not go toward the envisaged improvements. Nor were the promised donations from the community leaders handed over. The reasons for this failure were not revealed, but they may have been connected to the resistance of the priests, who up to then had collected this tax, keeping a commission for themselves. Earlier government efforts to ban this practice had failed through lack of enforcement by local authorities. This time township authorities nominally did as instructed, but the priests continued to receive a small allowance because they were closely connected with better-off merchants and the Sun lineage. When no funds were forthcoming, town leaders applied for a special county grant, which was denied on the grounds that Prosperity was one of the better-off townships in the county. And so yet another school term passed with the timber stacked in the courtyard and the classrooms short of furniture.

When Tang Gongyi left office, as mentioned above, he fled with one thousand yuan of teacher salaries. His successor, Tang Youtan, took over as township head in February 1941. Tang Youtan was a modernizer, committed to improving education and determined to keep close tabs on the disparate *bao* heads. However, his focus was on streamlining and economizing his administration. His predecessor had left him with muddled accounts. Whether outright embezzlement was involved, or merely confusion in shifting funds from one account to another, was never made clear. But as a result, Tang Youtan was hesitant to pay the teachers' salaries until the financial office matters had been straightened out. Teaching conditions were never particularly good to begin with, and Tang's refusal to pay the teachers intensified the hardships they faced. Now lacking income, several teachers were forced to seek temporary employment elsewhere until the crisis was solved, and consequently, classrooms were left without teachers. Finally, toward the end of the year, a teachers' strike brought classes to a halt.

The strike dragged on for over a week before the school inspector from the county, disgusted by the unsupervised classrooms, took Tang Youtan to task. Unwilling or unable to pay the teachers, Tang responded by ordering the pupils of the top class of senior primary to teach the juniors. Then, after fruitless efforts to muster local support to force the teachers to return to the classrooms, Tang called a meeting of the teachers to announce that he would pay them shortly, but in the meantime they must either return to teaching at once or resign. But the teachers were not intimidated, and at last Tang was forced to give each teacher twenty yuan and a promise to hand over the rest of the back pay within three days, along with their overdue rice allowance. Only then did teaching resume. Tang Youtan subsequently fled office, and in the summer of 1941, new township head Guo Ankang immediately implemented the government's directive to improve the pay and conditions of the teachers (see table 6.2).

Guo himself took up the duties of principal and renewed efforts to improve conditions in the school. He was fiercely dedicated to carrying out Nationalist policies to reform and modernize the education system in Prosperity. He called a meeting of leading citizens to launch a fresh fund-raising campaign. Commander Cai of the Paoge took the opportunity to attend in person and, on behalf of the society, offered to set aside a certain percentage of its gambling profits for the school. As an immediate first step, he promised twenty-four hundred yuan to pay the carpentry costs of having sixty desks and benches made from the timber already purchased. Since Guo had already taken initial measures to carry out a Nationalist government ban on gambling, Cai's reasons were obvious to all. But Guo dared not reject the public offer, for this would have amounted to a public humiliation of Prosperity's most influential figure.

Soon thereafter, disaster seemed imminent for Guo's reforms when Yang Huanzhang, a litigation specialist who was already conducting a court case against the township head, quickly seized the chance to accuse Guo of accepting payoffs from illegal gambling. But before Yang could press the new charge, the ruling on the impending case went against him and he was sent to prison. With Yang out of the way, Guo proceeded to collect the promised

Table 6.2. Pay Scales for Primary School Teachers

Qualification	Monthly Rate of Pay
Primary school graduate	At least 20 yuan
Junior secondary school graduate	Less than 50 yuan
Teacher training program graduate	50 yuan
Senior secondary graduate	More than 50 yuan

contributions, and by late November he had raised fourteen hundred of the twenty-four hundred yuan promised. He rehired carpenters, and they set to work in the temple courtyard making desks, benches, and blackboards. At last, Prosperity's main primary school boasted a cleaner, quieter, and more adequately equipped atmosphere for modern learning.

While Guo may have partly resolved the problem of teachers' pay, his attempt to streamline the budget for education by reducing other employees was less successful. Guo arranged for the teachers to eat with his family so that only one cook need be employed. Before long the teachers were complaining that after paying their board they had "scarcely enough for a cup of tea with friends." Convinced that Mrs. Guo was cheating them, they asked that the accounts be posted each month. Mrs. Guo indignantly refused, so the joint dining arrangement broke up. Once again the teachers ran their own kitchen with their own cook. But by the end of October, they were no better off and again began looking for better-paying jobs. One succeeded in securing a post in Chongqing and left before a replacement could be found. Fearing that he would lose more teachers, Guo asked permission from our director to submit the names of two of our highly qualified staff members, whose services we had provided free to the village school to promote our own public relations. This would mean that their salaries could be included in the budget submitted to the county. The increment would then be distributed among the regular teachers. This was agreed to, and in due course the extra salaries were paid by the county. But again the teachers were left dissatisfied when Guo divided the sum from the county into three equal parts: the first for the principal, the second for "administrative expenses," and only the final third to be divided among the teachers. Disgusted, a number of teachers skipped classes to take on outside jobs, leaving the pupils to get on with their studies on their own. In spite of the significant improvements Guo Ankang made in education as Prosperity's township head, it seems he was unable to fundamentally alter conditions for perhaps the most important aspect of schools: their teachers.

Bao schools, too, suffered from lack of funding. An irregularity in the running of one of them illustrates how one principal sought to overcome his financial difficulties. The principal in question found that his thirty-yuan salary hardly covered the cost of his tea. Noting that the county education department authorized the hiring of an additional teacher for every fifty pupils enrolled, he submitted a list of over fifty names of children in the *bao* who were not in school but whom he claimed to have enrolled. He requested and received the salary for an additional teacher.

During the year, the old county school inspector, who never moved outside his office in town, was replaced by a young man committed to the reforms. When the principal learned that the new man was planning a tour of inspection, he covered himself by lodging a preemptive protest with the county educational authorities, claiming that the illegal conscription of schoolboys had caused a sudden falling off of attendance in his school. He went on to blame the county health authorities for the absence of younger children, due, he claimed, to the failure of the public health nurse to come and vaccinate the children, a dereliction of duty that had resulted in an outbreak of smallpox. There had in fact been one case.

The newly invigorated education department was quick to act on the protest, notifying the township authorities that the *bao* head responsible should be dismissed. This was done. But the military department, the most powerful of Bishan County government's three major departments of finance, military, and education, protested that dismissal for an alleged conscription offense was an encroachment on its realm. The investigation that followed showed that only one pupil had been conscripted, and the *bao* head was reinstated. Still, the education department refused to take disciplinary action against the principal. This had the full approval of local opinion, shown in such comments as, "Of course the education department should not allow itself to be pushed around by the military department," and "How could one condemn the principal when he was so poorly paid, and when getting a rural school going was so difficult?"

MASS LITERACY CAMPAIGN

In addition to reforming the schools, the government sought to address the more widespread problem of illiteracy. According to our survey, roughly 70 percent of men and 98 percent of women (fifteen years old and older) had never gone to school. Among those who did attend, the majority had only had one or two years of schooling and had since lapsed into complete illiteracy. It took at least four years of schooling to become literate, a feat that was difficult for poor farming people to attain. The majority of Prosperity's functionally literate were either well-off merchants and professionals (stratum 2) or small-scale rice land farmers (stratum 3). Only seventy-five adults (seventy-one men and four women) had attended secondary school: some for one year, a few completing junior secondary, and at least one completing senior, or twelve years of schooling. Included were several of the ten teachers from the main primary school, most of whom were outsiders, but the rest who were of local heritage were from local gentry and merchant families (see table 6.3).

In October 1940, Prosperity received its first government directive calling for a literacy drive. This reflected the government's embrace of Dr. James Yen's Thousand-Character Mass Literacy Movement, pioneered in Dingxian, Hebei Province, which had received wide publicity and support in China and abroad and had given impetus to the literacy campaigns that were

Table 6.3. Educational Profile of Prosperity's Residents

Years of Schooling	No. of People	% of Total	No. of Men	% of Male**	No. Women	% of Female**
None	3,052	84	1,327	69	2,175	98
1–6 years	573	14	528	27	45	2
7+ years	75	2	71	4	4	.2

*Fifteen years old and over.
**Percentages are rounded.

part of the central government's program of rural reconstruction.[16] In 1940, official reports claimed that forty-six million people had learned to read in the preceding two years.[17] In Prosperity, however, the only efforts to tackle adult illiteracy before 1940 had been the semiannual three-week Bible schools, organized and run by an American woman missionary coming from Chongqing and her Chinese Bible women. These classes, which taught elementary literacy along with Christian precepts, had an attendance of one or two dozen women and girls.

The new directive required the township government to have all illiterate villagers attend a compulsory three-month course to be run by local government schools. First, the teachers were to carry out a census to determine literacy levels throughout the township. Then they were to enroll all illiterates between the ages of sixteen and forty into classes, which were to begin on November 1, using the approved mass education reader. Anyone who failed to enroll and attend could be subjected to a fine of one to five yuan.

Prosperity's main literacy drive got off to a slow start. The instructions arrived just as an opium suppression drive was being launched, and the teacher in charge of the literacy program had to go into hiding because he was an opium addict himself. Ten days later, he returned when the coast was clear and called together his colleagues to divide the *bao* among them. The next afternoon all classes were suspended so that the teachers could take the required census. Soon afterward, the literacy course started, but it had unaccountably been whittled down to a one-month session.

In the short run, the literacy drive was a failure as a mass movement. The vast majority of Prosperity's illiterate masses remained untouched. Despite legislation and official support, it was impossible to duplicate Dr. Yen's results by relying on the already burdened primary schools with their inadequate and underpaid staff to do the job. Teachers were expected to conduct the literacy work while continuing to do their regular teaching. But far more telling, the drive also failed because small-scale rice farmers and non-landowning laborers (strata 3 and 4, respectively) did not attend class. The younger men stayed away from the market village because they were in constant danger of being conscripted, while the rest had to labor to support their families. It appeared that families were willing to pay a considerable amount so as not to have to attend the classes.

The government did not, however, abandon its efforts to increase literacy in Prosperity. After we left, a January 1942 letter from Prosperity reported that a more vigorous and better-organized literacy drive was setting up regular night schools for adults. First, the Bishan County government called together about one hundred primary school teachers from various township schools and conducted a training class on how to run adult literacy schools. This was a forty-day session that took up the teachers' entire Lunar New Year Festival holidays and went on to overlap the first week of spring term in regular primary schools. According to the plan, the teachers would continue their daytime teaching. We had no reports from Prosperity on the results of the overall scheme, but it seemed likely that the same obstacles that plagued the first literacy drive would obstruct the second.

ROUSING THE NATIONALIST SPIRIT

One final aspect of the efforts by the Nationalist government to improve education and literacy in Prosperity is worth noting. Although the government clearly saw education as a marker of modernity, it also recognized that education could play a crucial role in garnering peasant support for the government's war against Japan and, more generally, for the government itself. A new China needed youth who thought of themselves as citizens of a republic governed from a central seat of power, as subjects of a common legal system, and as protected by a single military establishment committed to the defense of national security. The Nationalists aimed to expand education beyond traditional Confucian doctrines and to in turn foster a patriotic spirit that would encourage more widespread popular support for the war against the Japanese invaders.

In Prosperity's central school, the principal Sun Zhongyao and other teachers taught the Three People's Principles: nationalism, democracy, and livelihood. They linked this with current affairs, patriotism, and opposition to the Japanese. Music teachers taught patriotic resistance songs, including Nie Er's stirring "Arise, You Who Refuse to Be Slaves!" which pupils sang when seeing off conscripts. Another patriotic activity was writing slogans on the temple walls. Not all these slogans, however, represented Guomindang philosophy or policy. The most prominent slogan was "Benevolence, Loyalty, Ethics, Wisdom, and Faith" (*ren, yi, li, zhi, xin*), the ingredients of the feudal hierarchical ethics promoted by the Robed Brothers secret society, and, in retrospect most surprising, there was also "United, Alert, Earnest, and Lively" (*tuanjie, jinzhang, yansu, huopo*), which apparently no one recognized as a slogan of the Communist Eighth Route Army. In the latter half of 1941, with the appointment of Guo Ankang as township head, fresh efforts were made to promote nationalism. Modern patriotic plays were performed for the first time, arousing enthusiasm in the community.

In spite of obstacles to and the unevenness of progress, the Nationalist government had a significant impact on Prosperity's education system between 1940 and 1941. By 1940, one-third of all children ages five to fourteen years were officially enrolled in school, and one-fifth of them were girls, although, as we will see below, credit for this achievement did not rest with the government alone. Moreover, reform enthusiast Guo Ankang had a definite impact on education, despite the persistence of crippling systemic poverty and conflicts in local politics. In the fall term of 1941, Prosperity's central school had an unprecedented enrollment of 416 pupils in eight classes with ten teachers (see tables 6.4 and 6.5). And the full curriculum called for in central six-grade schools was being offered. A new directive, issued toward the end of 1941, authorized township governments to make a local levy to raise the money necessary for improving education and renewed the promise of outright aid to the poorest townships.

Positive results were achieved in the drive to promote rural schooling, although they fell far short of those legislated by the central government. In Prosperity, more children were in school than ever before, and better-off families who formerly had sent only their sons to school were now beginning to send their daughters in small but increasing numbers. However, progress was slowed by lack of funds and by the excessively close ties between local government and the schools, which caused the latter to become destabilized with each local political crisis and exposed their finances to various corrupt practices common in local administration. But this was still progress. Up until this time residents had picked up news of national and international significance from the teahouses where gentry, merchants, and other persons whose work took them to Bishan County town or Chongqing reported back the news of the war to interested listeners. Now children returning from school spread news. But even with this newly added source of information, few of the poorer farmers and almost no farm women had even the sketchiest ideas about national and international events. The Office of Cultural Affairs was the only one of the four township government offices sufficiently free from the indigenous power structure to be able to reflect progressive trends and achieve some successes in reforms in education.

Table 6.4. School Enrollment

Total Enrollment	Sex Composition of Students (%)	% of Each Sex Attending School
669 out of 2,011 children 5–14 (inclusive)	Boys: 81 Girls: 19	Boys: 45 Girls: 15

Table 6.5. School Enrollment by Grade

Junior Primary	260 Pupils	Senior Primary	156 Pupils
1st grade	91	5th grade (1st term)	47
2nd grade	87	5th grade (2nd term)	41
3rd grade	37	6th grade (1st term)	36
4th grade	45	6th grade (2nd term)	32

RURAL REFORMERS: THE NATIONAL CHRISTIAN COUNCIL

The Nationalist government was not alone in its efforts to institute reforms in Prosperity. The war with Japan caused a massive migration from the occupied parts of China to the interior, including leaders and intellectuals from some of China's most progressive and reform-minded universities and movements, who brought with them new ideas for promoting economic and government reforms, education, and science. These intellectuals and reformers often worked together and in collaboration with officials overseeing Nationalist government programs that were set up for rural development.[18] For a short period, the corridor between Chongqing and Chengdu became a site for experiments in rural reform.

In late 1939, one of these reform projects was set up in the market village of Prosperity, under the direction of T. H. Sun, a professor at Cheeloo (Qilu) University in Shandong who had attended Cornell University in 1936–1937 and had many years of experience in rural reconstruction work in Dingxian sponsored by the National Christian Council. Devoted to developing a modern rural society that was solidly anti-Communist, he accepted the NCC invitation to lead an experimental project in rural Sichuan that was intended to both ease rural poverty and expand the social base of Christian churches in the Chinese countryside.

At first glance, Prosperity was a somewhat strange choice for an NCC rural reconstruction project. Although Western Protestant missionaries had been active in this part of Sichuan since Chongqing had become a treaty port in the 1890s, their work had always been centered around Chengdu, where the NCC maintained a regional office. If the main criterion for selecting a site had been the ability of the local Christian church community to serve as a base for the rural reconstruction project, then the Chengdu area would have been preferable. As all missionaries who had come to Sichuan during the war readily acknowledged, the Chengdu area provided a much more hospitable environment for downriver people to resettle. Its weather and living conditions were better and its populace more open to outsiders. However, T. H. Sun chose to locate himself in the Chongqing vicinity because he sought to maintain close connections with the Nationalist government, which he felt would be beneficial for the success of his project. Furthermore, the NCC headquarters had moved from Shanghai to Chongqing at the beginning of the war. The NCC had worked in the areas of education and health for many years. Realizing that poverty alleviation was the underlying issue, it wanted an experiment to demonstrate how a rural church could address this issue.

Prosperity was one of two places in the county of Bishan that were proposed by the NCC and was most likely chosen because it had a Christian population dating back several decades.[19] In 1908, women missionaries of the American Methodist Episcopal Mission (AMEM) had begun evangelizing work in the villages of the small valley of Fulu and Xinglongchang. In 1924, the AMEM had set up the first coeducational school in this locality. Although the school had only lasted for four years, as mentioned earlier the AMEM continued to hold a three-week Bible school session every six months to educate girls, taught by American women missionaries based in Chongqing. They taught them literacy and homemaking (hygiene, thrift, and child care), making the girls more desirable as wives. Meanwhile, in 1928, a church was established in Prosperity. Attending church provided women an opportunity to leave home, and so, even though a number of village men became Christians, far more women than men went to services.

LAUNCHING THE NCC RURAL RECONSTRUCTION PROJECT

The NCC made its first appearance in Prosperity shortly after the end of the Lunar New Year festivities in 1940, when T. H. Sun arrived with his five healthy and boisterous sons, who moved into Prosperity along with their well-educated Shandong mother. The NCC's agenda was largely shaped by Christian priorities, but with some significant modifications due to wartime influences. The team's stated goal was to strengthen the small Christian community living in Prosperity by undertaking a number of projects that would address the "felt needs" of rural residents and thereby demonstrate that Christians not only cared about saving souls but also about improving the well-being of Chinese farmers.[20] The three projects that the NCC team launched were all built on existing strengths of previous Protestant proselytizing work in the areas of health care, education, and Christianizing the home. However, these programs also bore the imprint of wartime nationalism in that they were designed to support the Nationalist government's initiatives to foster the establishment of public schools, health care delivery systems, and economic co-ops in rural areas of Free China. T. H. Sun faced multiple challenges launching this project. He had to develop a creative approach to extract personnel and funding from various parts of the NCC. At the same time, he had to design programs that both facilitated NCC objectives and complemented Nationalist government initiatives at a local level.

T. H. Sun began by assembling a team with strong credentials: they were all young women professionals, three having graduated from Chinese universities and one from a Canadian university. As his strategy was first to forge goodwill in the community by providing health and education services to respond to what he called "felt needs," he recruited Zhu Xiuzhen, a public health nurse and midwife who had been trained and had worked at the Canadian-run missionary hospital in Xingyang, Henan, to head up the medical work. He selected Li Wenjin, a recent graduate of Jinling Women's College in Nanjing, to lead the educational work of the project, including starting a kindergarten. The AMEM contributed the funds for their salaries and for the operating costs of the clinic and the kindergarten because they were compatible with its China work. In addition, an AMEM district supervisor of nursing supervised Zhu's operation. T. H. Sun was able to recruit Yu Xiji, who had been trained at Peking Union Medical College as a medical social worker under Ida Pruitt, to serve as a field researcher, teacher, and health clinician to support Zhu Xiuzhen, and to serve as an unofficial project manager of the embroidery program.[21] Yu's salary was drawn from NCC funds connected to her uncle, Bishop Chen Wenyuan, the general secretary of the NCC. Later in 1940, after T. H. Sun had decided on a centerpiece poverty alleviation program that required social surveys, he also hired Isabel Brown, the daughter of Canadian missionaries in Chengdu who had returned after her graduation from the University of Toronto and was conducting anthropological research in Sichuan and Xikang. As she was a Canadian, he was able to obtain funding for her salary from the Canadian Women's Missionary Society.[22]

The recruitment of an all-female team was risky. The appearance of these unmarried young women on the village street without an escort most likely caused some concern, as it did not conform to customary practices at the time. However, their dress, manner, and language marked them as modern-minded downriver women who were presumably not expected to abide by the dictates of local gender codes. Although they wore the same long blue gowns worn by local women, they assumed the self-assurance and poise of intellectuals who had important work to accomplish, and referred to each other in public as Miss Zhu (Zhu Xiaojie), Miss Li (Li Xiaojie), and Miss Yu (Yu Xiaojie).

The all-female composition of the NCC team replicated prior work done by missionaries in this part of Sichuan. For example, two of the American women missionaries who began work in the village and in Bishan, Annie Wells and Orvia Proctor, always worked with a female Chinese partner: the Chinese partner conducted the evangelizing, as she had the linguistic skills, while the American partner proposed projects. They generally chose to base themselves in places where they could both convert local residents and also help improve the welfare of the community. Male missionaries did not do this sort of work because they could not enter people's homes with the ease enjoyed by their female counterparts.

Soon after the Lunar New Year festivities in 1940, when the NCC project team began to assemble in Prosperity, it became evident that the local church could not be of much use to their endeavor beyond supplying them with living accommodations. Two of the women staff members who had been sent by the AMEM questioned how it was that this church in Prosperity could be held in such high regard by the AMEM when its so-called active members were nowhere to be seen and no weekly church services were held. Living in the compound along with the kindly old Pastor Xu, these NCC project staff members were in a prime position to see how his meager fixed salary could not be stretched in this era of steady inflation to meet the needs of his family, particularly the education of his children.[23] Dismayed by the situation, T. H. Sun asked the AMEM to replace Xu. The AMEM responded by sending out the Chongqing district superintendent, Liu Zhiguang, who was happy to relocate his family into this Bishan market village to avoid the frequent Japanese bombings of Chongqing. His main job continued to be the supervision of all churches in the district, but by living in Prosperity, he was able to support the work of the pastor and the rural reconstruction team.[24] Before long, the team succeeded in encouraging Pastor Xu to divert some of his attention from his time-consuming small private business ventures to reinvigorating the church. With their support, Pastor Xu resumed weekly services, which drew a small group of women and girls from the community.

An important part of T. H. Sun's strategy for launching the NCC Rural Reconstruction Project in Prosperity was to create a strong impression in the community about the organization's durability and ability to finance the projects it promised. He therefore worked to create a compelling physical presence on the market street and in the church compound. The market village residents witnessed a flurry of new construction and renovations in the church compound, including the row of shuttered shops along the streets, that commenced soon after the Lunar New Year holiday and lasted almost eight months. The most impressive undertaking was the construction of an imposing director's residence where T. H. Sun, his wife, and his five sons would live. This structure was Prosperity's first brick building and its first two-story building, boasting as well a conspicuous staircase. Although this structure was inside the church compound, local residents felt free to wander about the courtyard to witness this major undertaking.

While T. H. Sun's new home underscored his importance, the renovations of the four rooms on the street front reinforced the message that the NCC project aimed to serve the community. One room was converted into a library with a long table, two benches, two maps (of China and the world), and shelves, which displayed books on a variety of subjects in an attractive manner. One of the old shops was converted into a recreation room with a ping-pong table and a deck tennis court marked on the floor. The third room became a waiting room for the public health clinic, which was housed in the fourth room.

T. H. Sun followed this with a series of moves that revealed a sense of rural diplomacy. Based on Pastor Xu's urgings that the approval of Commander Cai of the Paoge had to be obtained in order for the project to function in the community, T. H. Sun paid a courtesy call on the commander, as Guo Ankang had done when beginning his appointment as township head. Seeing that the Paoge was clearly a formidable force in the community, T. H. Sun and his team members accepted an unusual invitation from Prosperity's Paoge lodges to attend a banquet to celebrate the annual festival, *dandao hui*, one of two religious ceremonies held each year by the Paoge to worship Guan Gong. The four lodges in the community had decided this holiday would be an appropriate occasion to welcome significant newcomers to Prosperity: the newly arrived township head, the teachers at the central primary school, and T. H. Sun. Normally, women were excluded from the functions of the all-male Paoge organization, but the strong representation of women among the teachers and the NCC team inspired them to be innovative.

T. H. Sun further marked the rural reconstruction team's entry into the community by orchestrating a huge welcoming ceremony in Prosperity. On May 3, 1940, an unprecedented gathering of three hundred members of the local community, including all the local gentry and government-appointed leaders throughout the township, assembled in the market village's Wenmiao. T. H. Sun's ability to attract prominent personages, including the Bishan County head Wang Shidi, created a strong impression. Wang and his chief assistants gave speeches on the importance of rural reconstruction, the value of the Christian contribution to it, and the need for the county government to cooperate wholeheartedly with this initiative. Also present was the general secretary of the NCC, Bishop Chen Wenyuan, recently arrived from NCC headquarters in Shanghai.

The scale of this opening not only demonstrated Sun's ability to promote the project among people of influence, but also his strategy to gain strong Nationalist support for his rural reconstruction project. He designed his local programs in ways that were compatible with Nationalist rural policies in Sichuan. For example, in looking for a suitable economic venture that tackled the urgent problem of rural poverty, he consulted an old colleague who held a post in the Nationalist Ministry of Foreign Trade who was eager to expand exports of the famous Sichuan blue cross-stitch embroidery. Because the neighboring county of Yongchuan produced an excellent quality of fine linen, Sun realized that setting up such a program in Prosperity would be feasible. In the early spring of 1940, under the direction of project staff member Yu Xiji and the assistance of Miss Earnshaw, an American missionary, the project recruited twenty local farm girls, most of whom came from Miss Wells's Bible school,[25] and started them on a three-month course in cross-stitch, taught by two competent teachers loaned by a foreign trade section of the ministry. He also was able to negotiate an agreement that the ministry would purchase the embroidery and find outlets for its overseas export. Unfortunately, this project lasted only a few months, as the Nationalist government encountered difficulties in shipping the embroidery products to Hong Kong because of the intensifying war situation, and therefore discontinued its purchases. The embroidery school was closed down, and the NCC project lost its economic centerpiece. It was in the field of education (and, as we shall see in chapter 7, health) that T. H. Sun devoted more longlasting efforts to working with Nationalist government offices and programs.

MEETING RURAL "FELT NEEDS" THROUGH EDUCATION

The NCC rural reconstruction educational initiative was aimed to support and enhance the government's program of education reform. Li Wenjin was designated as the team member responsible for promoting education initiatives in Prosperity, but the three other team members were often called upon to participate, as the task of implementing the Nationalists' educational plan was so immense and resources so scant. For the next two years this team both responded to requests from the local authorities and took some of their own initiatives to improve Prosperity's educational program.

The first request, as discussed earlier, was for team members to serve as teachers in the school when some of the teachers, frustrated by the township's failure to pay their salaries, curtailed their work. T. H. Sun responded by assigning Li Wenjin and Yu Xiji as full-time teachers donated from the rural reconstruction team. The second request was for the team members to help build enrollment, particularly of girls who had been barred from attending school in the past. Li visited their homes to persuade parents to allow their daughters to enroll in school, something that a number of women remembered decades later. It was particularly challenging to persuade families to send daughters with bound feet to school. Ultimately, the school managed to attract one-third of all children in the community of ages five to fourteen years, one-fifth of whom were girls. Within the schools, the team also augmented the efforts of the township head and teachers to teach Prosperity's children about their duties as citizens of the Republic of China by organizing a patriotic rally of students on October 10, National Day. It was well attended and children seemed to enjoy the experience.

Less successful were the team's efforts to promote adult literacy. In October 1940, when the Nationalist central government ordered all townships to conduct a compulsory campaign to wipe out illiteracy, township authorities asked T. H. Sun to have his team take charge of literacy for women. Unwilling to engage in a program that the Guomindang deemed compulsory, the NCC declared that it would teach literacy only to individuals who participated voluntarily.

As indicated earlier, 98 percent of women fifteen years old and older had never gone to school. Classes for women had to be conducted separately, since it was not considered socially acceptable to have them study in the same space as men. Members of the rural reconstruction team took charge of the campaign among women and taught anyone who turned up. Using James Yan's mass education reader as the main text, Yu Xiji planned to teach home economics to the women, while Isabel Brown would teach folk dancing to the girls.

On the opening day only a few more than twenty attended, half of whom were teenage girls who were the daughters of well-off literate men, and the rest were older women. It quickly became clear that the married women had come primarily to enjoy the rare opportunity to get out of their homes and socialize. So the students were divided into two separate classes. By the end of the session, the girls had achieved the limited goal of reading and writing several hundred characters. As for the older women, all turned up regularly and enjoyed themselves thoroughly, even the woman who was too blind to see the characters in the book. But few learned and remembered more than several dozen characters.

In addition to, or perhaps confounding, the challenge of compelling attendance, the quality of teaching in the literacy programs was uneven. In one case, Daniel Li, the religious education supervisor for the AMEM in Sichuan, visited Prosperity and gave a talk about current affairs to the class. Students could not understand his accent, so he wrote the words on the blackboard, apparently forgetting that this was a beginning literacy class and the characters were far beyond the ability of the students to read and comprehend.

The most perplexing difficulty encountered by the team in its educational work stemmed from the rising anti-Christian sentiment spilling out from urban centers. Anticipating that the team might start to feel pressure from such popular sentiments, T. H. Sun had decided that his project had to be distanced from the local church in Prosperity. This meant abandoning one of the four central missions of the project, reasoning that his endeavor was not an experiment in running a rural church, but a Christian program of community service. He feared that his project's close association with this particular church could jeopardize their work in two ways: higher-level government officials might be antagonized if they thought the project's community efforts were primarily for the sake of proselytizing, and the connection might prejudice local people against them, since the local church was viewed as corrupt (a notion that later proved to be substantially false).

T. H. Sun's defensive strategy did not shield the team from a local official's wrath about the lack of clear boundaries between church and state in Prosperity. The conflict occurred in late 1941, when Sun Zhonglu and Sun Zhongyao, heads of the local branch of the Nationalist Party, persuaded the township government and the church to collaborate in organizing a two-day festival to arouse patriotism throughout the community. Although the festival was to occur on December 25–26, it was defined as commemorating People's Resurrection Day (not Christmas) to commemorate the popular uprising in 1916 that forestalled Yuan Shikai's attempt to make himself emperor. The centerpiece of the celebration was a modern play that was going to be performed by students from the missionary-run Shude Girls' School in Bishan. Township head Guo Ankang, in spite of his skepticism of missionary-sponsored events, decided that the play would be patriotic and earn him credit in both Prosperity and Bishan County; the church imagined the event would draw a much larger audience than the twenty to twenty-five women and teenage girls that it could ordinarily muster. To prepare for this event, Guo ordered his guards to sweep out the Wenmiao temple and festoon it with the traditional boughs of pine. On December 26, the girls from the Shude school were to stage plays all day, interspersed with performances of Sichuan opera by members of the former music club of the Paoge. To thank the performers, the township government budgeted for a banquet of eight tables that evening.

Not all went according to plan. When the girls from Shude were about to begin the evening performance in the Wenmiao temple, it began to rain. Although the temple stage was covered, the audience had no shelter. The pastor invited everyone to move to the church. He lit the bright pressure lamp, the audience flocked inside, and the performance began. The township government guards ordered everyone back to the temple, and when no one budged, they stalked up to the stage and began to tear down the curtain. One of the guards threatened to shoot if the audience did not relocate, and when a volley of shots rang out, the play stopped and the audience dispersed.

Guo Ankang was enraged, both because he felt it was inappropriate for a modern patriotic play to be performed in a church, and, perhaps more importantly, because rather than the throngs of people passing in and out of the township office in the Wenmiao temple, they had instead thronged in and out of the church. Ultimately, the event did not enhance his prestige in the way he had hoped. He expressed his disappointment and displeasure by dismissing the two members of the NCC assigned to teach at the central primary school.

CONCLUSION

Nationalist rule during the wartime era, often dismissed as passive and ineffective in rural areas, needs to be reconsidered. To some extent because of the war, the government continued earlier efforts to introduce reforms into rural areas. Through administrative reforms, it claimed control over place names and the appointment of township heads. At the same time, however, it could not control the names local residents used to identify their towns, nor could it determine what would happen once a township head arrived. Furthermore, the efforts of township heads to govern a particular locality were often thwarted by resentful local elites, the military, and secret societies such as the Paoge. Although the Nationalist government achieved some improvements in providing education and literacy training for rural residents, these initiatives often foundered because of instability in personnel and inconsistency of funding. The NCC, for its part, was most successful in education, particularly in providing schooling for women. Its success might also be attributed to the fact that the Paoge had no economic stakes in education, and thus no motivation to undermine efforts at reform in this domain.

By looking at the NCC's arrival in Prosperity and its attempts to improve education, we can see the ways in which wartime conditions provided an opportunity for a more collaborative relationship with the government than had previously been the case. The Nationalist government's projects turned out to be most successful when the NCC team provided support and supplemented their efforts. Meanwhile, the NCC was particularly effective when it piggybacked onto government initiatives, as it did with education. The complexity of the relationship between rural reconstructionists (such as the NCC) and the Nationalist government in the context of wartime China becomes even more evident in the context of health care, the subject of chapter 7.

NOTES

1. According to Sichuan sheng Bishan xianzhi (1996, p. 106), more than sixty thousand downriver people found their way to Bishan County during the war.

2. Perhaps the reason for the shift from *lianbao* to *xiang* was the concern that *lianbao* implied collective guilt.

3. "The New County System in China" (1942).

4. The Qing dynasty gazetteer of Bishan that was compiled by the county's elite in 1872 contained a map which used the name given by the community for this place—Prosperity Market (Xinglongchang) (*Bishan xianzhi*, 1992).

5. It seems unlikely that Prosperity could have avoided losing its name at some time during the twentieth century, as it was smaller and had less political clout than a township with the same name in the neighboring county of Baxian. Between 1940 and 2000, all these province-wide duplications were eliminated.

6. According to Isabel Crook's manuscript, these two were Yang Ronting, *bao* head and head of the fourth lodge of the Paoge, a farmer in his thirties who ran a profitable noodle shop

in the village on market days, and Wei "*Laoqi*," the seventh brother of the bristle merchant Wei Shuyao, a young idler and gambler in his early twenties.

7. Dapeng acquiesced to the loss of its township status, albeit reluctantly. In contrast, Prosperity's southwestern neighboring community of Sanjiao resisted its proposed merger with Danfeng. Given that Sanjiao was the youngest of the periodic markets in the area, having just been founded in 1915, as well as comprising the smallest population (approximately eight hundred households), its ability to launch a major challenge to this government directive was all the more remarkable. Sanjiao's first defiant move was to claim that its household register was out of date, and it soon produced a new one which showed more households than the required number of one thousand. Government authorities were distracted by the work involved in overseeing the other mergers for several months, so there the matter rested until after the New Year in 1941. This time the government first tried to use the positive example of Dapeng's experiences, arguing that it had not suffered in the merger, and then when that tactic failed, it threatened to close Sanjiao's market and divide its business between the three neighboring marketing communities of Zitong, Daxing, and Danfeng. The official closing of a market was a far worse prospect than the loss of a township government, for it was the market which made the surrounding households an intimate community. In practical ways its demise would have had a more fundamental impact on the day-to-day life of the ordinary people. Most important, the leading members of the community would lose profitable tax collection rights and other privileges associated with the periodic market. Hence Sanjiao finally capitulated, its township head fled the locality, and its merger with Danfeng was carried out. However, Sanjiao continued to find ways to resist its downgrading, with the result that it regained its township status (*xiang*) in 1943 (Sichuan sheng Bishan xianzhi, 1996, p. 63).

8. "Bishanxian Bihan zongshe" [The General Headquarters of Bishan County's Han Order], file 13/1, Bishan County Archives.

9. Zheng Dengyun (1994), p. 342.

10. The Nationalist government was required to put at least 15 percent of its budget into education, whereas the provinces and counties had to allocate at least 30 percent of their budgets (Zheng Dengyun 1994, p. 356).

11. The issue of control over the content of textbooks surfaced as a major issue soon after the 1911 Revolution. At that time many Chinese educators were beginning to notice that some other nations centered much of their educational curriculum around nationalism and ethics. In turn, there was an active push for Chinese textbooks to be revamped so as to emphasize concepts of citizenship, as seen in more Westernized education systems. Two resolutions were passed at the fifth conference of the National Educational Association in 1919: (1) a compromise with teachers to allow texts to have "local material" rather than a solely nationalist character, in exchange for (2) the teaching curriculum having distinct lessons of "national citizenship," including such subjects as hygiene, morality, law, and economics (Culp 2007, pp. 47–53). The debates did not end there. Throughout the mid-1920s, many primary school teachers continued to push for more local material in textbooks. However, according to Cyrus Peake, "with the advent to power of the nationalist party after 1927 the educational aims, curricula, and textbooks were revised in accordance with the most advanced form of modern nationalism" (Peake 1932, p. 117).

12. Between 1929 and 1936, the number of elementary schools increased from 212,385 to 320,008 and the number of students increased from 8,882,077 to 18,364,956 (Zheng Dengyun 1994, p. 360).

13. Sichuan sheng difang zhi bian zuan weiyuan hui (1996), p. 15.

14. Sichuan sheng difang zhi bian zuan weiyuan hui (1996), p. 14.

15. All these figures, however, should be viewed with caution. First, rolls were padded particularly at the *bao* level, for the sake of bringing in a bigger subsidy from the county education authorities to augment the woefully low pay of the teachers. As for any pupils as young as five years old, we never saw one even in the central school. Second, attendance was not regular. Farm families often kept schoolchildren at home. Finally, even those actually in attendance were not necessarily receiving regular instruction, for teachers sometimes had to be absent themselves to engage in other jobs for supplemental income.

16. Hayford (1990). Hayford specifically discusses James Yen, Sichuan, and the Nationalist government's education policies on pp. 189–195. See also Pearl S. Buck (1945).

17. Lattimore (1945), p. 194.

18. The papers of Dr. Theodore Dykstra, one of these agricultural specialists, are housed in the Yenching Library, Harvard University. The specialists included James Yen (Yen Yangchu), a Sichuanese who founded and led the Mass Education Movement (MEM); Liang Shuming, an educator who led the industrial cooperative movement; Wu Wenzao, professor of sociology at Yanjing University and the mentor of Fei Xiaotong; James Buck, a professor of agriculture at Nanjing University who was well known for his rural surveys; and other Christian missionaries and reformers who were preparing their own programs of rural reconstruction in the Great Rear. Their rural research and reform efforts were buttressed by U.S. agricultural specialists who were sent to advise on ways to increase food production.

19. According to files in the AMEM archives at Yale University, the first Protestant missionaries came to Prosperity in the final years of the Qing dynasty. The community's first Christian was baptized in 1904, and during the next twenty years slow progress brought another fifteen local people to Christianity, thirteen men and two women. Then in 1927, at a time when the Nationalist Revolution was fomenting much anti-Christian sentiment, six new male converts joined. This new influx spurred the AMEM to commit funds to building a church in Prosperity Market Village. The AMEM spent four silver ingots that were valued at fifty-six yuan at the time to buy two sections of housing on the market street, while a Christian from the nearby market village of Fulu, whose daughter had attended several sessions of a women's Bible class, donated the land just behind these buildings for the church and the pastor's manse. Unlike many market towns with Christian churches, the two Western structures, built in 1928, were located behind older Chinese buildings and thus did not mar the Chinese appearance of the village. In 1932, the church reached its peak year for recruitment, gaining twelve new members. Membership continued to rise slowly, so that over the course of the first thirty-five years of Christian activity in Prosperity, a grand total of seventy-seven members were baptized.

20. Beginning in the 1930s, the NCC deemed it important for its missionaries to develop proselytizing programs that responded to the economic and social needs of their constituencies.

21. The AMEM had a rural medical team under Alma Ericksen, an American missionary nurse who supervised a circuit of rural clinics in Sichuan. She was responsible for ensuring the quality of the medical work and the supply of medicines and equipment. She was appreciated by all of her colleagues for her strong support and her fun-loving nature. When she visited, there was much folk dancing and advice and supporting help.

22. T. H. Sun asked Isabel Brown to approach the Canadian Women's Missionary Society in Chengdu for funds to cover her salary. Using family connections, she was able to secure the agreement of Miss Harris to this proposal.

23. His financial situation was fairly common in the Chongqing district. As early as 1922, pastors were asking the AMEM to relieve them of their duties in order that they could find other employment that would enable them to support their families ("Report for 1922" in Official Minutes, West China [Chongqing] Conference of the Methodist Episcopal Church, Yale University Archives).

24. The rural reconstruction team was particularly grateful for his willingness to explicate many aspects of rural life in Prosperity that were difficult for them to understand. He was a particularly strong informant about conversations, mediations, and activities in the teahouse and other aspects of the Paoge.

25. Annie Wells had a long history of rural mission work in Sichuan. She was first sent to China in 1908 by the Women's Missionary Society of the AMEM. At the Fourteenth Annual West China AMEM Conference in 1923, held in Chongqing, she was highly praised for devoting "almost her entire time to the outstations," which would have included years of work developing evangelistic work in Prosperity.

Chapter Seven

Taking Health Care Public

A sickly fifteen-year-old boy, son of a teacher's impoverished widow, contributed to his family's spartan living by helping his mother make cakes to sell at the stall outside their home and by carrying coal when he felt up to it. In June 1941, the boy began to suffer from severe headaches which grew progressively worse. (He was apparently suffering from tubercular meningitis.) The mother reluctantly decided to spend the money necessary to consult a doctor and called in one of the *zhongyi* (practitioners of traditional Chinese medicine). Given her minimal economic resources, she chose Dr. Deng, who was less expensive—and less qualified—than the other *zhongyi*. He would come to Prosperity on market days. Examining the patient, the doctor explained that the boy's nasal discharge, instead of coming down his nostrils, was going back into the brain, causing the headache. He prescribed medicine, which the mother bought and administered. But within an hour the boy was noticeably worse. The medicine caused internal burns, and by nightfall he could no longer speak but only tossed in his bed, moaning and tearing at his nose, throat, and chest. The following day the mother went for the doctor, who refused to come. But she would not leave him in peace, so he eventually came and discovered he had given the wrong medicine. Although the doctor prescribed another that did relieve the boy's suffering, the mother abandoned Dr. Deng and sought out a well-known diviner who predicted that the boy would die, which he did shortly thereafter.

This incident reflects some of the ways in which poor villagers in Prosperity dealt with illness on the eve of the war with Japan. It was a stretch for the mother to pay for Dr. Deng, and more frequently poor villagers relied on shamans, diviners, and exorcists. The war years, however, marked a dramatic shift in the nature and delivery of medical services in Sichuan. For the first time in the province's history, the government took a strong interest in developing a public health program.[1] Its agencies were aided by a variety of religious and secular reformers, including those associated with the Rockefeller Foundation. Government planners envisioned a dramatic expansion of state and private Western medical facilities, to be built on the modest medical infrastructure concentrated in the urban centers of Chengdu and Chongqing that had been established earlier in the century. The government goal to deliver health care services to Sichuan's rural people, who accounted for approximately 90 percent of the population, proved daunting. In the end, many of the plans that were so meticulously presented in the reports of the government agencies and the reformers were never executed because of shortages in qualified personnel and funds. The task of improving the rural health care system in Sichuan was mostly left to the religious and secular reformers.

A health clinic was set up in Prosperity in 1940 as part of the National Christian Council's rural project. This chapter, after examining government efforts at health care reform, will turn to the efforts of the NCC clinic's staff to win the trust of the community over a two-year period, an endeavor that revealed much about the complex interplay between indigenous and outside medical practices. Because of the efforts by one Western-trained Chinese nurse, this project ultimately proved to be the most successful among the various undertakings brought into Prosperity by outsiders in the wartime era.

GOVERNMENT HEALTH INITIATIVES IN SICHUAN

After the Nationalist government had transferred its capital from Nanjing to Chongqing, it initiated steps to establish a Sichuan Health Administration. In comparison with the downriver provinces, this government public health initiative was considered to be relatively late.[2] However, the appointment of C. C. Chen in May of 1939 as the first director of the Sichuan Health Administration was a strong indicator that the government was serious about instituting a reputable public health program. A graduate of the School of Public Health at Harvard University, Chen had cultivated close connections with the Rockefeller Foundation, a major international funder of medical services in China, and had worked on medical projects in the Hebei county of Dingxian before coming to west China.[3] He moved quickly to define the scope of activities of the new health institute more broadly than the Nationalist government's original mandate to bolster the war effort, particularly to handle civilian and military casualties from Japanese air attacks, by publicly announcing that the mission of his ministry would include the prevention of communicable diseases, the establishment of county health centers, the reduction of maternal mortality, and the bolstering of children's health.[4]

Turning this rhetoric into reality was no easy task. C. C. Chen and his staff soon discovered the limits of Nationalist government support, which one NHA (National Health Administration) report characterized "as a matter of theoretical and remote importance."[5] Local resources for tackling major health problems were scant. In 1939 one study estimated that there were only 298 modern-trained physicians in this province of forty-five million people and that nearly one-fourth of the counties—approximately thirty-five—had no medical facilities at all.[6] Chen set to work to find foreign donors. In 1939 the League of Nations presented the National Health Institute with fifty-eight thousand quinine tablets to combat malaria. A much larger source of foreign funds came from the Rockefeller Foundation, which generously donated funds for the training of personnel and the purchase of necessary equipment and medicines.[7]

Over the next few years, the government health program officials focused attention on building a strong bureaucratic infrastructure. Each county was supposed to build a health center. In Bishan County the goal was four rural district health stations and twenty-six village health aides in 1942. However, it seems that the village aides were not functioning, and some suspected that many of them might only exist in government reports.

Designing a public health program for Sichuan was complicated by the lack of comprehensive information about the major health problems plaguing the province's populace. Chen was able to locate one study of communicable diseases in Sichuan from the early 1930s that found a high incidence of syphilis, gonorrhea, tuberculosis, malaria, and dysentery.[8] Another study reported that one out of every three stillborn births in the province was due to syphilis. Very high rates of parasitic infestations—85 and 96 percent of those examined—were revealed in another local study.[9] Although the NHA reports made no mention of typhus, which was spread by hordes of rats, it was also quite widespread.[10] Nor did these reports take note of the prevalence of blindness, which was usually caused by trachoma. While no specific data existed for maternal mortality rates or infant mortality rates, the NHA recognized that childbirth was particularly hazardous because of unsanitary methods of delivery. It also noted that in one major town in Bishan, the life expectancy for females was twenty-six years; for males, thirty years. Lastly, its reports noted that opium addiction was widespread. Among poor laboring men who hired themselves out as coolies, especially as porters, addiction was often unavoidable since many were forced to take the drug to stop dysentery so they could reach their destination on time.

In its first two years of operation, the Sichuan Health Administration focused attention on combating the spread of communicable diseases. One of the first projects was to establish the Institute of Infectious Diseases in Chengdu, which in turn targeted certain "strategic" county towns for the placement of health centers to carry out this work. The work was supported with a direct grant of three thousand dollars for equipment by the Rockefeller Foundation.[11] The Health Administration also expended a great deal of energy to deal with a major cholera epidemic that broke out in the province, especially the Chengdu area, in late 1939 and 1940. Its records showed that in 1939 it inoculated 648,000 people against cholera; and in 1940, 540,000. It also vaccinated 220,000 against smallpox in 1940.[12] This work was combined with a campaign to eliminate opium addiction in the province by March of 1940, as stipulated by the Nationalist government. Indeed Generalissimo Jiang Jieshi himself had ordered that the Health Administration should quickly produce and distribute large quantities of anti-opium pills for this purpose.[13]

Before long the Sichuan Health Administration focused on its mission to reduce infant mortality rates. In November 1939 a Maternity and Child Health Center was established in Chengdu, where twenty-three babies were born by the end of the year.[14] The Rockefeller Foundation gave more than thirty thousand yuan in 1940 to expand this work.[15] In 1940 the Health Administration also created a Central Field Health Station and a Public Health Personnel Training Institute near Chongqing which had a midwifery school, a nursing school, and a hospital.[16]

Just prior to the arrival of the Nationalist government in Chongqing, most babies born in Sichuan were delivered at home by either self-delivery (88.28 percent) or midwives (10.3 percent).[17] Because of a high maternal mortality rate, the Nationalist government decided to regulate midwifery in 1941 by demanding that all practitioners take special classes. By 1942, the government had licensed 401 midwives who had passed a course in new methods of delivery. One of the most important aspects of this training included the practical aspects of germ theory, a concept that was unknown in Chinese traditional medicine. Midwives trained to deliver babies in a sanitary fashion, including cutting the umbilical cord with a clean utensil and getting rid of the ashes that were usually placed on the dirt floor in order to restrict the flow of blood. The use of a pan instead of the ashes dramatically reduced the incidence of tetanus in newborns.

Under the auspices of the Sichuan Health Administration, a health demonstration center was set up in the county town of Bishan. The old Jiangxi Guild House, which served as the headquarters for the center, was spacious enough to hold a clinic, office, staff dorm, and hospital with thirty beds. Two doctors trained in public health were hired to initiate the work to control communicable diseases and to collect vital statistics.[18] The major sources of funds for the Bishan health center came from the NHA, the Bishan County government, and the Rockefeller Foundation, which contributed three hundred thousand yuan.[19] By 1940, the health center had four doctors, seven nurses, and three maternity nurses.[20] C. C. Chen was personally responsible for inspecting the Bishan demonstration center.[21] Through such centers the government initiated a vaccination campaign to reduce smallpox. By 1940 everyone in Prosperity had been inoculated,[22] constituting the major impact the government program had on the township.

The government was not the only promoter of public health initiatives in Sichuan. Since the end of the nineteenth century, Christian missionaries had been working in this arena. Protestant missions had proceeded from evangelizing to education and health care as a service and as outreach. A survey of Protestant institutions in Sichuan in 1939 showed that the province had one Christian university with a major medical college and twenty-five Christian hospitals.[23] Most of these were confined to the cities and towns, with little impact on the countryside. When the NCC team in Prosperity opened a health clinic in 1940, Prosperity became one of the few townships to boast an institution offering Western medicine. In order to understand the experience of the NCC clinic in Prosperity, it is necessary to first know something of the medical practices of villagers that were prevalent before its establishment.

TRADITIONAL MEDICINE IN PROSPERITY

Prosperity was plagued with disease, a product of inadequate nutrition, abysmal sanitation, and the prevalence of rats, flies, mosquitoes, and a variety of parasitic worms. The moist, temperate to hot climate enabled germs to thrive and spread freely in rural tenements. Smallpox, tuberculosis, and malaria were endemic; cholera and typhus struck from time to time. Poor eyesight and blindness, caused mainly by trachoma and vitamin A deficiency, reduced people's work capability. As in Sichuan more generally, midwifery practices added to the health hazards for both mother and child, while inadequate care after childbirth left many women with gynecological problems. Infant mortality and death in childbirth were common.

Before the establishment of the NCC Western clinic in Prosperity, customary measures of coping with illness included consulting either a practitioner of traditional Chinese medicine or a diviner, exorcist, or other expert in the field of the unseen world. Most people's choices were limited by cost, so hanging a patch of red cloth, brewing home herbal remedies, or petitioning the gods were the most common responses to illness.

For the more prosperous and literate people in Prosperity, the most competent medical personnel in the community were the *zhongyi,* practitioners of Chinese traditional medicine, which embraced a number of specialties including internal medicine, gynecology, pediatrics, and surgery. This expertise was passed down for generations through families or might be acquired through a longish period of apprenticeship with an experienced doctor. Even a preliminary knowledge of the medical and pharmaceutical classics required a fair degree of literacy and careful study. Hence, in Prosperity traditional-style doctors were respected as learned men and addressed as *xiansheng*, like teachers. Of the six or seven *zhongyi* in the community, four had offices and pharmacies in Prosperity Market.

The most highly regarded of these was Dr. Yang Huaqing, a well-educated man in his early thirties, owner of a fifty-*dan* rice farm, and dealer in medicine. Two other traditional doctors were brothers. The elder, Dr. Zeng Peiyuan, was a medium landowner, wielding some political power as *bao* head in his rural neighborhood, although he chose to live in his village home. But he suffered from an advanced case of tuberculosis, and much of his practice had already been taken over by his thirty-eight-year-old brother Zeng Deyuan who had his office, pharmacy, and home in a spacious house on the street. The fourth doctor, Deng Yuling, lived in the countryside but rented a room in the village as office and pharmacy on market days. The most prosperous doctor, Xiang, carried on his practice as doctor and pharmacist in Bishan County town, although he made his home on his estate in the countryside of Prosperity.

These *zhongyi* earned most of their money from the sale of medicines that they prescribed. They based their practices on centuries of research into the medicinal properties of herbs and minerals. The resultant development of pharmacology in China owed much to Daoist alchemy and the search for elixirs. These various approaches were not mutually exclusive, and families of some means tried a variety of treatments either simultaneously or consecutively. China's rich, centuries-old medical science was summed up in a philosophy of the human body and its functioning and a pharmacology defining the properties and uses of a vast array of herbs, minerals, and animal products and how to compound them into medicines for various ailments.

While mastering this body of knowledge would take years, some of it had become widely disseminated, giving rise to popular—and often very effective—folk remedies for fevers, headaches, flu, measles, and poisonous bites, making use of locally available herbs, roots, or other ingredients. It was mainly older women in the community who served as the custodians of this knowledge. In addition, other specialists offered secret prescriptions for specific ailments, which were handed down through generations within certain families.

Herbalists were often possessors of a secret prescription for a specific disorder (*danfang*) handed down through the family and carefully guarded. Some of them were itinerants covering a broad territory. The most colorful of these itinerant herbalists were the specialists in antidotes for bites of "the five poisonous creatures": the snake, scorpion, spider, centipede, and lizard. Each year on the fifth day of the fifth month (Duanwu jie), the date when insects and other such creatures officially emerged, a special fair was held in Prosperity. The evening prior to the fair, the monks would beat the temple drums long into the night, just as they did on the eve of every first or fifteenth of the month, and on the following morning people would eagerly crowd the village street to watch the snake doctors prove the efficacy of their potions by allowing snakes to crawl over them and bite them so that the potency of the medicine could be demonstrated.

Among *zhongyi* and the lay herbalists, medical knowledge was usually passed down through families and reinforced through experience. Some well-established *zhongyi* were willing to train apprentices for a fee, which in the early 1940s amounted to two to three *dan* of rice for the first three years. During this time apprentices were trained in three basic areas: brewing the medicines, diagnosis, and the nature of medicines. There were also some specialized classes, like bone setting and how to handle typhoid fever. Once a basic working knowledge was acquired, apprentices were put to work for several years under the direct supervision of their mentors. Their graduation was marked by a feast they were required to hold for their masters, who presented them with a medical book. The apprentices then set up their own practices, posting a plaque with their own names and those of their teachers. Although the graduates were often still in their teens, they were trusted if they had studied with a highly revered *zhongyi*.[24] People who tried to circumvent this apprenticeship and hoped to rely only on the study of the classics without sufficient practical training could get themselves in a lot of trouble. Pastor Tang Tianran had served as an evangelist of the AMEM in various mission stations throughout the province for many years. In 1941, when he reached the age of sixty, he resigned and returned home to Prosperity to seek some way of making a more adequate living. The field he chose was medicine because he believed that his ability to read the medical classics could enable him to be a better doctor than those with more limited literacy. But he needed practical experience so he went into partnership with Dr. Deng, who was also known to have a poor grasp of traditional medicine. The first case the partners took on was the one described at the opening of this chapter. Later, on his own, he tried to induce an abortion but failed miserably.

One specific branch of *zhongyi* was bone surgery.[25] The most famous bone surgeon in the area was Dr. Zhang in Dapeng Market, almost an hour away on foot. For serious injuries, people from Prosperity would send for Dr. Zhang. When, for example, the prosperous young weaver, Zhang Shaohua, had his left hand half severed while trying to prevent robbers from grabbing his stock of machine-spun cotton yarn, Dr. Zhang was called to treat him. Patient and doctor drew up a contract whereby the former would pay fifty yuan for a successful treatment. The down payment was twenty yuan. The remaining thirty would be paid only when Zhang was able to return to weaving. Following the signing of the contract, the doctor called daily to dress the wound. When we happened to visit this family two weeks after the disaster, we found the patient making good progress. No infection had set in, testifying to the surgeon's competence.

DIVINATION

Seeing a *zhongyi* was beyond the means of the majority of Prosperity's residents, and for them the cheapest alternative was the *guanhua*, or diviner, a diagnostician who explored the unseen world and discovered the cause of an ailment. Divination was based on the belief that illness was caused by unfortunate encounters between people and malevolent spirits bent on causing harm, or easily offended spirits who inflicted punishment for unintentional slights. Diseases could also be inflicted by an unhappy ghost that had not found repose, or they could be punishment for crimes a person had committed in a previous incarnation.

There were two diviners in Prosperity, both middle-aged women. One was from a middle-income farm family. She rarely came to the village but was consulted in her home or was called to the home of a client. The other was a blind woman from a poor farm family. She had been in the business for over twenty years, coming regularly each market day to the village where she held her consultations at the home of a widow.

While divining was hardly considered a sacred calling, it was nonetheless open only to the chosen. A diviner might diagnose the delirium of a young girl as an indication that the goddess Siniangzi had selected her for this calling. The parents then had to call in a Daoist folk priest to treat the girl, at the same time pledging her to the profession if she recovered. The priest, through chanting certain formulae, enticed the spirit possessing the patient into a vessel and wrapped it in red paper. The vessel was placed on the table, with lighted candles on either side and sticks of burning incense in front. The enshrined spirit was then worshipped. If the young patient subsequently recovered, the Daoist priest might teach her to chant a number of sacred formulae, or an experienced diviner might take her on as an apprentice and train her. When this teacher in due course proclaimed her competent, the fledgling diviner gave a dinner in her teacher's honor and set up a practice. A diviner, after her initiation, continued to live a normal life, marrying, having children, and doing farming and household chores.

Diviners often conducted séances to promote healing. There was no sense of mystery or sanctity about the séance or the diviner herself. She wore an ordinary blue cotton gown, which gave no inkling of her calling. When the day was fine, her landlady in the village set out a table and two benches in front of her house, and here the séances took place in a peaceful eddy in the thronging, noisy market day street. The diviner sat at the table with her bundle of wares beside her—sticks of incense, candles, and bundles of pic-

tures and inscriptions, which were esoteric drawings and characters, meaningful only to the initiated, done by a geomancer or Daoist folk priest in red
ink on a sheet of yellow paper. The pictures, which were printed, depicted
various situations that might be found in the unseen world. Clients sat on the
two benches on either side of the table. These were usually women who had
come on behalf of some family member who was ill. Waiting their turn, they
chatted with each other, completely ignoring the diviner as she carried on her
routines.

When a client's turn came, she took her place at the end of the bench next
to the table and the consultation began, with the diviner first establishing the
year, month, day, and hour of the patient's birth, then the home address, and
finally the nature of the patient's symptoms. For the simplest and cheapest
consultation, or "seeing reality" (*kanshi*), the diviner would light an incense
stick to help her on her voyage into the dark world. For the more probing
kanhua consultation, the client would purchase a candle so that the diviner
could see more clearly.

After lighting the incense or candle, the diviner would begin a monotonous incoherent chant to the accompanying clatter of a pair of *gua* (two
fitting, polished halves of a bamboo root), which she repeatedly tossed and
let fall on the table. Sometimes she chanted in a low nasal voice, and at other
times in loud urgent tones, as her spirit proceeded with its investigation of the
unseen world. Whenever the diviner discovered anything of significance, her
speech would become coherent as she divulged it to her client, then revert to
incoherence as she continued her investigations. Finally, when the cause of
the affliction was fully established, she would return to the present to explain
her findings to her client and advise her on how to appease the offended and
offending spirits.

Propitiation usually called for lighting candles and burning incense sticks
or mock paper cash. In more serious cases the evil spirit might be driven
away by pasting a sacred *fu* inscription on the wall above the patient's bed.
The various articles which the diviner might recommend lay in small piles at
her side, ready for sale to her clients. Sometimes the spirit afflicting the
patient was deemed too potent or implacable for these, and the client was
advised to invite either a Daoist folk priest or a shaman to exorcise them.

The first séance we witnessed was for a woman client of about thirty who
was concerned about the illness of her baby son, whom she sat nursing. After
the woman had answered the routine questions, she gave the unsolicited
information that the baby was her third, two previous sons having died in
infancy. With the lighting of an incense stick, the diviner began her voyage
into the unseen world. As this was a frugal "seeing reality," the diviner made
a rather quick investigation, then announced that she had discovered the
facts. Showing the woman the picture of a naked baby on a lotus flower with
a ghost on either side, she said, "You buried a child without clothing him.

Because he is naked he's inflicting illness on the baby." Such pronounce-ments showed little mental telepathy. Since the poor could scarcely afford to bury clothing for a dead infant, it was customary for the father to dispose of the little body unclad or wrapped in a bit of old straw matting. The diviner then advised the mother to make a tiny pair of shoes for the deceased baby and burn them. She also recommended that an inscription be pasted above the bed for the sick baby. But this would have cost 3.30 yuan, which the woman did not have. She simply paid the 0.40 for the consultation. As she left, the diviner pressed her to return the following market day with the money for the inscription, but the woman only mumbled that she would ask her husband.

The second client, a woman of about forty-five, was from a better-off farm family. She chose to have the more expensive *kanhua* consultation with a candle. She sat nursing a six-month-old baby girl, who had been suffering for two months from diarrhea and vomiting. The diviner ascertained that the child's illness was caused by a spirit that had accidently been jostled by the child's father and was venting its anger on the child. The mother asked the diviner to chant an incantation to appease the disgruntled spirit.

While the diviner was engaged in this chanting, the mother became en-grossed in a conversation with a waiting client. The conversation centered on a quarrel which her husband had had that very morning with the *jia* head, who had come to notify him that he had to perform one month and five days of corvée labor at the new military airfield or else pay for a substitute. The husband indignantly insisted it was not his turn. During the women's conver-sation, the diviner was continuing her incantation in the usual monotonous nasal tone, but toward the latter part of it, she became more and more excited, until at last she broke into coherence to inform her client that she had come upon some important information concerning the woman's husband and of-fered to divulge it in a separate consultation, for an additional 0.40-yuan fee. The client readily agreed, and the diviner told her that she had discovered that her husband was about to be separated from his home or from a large sum of money. Both client and neighbor were impressed, with the client exclaiming over and over again, "That's right!" Then she remarked how strange it was that her husband thought divination was just silly superstition.

This whole session cost the woman more than two yuan: two consulta-tions at 0.40 each (plus the cost of a candle to make the first one more probing), 0.80 for the incantation to placate the offended spirit, and a further 0.50 to cover the cost of the incense and mock paper cash needed for the incantation. This cost was quite extravagant, a little less than a week's worth of food for an ordinary person. Payment for a consultation had traditionally been one ordinary bowl of uncooked rice. But clients now paid in cash at the current price for a bowl of rice, which in March 1941 was 0.40 yuan. However, most séances brought in more than this, for the diviner sold incense, candles, and mock paper cash, as well as *fu* inscriptions.

EXORCISM AND INTERCESSION

While the diviner could placate minor spirits, major malevolent ones or angry gods were beyond her power. In such cases she advised her client to seek a shaman to exorcise them. Prosperity had two shamans (*dasheng*), although locals often consulted Shaman Su from a comfortably off family in the neighboring township of Dapeng. She was a dignified elderly woman, with a well-groomed appearance and tiny bound feet. On one of our visits we came upon the Dapeng shaman engaged in exorcising a malevolent spirit. The patient, a tenant farmer who supplemented the meager family earnings by carrying a litter, had become too ill to work in the winter of 1941. His skin was yellow and his legs swollen, presumably from heart trouble or nephritis. The family had first consulted an herbalist, but his special secret prescription (*danfang*) had failed and friends had recommended the Dapeng shaman. Though they could not afford it, they had invited her.

The door of the central "guest room" of this mud cottage was open, and behind the door sat the patient, a feather stuck to his forehead with a daub of rooster's blood. In the middle of the room stood the square table on which were set a bowl of water, a bowl of rice, two candles, four sticks of incense, and two eggs on a red cloth, while under the table was the rooster. The shaman was chanting scriptures from memory, alternately kneeling and standing. In her hands were four large and very shiny coppers which she would toss and let drop to the floor, then pick up and toss again, just as the diviner had tossed her polished bamboo root.

In fact, she was in the process of preparing a special potion. Having completed her recitation, she moved to the table, picked up the two eggs, and dexterously wound some red cloth around them into a shape suggesting a cat's head. Holding the eggs ceremoniously before her, she bowed to each of the four corners of the room, chanting a short text. She then placed the wrapped eggs on a small fire made of dried beanstalks and added more fuel on top. When the eggs were thoroughly burned, the remnants became an additional ingredient for the potion to be added to the water in the bowl, in which particles of ingredients already added could be seen floating.

Throughout the performance, the shaman appeared completely oblivious to her surroundings. She had an air of authority as she performed her rituals and barked out her commands to the family members who served as her assistants. The Du family showed great reverence for her, especially the patient's mother, who acted as chief assistant. When we spoke of the shaman as a diviner, Mrs. Du was indignant, so we corrected this to *lao taipo* (elderly woman from an upper-class background). But she was still dissatisfied, insisting that we refer to her as *dasheng*.

Another shaman sometimes called in by local people was a woman from Luopansi. She was consulted in the case of the mentally ill wife of the tenant farmer Zhou. Her mental illness was attributed by some to the fact that she had given birth to ten children, only one of which, a daughter, survived. When she began destroying household property and refused to work in the fields, Zhou first consulted a doctor, who proved unable to cure his wife. He then invited the Luopansi shaman to exorcise the malevolent spirit. When the exorcism rituals had no effect, the shaman explained that it was necessary to know more about the cause. Since she herself did not divine, she unsuccessfully attempted to send one of the members of the family into the unseen world. Finally she sent for a diviner who discovered that the patient's insanity was the punishment inflicted on the husband for nonpayment of debt in a previous existence. This accounted for the uselessness of exorcism, and the shaman gave up her efforts. Nevertheless it was a rather costly matter, for the performance had lasted a whole day and the shaman had been given special meals in addition to the fee and the cost of the incense and other materials required. Zhou, hoping for better luck in his next incarnation, eventually took a second wife to help with the farming and housework.

There were also male shamans called *fangying*. Unlike the women, they combined divination and exorcism. Prosperity residents sometimes consulted a Zhang *fangying* in Taihe market. One local case involved Sun Qingwu, a small owner-farmer in Prosperity with six *dan* of rice land. He and his wife had a son (now sixteen) who had suffered a severe illness four years before which left him with both legs paralyzed and unable to speak coherently, though his mind seemed clear. It appeared that when he tried to express himself and failed, he would fall into a rage and chew his bedclothes in frustration. To make matters worse, in the winter his paralyzed legs were covered with chilblains which became open running sores. At last the parents became so concerned that they called in the male shaman from Taihe.

During the séance the shaman discovered that in a previous incarnation the patient had been a butcher and had slaughtered thirty-seven buffaloes. Since slaughtering them for meat was taboo, the ox/buffalo deity (*niu wang*) had possessed the boy as punishment. This accounted for his chewing the bedclothes in cowlike fashion. The shaman then took measures to propitiate the buffalo deity in an expensive daylong ceremony costing forty-four yuan (at the inflation rates in April 1941). Of this sum, twelve were spent to bring the shaman from Taihe market by litter, and the remaining thirty-two covered the divination and exorcism fees, plus the necessary incense and candles, as well as the cost of festive meals which had to be served to the shaman throughout the day.

When this effort failed, the shaman declared the case hopeless. The Suns rejected the prognosis. After the shaman left they called in the boy's maternal grandmother to perform a "hang up the red" exorcism. Despite their manifestly poor results, the people of Prosperity continued to call upon shamans for their services out of desperation in the face of serious illness. As far as we could see, unlike diviners, shamans resorted to no special techniques to build up their credibility. They relied on the strong impression created through rituals and magic. Members of the patient's family appeared to get emotional relief from the shaman's esoteric performance in which they themselves actively participated.

Daoist folk priests could also be called in to intercede with the heavenly officials in a *tiao duangong* ritual. This was a more ambitious and costly ritual which only better-off families could afford and which usually was held only after a doctor had been unable to effect a cure. In one case, Sheng Huaiqing, proprietor of the most flourishing restaurant in the village, hired five priests to recite twelve scriptures in an all-night ceremony in Sheng's home when his wife became critically ill during her third pregnancy. When the priests arrived they set up two tables inside the main room of the house. On each table they placed two candles and some incense, and on one they placed five cups of spirit, and on the other, four. Above the five-cup table was a drawing covered with feathers that had been smeared with rooster's blood (the slaughter of a rooster being a crucial part of *tiao duangong* ceremonies). Four of the five priests sat on two benches on either side of a third table which had been placed against the wall by the bedroom door and furnished with two candles and some incense. These four priests beat out the music, while the fifth paced the floor chanting the scriptures. As the evening progressed, the priests took turns chanting.

Two cardboard figures with clay faces had been set up, one of a man and the other of a woman. The former wore straw sandals, while the latter wore a pair of Mrs. Sheng's own shoes. Holes were pierced in the eyes, ears, and mouths of the two figures to endow them with the respective senses. Each was clad in garments with pockets, and in the course of the rituals, gifts were thrust into these pockets, first rice, then bean curd, and so on. Toward dawn the two figures were taken out and burned along with a banner from which hung a number of letters addressed to various heavenly officials. This was considered a successful exorcism, for Mrs. Sheng came safely through this particular crisis—although she died shortly afterward in childbirth.

The ritual had cost Sheng a fair sum. Apart from the four yuan he paid each priest for the nightlong performance, he provided three banquets, one before the chanting started, one in the middle of the night, and the third in the morning. Many guests had also been invited to the evening meal, making up five whole tables, or forty people. Although each guest contributed either a *sheng* of rice or two or three yuan, as was customary, the performance was a costly matter. But a ceremony on such a scale was not solely for the sake of a patient's health. It was also a social display. In this case it showcased the growing prosperity of the restaurateur in such a way that it brought him praise for his propriety rather than criticism for conspicuous extravagance.

PRAYERS AND THE TREATMENT OF DISEASE

Unlike divination and exorcism, which were closely related to Daoism, prayers, vows, and thanksgiving ceremonies belonged to the Buddhist tradition. For illnesses big or small the sufferer, or more often some woman member of the family, would visit the shrine or image of the goddess of mercy, Guanyin, to light incense sticks and murmur a few prayers. Prosperity had twenty-one shrines to Guanyin scattered throughout the community. If the disease was incapacitating or alarming, the petitioner might make a vow, pledging that if the patient's health was restored she would, for example, become a vegetarian (either fully, or partially—which meant abstaining twice a month). Or she might vow to repaint the goddess's image, repair her shrine, or conduct a thanksgiving ceremony in the goddess's honor. A thanksgiving ceremony was a somewhat costly affair which required the hiring of priests to chant a number of scriptures for one or more days and involved various other expenses, not least the banqueting. Only better-off families could afford this ceremony, and even they usually postponed the thanksgiving (should the patient recover) until the following Lunar New Year when the feasting for the festival and the thanksgiving could be combined, thereby cutting costs. Several such thanksgivings took place during the New Year festival in 1941.

Men and women had somewhat different attitudes toward all these ways of dealing with illness. Many men were skeptical of traditional practices and often joked about them. Those with old-style learning gave little or no credence to the idea that disease was inflicted by supernatural beings, but they did not discourage ordinary folk from their beliefs. Those with modern education deplored divination and exorcism but generally ignored it. The few who spoke out against these practices were the primary school teachers— young outsiders from the towns. The one local exception was Wu Huanyun, onetime township head, who as a young man returning home after graduating from a town secondary school beat a diviner to death in the mid-1930s in his one-man drive to eradicate superstition in Prosperity. Ordinary working farmers might express skepticism, but if they themselves or a member of their own family suffered a disease that did not yield to treatment, their disbelief was easily shaken. A major misfortune could even turn a man into an ardent believer, as was the case with the skeptical miller who turned to religion when his eight pigs died.

Women, on the other hand, held strongly to their belief in the unseen world of spirits, ghosts, and gods. And whether the patient was a man or a woman, the client who consulted the diviner or shaman on behalf of the patient was usually a woman. Even when a family could not afford the services of a diviner or shaman, it was the maternal kinswomen who were called upon to administer the simple home remedy of binding the patient's head with a piece of red cloth for a headache, or putting a red cloth on the stomach for a stomachache. For more serious diseases, the maternal grand-mother would be asked to perform a simple form of exorcism called the *guahong,* "hang up the red cloth." On one home visit we found a grandmoth-er hanging strips of red cloth like small banners on bamboo sticks outside the door of the room where the patient lay to exorcise a malicious spirit harming her grandson. The old lady was treated with the greatest respect by the family members as she performed her rituals. In matters of health in the family, then, it was women who took charge. Attending to matters of illness in the family gave a woman some respite from her household and farm chores and seemed to give her special status. The role women played in local medical practices was central to the ability of the NCC to establish an effective clinic, providing Western medical treatments.

THE NCC CLINIC IN PROSPERITY

The first group to bring new medical practices to Prosperity was not the Nationalist government, whose health programs had extended no further than the county town of Bishan, but rather the NCC. Many Western and Chinese Christians had come to appreciate the struggle against illness as one of the most important "felt needs" of Chinese peasants.[26] T. H. Sun sought to establish a clinic in Prosperity as a part of his project because he recognized its potential importance in the overall effort to "draw the Church from the margin toward the center of Chinese national life."[27] To this end, Sun con-tacted Miss Alma Ericksen, an American Methodist Mission public health nurse based in Chengdu who oversaw various rural health clinics, including the ones at Longchuanyi, Ziliujing, and Laifengyi.[28] After Miss Ericksen agreed to open up a clinic in Prosperity modeled on her Longchuan center, Sun hired a dedicated Chinese Christian nurse and midwife, Miss Zhu Xiu-zhen. Miss Zhu had been trained in the Canadian-run missionary hospital in Xingyang, Henan, where she worked until the Japanese invasion.

Miss Zhu was paid by the AMEM and supervised by Alma Ericksen, who was stationed in Chengdu and who spent a lot of time on the road visiting the health stations under her supervision. She was very popular with Chinese and Westerners because of her sparkling personality, love of Danish folk danc-ing, and lively teaching style. Ericksen's clinics were not in contact with the government health project. Miss Zhu, for her part, was not even registered with the government,[29] although she was a graduate of Peking Union Medical College and had credentials as a maternity nurse, which was the highest rung on the nursing hierarchy.

In early 1940 the clinic in Prosperity began operation, constituting the only source of Western medicine in the community. The clinic was open every day from 9 a.m. until 12:30 p.m., except Sundays when it was only open in the afternoon. Initially the people most responsive were those who had some experiences outside of Prosperity, such as the Cais, Caos, and Suns, as well as merchants like Cheng Songling and Dong Taibang. The vast majority of people in Prosperity ignored the clinic, relying on their familiar ways of treating illness. At most, they hesitantly looked at the clinic. Eventually, a few brave souls went in to rest on one of the benches in the waiting room and chat with friends. Gradually a few felt comfortable enough to ask for treatment.

Miss Zhu worked hard to build up confidence in the clinic. She held a physical exam of the students in the school and conducted hygiene classes there as well. She also gave classes to the girls in the Bible school, twice a year for three weeks. She looked after the health of the girls in the embroidery classes as well. In 1940 she gave a physical check to the 329 pupils enrolled in the central primary school (all from better-off families) and found that 314 of these children had ailments, mostly trachoma, scabies, ringworm, or tinea, all easily curable with modern medicines and many with local remedies. Yet they went untended. Only if an ailment persisted and grew worse, threatening incapacity or death, would the patient or family take measures.

The clinic's reputation for treating wounds was greatly bolstered by its handling of a critical wound suffered by a farmer. On this occasion, Miss Zhu was away, but she had left her medicines for Yu Xiji, who was standing in for her. It was expected that most of the patients that day would be coming for ringworm or scabies, or perhaps diarrhea. But it happened that a man in his thirties was carried into the clinic with a horrendously swollen leg and a large cut on his foot that had been coated with ashes to stop the bleeding. He had been cutting bamboo to make baskets and chairs when the accident occurred. Yu Xiji immediately realized that he was being brought to the clinic as a last resort. While most people in Prosperity at that time did not have much faith in the Western clinic, when all else had failed they thought it would be worth a try. She cleaned the wound, washed it with a disinfectant, *pengsha*, and then had him soak it in a basin of warm water for several hours. After some of the pus came out, she was able to apply Miss Zhu's medicines, and the man was carried home with the instruction that he should return to have the bandages changed when Miss Zhu returned. His recovery earned much respect for the clinic.

The ability of Miss Zhu to attract patients was greatly aided by a case involving Dr. Yang Huaqing. When his infant son became seriously ill from dysentery, a local diviner interpreted this development in a way that reinforced the legitimacy of the landlord code. He claimed that in a previous existence, Mrs. Yang had owed another individual a considerable sum of money which she had failed to repay, and in order to secure repayment the lender had been reborn as a son to his debtor. During the two years he had already spent in the Yang family, he had received full reimbursement, so he was now taking his leave. Nothing could be done to persuade him to remain on earth. But Mrs. Yang was not prepared to give up her precious son so readily and brought the baby to Miss Zhu's clinic, where it was cured. Thereafter Dr. Yang did not hesitate to recommend any patient he failed to cure to consult our nurse. One market day, when he found he was achieving poor results in his treatment of the epileptic wife of the prestigious landlord Wang Junliang, he requested Miss Zhu to come for a consultation. As this took place in his open-fronted office in clear view of the public, it was a calculated display of recognition and approval of her expertise.

One incident related to the war that further enhanced the clinic's status occurred on August 13, 1940, when a major air battle took place over Chongqing involving sixty-six Japanese planes and thirty-six Nationalist aircraft. Of the thirteen Nationalist planes that were shot down, six or seven fell in the vicinity of Prosperity. Miss Zhu administered first aid to the inexperienced pilots, but she recognized that their wounds were quite serious and would require treatment at the hospital in Bishan. Carriers were unwilling to carry them into Bishan because no one would pay them for this service. It was only when Commander Cai appeared on the scene and agreed to pay the carriers in advance that they took the injured airmen to the hospital. An air force official later sent someone to thank Miss Zhu for her help, which contributed to the enhancement of her status in the community.

Miss Zhu's practice built up gradually, through the combination of her expertise and her personality. Her success may also be attributed to her respect for traditional medicine and her willingness to find local substitutes for ingredients that were expensive or hard to procure. For instance, in treating scabies she mixed sulfur with pork lard instead of Vaseline. Such adaptive practices sometimes concerned T. H. Sun who, as a graduate of a missionary university, distrusted traditional Chinese medicine and feared the clinic might be discredited by the adoption of treatments not vouched for by Western medicine.

The most challenging area of medicine to break into concerned childbirth. Miss Zhu was initially not able to get any business in midwifery, as people stuck to their customary practice of having babies at home and consulting a traditional midwife if necessary. Few families would permit a woman to deviate from traditional practices because childbirth was considered fraught with supernatural dangers.

After six months of exclusion, Miss Zhu was able to make inroads into this area of health care delivery when in one difficult labor she was called in and saved both mother and child. The family had already consulted a Daoist folk priest for a *fu* inscription that was pasted on the head of the bed to keep evil spirits at bay. However, this remedy was seen by the family to have the opposite effect, for that night the rats were unusually active, jumping all about the rafters of the room. In alarm the family sent for one of the most respected shamans, an imposing middle-aged deaf woman surnamed Wu. When she arrived she shut herself in the bedroom with the patient, recited sacred words at the bedside, lit candles, and burned mock paper cash. But that night the rats were still more obstreperous, and even the dogs outside barked and tore around the house as if chasing evil things. As the wife was suffering acute abdominal pains over such an extended period, the family finally decided to call in the Western nurse. The staff explained that she was out of town but would come the next day. That night the rats were extraordinarily quiet, an auspicious sign, and the following day when Miss Zhu arrived, she delivered the baby, and both mother and child were fine. Her success was lauded, but she was sought only for difficult cases until the tragic, much-talked-of death in childbirth of a young woman whose family did not seek Zhu. Suddenly she was in great demand, with an average of one midwifery case a day by mid-November 1940.

Clearly, the clinic flourished. A few months after the clinic began treating patients, Zhu was seeing twenty patients a day on market days, and ten on other days. Within a year, the clinic had become Prosperity's most popular center for the treatment of wounds, injuries, boils, and skin troubles. The head of the county health department, on a visit to Prosperity, was quite impressed with the quality of health care delivery by the Rural Reconstruction Clinic. Moreover, T. H. Sun was able to supply an impressive set of statistics on its overall accomplishments, including the number of individual patients (985) who had been treated at the clinic in its first eleven months and the number of smallpox vaccinations (237) given. After assessing the performance of Prosperity's clinic, the county's health department official decided to provide the total funding for its operating costs, including medicines, bandages, and vaccines. In endorsing this rural clinic, he vindicated T. H. Sun's approach to rural health programs. [30]

CONCLUSION

The Nationalist government was able to establish a health care infrastructure based in urban centers and to begin to reach out into rural areas. Much was accomplished in terms of sanitation, training some midwives, and inoculation. However, the vastness of the countryside, where 90 percent of the population resided, presented a formidable challenge. Religious and secular reformers seemed more effective in small towns and rural areas, as was evidenced by the expansion of Western-style medical service in Prosperity.

The success of the clinic in Prosperity depended on many factors. The efficiency of Western medical treatment in terms of bacterial infections was key. But modern practices were alien to Prosperity and probably would not have been accepted so quickly without the patient and persistent efforts of Miss Zhu. The fact that women played an influential role in Chinese traditional medical practices may have facilitated Miss Zhu's efforts, because the local community was accustomed to female practitioners. Miss Zhu created a channel between the modern health initiative and the local tradition, thereby linking the two endeavors rather than placing them in opposition to each other.

NOTES

1. Liu Xiang's warlord government had shown some interest in health care, but it was not a major concern.

2. The National Institute of Health (also sometimes translated as the National Health Administration) was founded in Nanjing in 1928 and established a number of provincial public health care programs in the late 1920s and early 1930s, including the Jiangxi Provincial Health Administration in 1931 ("Szechuan Provincial Health Administration, 1942," p. 2).

3. Chen Zhiqian first became active in Sichuan in 1936 when he and James Yen were invited by the Sichuan governor, Liu Xiang, to visit Chengdu. As a result of the visit, an experimental county was created on the basis of earlier work done at Dingxian, which included a fulltime health center. "A Review of Government Health Service in Sichuan, China for Period 1939–1945," p. 1.

4. "First Report of the Szechuan Provincial Health Administration" (1941), p. 1.

5. "A Review of Government Health Services for Period 1939–1945," p. 8. Later in this same report (p. 14), the government was criticized as being "highly bureaucratic" and "dreadfully inefficient," and as having a large number of leaders who were "ignorant of modern civilization."

6. "First Report of the Szechuan Provincial Health Administration" (1941), p. 2.

7. The Rockefeller Foundation made the following contributions to the Technical Division of the Sichuan Provincial Institute of Health: 1941, $10,000 (U.S.); 1942, $15,000; 1943, $18,000; and 1944, $20,000 ("Preliminary Report of the Szechuan Provincial Health Administration," 1942).

8. "A Review of Government Health Service in Szechuan, China for Period 1939–1945," p. 6. Chen's lamenting the lack of data on communicable diseases in Sichuan when he assumed the leadership of the Sichuan Institute of Health was also contained in this report.

9. Of the 574 people in Lanchung examined, 85 percent were infested; in Yingshan, 96 percent of the 166 people who were studied were found to have parasites ("Report of the Sichuan Provincial Health Administration, 1942," p. 5).

10. Yu Xiji was afflicted in the summer of 1940 by this disease.

11. "First Report of the Szechuan Provincial Health Administration" (1941), p. 3.

12. "A Review of Government Health Service in Szechuan, China for Period 1939–1945," p. 10.

13. "First Report of the Szechuan Provincial Health Administration" (1941), p. 3.

14. Chen (1944), p. 1.

15. Balfour to Sawyer (December 24, 1940).

16. "Annual Report of the National Institute of Health, 1942."

17. Sichuan sheng Bishan xianzhi (1996), p. 709.

18. "Annual Report of the National Institute of Health, 1942," p. 35.

19. The NIH contributed four thousand yuan a month from January to July 1940, and thereafter nineteen thousand yuan a month. The Bishan County government's contribution was forty thousand yuan ("Annual Report of the National Institute of Health, 1942," p. 35).

20. Sichuan sheng Bishan xianzhi (1996), p. 698.

21. The other county health demonstration center under his personal supervision was at Pixian, on the Chengdu plain ("China-Szechuan Provincial Annual Report Health Administration," 1941–1942, p. 7).

22. Interview with Yu Xiji, June 2001.

23. Price (1948), p. 232.

24. Interview with Luo Minchen, *zhongyi* in Daxing, in May 1997 and April 3, 2001.

25. Now it is called *guwaike*.

26. For an example of an articulation of this line of approach, see Hubbard (1947).

27. T. H. Sun (1940), p. 501.

28. Other Methodist medical centers with major hospitals included Chengdu, Chongqing, and Luzhou.

29. Interview with Yu Xiji, June 2001.

30. Our medical check on the pupils of the central primary school in 1940 listed the following ailments from which 162 pupils (ranging in age from five to eighteen) suffered:

- skin diseases: roughly 20 percent
- eye trouble: over 60 percent
- ear and hearing problems: over 20 percent
- conspicuous dental caries: about 15 percent
- TB glands: over 50 percent
- enlarged tonsils: over 20 percent
- signs of secondary anemia: under 10 percent

Chapter Eight

Marriage

Reformed and Unreformed

Two neighboring middle-farmer families, the Xiangs of Gaoyuan Temple Corners (*Gaoyuan sijiao*) and the Yangs of Yangjia Bend (*Yangjia wan*), had betrothed their children when the Xiang boy was three and the Yang girl two. When the girl was four, her mother died. Not long after, the father went on business to Guizhou, leaving her in the care of his brother. The father was never heard from again, and when the girl was eight her uncle was conscripted, leaving her on her own. To provide a home for the child, the boy's mother, who had been widowed the previous year, celebrated the marriage of the children, now aged eight and nine. Six months later she too died, and the juvenile couple was taken in by relatives. When Xiang was fifteen, they helped him rent a small farm of one *dan* of upland fields with a tiny three-room cottage. With less and less help from his relatives, the boy and girl were able to support themselves. By the time Brown and Yu knew them, they were twenty-two and twenty-three years old, had been married fourteen years, and had a two-year-old baby daughter whom they treasured.

Marriage practices were embedded in a web of social relationships and practices, as well as economic and political realities. In this case, the consequences of a child marriage were shaped by work, death, widowhood, and conscription. In spite of the seemingly positive outcome of this particular marriage, the arrangement of childhood marriages was one of many social practices that reformers sought to change. Although rural marriage reform was not a central element of the Nationalist government when it moved its capital to Chongqing in 1938, the Nationalists did articulate a modernizing program that envisioned the curtailment of traditional marriage practices. Limited as their effects may have been, Nationalist government directives, laws, and political campaigns touching upon marriage serve as a useful lens for examining gender changes in society. These government initiatives were applicable to almost all women and most men in rural Sichuan, a society in which marriage was generally regarded as a socially sanctioned norm for all. It was considered a great misfortune for any individual to remain unmarried. In Prosperity, no daughters were left unmarried beyond their early twenties, with the sole exception of two Buddhist nuns, women who had come from comfortably well-off pious families. In contrast to this compulsory marriage pattern for females, many poor males remained bachelors, not out of desire but because they could not afford the required bride price.

The marriage codes in the Nationalist Family Law of 1930 stipulated that the decision to marry should be made by the individuals involved and that marriage should be monogamous, although some articles also protected the rights of concubines. The Nationalist code specified that an engagement should not take place until a woman was fifteen years of age (*xusui*) and a man seventeen years of age. It devoted much more attention to the nature of the marriage contract than the engagement contract. These laws asserted the state's authority to set the terms of marriage, including stipulating a minimum age (sixteen for women and eighteen for men), expanding the prohibition of the marriage between close relatives to include a ban on first cousins on the maternal side, and setting the basis on which a marriage could be terminated. Most important, women now had the right to divorce their husbands, while men lost the right to divorce on the grounds of barrenness, jealousy, loquacity, or theft. The law also included a liberal provision for divorce based on mutual consent.[1]

At a local level, these Nationalist legal codes conflicted with customary laws. In some cases, the differences between the two sets of legal practices were huge. Although free-choice marriages occurred in urban areas, they were very rare in rural Sichuan before the war. Engagements were usually contracted well before children reached their teenage years and were considered binding. Marriage age was one area where the codified laws were fairly close to long-standing customary laws that regarded a girl over sixteen (*erba*) and a boy over eighteen (*ruo guan*) as having reached adulthood. Already by the 1930s most urban women married in conformity to the marriage law age, though 10 percent were less than fifteen years of age by the traditional way of reckoning, or fourteen by present-day calculations of age.[2] But in many respects, marriage rather than age in Chinese rural society was the determinant of adulthood. Those who married early were considered adults. Early marriages were more common in some parts of China than others. Martin Yang found that early marriages were virtually unknown in the village of Taitou, Shandong.[3] In contrast, early marriages were evident in many Sichuan rural communities, including Prosperity.

As the force of law was generally weak in rural Chinese communities, the government used several means to educate the people of Prosperity and other rural areas about its provisions: articles in its party newspapers, government ordinances, and social movement organizations. The *Central Daily* (*Zhongyang ribao*) in Chongqing carried many articles advocating the end of arranged marriages, the promotion of group wedding ceremonies to be conducted in a frugal manner, and the introduction of free-choice marriages. The local Bishan newspapers also carried a few articles on raising the status of women. For those issues of greatest concern, the central ministries in Chongqing issued directives requiring enforcement of certain laws to the county governments, who then usually passed them along to the township governments.

FOOT BINDING AND EARLY MARRIAGE

Government directives on reforming marriage practices began with the issuance of an order to rural townships in 1938 and again in 1940 to eliminate the "evil" custom of foot binding, a practice that had once served as an important condition for marriage.[4] The Nationalist government argued that this practice should be terminated in order to increase girls' and women's involvement in the anti-Japanese war effort. This directive instructed township heads to impose fines on all families whose women had bound feet. However, it also noted that this practice could only be found in remote areas of the county, as confirmed by the observations of Isabel Brown and Yu Xiji. They saw no evidence that young girls' feet were being bound in 1940, and from what can be reconstructed, it seems that this practice was rarely practiced in this community after 1929, though there is some evidence that it continued into the late 1930s in some mountainous communities on the edges of Bishan County.[5] Thus the Nationalist government first chose to target a marriage-related practice that was definitely on the wane, where it would not be difficult to secure further compliance.

A more difficult issue was addressed in December 1942, when the Sichuan provincial government issued a mandate calling on each county to restrict the incidence of early marriages in its areas and to write up a report about its prevalence.[6] Once again it used a war-related rationale: that early marriages were bad for one's health and thus detrimental to the war effort. Some county reports indicated that the incidence of early marriage was fairly high, as much as 50 percent of the marriages in Dazu, for instance. County officials believed it was impossible to use legal means to eradicate early marriages, as it clearly was a survival strategy of the poor and desperate. One report suggested that the government should hire poor young girls in its textile factories as a way to delay their marriages.[7]

In Prosperity, Brown and Yu found that many girls married around the age stipulated by the civil code, that is, sixteen (*xusui*). To wait much beyond this age caused great concern, for with every passing year a young woman's worth was considered to have diminished except in the case of more educated peasant families. However, occasionally a girl in Prosperity reached her twenties still unmarried, often because her family was dissatisfied with the candidates put forward by matchmakers, believing they fell short of the "matching doors" principle that guided families to seek spouses for their children from families of an equivalent social and economic standing. But this was not the only reason for delay. Parents could be loath to lose a daughter who was a major income earner. Such cases were chiefly found in comfortable and middle-farm families who supplemented their income through cottage weaving, for the weavers were often their unmarried daughters.

The most extreme case of putting off a daughter's marriage was that of Sun Yichang, one of the young women who attended the Bible school sessions. A skilled weaver, good looking, healthy, industrious, and from a comfortably off farm family, she was still not engaged at the age of twenty-three. The explanation given by friends of Yichang was that in "matching doors and households," the Suns overrated themselves: candidates they considered appropriate were not satisfied, while those who sought their daughter were not good enough (*gao bucheng, di bujiu*). But there was an equally compelling reason. The longer the Suns postponed their daughter's engagement, hoping for a better match, the longer her family could enjoy the income from her skilled labor. Yichang herself was in no hurry to give up her current status of favorite daughter in a loving home for the status of daughter-in-law in an unfamiliar and possibly uncongenial family.

A similar case that turned out differently was that of Cao Ziyun's daughter, another one of the Bible school girls. The Caos owned eight *dan* of rice land and had a thriving cottage weaving industry with two standard looms. One of the weavers was the seventeen-year-old daughter. The parents were modern-minded people who had sent their son to secondary school in Bishan, after which he had taken a job in Chongqing. After two years there, he had just returned to Prosperity to take up the post of clerk in the township government office. When he found that his parents had not arranged a match for his competent young sister, he remonstrated with them, saying, "If you're going to be new-fashioned, then send her to school to get a regular education. If you're going to be old-fashioned, then arrange the match and marry her off." The parents took his advice and, choosing to be modern, sent her to school. As the farm was eight *li* (three miles) from the village, they rented a room for her in the home of Zhang Yunheng, whose daughter was the same age and attending the same school. The brother, as village clerk, lived in the village and kept an eye on his sister.

In theory, as a daughter grew older, her marriage value decreased and it became more and more difficult for the family to arrange as advantageous a marriage as they wished. In the end the girl might find that she was worse off than she might have been if her family had accepted an earlier offer. But this did not necessarily hold if the young woman was a substantial money earner or if she was literate.

Brown and Yu found that these instances of delayed marriage stood out much more than the early marriages for their rarity. According to their survey of families in Prosperity, early marriages were not as common as in Dazu or as reported by John Buck in his surveys of Sichuan,[8] but they were nonetheless somewhat common. Among nine- and ten-year-old girls, one in forty-two was married; among eleven- and twelve-year-olds, one in eighteen was married; and among thirteen- and fourteen-year-olds, one in three was married. Moreover, at least some of these girls had already been married for a number of years.

Although girls were more likely than boys to be married early, several well-off families in the community chose to arrange the marriages of their sons under the age of fifteen. One example is the marriage between the fourteen-year-old son of a prosperous family, Sun Shaoliang, and the sixteen-year-old daughter of Cao Guoliang, whose family fortunes fell short of Sun's. Another example is the marriage between the sixteen-year-old son of a powerful landowner, Wang Junliang, and a daughter of the landowning Zhang family of Zhongxin Market.

The promulgation of a marriage code prohibiting early marriages had little impact on curbing this practice in Prosperity. Families who deviated from the customary practices of marrying children off after they had reached the age of sixteen mostly did so out of economic necessity. It was a strategy for survival that could not be altered by law alone.

WEDDING EXTRAVAGANCES

As part of its "New Life Movement" in 1934, the Nationalist Party had promoted the idea of group weddings, based on the belief that marriages should be simple and frugal rather than extravagant and elaborate. After it set up its capital in Chongqing, the government once again promoted group wedding ceremonies as a new marriage style during the war. It furnished the food and space for these weddings, thereby enticing many young urban couples who lacked the money to hold a wedding party. In 1941, the Chongqing-based government tried to spread this practice to the county towns and townships by telling local officials that they needed to promote frugal group weddings among their citizenry. This practice did not attract many followers in Bishan or Prosperity, as weddings were still seen as the occasion for display, affirming or enhancing the standing of the family in the community. Elaborate local wedding ceremonies also served to publicize and document the marriage because it had many witnesses in the community. This occasion provided a more immediate legality than could be afforded by a written document dispensed by the county.

Symbolically, too, both scale and style mattered in local weddings. Crowds, bustle, and noise augured prosperity, happiness, and many sons. The greater the furor, the more auspicious the occasion. In a community starved for entertainment, any wedding attracted some attention. But when leading families were involved they provided colorful display and excitement, enlivening the social scene and remaining a major topic of conversation in the neighborhood for days.

When the day of a wedding arrived, the bride was carried in a sedan chair to her new home, escorted by relatives and bringing a dowry. If she came from a family of means, the wedding procession included a whole set of furniture together with chests of clothes and quilts and other items borne along by young relatives, friends, or tenants. The ceremony itself entailed the familiar honoring of ancestors and kin, with the young couple kowtowing in turn to the ancestral tablets, the groom's grandparents, his parents, the bride's relatives, and all the honored guests, in strict order of precedence. The ceremony combined formality and celebratory fuss.

A marriage connecting two prosperous and/or influential families could be a social affair involving hundreds of guests and many more onlookers. Few received invitations to the wedding. Most came unbidden to honor the family because they were duty bound to do so as relatives, friends, secret society brothers, neighbors, or tenants. The greater the number of guests at the wedding banquet, the greater the honor bestowed on the families involved. Since the host could only guess at the number of guests, it was necessary to underestimate, for empty places would discredit the host. Underestimation had the additional advantage that a pleasant fuss was created as more tables were set up and more cured pork brought down from the kitchen rafters, bringing attention to the size of the crowds.

Wang Junliang, at the age of forty-five, was one of Prosperity's most prosperous and influential citizens, with an estate of one hundred *dan* of rice land and a high rank in the most powerful local lodge of the Paoge. When Wang hosted a betrothal party for his son, he prepared thirty tables of guests, but six extra tables were required to seat all the well-wishers. When the time came for the son's wedding party, it had to be on an even greater scale. Such crowds came to honor him that there was no counting them until they sat down to eat. By the time the banqueting was over, Wang had fed one hundred tables of guests—eight hundred people in all. The strain on Wang's financial resources was heavy, but such extravagance was obligatory for a man of his status.

Wedding ceremonies were not only an occasion for male heads of household to display their wealth and status but also provided women a public opportunity to display their talents and status. In the wedding of Wang Junliang's son, for example, the bride's middle-aged aunt played a prominent role, trying to protect her niece from criticism from Wang Junliang about the size of her dowry. He had only agreed to a match between his son and the daughter of a less affluent landowning Zhang family of Zhongxin because of the skillful negotiating tactics employed by the matchmaker, a woman in her fifties who was related to both families. Soon after the arrival of the bride, carried in a sedan chair, her dowry, and three attendants—her ten-year-old brother, an adult male relative, and her middle-aged aunt—Wang had shown his displeasure at the amount of money that was presented in lieu of furniture.[9] Soon afterward, Wang Junliang's friends and relatives began, as was the custom, to look at each item of the dowry, murmuring softly or loudly their praise or disparagement so as to exert social and psychological pressures for the advantage or discomfort of either side. Some commented on the locked chests of clothing, suggesting that the bride's wardrobe was poor and meager.

The dowager aunt, along with the rest of the bride's party, showed no visible reactions to this chitchat and deported herself with complete aplomb. She then launched an offensive to counter the criticism of the bride's family for offering too small a dowry by gaining the guests' respect for their strength of character and valor. To this end, the aunt first responded effectively to a servant's refusal to accept a tip of fifty *fen* (the absolute minimum appropriate for a tip) for a hot towel he had supplied after her long journey of several hours by offering him another ten *fen*. When he still hesitated, she fixed him with her eye and did not withdraw the offered tip until he reluctantly accepted it. She continued her performance at dinner. As the aunt was a Buddhist and vegetarian, the top table for women served no meat. Seated next to the groom's grandmother at the women's table, she was offered a water pipe by one of Wang Junliang's lesser relatives. She offered him a scant ten *fen* rather than the appropriate amount of fifty. The aunt then turned to face him with an expression of withering scorn while continuing to hold out the ten *fen* note. When Wang Junliang's sister tried to break the tension by asking a question, the bride's aunt replied courteously without for a second removing her scornful eye from the man's face. After a moment, the man accepted the tip, as he could hardly bear responsibility for an incident created by this strong-minded woman.

The next act began when the bride was expected to give all the children at the wedding a present of five *fen*, which was believed to bring good luck to the young couple. With great composure, the bride opened one of her locked chests, in view of the guests, to remove a wad of brand new five-*fen* notes, while also revealing a chest full of fine clothing. In an instant, the criticism was stifled, as the dramatic opening of the locked chests showed the guests that they had been mistaken. No more complaints were uttered, and the atmosphere of the wedding became very jubilant. By showing herself to be both strong-willed and a master of the codes of conduct in a male-dominated culture, the aunt had engineered a successful entry for her niece into a very powerful landlord family. Such opportunities for older women to strengthen their positions in male-dominated families meant that for women, as well as for men, elaborate weddings were desirable and that far more than a government directive would be required to persuade them to engage in group weddings.

ARRANGED MARRIAGES

Although the Nationalist government invested its resources and energies in ending foot binding and early marriages, as well as in promoting group weddings, it did little to enforce or educate the populace about the legal provisions to terminate arranged marriages. In Prosperity, there was no indication in the early 1940s of voluntary marriages contracted by the couples themselves as stipulated in the Nationalist civil law. Instead, marriage making continued to be seen as the responsibility and right of parents.

The silence of the government on this issue constituted recognition of its inability to use state mandates and laws to transform this family practice. In many ways, it is not surprising that the government did not make a strong effort to enable young people to make betrothal decisions on their own. There was little economic or social basis for voluntary marriages, particularly as most young people were dependent on their families for their livelihood. Unlike the process of ending foot binding, the better-educated and more open-minded families in Prosperity were not willing to tolerate free-choice marriages in the early 1940s.

Brown and Yu did learn of one attempt by a young couple to negotiate their own marriage. This was undertaken by Dr. Yang Huaqing's adopted son, whose family had set him up in business in Bishan County town when he reached adulthood. There he became interested in a stylish modern young woman, who sent a matchmaker to him suggesting marriage. As he was willing, he brought the young woman and her matchmaker to Prosperity to obtain his parents' approval. The Yangs held a dinner and the parents and the matchmaker negotiated late into the night. The following morning the young woman and her matchmaker departed for Bishan in style, riding in litters paid for by the Yangs. When no engagement ensued, it was understood that the negotiations that had transpired that night were not to set the terms of the marriage but rather to fix the amount of compensation to be given to the young woman for a rejection of the suit. Word later spread that the young woman had doomed her cause when she tried to create a favorable impression by saying, "I'd like you to know I have high-ranking friends in the Twenty-Ninth Army." Rather than indicating her high connections, it suggested to the Yangs that she was a woman of questionable virtue. The young man appeared to accept his parents' verdict calmly. With an inheritance at stake, it was highly improbable that a young man in Prosperity would have challenged his parents' disapproval.

Families took into account a number of considerations when arranging a match. One was the principle of "matching doors and households," meaning that the socioeconomic status of the two families should be equal. A second was the much less mentioned principle of adjustments for special positive or negative qualities in the individuals involved. On the positive side, a girl might be valued for special household or production skills or her beauty or education. A young man might be valued for his special capabilities, his education, or his prospects. On the negative side, flaws of one kind or another—physical or mental—would be taken into account, though each family did its best to hide these.

Orthodox marriage-making practices started with the aid of a matchmaker approached by one party or the other. This third party was important since, for reasons of face, it was inconvenient for the two parties to deal directly with each other. The matchmaker, often a woman, could be a relative of both sides who matched up cousins of different surnames. Among influential landowners, however, the initiator might be a member of a power faction, proposing a match between eminent families in order to consolidate property and strengthen a political alliance.

Once the initial approach had been made and tentatively accepted by both families, the horoscopes of the proposed couple were checked. While this was a necessary procedure, Brown and Yu were told by a skeptic that a competent horoscopist (*bazi xiansheng*) could accommodate any match that might have been decided upon by influential families. Likewise he could be persuaded to declare horoscopes incompatible should one family wish to avoid a match without offending the family seeking the marriage. Once the horoscopes were found compatible, the matchmaker helped the two families reach agreement on guidelines for the dowry and gifts to the bride. A banquet sealed these agreements and made them almost as binding as the wedding itself. No matchmaker would dare suggest alternative matches, and if either side backed out at this point, a legal case could result, with demand for compensation. When the entire family decided it was time for the wedding, the matchmaker was again approached to put forward the request to the other party. If agreeable, the horoscopist was again consulted to determine an auspicious date for the wedding. The bridegroom's family now presented gifts to the girl's. If these met their expectations, everything moved forward smoothly.

Betrothals traditionally took place when children were small, as parents were eager to seal a good match as early as possible. This meant that in difficult times, families of similar economic and social standing at the time of betrothal might more easily find themselves in drastically different financial situations by the time the marriage was consummated a decade or more later. Perhaps for this reason, betrothals in the early 1940s often took place not long before the marriage, when the young people were already in their early or mid-teens.

Although the traditional marriage system remained quite vibrant, one marriage-related custom that was beginning to show signs of change among the well-to-do was the strong prohibition against the couple seeing one another before the wedding day. In many cases, the engaged young people would be allowed to catch a glance of their future mate from afar. In a few cases, an "accidental meeting" of the couple was concocted before the wedding day in order to win the enthusiasm of the two teenagers designated for marriage. These meetings had to be set up in a fashion that made them seem to have happened as a coincidence, as is revealed in the chance meeting one January morning in 1941 between Wang Junliang's eighteen-year-old daughter, Wang Zhengbi, and her fiancé. Wang Zhengbi joined a group of eight of her women relatives who were making an unexpected call on the wife of Mr. T. H. Sun, the director of the National Christian Council Project in Prosperity. The party filed straightaway upstairs to the surprise of the hostess, who followed them up. At this moment a second party of unexpected guests arrived, led by the wife of the biggest landowner, Mrs. Cao Yuexian, with her sixteen-year-old nephew (the prospective groom), who was heir to the large Zhang estate. She was accompanied by Commander Cai Xunqing's wife, as well as three of her own daughters. The Wang party upstairs took this as their cue to file downstairs in full sight of the Cao party below. As the boy and girl came face to face, Mrs. Cai introduced them. The girl bowed to the boy, and he reciprocated. The girl and her party left while the boy's party lingered, but only briefly, for the mission was accomplished. This little operation not only succeeded in winning the support of the two teenagers, who were highly satisfied with each other's appearance, but it also exhibited style. The practice of "accidental meetings" deviated sharply from the traditional conventions which prohibited social contact between unmarried adolescents of the opposite sex. Yet this type of premarital encounter was beginning to be accepted by Prosperity's better-off families who showed some modern influences.

However, these erosions in betrothal customs were limited. Wang Zhengbi's orchestrated outing was not an indication that a significant loosening had occurred in the strict regulation of proper conduct by young unmarried women. In Prosperity there was a strong sense that it was unseemly for engaged women to have a visible presence in public, as Cao Hongying sadly discovered when she tried to attend the three-week Bible classes offered by Orvia Proctor as part of her regular biannual circuit around Sichuan. These classes were appealing to a select group of young educated women like Hongying because they offered an opportunity both to increase literacy skills and to learn about modern ways of managing a family. However, soon after these classes began, an anonymous note was found pasted on the wall opposite the South Gate of the village, stating that Hongying had been seen attending the market, an oblique but unambiguous way of saying that she was meeting a boyfriend. Although Hongying had always been careful not to use the public street when attending these meetings, but rather to arrive discreetly by the back gate, she and her family took the warning seriously. She gave up the literacy classes and stayed at home until her wedding.

MINOR MARRIAGES

The Nationalist legal codes pertaining to marriage did not outlaw the practice of minor marriages. This arrangement was widespread in the entire county of Bishan.[10] Stark poverty made it impossible for poor farm families to follow standard practices in arranging marriages for their sons and daughters. The most common solution was taking a young girl to raise as a future daughter-in-law, a little "foster fiancée" (*tongyangxi*). A large number of girls moved into the homes of their future husbands when they were quite young, perhaps even babies, and were raised by their future mothers-in-law. If the girl was two or three years old, the boy's family might give a small sum to the girl's parents in recognition of what her parents had spent on feeding her; if she was older, they would give somewhat more; if she was already ten or twelve and able to earn her own keep through work around the house or in the fields, they would have to present a more substantial sum. Despite the transfer of money, the system was not spoken of as purchasing a girl.

This method of contracting a marriage had advantages for both families involved. For the boy's family, it ensured them a future daughter-in-law in a community where boys outnumbered girls by fifty-five to forty-five.[11] It also reduced the expense to the relatively small initial payment and spread out the cost of feeding the youngster until she was old enough to pull her own weight. As for the girl's family, it relieved them of the expense of raising a daughter and providing her with a dowry. Both sides also suffered a loss. Unlike the standard marriage, which forged a link between two families, this type of marriage rarely established an ongoing link. Poverty steadily broke up scores of poor and landless families, causing them to disperse. Even where both families remained, the tie between a girl and the parents who had not brought her up often weakened.

In 1940–1941, there was a slight trend away from the foster fiancée pattern of marriage, due more to economic conditions than government initiatives. The price of rice, which before the Sino-Japanese War had sold at 1.40 yuan a *dou*, by December 1941 was up to 120 yuan a *dou*. Calculating the monetary cost of feeding a girl, some poor families decided against taking an extra mouth to feed. Others regretted having already brought in a foster fiancée, and if they had not had her long might look for an excuse to return her.

Life could be exceedingly harsh for these little fiancées. They were typically overworked and underfed. Often by the time these girls had reached their mid-twenties and thirties, they had become the mainstay and even the family head, having lost their parents-in-law or even their husbands.

While this form of marriage making was typical of the poor, some better-off families also took foster fiancées. This was often because a farm family had several sons and could not afford a traditional marriage for all of them. Since Brown and Yu's questionnaire was not designed to study internal family relations, they had no precise statistics on the prevalence of this form of marriage. But based on fourteen months of field research in Prosperity, Isabel Crook estimates that foster fiancées made up the majority of brides.

COMMON FORMS OF DIVORCE

Equally difficult to institute in the community of Prosperity was the notion that the state had the power to determine the terms for ending marriages. Although the municipal courts in the large cities of Beijing, Shanghai, and Chongqing had been issuing divorces for a number of years, legal divorces in Bishan were quite rare before 1940. One of the few suits filed with the Bishan court in the early 1940s was brought by a woman from a wealthy family, as was evident by the fact that she was willing to hand over the very large sum of one thousand yuan in the settlement, more than enough to enable her ex-husband to find another wife. She wrote in her divorce statement that there had been no happiness in the five years that the couple was married. But what is most interesting about this case is that she did not seek a judgment from the court. Rather, she just wanted to register her divorce agreement with them as a way of legitimating it. This action was similar to her decision to buy an advertisement in a Chongqing newspaper publicizing the fact that the couple had decided to divorce.

Few people in Bishan seemed interested in obtaining a legal divorce. Often the plaintiff did not seek a divorce but rather asked the court to make a wandering wife come home. In one case a woman who remarried for financial reasons after her husband had been away in the army for several years was charged with polygamy (*chonghun*).[12]

The few cases brought before the Bishan court that were connected to marriage issues were not primarily about divorce but rather were related to the complications connected with executing or enforcing a marriage agreement, with wartime disruptions adding to the difficulties. In one contentious case, forty-three-year-old Chen Nanxuan from Taihe Township petitioned the Bishan court to stop Luo Xingwei of Zitong from pestering him, sometimes in a belligerent manner, about honoring the marriage agreement they had entered into some years earlier. As Chen's son had been conscripted into the army in August of 1938, he was reluctant to incur the expense of the bride price plus the upkeep of the prospective daughter-in-law until his son returned home. The court in effect decided in favor of Chen by ordering the township authorities to prevent Luo from continuing to badger Chen, but it also indicated that there was no basis in the law for determining the validity of the marriage contract.[13] In another case, Gan Xiangquan, a Daoist priest, filed a petition with the court claiming that his wife had run off with another man who was quite wealthy, leaving him with two kids to raise. He sought to call the integrity of his wife into question by asserting in his statement to the court that his wife had a history of being unfaithful to him. While he asked the court to force his wife to come back to him, in fact he seemed more interested in gaining compensation for his loss, including the jewelry that he had given her. In yet another case, relatives of a man who had been conscripted into the army asked the court to take action against his wife. She had gotten a job in a small textile workshop in Danfeng in order to make ends meet after her husband went to war and had then moved in with a male coworker. Her incensed husband's relatives succeeded in having her imprisoned.[14]

For women, appealing to the law or courts might have seemed futile. Legal authorities were all male, and in general they did not want to become involved in family problems. When an occasional woman did appeal to the government, it was usually fruitless. For example, when Bishan began to be the target of Japanese air raids, Sheng Qingchen and his wife, residents of Bishan, moved to Prosperity where they rented some land and two rooms in the countryside. They brought with them their four children and their most prized possessions, which they crammed into the two rooms: fine carved furniture, lacquered red with gold trimmings, and pairs of porcelain vases with bunches of artificial glass and paper flowers.

But the husband, forty-two, treated his thirty-two-year-old wife badly. Apart from beating her, he banned her from the kitchen, claiming that she was a bad cook. The cooking was then entrusted to the eight-year-old son, while the wife was forced to work all day in the fields. On one occasion the beating was so brutal that the wife went to the township office in Prosperity to ask them to lodge an appeal in the Bishan County court over her maltreatment. The husband followed her to Prosperity where he beat and cursed her mercilessly in the street outside the government office. In this particular case bystanders did intervene to stop the beating, but they allowed the husband to drag his wife home before she could lodge her complaint. The township government was loath to get involved in family quarrels, so this woman had little hope of help from that source.

The difficulties of persuading married couples to use legal methods to end an unsatisfactory marriage may in large part have been a result of the myriad customary ways of contending with such situations. When a woman was abused by her husband, for example, she had a number of options. The simplest counter to a beating was to emit piercing screams, guaranteed to disturb the tranquility of the entire neighborhood. This would draw neighbors who in conciliatory tones would urge that the punishment was already adequate, or in irritable tones demand an end to the disturbance. Another option was the noisy quarrel, which could become violent with scratches, bites, blows, and tearing out of hair. Such quarrels inevitably drew public attention, but no matter how sympathetic the onlookers, no one would do more than urge conciliation. Even the local officials would refuse to intervene, since such quarrels were considered internal family matters. An abused woman's third option was to return to her maiden home, taking any children with her. Since her labor was important to the husband's farm and home, leaving was a powerful weapon. However, women's natal families usually believed in a husband's right to beat his wife and would only shelter her for a few days, perhaps slightly longer if she was conspicuously bruised and battered.

A final, and most extreme, way in which women contended with an abusive marriage was to commit suicide. A poor tenant farmer, Cai Shuting, married his daughter to the son of another poor farmer. The young husband, Yang Zhongchen, went to Chongqing as an apprentice, leaving his wife at home to help with the farming. But the twenty-year-old wife did not get along with her in-laws. She was so ill-treated that she committed suicide. Her natal family accused the Yangs of murdering their daughter. The Yangs were frightened and immediately invited priests to perform a funeral ceremony for the daughter-in-law. The Cais dropped the charge. No matter how angry they might have been over the death of their daughter, once a good funeral had been provided they could not expect to win a court case to have the Yangs punished.

Perhaps the most common way in which women dealt with problematic marriages was simply to leave. There were numerous examples in Prosperity of women who walked out of their marriages and found another spouse. Commonly referred to as runaway wives (*taoqi*), these women were compelled to flee because of unbearable ill treatment or poverty. Some might support themselves as day laborers, but many sought a better husband. They would travel by foot a distance of an hour or two from their fiancé's or husband's home and then begin loitering along the way, lingering especially on the outskirts of a market village, waiting to be picked up by someone looking for a partner either for himself, for a son, or for a poor relative. If the fugitive was not picked up in one place, she moved on to another, keeping a distance from her partner's home, for she was family property and a valuable source of labor.

The appearance in the village of a runaway fiancée or wife aroused the eager interest of those seeking a partner. Still, they were viewed with uneasiness. Might the woman be a perennial runaway and perhaps even have run off with some of the family's meager possessions? Or might she be the quarrelsome type? Might she commit some crime for which the new husband would now be held legally responsible? Yet despite these apprehensions, the fugitives almost always found partners, as women were in short supply.

In September 1940, a young woman appeared in Prosperity Market and hung about for a day or two. She freely replied to questions posed her. Soon everyone knew that she was the daughter-in-law of Wu Hailu, a small farmer up the hill at Xueyakou, that her husband had been conscripted the previous year and had not been heard from since, that her parents-in-law maltreated her, and that she was determined to leave them for good. Immediately a number of people were interested. Peng Shaohui, a twenty-nine-year-old laborer in the village still unmarried because of poverty, asked his widowed mother for permission to marry the woman. She refused. She had come from a prosperous farm family bankrupted only a decade earlier and could not relinquish hopes of a standard marriage for her eldest son. He reluctantly dropped the matter.

In another poor household in the village, Wu Chunzhi and his wife were on the lookout for a bride for their eighteen-year-old son, the eldest of three. They agreed that the woman looked promising, so Wu invited her to live with them and marry their son. The young woman, for her part, thought the prospect satisfactory and moved in. But she had no sooner done so than her father-in-law, Wu Hailu, arrived in Prosperity and compelled her to return to his farm. The young woman, however, did not submit to her forced retention and quarreled unremittingly. After a whole month of this, Wu Hailu and his wife could stand it no longer. The father-in-law himself brought the young woman to the village and negotiated with Wu Chunzhi for compensation. A sum was agreed upon, Wu Hailu relinquished his claim to the woman, and she was publicly recognized as Wu Chunzhi's daughter-in-law. During the following year the young woman made a name for herself in the village as a quiet, industrious, well-behaved daughter-in-law. People commented on the Wus' good fortune, and even Peng Shaohui's mother berated herself for having thrown away such a golden opportunity.

This example was not unusual. Families who lost a daughter-in-law or wife would seek to track her down, for her disappearance represented an economic loss, and they were legally entitled to seize her and take her home.

But often they found it preferable to settle for compensation instead. For the new husband, even if he had to pay compensation, the cost of the marriage with a fugitive was greatly reduced.

Among the poor, the accepted practice of marriage with a runaway wife meant that in reality a woman could divorce her husband, and her remarriage became legal when her new partner paid compensation to her former husband. This was in contrast to the accepted marriage practice that permitted only men to seek divorce (although women also had the legal right to do so). It was a reflection, on the one hand, of the crucial economic role played by women in poor families and the shortage of women in the community. On the other, it was a reflection of the harshness of the life for women among the poor. Unlike women in better-off families, they had little to lose.

While taking in a runaway was primarily a marriage stratagem of the poor, well-off families were also known to adopt such tactics in order to avoid expensive marriages for second or third sons. Such a case occurred in Prosperity in 1938. It began when a woman stranger arrived in the village. As she refused to say who she was or where she came from, someone suggested she must be a fugitive from the law and she was placed in the township lockup. No one turned up to lay any accusations against her, so after a few days she was released. She then went to Prosperity's cheapest inn, where she unaccountably stayed for another couple of days before disappearing as mysteriously as she had come.

Not long after this, the thriving but thrifty butcher Wang Chang'an announced that his twenty-five-year-old second son, Wang Haiyun, was engaged and soon to be married, the matchmaker being the young man's older married sister who lived in Bishan. On the appointed day the bride arrived in a red wedding sedan chair, clad in red and with a modest dowry. Guests and onlookers were impressed until one of them recognized the bride as the stranger of a few weeks before. Clearly Wang's subterfuge had enabled him to greatly scale down the cost of his second son's marriage. But it caused a storm of gossip and further confirmed Wang Chang'an's reputation as a miser. People speculated that Wang's daughter in Bishan had found (or enticed away) an unhappily married woman and had sent her to Prosperity to look over and be looked over by the Wangs, and that a secret agreement had been reached while she was staying at the inn.

This bride, like her new father-in-law, was the subject of unfavorable gossip. She was categorized as a brash woman and a perennial runaway type. But two years later the marriage was still holding, despite incessant quarrels between the couple in which neither side had any sympathizers, for both were considered equally at fault. Proof that the marriage was nevertheless acceptable to all concerned came when the Wangs paid a sizable indemnity to the woman's previous husband when he finally managed to track her down after a two-year search.

Wang Chang'an had made a decent traditional marriage for his eldest son. But he begrudged this expense for his other three sons. In addition to providing this mock-traditional marriage for his second son, he left his third soldier son unmarried, and his fourth son he allowed to marry out of his family and into a farm family with a daughter but no sons. While this type of marriage was considered very demeaning to the man, it provided him with an inheritance and relieved his family of an expensive wedding party.

The neighbor across the street was Zhou Dongchang, a forty-year-old laboring man who earned his living by helping the restaurateur, Zhang Yunheng, with such heavy jobs as butchering and carrying water. He had obtained the job through the offices of Zhang's wife, who was also of the Zhou lineage. In 1939, Zhou Dongchang had picked up a runaway wife and was considered a lucky man, for she turned out to be a quiet, hardworking woman who contributed to the couple's livelihood by hiring herself out by the day as a farm laborer. But no one in the village, even Zhou, learned anything of her background, for she hardly spoke at all.

Then in October 1940, Zhou's wife disappeared without explanation. Two months later she returned, saying only that she had taken employment as a live-in domestic. But a few weeks later, three men seized her in front of her home and took her to the township office, where she was charged with having stolen a peddler's stock of needles and thread. She was put in the village lockup to await the hearing of her case by the township head. Throughout the incident, Zhou stood in his doorway, apparently an indifferent spectator, though his kinswoman negotiated the woman's release, promising to stand guarantor.

In the course of the hearing the next day, the following story emerged. One market day back in October, a couple of fortune-tellers from Shizi market town came to Prosperity to set up their stands. When the pair returned home at the end of the day, Zhou's wife went with them. She stayed with the couple for a time but could find no way to earn her living, so she suggested that they arrange a match for her with their bachelor neighbor, a peddler named Lai. This was done. Lai was highly satisfied with his new wife, who even on occasion accompanied him on his rounds, carrying his wares for him. After two weeks the wife suggested they move to a safe place in the countryside, saying she feared that living in town she might be recognized by people who knew her husband in Prosperity. Lai agreed. A week after the move, the wife sent her husband off on an errand. When he returned, he found that she had absconded with his stock-in-trade. The woman had in fact returned to Shizi market town to the home of the original couple of fortune-tellers. But they in turn ran off with the needles and thread, leaving her stranded. It was at this point that she returned to Zhou. Lai, having lost his precious stock, now peddled cheap gourd dippers. As he traveled around the countryside he kept on the lookout for the wife who had robbed him. It took a month or more before he set up his stall in Prosperity and happened to catch sight of her. He immediately accosted her, but she insisted it was a case of mistaken identity and Lai let the matter rest. However, that very night when he returned home, he rounded up two young men friends, and the three of them came to Prosperity, where they put up in the cheapest inn to watch for the woman. But each morning before dawn she rose and went into the countryside to work as a farmhand, so it was not until the third day that they finally caught her.

When the hearing was over, the township head ruled that the woman was guilty of robbing Lai of his stock-in-trade valued at thirty yuan; he ordered Zhou to pay the sum to Lai; then he advised both Zhou and Lai to disown the woman publicly so as to clear themselves of responsibility for any future crimes she might commit. Zhou paid the indemnity without a murmur, the two men disowned her, and the woman departed for an unknown destination.

Six weeks later, the disowned wife returned to Prosperity. She walked into Zhou's house and set about tidying the place, ignoring Zhou, who stood in the doorway loudly ordering her to clear out. Next she prepared a meal. When it was ready and set out on the table, she took a hoe and went into the back garden to tend the vegetable patch. After some delay and seeming reluctance, Zhou sat down and ate the food. Toward evening the woman gathered some twigs and heated water for her husband, and Zhou enjoyed the rare luxury of washing in hot water. The following morning Zhou and his ex-wife could be seen silently hoeing the vegetable garden side by side. As one neighbor commented, "He would be a fool not to take her back. Where could he find another woman who is so quiet, able, and hardworking?"

Anyone could see that the quality of Zhou's life was immeasurably better when his wife was with him. But what of the woman? Why had she run away from Zhou? What was she seeking? She never gossiped or quarreled or even talked much. No one knew where she had come from, what sort of life she had led, or what she thought. And few, if any, knew her name or if she had one. Such self-effacement was a much-praised virtue in a woman.

Abusive treatment by husbands or mothers-in-law may have been the most common reason for women to leave and become "runaway wives," but it was not the only reason. Zhang Taizhi, for example, had married Hu Yunhua, the son of the poor village washerwoman Wu-Wang shi. When Hu went to Chongqing to seek work, Zhang was left to fend for herself. She left her mother-in-law's home and moved in with a widow friend of hers. Before long, teahouse proprietor and opium dealer Feng Qingyun started visiting her, and soon they were living together quite openly in Feng's village home. Feng had another home on his estate in the country, where his first wife and his children lived. Before long, Feng took Taizhi as a secondary wife, although not without some skirmishes with Zhang Taizhi's husband. When Hu learned the news of his wife's defection, he returned promptly to Prosperity and launched a protracted noisy quarrel demanding his wife's return. But in fact Hu had found work in a factory in Chongqing and had taken a wife and settled down there. He was simply hoping to make a profitable deal with the prosperous Feng. But Feng moved Taizhi secretly to a place in Bishan, and when Hu tracked her down, he moved her to Chongqing but was again discovered. Since Feng still did not offer to compensate him, Hu took the matter to court in Bishan. Smart young men of the village poor, unlike the ordinary country poor, had strong patrons and dared tangle with the prosperous and influential. In this instance, the two parties had a seeming parity, so the outcome of the court case was satisfactory all around. Hu was deemed to have deserted his wife, since he had left her unprovided for; hence she had been entitled to remarry. Still, Hu was a poor man and hence was entitled to compensation "so that he could afford to remarry." The prosperous Feng was directed to pay him eighty yuan in compensation, a fairly sizable sum in 1937 when inflation rates were far lower than later. Nevertheless, even Feng was satisfied with the ruling, for it legalized his possession of this attractive woman. He was careful to make a public display of handing over the sum so that Hu could not claim later that Feng still owed him the money. Hu returned to his second wife in Chongqing well satisfied. As for Taizhi, the transaction had elevated her position from mistress to secondary wife.[15]

CONCLUSION

The war stimulated some major changes in Chinese politics and society, including marriage practices in the rural township of Prosperity, but they were limited and more connected to indirect influences than to the efforts of the government to enforce its legal codes. The large influx of downriver people who brought many new ideas and practices facilitated some minor shifts, as did the rapidly shifting economic realities. The arranged marriage system remained unchanged. The gap between what the government aimed to achieve and what it was actually able to accomplish was large. Government directives, laws, and propaganda campaigns to alter marriage practices were based on a bold vision by Nationalist reformers who sought to modernize the family, a vision influenced by Western models and supported by Christian and secular reformers. But in large part, the Nationalist government failed to implant its urban-based vision in rural society, as it was unable to create social legitimacy and support for its proposed reforms, particularly in its efforts to replace customary marriage practices with codified laws.

NOTES

1. Bernhardt (1994), pp. 190–191.
2. Zang Xiaowei (1999).
3. In Taitou a young bride was not desired because she was not yet capable of taking on a heavy workload. As a result, no woman in this community married before the age of seventeen. The average age of a couple at the time of marriage was twenty (Yang 1945, p. 113).
4. Bishan dang'anguan (1940). These Bishan County archival materials, as well as others discussed in this chapter, were provided to us by Liu Jing, an archivist at the Chongqing Municipal Archives. Unfortunately, these files did not have case numbers attached to them.
5. This assessment was reached through a combination of observations by Isabel Brown and Yu Xiji in 1940 and 1941, and interviews with fifty elderly people in the community in late January 2004.
6. "Jianchabao zaohun" (1943).
7. "Jianchabao zaohun" (1943).
8. John Lossing Buck (1937/1964).
9. Because Wang Junliang had asked for an immediate date for the wedding of his son, giving the Zhang family only two weeks' notice, it was acceptable for the bride's parents to send money rather than a complete set of furniture, which normally would have included a large lacquered wardrobe, chests, tables, and chairs.
10. The 1996 Bishan Gazetteer did not provide any exact figures for *tongyangxi*, merely stating that the practice was very common (Sichuan sheng Bishan xianzhi, 1996, p. 74).
11. This ratio was determined by Crook and Yu and is included in table 3 of chapter 1 in Isabel Crook's manuscript.
12. Bishan dang'anguan (1940). See note 3.
13. Bishan shiyan difang fayuan (n.d.).
14. Bishan shiyan difang fayuan (1941).
15. For a detailed analysis of runaway wives among lower-class women in Beijing, see Zhao (2007).

Chapter Nine

Of Money and Men

Late one night in June 1941, a prosperous farmer was awakened by the sound of guards hammering on his door and then battering it open. They had been sent by the township head to raid his home and seize at least one of his sons to serve in the army. He put up stiff resistance, long enough for all his sons to escape. However, realizing that he was going to be in trouble, the next day he sent one of his sons to volunteer for military service. As he had anticipated, the guards lost no time in formally charging him with violent resistance. He at once filed a countercharge, accusing the guards of breaking in and stealing several bundles of cotton yarn and other property, and demanding reimbursement for his losses as well as a prison sentence for the culprits. The guards claimed they had taken nothing and stressed that they had identified themselves as guards when they knocked at the door. When the dispute was mediated, the farmer reportedly declared, "Bandits always claim to be guards when breaking in at night. If you were coming as guards, why didn't you come in the daytime?" To which the guards replied, "We had to come at night because we were trying to conscript one of your sons." The farmer retorted that his sons were happy to serve in the army, as evidenced by the fact that one had already volunteered. He not only won the suit but received compensation for his alleged losses, even though one son was sent to the army.

For many of Prosperity's residents, the threat of conscription intensified during the wartime years. Although the goals of army service may have been more compelling than during the warlord era, the methods of recruitment and conditions of army life continued to be dreaded by rural families. Furthermore, wartime conditions caused the government to escalate its demands for military recruits. This was accompanied by an intensification of taxation. Township or *bao* heads were required to turn over the grain and manpower

225

demanded by higher levels or face punishment. This chapter explores the fact that in spite of its attempts to modernize rural China through such projects as administrative and marriage reform, and by increasing the availability of education and health care, the most significant experience of the Nationalist government for many residents of Prosperity was its demands for taxes and for young men to serve as soldiers and laborers.

TAXATION

When the Nationalist government was established, one of the major problems it had to address was the extreme burden of taxation on peasants that had been imposed by local warlords. Tax reform legislation introduced in 1935 sought to provide some relief. However, the outbreak of war with Japan in 1937, subsequent military defeats, and the relocation of the central government to Chongqing resulted in an increased need for food and finance from a diminished territory in order to support the army and civil administration. In spite of fresh efforts at tax reform in 1939, demands for money and grain from the countryside became even more intense.

The traditional land tax (*zhengliang*) was payable in money. But with the heavy wartime demand for grain along with rapidly rising inflation, the central government decreed that the tax be paid in kind. This increased the center's power over the provinces where the grain was collected and provided the government with revenues that could actually feed the armies and provide food allowances to officials to compensate for the steady devaluation of their salaries. [1]

In Prosperity in 1940 the man in charge of the collection center as well as the public granary for storing grain against famine was Feng Qingyun, whose career is discussed more fully in chapter 10. The nonstandard instruments that Feng used to measure the grain compounded a situation in which assessments of land ownership were anything but uniform.

The amount owed was based on the land deed issued by the county authorities, which included the size of the field and a detailed description of its boundaries. It also included the tax assessment, and no new deed was issued until all outstanding land tax had been paid to the authorities. Each division of the land, whether through inheritance or sale, brought with it a division of the land tax. This was not necessarily proportionate but was open to negotiation. A man whose desperate need for cash forced him to sell a portion of his land could get a higher price for it if he passed over a smaller proportion of the tax. In the course of over two centuries of division and redivision, anomalies had appeared, with some fields becoming more heavily taxed than others and more of the tax burden being shifted onto the poorer and weaker landowners.

It seemed unlikely that there was any unregistered rice land in Prosperity, since the official land deed afforded legal recognition of ownership in a situation where acute land shortage inevitably led to disputes and litigation. However, the officially registered figures did not accurately reflect the size of holdings, nor did the tax assessment bear close relation to the yield, especially in the case of well-off and influential families. The central government was well aware of the flaws in tax assessments, which were affecting state revenues, but solving the problem was not easy.

The system of land measurement was one complicating factor. The uneven terrain in much of Sichuan made linear measurement difficult, and a system of computing area by yield had evolved. This adopted the volume measures for grain—the *dan* and *dou*—as area measures. (A slight modification in the writing of the characters distinguished each of these two pairs of homophones.) One *dan* was the area of land required to produce one *dan* of unhusked rice. The *dou* was a tenth of a *dan*. The actual yield of a particular field naturally varied from year to year, but its output figure on the land deed was fixed, based on the results achieved in earlier years. Even if the land improved or deteriorated over the years, this did not alter its registered size. Instead, people spoke, for instance, of a "good" two-*dan* field or a "poor" one. Since rice land was more productive than unirrigated land, there was a big discrepancy in the area of a *dou* or *dan* of these two types of farmland. To rectify tax assessments, the government called for a re-registration of land throughout Sichuan. By 1941, according to John Lossing Buck, three-fourths of all counties had completed it, thereby increasing taxable land by at least two-thirds.[2] In Bishan County, however, no signs of this were visible.

Nonstandard systems of measurement had a social significance beyond simple tax evasion. They put any outsider wishing to buy or rent land at a disadvantage. He could not easily make an accurate estimate of the size of a field. And for him an additional complication was the local custom of taking the many irregular patches of arable dryland which knitted together the innumerable tiers of paddy fields or upland fields as adjuncts of their bordering fields. These served as bargaining points when fields were being rented or sold. Unless the would-be buyer or renter could find a local middleman he could trust, he could easily be cheated. Such factors played some part in keeping the land in the hands of native-born families of the community and bolstering localism.

Any outsider involved in land surveys encountered a further complication. The units of weights and measures used in Sichuan at this time were still not standardized, despite the efforts made by Republican government to introduce the metric system nationwide. In Prosperity in 1940, there were three different-sized *dan* and *dou* in use: the "old" *dan*, the "new" *dan*, and the "standard" *dan*. Throughout this book, we use the "new" *dan*, since this was what Crook and Yu's informants favored and because in Sichuan at this time it was equated with a *mu*, the unit of land measurement common throughout the rest of China. Officials in their dealings, however, used the "standard" *dan*.

As for the system of land measurement by yield and the faulty land registration and tax assessments, local people took these anomalies for granted. We heard no complaints even from those with poor-yield, overtaxed land. Seemingly anything that strengthened the community against outside interests was seen as protection for all. Furthermore, the chief beneficiaries were the leading local landowners, whom many members of the community cultivated as patrons that they could turn to in time of need.

More burdensome than the land tax were the various grain levies: the military rice levy for the army, as well as a fodder (grain and straw) levy for its horses (*junxu fei* or *maliang macao*); the rice allowance for soldiers' dependents in the *bao* (*zhuangding liang*); the levy of rice for storage against famine (*jigu* or *yigu*); the supplementary grain allowances for township officials and teachers; and the rice levy for the maintenance of the local militia (*mintuan fei*). In addition to the grain levies, there were monetary ones; for instance, there was a levy to pay the wages of men sent by the *bao* for corvée labor on public works, and another to provide gifts to soldiers' families on various occasions or to pay for such things as army uniforms. In Prosperity, complaints about the grain levies were endless.[3]

The most onerous levy was rice for the army. Several times a year the township head would be notified that within three days a specified amount of unhusked rice should be brought to the township collection center for shipment to the county. The township head would notify the *bao* heads, and they in turn would notify the *jia* heads. Officially only those with twenty *shidan* (market *dan*) or more were liable to pay. But a *bao* head, especially one with a strong patron, could adjust payments to some extent, shifting the burden from some to others. Furthermore, there were loopholes. Small farms were typically the result of a partition of the land that took place with the division of the family, usually at the death of the parents. However, to avoid eligibility for grain levies, and likewise conscription, some households had carried out a nominal division of the family and the property. The *bao* heads used their own discretion in deciding which household divisions were genuine and which false.

Sun Juchang, for example, after the division of the family several years earlier, owned a farm of eighteen market *dan*, just two under the limit for paying the rice levy. It was difficult to determine whether the division was genuine or not. Sun was a young man in his twenties, and his parents were still alive. Sun's wife had become mentally deranged, and no one but he could or would get along with her. Nevertheless, the *bao* head decided he should pay. Sun refused, and the *bao* head reported him to the township head, who put pressure on Sun personally. "Think of the soldiers fighting at the front," the township head pleaded. "All we are asking of you is a trifle. Contributing rice is the honorable duty of those not in the army." Sun replied that he would just as soon be a soldier as pay an unjust levy. On the grounds that he had thus volunteered for service, the township head had him thrown into the village lockup to await transfer to the army induction center in the county. Early the following morning, before the young man had been sent off, influential kinsmen called on the township head to apologize for the young man's behavior and to ask that he be forgiven. That evening Sun was released and returned home quite chastened. As this instance shows, despite official regulations, which individuals were expected or forced to pay, the tax was to a considerable extent in the hands of the local officials.

Similarly, local officials had considerable say in how much was actually collected. When a delivery of public grain fell due, the county authorities notified each township head of his quota in strict confidence. The latter could then inflate the figure and divide it among his *bao*, notifying each *bao* head of the amount to be handed over, again in strict confidence. The *bao* head could in his turn inflate the figure before openly announcing to the eligible households of the *bao* the quota they must fulfill. After the collection the *bao* head turned over to the township what had been demanded and kept the balance. The township head did likewise. Local inhabitants therefore paid more than the central government authorized, subsidizing local officials at all levels.

Once the military rice levy was collected in Prosperity, the army was responsible for transporting it to Bishan. On the appointed day, a contingent of soldiers would arrive with carrying poles and baskets. At such times, the underlying resentment over the levies could cause considerable friction between the soldiers and local inhabitants. For example, one day in September 1940, just after the rice harvest, fifty-odd soldiers arrived to transport a consignment of rice. But despite three days' notice, the quotas had not yet been delivered from the *bao*, and messengers were sent out to hurry them along. The soldiers, eager to get back before dark, became increasingly impatient. But the township head was able to silence the grumbling by pointing to the office clock (the only clock in the village, apart from that belonging to the NCC team), which he had turned back a few hours. By the time all the rice reached the village, the clock said 3 p.m., even though darkness was falling. Forced to spend the night in the village, the frustrated soldiers devoted the evening to picking quarrels with local inhabitants.

If the rice was to be consumed by troops stationed in Bishan, the soldiers were required to bring back the grain already milled. This meant commandeering mills in farm homes. On such occasions, more serious problems could arise. It was hazardous for a local official to intervene. As described in chapter 6, one inexperienced young township head was thrown into a military prison because he chastised soldiers for beating up a local farmer.

SALES TAXES

In addition to the levies, Prosperity residents also had to deal with the burden of numerous sales and enterprise taxes. The rates were legislated by the state while the collection was the responsibility of the county authorities. Having no way of monitoring the myriad transactions taking place in the dozens of market villages under its jurisdiction, county officials auctioned tax collection rights to local bidders who knew their own market. This practice, dating back to the Qing, was not affected by the Nationalist government's tax reforms.

At the end of each year the Bishan County government auctioned off the following rights for the coming year: the rice sales tax (along with a 1 percent surcharge toward school expenses); the livestock sales tax of 3 percent; the retail sales tax on shops and street stalls collected separately at 2 percent of monthly profits (with a recently added surcharge of 0.4 percent to be handed over to the township authorities for "self-governing" expenses); the coal sales tax of three *jin* per *dan*, paid in kind; the salt sales tax; the pig-butchering tax (*tuzai shui*) at 3 yuan for pigs slaughtered for sale, and 1.50 for those butchered for home consumption (rates which rose to 5 and 3 respectively in 1941); and the cotton home-weaving tax of 1 percent of profits. While the collection rights for all these taxes were auctioned off separately for each market village, the collection of taxes on larger enterprises, like the distillery and the flour mill, was auctioned for a larger area of several market villages. These enterprises were taxed for each day of operation, the former at 7 yuan per day, the latter at 1.40 yuan.

A contender for a particular tax, such as the rice sales tax, estimated how great the sales of rice might be in his particular market in the coming year and on this basis made a bid, allowing a margin of profit for himself to repay his efforts. The county government then awarded the collection right to the highest bidder. Competition was counted on to bring the bids up to an optimum level. In Prosperity, however, aspiring local tax farmers colluded to keep the bids low. Sometimes, as a result of private bargaining among contenders, only one attended the auction and won the bid uncontested. At other times the rivals submitted precisely the same bid and then used political maneuvering to secure the prize. The three most desired tax farming opportunities were the rice sales tax, the livestock sales tax, and the pig-butchering tax.

TAX COLLECTION AND THE RISE OF FENG QINGYUN

The problems the central government encountered in trying to extend its authority to the local level were epitomized in the person of Feng Qingyun—

opium dealer, teahouse proprietor, and a member of Commander Cai's informal power faction. Feng's original capital was derived from his estate, which he used to become an entrepreneur in the market village. Capitalizing on his Paoge connections, he added greatly to his assets by becoming one of the three main opium dealers in Prosperity, an activity tied to the Paoge ports. His success in the teahouse and his opium dealing in turn allowed him to develop his connections sufficiently to be appointed keeper of the Famine Relief Granary. This practice, which dated from the Sui dynasty (589–618 CE), was intended to provide a reserve store of publicly owned rice in times of famine.[4] The storage-against-famine rice levy was payable by owners of twenty *shidan* of rice land and collected by the *bao* heads. Feng was a formidable man, so though people grumbled about the oversized measure he used when they delivered the grain, we never heard anyone challenge him openly over his cheating.[5] The grain was supposed to be stored in the village granary in the charge of a locally appointed official, but during the warlord years the looting of granaries by warlord armies became so rife that the public grain was lent out to private dealers for profit. Feng Qingyun, as keeper of this public granary in these uncertain times, could take full advantage of the earning power of this stored rice without much heed for community interests. Thus, when a serious drought occurred in the early spring of 1940, Feng was able to resist pressures to call back the one hundred *dan* of public rice even though people suffered acute hunger.[6]

Related to the land tax was the tax or fee for putting the official stamp on any new deed of sale or mortgage of land or housing. Without this stamp, no deed was legally effective. The fee came to 3 percent of the value of the transaction. It was collected by a government-authorized agent. In Prosperity the man, again, was Feng Qingyun.

In Prosperity Market, the rice sales tax and the livestock sales tax had customarily gone to the same person. In 1939, the year prior to our arrival, both were collected by Sun Zhonglu, leader of the modernizer clique of the elite, who at the time was serving as township head. But at the end of the year, Sun did not attend the auction for the 1940 rights. Feng Qingyun's bid was uncontested. People surmised that Feng had given Sun some compensation, for there was no acrimony.

The following year, however, the bidding was a prolonged and contentious affair. Two men put in bids for the 1941 rights: Feng Qingyun and the newly appointed head of Prosperity Township, Tang Gongyi, whose brief career was discussed in chapter 6. The two rivals submitted precisely the same estimates. At the same time each went to the county financial committee to press his case. Feng pleaded that he was a local man and the current collector; Tang countered that his salary as township head was inadequate and he needed to supplement his income. The authorities acknowledged the legitimacy of the latter's claim and designated Tang. However, they were unable to finalize the appointment until they had investigated charges of corruption in the collection of military rice levies made against Tang by anonymous local inhabitants (that is, members of Feng's group). When New Year's Day came and went without confirmation of the appointment, both candidates began collecting both taxes. Here the township head had the advantage, since rice sales took place in the temple courtyard right where he had his office. But Feng had considerable success in collecting the livestock sales tax, with some unfortunate farmers being forced to pay twice. Since Tang had the local militia at his disposal, he decided to put a stop to such encroachment. One market day, he set a watch on Feng to catch him red-handed, but Feng had been tipped off and did not try to collect taxes that day.

At the end of January, the county reached a compromise settlement on the corruption charges against the township head. Tang was found not guilty of corruption, but nevertheless he was transferred back to his own home township of Zitong as head and replaced in Prosperity by a new man. Feng was officially confirmed as the collector. He lost no time in initiating a court case against Tang, suing him for a refund of the January taxes already collected. The county dismissed the suit. Feng then rounded up a bunch of tough-looking supporters, went to Zitong Market, and set up a commotion outside the township office, with his strong-arm friends shouting, "Haul out the township head and beat him up!" Tang was not intimidated, and Feng dared not have his men enter and seize him. In the end Feng never did succeed in collecting these back taxes.

Later in the year a quarrel brought into the open the fact that Feng, as collector of these two sets of taxes, was not operating on his own. He was the manager of a group of about ten local men whom he had banded together to put up the required capital for a number of moneymaking ventures, including tax collection. The group included Yang Heling, proprietor of a prosperous general store; Zhang Yunheng, proprietor of a village restaurant and a cloth trader; and a number of other comfortably off residents. The one incongruous member—incongruous because he lacked the capital to invest—was Yang Guifan, an intelligent, personable young farmer who had just set up his own tailoring business. It was through this young man that some of the inner workings of the group were exposed. Yang Guifan had been invited to join because the group wished to hide behind an innocuous front man for some of the ventures. He had thought he was a full-fledged member of the group until he found that behind his back, letters addressed to him were handed directly to Feng by group member Yang Heling, who also ran the village post office. The young man filed a suit against Yang for violation of his private mail. The quarrel escalated, and as a result the following confidential matters concerning the group's tax dealings became known.

The group had raised an initial capital of about 7,000 yuan, of which 3,010 were bid and went to the county finance committee for the rice and livestock sales tax concessions. During February, the group's first month of undisputed authority, it collected an average of around one hundred yuan each market day. With ten market days a month, it would meet its complete year's estimate of 3,010 yuan in three months, giving eight months' clear profit, or 8,000 yuan, even after deducting the 1,000 yuan lost to Tang in the first month.

For these two major taxes, the government received only one-quarter of the money collected by their agent. For the third major tax—the pig-butchering tax—it may have done somewhat better.

COLLECTING THE PIG-BUTCHERING TAX

In 1940, the collector of the pig-butchering tax was once again Feng Qingyun. At the auction on the eve of 1941, Prosperity's largest landowner Cao Yuexian and his friend Commander Cai Xunqing submitted a joint bid and won the concession uncontested. Yet in the new year Feng continued to collect, though now in the name of Cai and Cao. No details emerged on the manner in which Cai and Cao had cut in on Feng's profits, nor on how the proceeds were divided between them. What became public knowledge was that the bid Cai and Cao had tendered was based on an estimate of eight pigs slaughtered for sale each market day. But any local inhabitant knew that a realistic figure would have been thirteen. With one hundred market days a year and an intake of five yuan a head, the agents took in sixty-five hundred yuan, of which they handed over four thousand yuan to the state. Hence, a minimum of 40 percent of the state revenue from this tax on pigs slaughtered for sale was going into the pockets of the local tax farmers.

Having failed to keep their bids confidential, Cai and Cao did not deny the facts. Instead they talked much about their motive in underbidding, which was to accumulate funds for village improvement. However, no visible improvements materialized in the course of the year.

Unlike the taxes on pigs butchered for market, no information leaked out on the estimates made for pigs slaughtered for home consumption or the sums collected. This was a more difficult tax to collect. Only a local man with a wide network of friends and relatives could keep a check on over a thousand farm homes scattered over an area of twenty square kilometers. Anyone who detected and reported a tax evasion could expect a reward.

One day in the spring of 1940, Feng Qingyun's brother happened to meet a man carrying butchering equipment. It turned out that the man was going to Wujiaba to butcher a pig for the Wu clan's Qingming celebration. The brother hurried home at once to check whether the Wu clan had paid the tax. They had not. As a reward, Feng Qingyun authorized him to confiscate the pig and keep it. Taking two township guards with him, he hurried to Wujiaba and caught the Wu family red-handed. Rather than surrender their banquet pig, they paid a fine of eighty yuan. The guards each got ten yuan for their services and the brother pocketed the remaining sixty yuan.

Through tax farming, opium dealing, and a host of other ventures, Feng Qingyun continued to augment his power as a member of that segment of the Paoge involved in the underground economy. Unlike his fellow members of Prosperity's elite, Sun and Cai, he seemed not to care about his public image. He moved steadily to the fore during 1940–1941. By autumn 1941, Feng was not only the county-appointed collector of the land tax in kind for Prosperity Township and keeper of the public granary, but he had also won an increasing number of the most profitable farmed taxes, including the rice sales tax, the livestock sales tax, and the pig-butchering tax. The only field to which he had not gained access was the *baojia* collections. For this he would have to become township head. (Within a few years of our departure, he did just that.) Feng could only have accomplished this through powerful connections he had forged in the county and beyond. From the standpoint of the central government, unless such local tentacles of power were chopped off, reforms in the field of taxes could hardly be expected to succeed.

The central government had renewed its reform efforts in 1939, but by late 1941 the overall situation was not encouraging. A failure to dismantle local structures of power meant that taxes were falling increasingly under the control of the more venal figures in the community. In the course of these two years of reform, Feng had come to dominate tax collection.

The key to the enforcement of the promulgated tax reform lay with the county government. But despite the fact that the county head himself favored the reforms, he was an outsider and apparently could not function without the support of the local landowning elite. And it was certain members of the local elite that most profited from tax collection, at the expense of both local people and the state. The burden of grain levies fell most heavily on the middle and small farmers, who were forced to give more than was legally required while lacking the political strength to protect themselves against illegal exactions.

CONSCRIPTION

If government demands for taxes alienated the less prosperous residents of Prosperity, demands for conscripts proved to be even more damaging. The impact of conscription is suggested by the fact that by summer 1940 roughly two-thirds of the men of military age were absent from Prosperity. An estimated 1,123 were serving in the army, through conscription, press-ganging, or enlistment, while others left the area to evade service.

Conscription law defined three types of military or paramilitary service: active military service, reserve service, and corvée or conscripted labor for public works. Men were classified according to their eligibility for each. All men aged eighteen to thirty-six were eligible for active military service. Recognizing that most households, with wives and young children or with dependent parents, could not easily dispense with the man's labor or earnings, the state issued laws prescribing exemptions for heads of families; only sons; civil servants (township, *bao*, or *jia* heads, or guards in the local militia); students; and middle school graduates.[7] The number of sons that could be conscripted from one family was also fixed; in 1940 this was raised from two out of five to three. Men aged thirty-seven to forty-two were eligible for unpaid service in the reserve corps. Men exempted from active service were also eligible for the reserves, as were township officials. A 1940 directive required the township head to serve as captain of the corps. Corps members lived and worked at home but were supposed to undergo military training organized by the local government to prepare them for emergency call-up. Finally, men aged forty-three to forty-eight were eligible for conscription to work crews. When laborers were needed for construction of public works such as highways and airfields, men from this age group were pressed into service.

These exemption clauses affected Prosperity's residents differently, depending primarily on their economic status. Most young men of gentry and merchant families were exempted under the clause making secondary school graduates or students ineligible for conscription. A fair proportion of the young men of the typically small nuclear or stem families of the poor were exempt as well, being covered by the clause making the only son or the head of a family ineligible. Some men from poor families gained exemption by serving as guards in the local militia. Although most guards came from among the village poor, by 1941 at least two were from families of stratum 3 farmers who had joined simply to gain exemption from conscription. One of these was Zhang Fuliang, from a small farm on the outskirts of the village. Zhang had a brother, which made him eligible for service in the army. But his brother was still too small for heavy work, and his father was disabled. Serving in the militia suited Zhang Fuliang well since, being close at hand, he could return home for any heavy work that was needed. But such men were still the exception. Most country people considered the guards a disreputable and unscrupulous bunch.

It was the young men of farm families of stratum 2 and some of the managing-to-get-by farm families of stratum 3 who were legally most eligible because they were members of the ideal extended family which was granted minimum legal protection. In an undivided three-generation family, for example, the family head was exempt from service, while a proportion of his sons were eligible. Furthermore, even if sons in the extended family were already in their forties and thus too old for active service, some grandsons would be reaching military age. Since all grandsons in such a family counted as siblings, being an only son of a son did not exempt a man. According to the conscription law, therefore, most soldiers should come from strata 2 and 3. In fact, however, they were press-ganged from the poorest families of stratum 4.

The conscription regulations had a gendered dimension, as the clause "only son" referred to the only son of a man, not of a woman. For example, one woman we knew forced herself to drown her newborn only son. She had married a widower with one son. The man had become partially disabled, and the nineteen-year-old son did the major part of the work on the farm. The birth of another son deprived the older lad of his exemption. Since the family could not dispense with his labor, the mother had to give up her baby. In contrast, another woman we knew had three sons, each the only son of three different husbands, and thus none was eligible for military service.

At the county level, the conscription process was in the hands of the officer heading the county department of military affairs. He derived from the censuses the names of all those of military age not qualified for exemptions. When the army asked for a new batch of recruits, the officer divided the quota among the townships and notified each how many to send. The township head, in turn, notified each *bao* head to deliver to the recruitment center the men whose names were at the top of the list in his *bao*. The problem was that, although the quotas were secret, the name lists were public. Consequently the men high on the list were usually nowhere to be found. This procedural problem was solved in 1940 by making the lists confidential. The county department of military affairs now met four times a year in secret, drew lots among the men eligible, and sent each township a secret list. Then, when the township head was sent a quota, he made up a list for each *bao* of the names of the men to be turned over to the recruitment center. Although this procedure might have seemed straightforward, in fact its implementation was shaped by economic status in a way that made the poorest residents in Prosperity far more vulnerable to conscription.

Large families of relatively prosperous farmers were the most liable to be required to provide conscripts. However, they were also most able to use their wealth and status in a number of ways to avoid the conscription of their sons. The first means was to arrange for the falsification of the census by either changing a man's age or even deleting his name altogether. *Bao* heads did this for their friends and relatives as well as for those who paid them. In autumn 1941, for example, leading members of the Cao family issued vociferous complaints that the *bao* head, Wu Deqing, had omitted the names of young men with his surname from the census. As a result of the complaints, Wu was transferred to become head of a different *bao*, and Cao Dongyang, a fifty-year-old weaver, took his place. He restored the names of the Wu family, but omitted eligible men from the Cao clan. In another *bao*, the head had one of his relatives entered on the census as age twelve, even though he was sixteen; in another, a seventeen-year-old was recorded as thirty-four, and two brothers aged thirty and forty were entered in the census as forty-three and forty-eight, respectively. Falsification of age did not always prevent conscription, as in some cases local officials seized men who were obviously of military age.

In addition to offering financial bribes to falsify the census, prosperous peasants could also purchase deferments from the *bao* head, for whom the sale of deferments became a significant source of income. This was facilitated by the fact that both the quota and the list of names he received were secret. In his *bao*, he could notify any family with some economic potential that one of their sons was on the list. He would then offer to arrange a deferment or to find a substitute. At the beginning of 1940, a one-year deferment cost two hundred yuan. But as time went on, deferments not only became more expensive but also less reliable. By late 1940, the pressure for conscripts grew so great and the protests of families with sons in the army so vociferous that *bao* heads had little alternative but to try to conscript some eligible sons of better-off families despite their payments. In this context, these families employed several strategies to protect their sons: dividing an extended family so as to establish all the adult sons as family heads, securing an appointment as *bao* or *jia* head for the eligible family member, or sending that son to school.

These strategies are illustrated by the case of Wu Xueshan, a comfortable farmer with four sons, the youngest already fourteen. His wife explained how the family had protected them. "First, we divided our rice land, giving each son his share." (Whether in this case each son was actually given a deed for his share, which would make it a genuine division, was left vague.) "Our eldest son rented a twenty-*dan* farm on the boundary of the township, and our third son rented a farm in the neighboring township of Zitong. They have separate households, so both count as family heads. Besides, our eldest son got himself appointed as *jia* head, and this affords protection to our second son, who lives at home with us." (In fact, the whole farm was being cultivated by the father and second son despite the alleged division of the property.) "Our fourth son is only fourteen, and we're keeping him at school so he'll be exempt."

Family divisions had potentially negative consequences. For example, Zhou Shuming, eligible for conscription, left his father's home and rented twenty *dan* of land where he moved with his wife and two children. His father was shorthanded without Zhou's labor, so Zhou ended up taking his aged grandmother to live with him in an effort to reduce the burden on his father.

Wang Zhoulin of *bao* 8 was one of three brothers, the youngest of whom was serving in the army. Though the family had divided ten years before, Wang suddenly felt vulnerable when his soldier brother deserted. He disappeared, giving his wife no warning. We found her in a state of acute anxiety, for this was the busiest farm season, and it would be hard to hire help since most laborers had already been spoken for and most farmers were tied up with mutual aid.

Falsification of age or deletion of a name could keep a young man's name off the official county lists of those to be recruited, but it could not prevent him from being seized locally as a man obviously of military age. In *bao* 9, a certain Sun family had seven sons, only one of whom had his age correctly recorded. The seventeen-year-old was recorded as thirty-four, and the recorded ages of the others ranged from thirty-five up to forty-six. Despite this, the second and third sons had both been taken. In *bao* 4, as well, Yang Bailing, a tenant on thirty *dan*, had succeeded in having his two sons who were aged thirty and forty entered in the census as forty-three and forty-eight. But the younger son was conscripted regardless.

Under these circumstances, some well-off peasants preferred to send their young men away to seek jobs in government factories or offices in Bishan town or Chongqing. For instance, the brothers Sun Yichang and Sun Juchang were both of military age. The family had divided its eighteen *dan* of rice land some years before, but neither felt secure from conscription. The older brother rented out his land to tenants and went to Chongqing where he got a job as a laborer in the military oil depot, an achievement that could only have been accomplished with backing or a bribe. The second brother succeeded in getting into the local township militia, which required similar measures for entry. As half the young weavers in Prosperity were of military age, many of them left the town to seek jobs elsewhere and avoid conscription. They were sometimes able to gain work as skilled weavers in comfortably off households outside of Prosperity. As a result, a substantial number of both the native and standard looms in the village were idle.

Sometimes the evasion tactics of the better-off large families were enacted at the expense of poorer and weaker families. Two neighboring farm families each had four sons. The Huang family, which farmed a minute two *dou* of rice land along with one *dan* of dryland, already had two sons serving in the army. Meantime, the Luo family, prosperous tenant farmers on sixty *dan* of rice land, had no sons conscripted, but by 1941 they had become apprehensive. Luo approached Huang to see if he might hire his third son, now sixteen, as a farmhand. Huang was delighted, and the boy went to live in the Luo home. He had worked there only a little more than a month when guards made a night raid. Luo, on the alert, roused his own sons and sent them out the back door to hide up the mountainside. The guards seized the sleeping farmhand and took him to the assembly point in Prosperity. On learning the news, the boy's mother hurried to the township to intercede, but the guards claimed that because he had been taken into the Luos' home, he counted as a conscript of the Luo family. The Huang family, left with only their fourteen-year-old son, immediately sent him to Bishan to live with his married sister in the hope that he would be safe there.

Many families with large farms were unwilling to break up the family or to dispense with the labor power of their young men. They kept them at home in hiding and in moments of danger stood guard with guns to prevent their seizure. Hu Songling of *bao* 1, a farmer in his sixties, had three sons of military age. The family lived in trepidation, despite the fact that two of the sons had been entered as heads of separate households, the third was absent, and a close relative was their *jia* head. The two sons at home rarely ventured far afield. Everyone knew that the house was guarded by a pack of four fierce dogs and that the family kept a gun and a fair supply of cartridges. Another farmer, Shi Xiangling of *bao* 5, who had three registered sons of military age and a fourth unregistered, was put in the township lockup on two occasions for forcibly holding off the guards when they were sent to take a son. On each occasion he was released after a few days since there was no provision for holding prisoners in the township on a long-term basis, and a gift to the militia captain or township head might have helped.

Prosperous farmers who were caught evading the conscription of their sons could bribe their way out. Wang Hanchen, a well-off thirty-year-old farmer who engaged in the cloth trade, was seized one market day by the Bishan County guards. He had enough money on him to bribe one of the guards, a Prosperity man named Mao. Though Mao let him go, Wang had personal enemies who had connived to have him conscripted. Frustrated in their attempts, they went to the county office to demand that Wang be retaken and that the guard be punished. In the meantime Wang discreetly hid himself to await the outcome. When he learned that Mao had been arrested, he hurried to Bishan and filed a suit against the Bishan militia, claiming that he was not eligible for service and that the guards had seized him simply to extort money. He demanded the return of his three hundred yuan and Mao's imprisonment. The outcome of this case, however, remains unknown.

In Prosperity, Wu Zixuan, a comfortable landowning farmer of *bao* 1, held the record for success in preventing conscription of five sons, all living at home. In 1940, four of these five sons were of military age, while the fifth, aged fifteen, was registered in primary school. Each time his *bao* was required to turn over a batch of conscripts, other families grumbled that the Wus had no sons in the army. Finally a number of them got together and lodged a complaint against the *bao* head. Not wishing to be subjected to an investigation, he seized the fifteen-year-old schoolboy and sent him to the county recruitment office, where he was inducted into the army. The father protested to the county authorities, and the *bao* head was asked to account for his action. He replied that lacking accurate statistics on age, he had to judge by appearances, leaving it to the military authorities to decide whether the recruit was acceptable. He claimed that he would willingly have replaced the boy had the army rejected him as too young.

Despite the father's protest, the military authorities did not release the boy since by law two of Wu's sons should be in the army. Wu then went to the military authorities and pledged that if they returned his fifteen-year-old, he would turn in two of the older boys. The father stood guarantor for the two sons, while his *bao* head and *jia* head stood guarantor for him. The boy was released, but the two other sons were not forthcoming. Instead the father stoically allowed himself to be arrested and sent to prison in the county town.

Prison conditions for most were so grim that a two-year sentence was considered equivalent to a death penalty. But prison wardens, like other officials whose salaries were inadequate, granted favors to those few prisoners who could afford to offer bribes. Wang thus secured a degree of comfort. Furthermore, prison wardens, although having no authority to commute sentences, were allowed to release the dying. And it was customary for the family of a dying prisoner to petition to take him home to save him from an unmarked grave in a paupers' cemetery. This was how it came about that after only two months in prison, Wu returned home, having been officially released as a dying man.

PRESS-GANGING

While well-off peasants had myriad ways of using wealth and connections to avoid the conscription of their sons, the *bao* and township heads, who benefitted from the bribes, still had to meet their quotas for potential soldiers. Most commonly this was done by press-ganging the men in poor families. This involved the sudden seizure of a family head or only son, leaving a wife and children or parents to cope as best they could. In poor families, men living into their fifties often suffered from debilitating illnesses or disabilities. This made them particularly dependent on the labor power of a young man. Hu Xiancai, an elderly farmer of *bao* 2, and his wife were supported by an only son aged twenty-four. In the winter of 1940 the son was nabbed while attending market in Bishan town. The old couple could do nothing about this illegal seizure and were only able to survive because of the help of a married daughter.

In principle, a family could protest to the township or county authorities and demand the return of a wrongly conscripted man, but the poor rarely dared tangle with authorities. When on occasion they did, the response was minimal at best. The sympathies of the latter were with their subordinates, since conscripting eligible men in better-off families was such an arduous, even dangerous, task. This is illustrated by the experience of one of the Xie families. With two sons already in the army, the third, aged seventeen, joined a transport team. As he was small, thin, and undernourished, the other cart pullers paid him only 5.50 yuan instead of the 6.00 rate, claiming that was all he deserved. He was dissatisfied and quarreled constantly with the others, making himself unpopular. One day he dropped behind to relieve himself and was seized by guards of the district through which the highway passed. He called out for help. His comrades' protests could have saved him since members of transport teams were not eligible for service, and team members were numerous enough—and tough enough—to enforce the ban. But his mates ignored him. The following day when the cart was returning, the team members saw Xie being marched along with other conscripts to Tongliang. Hearing his cries, they felt regret, but all they could do was carry a message to his father to try to secure his release at the recruitment center in Tongliang. The father went at once, only to be told that the recruits had been sent on to some undisclosed destination. He hurried home and got the *bao* head to draft an appeal to the county government. Though both the *bao* head and *jia* head affixed their seals to the document, it remained on the desk of the township head, for as he remarked, "It's no use sending this in until we have more details, such as which army unit the boy has been drafted into." The young lad's eldest sister-in-law doggedly pursued the case, even going to Bishan County authorities to complain bitterly about the illegal conscription and the callous indifference of the local officials. The poor did not passively submit to press-ganging. Although, unlike the wealthier peasants, they owned no guns, some resorted to knives to prevent capture. In mid-November, the head of *bao* 2 went to the NCC clinic to have his wounded hand dressed. The previous night he had gone out to round up conscripts. Standing outside the door of a home, he had shouted, "Is anyone home?" In reply, the door flew open and a knife slashed down, cutting his hand. The guard accompanying him managed to grab the handle, but the farmer got away, fleeing naked into the night.

The *bao* head's responsibility ended when he turned over his full quota of recruits to the township. It was then the township head who had to make up for not meeting the quota. Having no pool of conscripts to draw from, his only option was to send out the township guards to press-gang whomever they could. One time this happened was toward the end of March 1941. The market village was in an uproar over the escape of five conscripts who were being held in the township lockup for transfer to the county recruitment center. It was a market day and the street was packed. The wife of one of the conscripts had to come to bring her husband a bundle of clothes. When she went to the lockup, she found the guards' attention fully occupied with other matters, so she slipped past, unbolted the door, and let all five conscripts escape. Then she calmly set off for home. Soon after, when the guards found the men gone, they remembered having seen the woman, so they arrested her and locked her up. But after a couple of days she was released. Some said this was because the guards had no proof that she had opened the door; others pointed out that the guards dared not press the case since it would highlight their own negligence; still others surmised that her husband's uncle had come and bribed the guards to release her, an allegation the guards indignantly denied. Whatever the facts, holding her was an inconvenience and expense and would in no way help the township head make up the quota. The sympathies of ordinary people were expressed in such comments as, "What a clever wife!" and "Won't this put the township head into a real fix!" Press-ganging created an atmosphere of tension, apprehension, and even terror, deeply affecting the quality of life and the state of mind of the poor.

RELUCTANT RECRUITS

By 1941, as it became increasingly difficult to fill the quotas, men were seized who were disabled, ill, weak, undersized, underage, overage, vagrants, or simply passing strangers. The poorest of the poor were particularly vulnerable. Even public opinion favored their seizure, on the grounds that they were ne'er-do-wells and probably thieves. While the military authorities could reject anyone who was obviously unfit, their standards were lax. However, on those occasions when a man was rejected, the township or *bao* head was obliged to find a replacement. In May 1941, three *bao* heads were detained in the county for failing to meet their quotas. They were released shortly. Two had presumably bought their freedom, while the third, who was short one conscript only, was freed when the *bao* guards' officers arrived with a destitute man who sometimes hung around the market hoping for a break. So, although a skillful *bao* or township head could profit considerably through the handling of conscription, he sometimes found himself forced to provide payoffs to county officials to overlook his failures.

In 1940 the government in Chongqing, well aware of the acute reluctance of farmers to serve in the army, chose to tackle some of the ideological obstacles. Knowing that the prestige of soldiers was very low (as reflected in the common saying, "Good iron is not used for nails, nor good men for soldiers") and that peasants ranked loyalty to their family higher than loyalty to the community or state, the government sent an order to townships such as Prosperity to arouse patriotism and to glorify soldiers as heroes. Teachers and pupils were delegated to take up this duty. One specific task assigned to Prosperity's central primary school was to turn out in full force and sing patriotic songs whenever a batch of new recruits was being dispatched to the county induction center. This produced situations such as the following: in March 1941, eight men, several of them bound, were assembled on the street outside Wenmiao temple, ready to march off to Bishan under armed guard. A wailing woman with a baby on her back clung to her husband's arm, while her four-year-old daughter looked on bewildered and forlorn. An old woman held on to her son in despair. A man with a large tumor on his neck, which pressed his head permanently to one side, stood waiting. A young farmer loudly cursed his bad luck in being a member of one of the three *bao* required to send conscripts on this occasion, to which one of the guards responded bitterly, "You fool, your bad fortune is being Chinese!" Then, at a sign from the singing teacher, the schoolchildren, who were lined up witnessing the scene, burst into song: "Arise, ye who are unwilling to be slaves!"[8] The contingent of fresh recruits moved off, while the guards pushed away the women who cried and clung to them. It is not at all clear that the conscripts or their family members were moved by the patriotism expressed in the song.

The government provided allowances for the dependents of soldiers. Officially, army families were entitled to a yearly allowance of two *dan* four *dou* of unhusked rice. This amounted to two *dou* a month, whereas the locally accepted rate of consumption of an able-bodied male laborer was 1.5 *dou*. However, if the soldier's family sold the rice and purchased some cheaper cereal, it could suffice to feed a small family. In addition to this food allowance, the soldier's family was entitled to help from its fellow *jia* members at the busy seasons, especially at rice-transplanting time.

Several other compensations were due a soldier's family. At the time of the man's conscription, other households in his *bao* were expected to take up a collection to present to the family. In the event of the death of the soldier, all households of the *bao* were asked to make a money contribution. And at the Moon Festival and other holidays, the *jia* was charged with providing small gifts to its army families. Finally, if calamity befell a soldier's family, such as a robbery or a fire, the township was required to provide relief until the family was able to get back on its feet. By prevailing standards, this package of family allowances, aid, and gifts seemed passable. But these payments were often not issued. *Bao* heads might wait to see what pressure the family could exert.

The soldier himself was entitled to an initial payment roughly equivalent to a month's pay (a sum which had risen from seven yuan in 1938 to forty yuan in the autumn of 1940) at the time of enlistment. Once in the army, in addition to his monthly pay, he was provided with a uniform, accommodation, and food. But how much food or pay he got depended entirely on the officers of his unit. Generally, rations were so meager that malnutrition and the diseases that accompanied it were rife in the army. This was exacerbated by poor sanitation and hygiene in most units. The result was that soldiers' bodies were covered with scabies and their clothes were full of lice. Furthermore, medical service in the army was inadequate, and casualty rates from illness and accidents were high. Those seriously wounded in battle had slight chance of recovery or of returning home if disabled, especially if the soldier was serving some distance from his home. Most disabled men had to resort to begging in whatever locality they found themselves. The only others who had managed to return to Prosperity during 1940–1941 were men serving in a unit posted nearby. One had gone blind as a result of vitamin deficiency. Although he succeeded in getting home, he and his family were in desperate straits, for no pensions were granted to disabled soldiers. In this case, the man's family of seven (himself; his wife, aged thirty-one; and his five children, aged one to nine) were supported solely by the wife. Such cases were not exceptional, and they did cause some public concern. In Bishan at this time, it was not unusual to see schoolchildren in the streets collecting money for wounded and disabled soldiers. They had been mobilized by progressive teachers appalled at the callous disregard shown to the men.

While no military units were stationed in the village of Prosperity Market, in late November 1940 a unit of over fifty conscripts from the surrounding districts was assembled in Prosperity for a period of training. In the bitter winter weather, the conscripts wore cheap green cotton uniforms with little padding, while the officers in charge wore well-padded blue cotton uniforms. The men ate their meals out in the street, squatting in groups of eight around an earthen bowl of spinach soup and a large vessel of the cheapest rice. They ate at breakneck speed, for they were allowed only a few minutes in which to eat what they could. The wife of one recruit each day brought her husband a dish of cooked vegetables that he shared with the other seven men in his group. Officers treated the soldiers with contempt: instead of shouting clear intelligible orders, the officers cursed the men and pushed them around to show them what they should do. Some men dreaded military service so much that they disabled themselves. The farmer Wu Rongguang chopped off his trigger finger, and some others did the same.[9]

Yet despite this dread, there were young men whose families were in such desperate straits that in order to obtain grain to keep parents or children alive they sold themselves as conscripts to a *bao* head or to a family wishing to keep a member out of the army. Liu Demin, who was an only son and hence technically ineligible for service, sold himself to his *bao* head for four *dan* of rice because of his family's hunger. He promptly deserted, which mattered nothing to his *bao* head, whose responsibility ended the moment he had handed him over. He sold himself again, this time for three *dan*. However, at the time of our visit, he had still failed to return, leaving his wife to support the old folks.

Apart from those like Liu, who sold themselves as conscripts, there was also an occasional volunteer, almost all of whom were school graduates inspired by patriotism. There were also a small number of men for whom army service worked out well. A stalwart of the Paoge might find little difficulty in making a satisfactory place for himself in the army, as he would already know how to make himself useful to superiors and how to be good company or a good gambling companion. Prosperity's Peng Shaohui, the eldest son of the NCC cook, was able to make a satisfactory niche for himself in his unit; he was promoted to squad leader, then to acting platoon commander; and he was lucky enough to survive numerous engagements with the Japanese unharmed. [10]

SERVICE IN THE RESERVE AND LABOR CORPS

In addition to conscription for the military, men in Prosperity were required to serve in the reserve corps or to work as conscripted labor. Men aged thirty-seven to forty-two who were part of the reserve corps, directed by the township head who served as captain, were to patrol their own *bao* at night and protect scattered farm homes from bandits. Men aged forty-three to forty-eight were liable for service as corvée laborers for one month and six days per year; responsibility for sending the men, replacing them, and paying them fell on the *bao*. They were to be paid at the current rate for unskilled labor, but the precise sum was fixed by negotiation between the *bao* and the conscript himself. In January 1941, the wage was roughly eighty yuan a month, but by September the same year it had risen to 150 per man. [11]

In supplying and paying its quota of five men on corvée, the *bao* called on its *jia*. Since most *bao* had ten *jia*, each *jia* of ten families carried the burden of supplying and paying manpower to do public service for half the year. How the *jia* chose the man and how it raised the necessary funds from among its ten or so constituent families was its own concern. If a *jia* was made up of discordant families, there might be considerable jockeying to shift the burden onto others and delays in providing a replacement. But in other *jia*, the families might reach a harmonious arrangement, with levies allocated according to the economic condition of each family. And in some cases, individuals not belonging to a particular *jia* were recruited in order to spare the families in the *jia*. This is illustrated by a meeting of a *jia* in *bao* 6. It was an informal affair, with six men and two women sitting or standing in one of the courtyards, discussing with the *jia* head the current task of finding a man to go. One man reported that he had found an outsider willing to go for sixty yuan. Everyone greeted this news with enthusiasm, for the going price was one hundred yuan. In high spirits at this excellent bargain, the members debated how to divide the sum among the twelve households and decided levies should range from three yuan minimum to nine yuan maximum, depending on the economic condition of each family. A literate member of the *jia* entered the assessment for each household reached by consensus of those present. But the meeting did not disperse without mild grumbling about the frequency of the impositions on the *jia*. One of the women recalled that just a few days earlier they had had to pay forty-five yuan for the purchase of one new military uniform for the army.

While a stint of corvée labor was not as dreaded as military service, few willingly agreed to take a turn. The better-off never went but instead bought their way out by paying a larger share of the cost. Since few went willingly, the *bao* often failed to send replacements. A man already serving might find himself doing indefinite corvée labor since the work site would not release a laborer until his replacement arrived. To make matters worse, considerable numbers of the men pressed into service were weak or in ill health and unable to tolerate the forced labor and harsh conditions. It was only when the authorities there feared that a man might die on their hands that they would release him, even then leaving him to make his own way home.

In March 1941, at dusk, a man lay groaning by the side of the road less than a kilometer from Prosperity Market. By evening he had dragged himself into the village and was making his way slowly along the street. As he passed the shop of the prosperous restaurateur and cloth cleaner Zhang Yunheng, Mrs. Zhang brought him a bowl of rice porridge. When he got as far as the shop and home of the well-off tobacco and wine merchant Rao Haiyun, Mrs. Rao asked a neighbor's boy who was loafing in the shop to take the man to the NCC clinic. But the nurse happened to be away on a case. As he waited outside the clinic, the opium dealer Zhang Guangquan noticed him and sent him to a nearby inn for the night, paying the cost. The man died in the inn, just before dawn. First thing in the morning, the village guards took up a collection to give the deceased a burial, simple but adequate to prevent his spirit from getting lost and remaining in the vicinity to cause harm to residents in Prosperity.

This might have closed the matter so far as Prosperity was concerned. However, the man turned out to be a tenant of a big Dazu County landowner known for his benevolence. As patron of the dead man, he demanded that the county authorities make a full investigation of the case. To complicate matters, it happened that the Prosperity Township head had an enemy looking for revenge. He seized on this death to file a suit at the county court accusing the township head of poisoning the man. In due course, however, the investigation by the county authorities cleared Prosperity's township head. Their findings were that the man's *bao* had pressed him into corvée duty, despite ill health, and had failed to provide his replacement, and that the captain of the labor corps, for his part, had driven him out when the seriousness of his condition became apparent. This left the *bao* head in Dazu and the captain at the work site to bear any punishment that might be exacted under pressure from the dead man's powerful landlord patron.

CALLS FOR REFORM

Prosperity had a shortage of land and a surplus of labor and might have spared manpower for the army without causing a labor shortage. But the loss of manpower from the farms because of press-ganging and the flight of able-bodied men had become serious enough to affect production. In the summer of 1941, with a serious drought in some parts of Sichuan and a shortage of able-bodied manpower to bring in what harvest there was elsewhere, the central government became so alarmed that it declared a moratorium on conscription for three months so that young men would dare to go home.

The effect of conscription practices on the army was equally disastrous. Under the system of recruitment, as it was currently enforced, considerable numbers of men recruited into the army were physically unfit. Death, disability, and desertion were common; morale was extremely low.

The essential problem with conscription, army service, and corvée labor was that it involved extortion and corruption. Feng Qingyun's rise to power provides an indication of the extent of the extortion. In the six years following his appointment as township head, he amassed enough to increase the size of his landholdings from twenty *dan* to one hundred, making him one of the biggest landowners in the community. This was credited in particular to his handling of conscription. [12]

The corruption and its devastating results, as seen in Prosperity, were so widespread that they drew the attention of the well-known reformer Liang Shuming. Soon after his arrival in Sichuan in 1938, Liang made a study of recruitment and army service. His findings noted that one-fourth of the massive numbers of peasants conscripted died of privation or disease before they even reached their assigned units. [13] Peasants arrived at the recruitment centers bound with ropes to prevent their escape. Liang concluded that there was a huge gap between national conscription laws and the actual recruitment process. At the local level, recruitment was basically in the hands of the local gentry, who took the poorest and weakest peasants. Liang drafted a plan of reform, emphasizing three points: the need for education to arouse the peasants' enthusiasm for the war effort, the need for peasants to understand the law and dare to demand its enforcement, and the need to choose local figures whom the masses trusted and who would guarantee care for the draftees' dependents. Liang also proposed improved conditions for the men in the army and punishment of officers guilty of corruption. To pursue these reforms he founded the Compulsory Military Service Implementation Association (*bingyi shishi xiejin hui*) in October 1938.

Liang's proposals would have been unenforceable in Prosperity, and they were completely inadequate to solve the problems found there. Yet even these reforms were impossible to promote. From early 1939, the association found its efforts blocked. And early in 1940, Generalissimo Jiang Jieshi personally ordered Liang's association disbanded. While Liang continued to work for conscription reform throughout the war, it was always in the teeth of Guomindang opposition. Finally, in 1944, the government did establish a Ministry of Conscription to carry through reforms. This, however, did little or nothing to alleviate the abuses. If taxation was a periodic irritant in the relationship between Prosperity and outside state authorities, conscription was a constant, escalating, and terrifyingly unpredictable reminder of every family's vulnerability to disaster.

NOTES

1. The tax was set at 5 percent of the registered yield of the land.

2. Concerning re-registration in Sichuan, see John Lossing Buck (1942, p. 155).

3. The levies were made through the *baojia* machinery. Some, like the military rice levy or the rice levy for storage against famine, were payable by owners of twenty *shidan* (6.44 local *dan*) and over—or roughly 70 percent of owners of rice land in the township. This meant that even small vulnerable farm families were subject to the levy. Other levies, like the rice allowance for soldiers' dependents in the township or the levy to pay the wages for corvée labor, were payable by every household, with the *bao* deciding how the burden was distributed among them.

4. An entry in *Cihai* on the origins of this practice dates it back to the Sui dynasty official Zhang Sunping, who sent a petition to the emperor recommending that all families be required to supply one *dan* of rice to the public granary that could be used in times of famine. Unfortunately this practice was easily manipulated by the elite of a locality for their own purposes (Wei Zheng 2006). According to Isabel Crook's field notes, Bishan County had fifty-four official granaries for this grain, one belonging to the county town, the rest to different villages and neighborhoods.

5. Measurement collection and delivery of the rice transactions was done by volume rather than weight, the standard equipment being a set of wooden boxes which were filled and leveled off. It was the common belief that Feng secretly had two sets of these, a larger one for collection and a smaller one for delivery.

6. The official figure for the amount of relief grain held in the county in 1938 (the figure for 1940 was not available) was 19,880 *shidan* (6,626.6 local *dan* of unhusked rice). Thus, Prosperity could be expected to have at least one hundred *dan* in its relief granary.

7. This is deduced from the official figure of 48,413 conscripts for the county as a whole given in the summer of 1940, when the population of Bishan was 332,847. With a population of 7,744, Prosperity accounted for 2 percent of the county's population. Hence its share of recruits would be well over one thousand.

8. This was Nie Er's popular song rousing patriots to resist the Japanese invaders which was later chosen to be the national anthem of the PRC. We were told this story by the singing teacher's cousin, Sun Zhongyao, when we were in Prosperity in 1983.

9. Apparently men kept their severed fingers, for during the Cultural Revolution (1966 to 1976), someone gathered these fingers for an exhibition of the "sufferings in the old society." Men also exhibited the scars they bore from floggings in the army.

10. In 1983 when we revisited Prosperity, we found Peng Shaohui working in a noodle restaurant in the village. He gladly recounted the tale of his exploits in the army. Peng had originally been conscripted in 1938 but had escaped and found work in Chongqing. But, falling ill, he came home and was caught a second time by his *bao* head, ex-captain Yang Desheng. After induction, he was assigned to the Fifty-First Infantry Division, a newly formed reinforcement division made up almost wholly of Sichuanese but officered by non-Sichuanese. The division left Sichuan in May 1940 and after being stationed near Yichang for a time was moved

toward Hankow. Then at Hengyang they met the Japanese in a major battle. Apparently Peng took part in no other large-scale encounters.

In 1945, when the Japanese surrendered, Peng and some fellow soldiers decided to desert and return to Sichuan. But hearing that their unit was to be flown to Beiping (to prevent a Communist takeover from the Japanese), they decided this was the chance of a lifetime to ride in an airplane, so they delayed their desertion until after the flight. Then, in return for a substantial gift (saved from his winnings at gambling), Peng obtained from his commanding officer an "errand-leave certificate" (*jia cai zheng*), enabling him to avoid the risk of arrest as a deserter.

When Peng reached home, he found that his mother and brothers had died some years earlier. A filial son, Peng had sent money home to his mother on many occasions. But no one had notified him of his mother's death, and so the money had been pocketed by the *bao* head. In the land reform, Peng received a portion of land. Decades later, with the economic reforms encouraging service trades and entrepreneurship in the countryside, Peng began augmenting his income by running the small noodle shop where we found him.

11. Isabel Crook notes that warlords treated their laborers better than the GMD, as they needed to prevent them from switching their allegiance to another warlord.

12. At the time of Liberation, Feng Qingyun was the most hated man in Prosperity. One reason given us was that as township head for six years (1944–1949) he had gone into the conscription racket in a big way and fleeced so many. See chapter 10 for further details of his activities.

13. The facts concerning Liang Shuming's efforts to reform the military conscription and service systems come from Alitto (1979, p. 295).

Chapter Ten

Trial of Strength

Among the numerous obstacles the reformers encountered in their state-building and nation-building endeavors in 1940–1941, the most formidable proved to be the Paoge. Because it was such an amorphous and dispersed patron-client entity, its responses to the reformers tended to be localized and varied. Two leaders of one lodge sometimes held sharply different positions on a specific reform or even on the merits of the reformers' overall programs. As a result, the reformers could not readily predict the intensity and modes of resistance that might be launched by certain sectors of the Paoge against specific reform programs.

Compared to the NCC reformers, the Nationalist government was much more direct in its assault on local power structures. State organizers realized that in order to extend central government power down to the local level, they needed to smash parallel local power structures and revenue bases. The Paoge, more than any other local institution, had the capacity to channel resources and allegiances away from the state.[1] Many Nationalist reformers were committed to weakening local practices that strengthened the sensibility that obligations within the community had to be placed above demands from without. In the urgency of wartime and in the desperate political struggle to maintain control of the state, the Nationalist government, despite its rhetoric, was more likely than nongovernmental reformers to see the competition between the locality and the state as a zero-sum game.

THE CAMPAIGN TO SUPPRESS OPIUM

The confrontation between local and provincial interest groups on the one hand and the central authorities on the other was nowhere more evident than in the implementation of the ban on the opium trade and opium addiction.

251

In the early twentieth century, Sichuan was widely believed to be home to the greatest amount of opium production in all of China.[2] A number of Qing dynasty officials launched opium suppression campaigns to no avail, and the situation only worsened after 1911 when the province was ruled by five warlords.[3] Drug trafficking helped these provincial warlords finance their armies. The initiative for suppression of opium in the province during the Republican era came predominantly from the central government. As early as 1935, when Liu Xiang appealed to the Nationalist government for help against the Communists, Chiang Kai-shek pressured provincial rulers into issuing a plan for the phased elimination of poppy cultivation and opium addiction.[4] But the trade did not diminish; it reached unprecedented heights by 1937 when, with the financial support of Chongqing bankers, provincial authorities together with private merchants organized a company to monopolize all purchase and sale of Sichuan opium. Prices were kept high, and the monopoly brought immense profits for the founders and backers. In Prosperity, prior to the arrival of the Nationalist government in Chongqing in 1938, the three big opium dealers—Feng Qingyun, Wang Mingxuan, and Zhang Guangquan—sold the drug openly.

Early in 1938, with the shift of the central government's wartime capital to Chongqing, pressure to ban the drug was renewed. The province complied by making the opium trade illegal and ordering the establishment of county bureaus throughout the province to deal with addiction.[5] By 1940, the Nationalist government had issued a dozen regulations banning the drug, and Sichuan had set up two provincial organizations to supervise the work: a section of the Civil Affairs Bureau (*Minzheng ting*) and a Department for the Supervision of Banning Opium (*Sichuan sheng jinyan dulichu*). Provincial authorities ordered that all addicts (it was estimated that Sichuan had 1.3 million of them) should be registered; have their heads shaved and washed, their fingernails inspected, and their urine and feces tested; and be cured under the supervision of county and township bureaus set up expressly for that purpose.[6]

A chronicle of efforts at suppression of the opium trade and addiction in Prosperity during 1940–1941 illuminates the difficulties of enforcing this ban. The Bureau for Curing Opium Addicts set up in Bishan County in 1938 first made a survey of opium addiction in the county. Apart from this, the years 1939 and 1940 saw little action by the authorities in Prosperity to clamp down on either sales or addiction. County authorities were more active. In April 1940, they caught a Prosperity man smuggling opium elsewhere in the county and threw him in prison in Bishan. The man was Zhang Dongchen, a day laborer in his mid-thirties, who attempted to supplement his meager living by smuggling opium. Zhang left a pregnant wife and a daughter of twelve to fend for themselves. When a baby son was born shortly after, the mother almost died of toxemia, having received no care. She was saved by our nurse, and with care and food she recovered. But she had no way to keep herself and her family alive, so she gave the baby out for adoption and hired herself out as his wet nurse. After about six months, Zhang was released and returned to Prosperity, where he was taken on as a helper in Feng Qingyun's teahouse. This revealed that Zhang had been in the employ of—and running the risks for—the dealer Feng, who was protected by his status as a member of the local elite and the Paoge. Often in opium dealings the risks were shifted to the poor.

In July 1940, the county militia were sent to raid the dens in Prosperity Market Village, since local authorities had done nothing to suppress opium. First they entered a "poor man's den" operated by Cao Ziyun. Cao and the patrons escaped while Mrs. Cao, a stout middle-aged woman with tiny bound feet, remained at home, believing herself to be safe since she was not an addict. But she was seized, perhaps because the militia dared not return empty-handed. As Mrs. Cao had no ready cash with which to mollify the guards, they were highly disgruntled and hurried her along the road to Bishan on this hot midsummer day. Halfway there she had a stroke and had to be carried the rest of the way to town, where she died on arrival and was forthwith buried in the paupers' cemetery.

On hearing the news, Mrs. Cao's married daughter promptly went to town to retrieve the body for a decent burial. She was refused on the grounds that in this cemetery no records were kept of who was buried where. Soon after, the Cao family brought charges in the Bishan court against the county militia for causing Mrs. Cao's death, a legal action supported by influential local patrons. But the court ruled that Mrs. Cao had died of a stroke, not maltreatment. Nevertheless, the death of Mrs. Cao did nothing to win the support of Prosperity residents for the suppression campaign.

Although the campaign achieved little, it continued to hang like a threatening cloud over the dealers, who took steps to protect themselves. Two of the four main dealers in Prosperity gave up serving opium on their own premises, shifting operations—and risks—elsewhere. Feng Qingyun no longer served opium at his teahouse but simply supplied smaller dealers like the widow Xiang-Tian shi. Zhang Guangquan arranged to cook and serve opium in a back room of the teahouse owned and operated by Cai Fangzhi. Cai was thought to be immune from a raid since he was a relative of the captain of the Prosperity militia and a personal friend of Prosperity's biggest landowner, Cao Yuexian. In payment for use of the room, Zhang provided Cai and his wife with several pellet-sized smokes (*kou*) of opium a day, which was still not enough to meet their daily consumption needs. Wang Mingxuan, on the other hand, showed no apprehension about the opium suppression campaign and continued to serve opium at his teahouse to a special clientele—the elders of his lodge and the guests they entertained in his teahouse. Since his teahouse served as the "port" of the most powerful local lodge of the Paoge, he was in a singularly strong position. Similarly, Tang-Nei shi gave no evidence of concern, perhaps because her clientele was private and she had a strong patron in Wu Huanyun.

Nevertheless, by 1940, opium was not sold openly by the township's three chief dealers but rather was retailed to the proprietors of small dens along the street in the market village. These dens were located in miserable, dark, cramped homes or tenements of the village; the proprietors were poor people providing service to both smokers and petty dealers. Here the opium was cooked and sold by the standard pellet to be smoked on the premises, with the smoker reclining on the host's bed.

While the important members of the Paoge—Feng, Wang, and Zhang—had opted to shift the risk of opium sales to Prosperity's small proprietors, they were quite willing and able to provide protection services in the unusual event of a raid, or to secure their release if arrested. In so doing, the Paoge showed that it was largely able to thwart the central government's opium prohibition in the first few years after it was enacted. At the same time it was also able to protect the traders from thieves, a major accomplishment in an area that was plagued by endemic banditry. In short, the Paoge continued to wield sufficient power in Prosperity and its environs in 1940 to ward off threats to its thriving opium business.

In September and October 1940, no fresh raids on dens took place, but a number of addicts were rounded up and placed in detention in Bishan to undergo compulsory treatment. One of those taken was the wife of Cai Yunqing, the forty-year-old proprietor of a particularly popular teahouse, with gambling often proceeding all night long. Mrs. Cai returned home, cured, two months later.

In October 1940, the county government sent an official to check on opium suppression in the township. This brought a rush of addicts to our health clinic, requesting certificates proving they had broken the habit. Among these was Commander Cai, who requested a certificate on behalf of his mother. He made no pretense that she was cured but said affably, "The old lady is over eighty and giving up opium would kill her, so I need a certificate." Fortunately our director's secretary, a lawyer by training, was able to draw up an impressive but noncommittal document that proved satisfactory. For Cai, his wife, and his mother, smoking opium was a pleasant pastime that did not strain their household budget; the government campaign for them was a nuisance, not an imperative to change their behavior.

Most who bore the brunt of this campaign in Prosperity were poor. One man who was rounded up at this time was an impoverished member of the Zeng lineage. He was a man of no fixed abode who slept in one or another of the various opium dens in Prosperity Market. Some months earlier he had aroused the ire of his kinsmen by stealing the ancestral tablets and selling them to a rival branch of the Zeng lineage. The tablets were never recovered, and Zeng had soon spent all the money he gained on opium. Three months after his arrest as an addict, he had still not returned. It was rumored that he had been turned over to the construction corps for corvée labor or conscripted into the army. This was what typically happened to those men pronounced cured.

Pressure on smokers and dealers continued to mount. In November 1940, the county militia caught a smoker in Zitong Market and gave him rough treatment until he confessed that he had bought his opium from Tang-Nei shi in Prosperity. Shortly thereafter, three county guards arrived in Prosperity to arrest her. But having received an hour's warning, she had fled into the countryside, asking a neighbor to feed her pigs in her absence. The guards, who settled into a neighboring teahouse to watch for her return, created such a disturbance that no one else dared enter the house. It was only when a friend gave the guards thirty yuan that they grumblingly returned to Bishan to report her absence. On their departure, Tang-Nei shi returned and promptly sought out Wu Huanyun, onetime township head and political activist of the Cai faction, and asked him to clear up the case for her with the county authorities. This he did at a cost of two hundred yuan. Here the reformist county head's efforts at suppressing the opium trade were being undermined under his own nose by influential people in the county who were accepting payoffs to protect their clients in the townships.

This same month the county militia launched its second raid on Prosperity Market, lasting several days. One den raided was that of Liu-Wu shi. Tipped off just minutes before the raid, she managed to lock up her house and disappear, also asking a friend to feed her pigs while she was in hiding. However, the house was so closely watched that the loudly complaining pigs remained unfed for two days. The source of these timely warnings remained secret, but their result was clear: no dealers were arrested, only addicts.

One of these latter was Luo Shuling, an impoverished villager. After being held in detention for some time, Luo was pronounced cured of his addiction and sent to do corvée labor at the military airfield. After a period there, he was drafted into the army. In this exceptional case the family's livelihood was not much affected by the loss of the head of the household. Luo's old mother, wife, and two young children were able to carry on much as before from the meager income they received from the barbers who rented their ramshackle buildings each market day, and by running a small cake stand in front of their home.

Three more addicts even poorer than Luo were taken at the same time. This was a family, Liu Fengyun and his wife, both around forty, and their thirteen-year-old son Hai'er, whose altercation with Commander Cai was described in chapter 5. The couple was employed by the innkeeper Zeng-Wang shi. Liu carried water and did other heavy tasks, while his wife served as a maid and prostitute for the guests. She was the only woman in Prosperity registered in the census as a prostitute. Hai'er, a cheerful, saucy urchin, was well known locally as a little beggar and petty thief. Since they could hardly have afforded enough opium for addiction, they may have been taken simply to make up a quota. After two months of detention, the wife and son returned, but not Liu Fengyun. Instead, he was sent to do compulsory labor on the airfield. Sometime later a rumor circulated that Liu had died at the work site. Hai'er cheerfully spread the story with the comment, "Everyone says I have eight fathers, so why should I mourn for one?" In July, mother and son left Prosperity and we lost track of them.

Another addict rounded up and sent off to Bishan for the opium cure was blacksmith Zhang. Zhang lived in Prosperity Market with his wife, two young children, and an apprentice of fifteen. For a month following Zhang's detention, the young apprentice strove to support the family of his master, but he could do only the simplest of tasks. When this proved inadequate he returned home. The baby son, aged two, soon died of dysentery. The wife and ten-year-old daughter moved to the home of relatives in the countryside where they tried to eke out a living making incense.

To sum up the results of the drive against opium in the autumn and early winter of 1940, no dealers were caught, thanks to forewarnings and payoffs; all the addicts caught and locked up were poor; no provision was made for the livelihood of families of addicts while they were being detained; and in the case of men, instead of being released after they were cured, they were sent to do forced labor, conscripted into the army, or first one and then the other.

In 1941, enforcement of opium suppression moved from the county level down to the township. The first opium raid conducted by local township guards, an unsanctioned one, took place in January 1941 and caused quite a stir. The Lunar New Year was approaching, and six guards found themselves in need of ready cash for the celebration. One day they happened to notice Cao Yuexian, Prosperity's biggest landowner, and his friend, the teahouse proprietor Wang Mingxuan, going into Cai Fangzhi's teahouse where the dealer Zhang Guangquan served opium. Guessing that the guests were there for a smoke, they decided to raid the place in the temporary absence of their captain and extract some bribes. Two guards were stationed at the back of the premises while the other four broke in at the front. But the timing was a trifle early. Though opium was being cooked, no one was yet smoking. Zhang Guangquan, Cao Yuexian, and Wang Mingxuan climbed out a high aperture and jumped from the roof, taking the opium with them. The guards chased the men through the paddy fields, knee deep in water, but failed to catch them. (The story of one of Prosperity's richest men jumping out the window and splashing through the paddies caused considerable hilarity on the village's next market day.) Afterward, since proprietor Cai himself was not at home, his wife gave the guards twenty yuan. But this did not mollify them, and they put her in the lockup for the night. The following morning her brother-in-law bailed her out and in great ire called for a mediation. The captain of the militia, their kinsman Cai Keming, attended and explained with considerable embarrassment that the guards had launched a sneak raid without his knowledge; but as he pointed out, it would not be expedient to punish the guards, since if word should reach the county, events would be hard to explain. The matter was dropped.

In July 1941, the local township authorities officially began to clamp down on opium for the first time. Prosperity had a new outsider township head, Guo Ankang, a young dedicated reformer determined to carry out Nationalist government policies. At about this time new and stiffer regulations were issued on the suppression of opium. These were purported to include extreme measures: opium dealers to be shot, incurable addicts to be severely punished (some said shot), and any landlord failing to report a tenant who was an addict—whether he was aware of the fact or not—to receive life imprisonment.

Early on the morning of July 30, Guo launched a surprise raid, sending the guards first to the home of the respectable and prosperous oil and liquor merchant Wu Wanlin to arrest the tenant renting his small back room, the widow Xiang-Tian shi, who was known to be in the opium business. They seized her and locked her up, taking as evidence a small pan for cooking opium and some ashes.

Next the guards raided the home of the widow Liu-Wu shi, likewise known to be in the business. She had been warned just in time to ask her own tenant to go out and lock the house door with a padlock on the outside while she hid herself under her bed and waited for the danger to pass. But the guards were accompanied by the brother of the township head, so they could not accept the evidence of the locked door but were ordered to break in. Once the door was down, one of the guards was sent in to search. He came out reporting no one at home. Since it was unimaginable that he could have failed to look under the bed, neighbors concluded that Liu-Wu shi had passed the man an adequate bribe.

The next house to be raided was where Cao Ziyun was known to carry on his opium business. This was the house entered by the county militia just one year earlier in the raid culminating in the death of Mrs. Cao. This time, though no evidence was discovered, Cao was thrown into the lockup.

The home of the dealer Zhang Guangquan was the next target, and then the home of the widow Wu-Wang shi, whose second son was a well-known loafer, opium addict, and gambler, and a close friend of Zhang Guangquan. But Wu and Zhang had learned of the raid in good time to escape together to Zitong Market. All of Guo's earnest efforts had produced only two prisoners. And only one of these got as far as the county jail, for on the day following Xiang-Tian shi's arrest, her landlord, Wu Wanlin, was taken to the township office for his complicity in not reporting a tenant's opium dealings. But not daring to risk having her case go to the court in Bishan, he approached the influential Feng Qingyun to handle the matter for him. Feng called on Guo, promising to stand as guarantor for the woman, and she was released.

The second prisoner, Cao Ziyun, witnessing her release, bitterly castigated the township head, saying, "You caught Xiang Erniang [Xiang-Tian shi] with evidence, but you let her go because she has a rich guarantor. You have no evidence against me, yet you're sending me to prison." Subsequently Cao sent an appeal to the county government accusing Guo of having taken a bribe to release Xiang-Tian shi, but he received no acknowledgment or reply. A few months later, he died in prison. His son, a gambler and popular member of his lodge of the secret society, brought back his body. His friends rallied around and collected several hundred yuan for a decent burial with a modest coffin and a one-day chanting of the scriptures by a Daoist folk priest.

Opium dealers like Zhang Guangquan were not easily intimidated. A scant two days after he had fled to Zitong Market, he arrived back carrying in his pocket a packet of opium worth two hundred yuan, which he accidently dropped. When he discovered his loss and tried to recover the packet, a noisy quarrel ensued. Although this attracted considerable public attention and comment, apparently no word of it reached the ears of the township head. Members of the local militia did not even use the occasion to extract a bribe from Zhang, who was an old gambling companion and well connected.

The summer raid ordered by township head Guo was the only official raid by the township militia that year. During the remainder of our stay in Prosperity, we heard no more of opium suppression. Our conjecture was that this one thoroughgoing effort in Prosperity, despite its meager results, had shown that Guo could make trouble for opium dealers and addicts if he chose. Then, by allowing the local power holders to continue their trade on sufferance, he put Commander Cai in his debt. This would help explain why Guo was the first of the outsiders able to maintain his hold on office, whereas his two predecessors had each lasted only a few months.

Many questions concerning the opium trade in Prosperity remained unanswered. We never learned precisely where the local dealers got their supplies, how much profit they made, or how much protection money they paid and to whom. But the course of these raids showed that leading figures in the local informal power structure had their patrons in the county who provided protection in return for payoffs. Consequently, the results of the opium suppression drive in the township were minimal. Out of our projected figure of 108 addicts in the township, no more than ten or twelve were taken in, a scant 10 or 12 percent. Even fewer dealers were detained for engaging in the opium trade, and these were not key people.

Socially, what success the drive had was at the expense of the poor. Those seized and punished as addicts or agents were all poor, underemployed men or women. Although some of those arrested were bailed out by patrons, others such as Cao and his wife got no protection. Furthermore, punishments that on paper appeared reasonable, even humane in the case of addicts, proved in practice to be devastating not only to the offender but to his entire family, who were often left without any means of support.

Politically, the course of the campaign showed that the newly appointed reform-minded township head found it expedient to reach a compromise with local informal power. He apparently concluded that with influential patrons at the county level protecting local dealers, he could not enforce the ban but could only use it to acquire some leverage. If the central government hoped to clear the province of opium, it would have to oust or weaken the local power holders with their vested interests in opium. And conversely, if the central government hoped to control local power holders, it would have to undercut their revenues from opium.

GAMBLING AND THE MILITIA

Apart from his efforts to straighten out township finances, township head Guo Ankang took an initial step against gambling by prohibiting members of the militia from gambling, on pain of imprisonment. In October 1940, the captain of Prosperity's militia was Cai Keming, a middle-aged man with six years' old-style education. Cai was a small landowner and onetime proprietor of a restaurant in Prosperity Market. But more important, he was a relative of ex-regimental commander Cai Xunqing. Until May 1941 the militia under Captain Cai remained a disorganized, undisciplined force. However, in the course of the reforms in local government, changes began to touch the militia. Between January and May, administrative reforms brought the amalgamation of parts of three townships, making Prosperity appreciably larger. At the same time the militia strength was raised from nine to over twenty. To prepare Captain Cai Keming for his increased responsibilities, he was called away to a training course in Bishan. Six weeks later, Cai returned elated and full of self-esteem, talking enthusiastically and knowledgeably about the state of the war in China and throughout the world. He spoke of his determination to shape up his new twenty-strong ragtag militia into a well-trained, politically motivated force.

Captain Cai's first measure was to concentrate all twenty guards in Prosperity and establish a strict routine, whereby they had to drill early each morning, report for duty assignments after breakfast, report again in the evening on the carrying out of these tasks, and finally be in bed by a fixed early hour. Gambling was forbidden. The central government had long since decreed it illegal, but this had not previously been enforced in Prosperity. Now Cai threatened to arrest and imprison any guard caught gambling and warned local people that he would only turn a blind eye to their gambling so long as they refused to permit guards to join them. One Sunday soon after, some of the guards, frustrated over not being allowed to gamble, were looking about for some other form of recreation. Cai, slightly drunk, suspected them of harboring a wish to gamble. He ordered them to line up and hold out their hands and then administered such a beating that they all had swollen hands and could hardly handle their chopsticks and bowls at suppertime.

Although Guo Ankang's efforts to stop the militia from gambling had the support of militia captain Cai, enforcement of even so limited a measure was not easy. When the guard Sun Bingcai was caught gambling a week or two later, Guo had him arrested and sent to prison in Bishan. But on his way there the prisoner met a distant relative who was a member of the local elite. The latter intervened and instructed the escorts to take the man back to Prosperity to settle the matter locally, pledging himself to stand as guarantor. Guo bowed to this pressure and sentenced the offender to fourteen strokes of a carrying pole and local detention. Already indignant, he became irate when he saw how gently the punishment was being administered and vented his anger by seizing the pole himself and giving Sun a couple of resounding wallops. Still, the matter did not end here. After Sun had been put back in the lockup, he escaped. Guo ordered the arrest of his guarantor, who protested that with the meting out of the punishment his responsibility had ended. Then it turned out that the guard on duty at the time of the escape was one of Guo's own men. The guarantor reported the matter to the county, demanding severe punishment for the guard. But Guo took the wind out of his sails by ordering the arrest of his own man. At this unexpected turn of events, Sun Bingcai, who had been hiding at home, fled, and we never saw him again. And so ended the first attempt to enforce the government's ban on gambling.

Though it was the Sun faction who had hindered Guo in this case, their interests were not involved. They had simply felt compelled to help a man who shared their surname. A more awkward confrontation came later with Commander Cai and the Paoge, whose interests were directly at stake with the gambling ban.

In the summer of 1941, Guo called a meeting of leading citizens of the community. He urged them to raise the funds necessary to carry out the improvements in rural education already agreed to by the local elite. It was on this occasion that Commander Cai confronted the township head with a dilemma by offering to fund the improvements by handing over a percentage of the profits from gambling. If Guo accepted, he would make himself a target for the charge of involving himself in the banned gambling racket. If he refused, the loss of face this would cause the community's most influential public figure could bring him dire consequences which he dared not risk.

And so Guo's efforts to curb gambling, like his efforts to suppress the opium trade, came to naught in the face of Paoge opposition.

THE RISE AND FALL OF THE PROSPERITY SALT COOPERATIVE

Salt was an indispensable commodity in Prosperity's subtropical climate, helping people who performed arduous physical labor to stave off rapid dehydration. It was the key ingredient in preserving food, preparing salted eggs that could then be coated with lime and mud to preserve them, and making brined vegetables (*paocai*) to accompany daily fare. (In Prosperity, the ability to make good *paocai* was a quality much desired in a wife.) Salt was also used in fertilizer, cattle feed, the production of medicine, metallurgy, the making of soap or glass, dyes, and leather goods production.[7] Fortunately, Sichuan was rich in salt, and Bishan was close to major supplies: the famous *ziliujing* ("self-flowing wells"; now called *zigong*) salt wells and those at Neijiang. These had been operated using remarkable technology both for extraction and processing of the salt.

State control of salt production and distribution had a record of several thousand years. By the early Republican era the warlords relied heavily on the revenue from three types of taxes: on land, opium, and the production and sale of salt. In 1933, taxes on trade had raised the prices of Sichuan's principal exports, including salt, so high that it caused a decline in demand, exacerbated by the worldwide depression. This caused a drop in revenues and threw as many as a million salt and transport workers out of their jobs.[8] Liu Xiang, Sichuan's leading warlord, had to seek help from the Nationalist government, and in July 1935 Sichuan received a massive gold loan, secured on Sichuanese salt revenue.[9]

With the outbreak of the war and the move to Chongqing, the Nationalist government lost access to most coastal sources and was left with only Sichuan and Yunnan salt wells and rock salt.[10] Not only were salt supplies reduced for this region, but the large-scale migration inland created additional demand.[11] The Nationalist salt supplies were also reduced by Japanese bombers, which deliberately targeted salt production areas.[12]

In order to cope with this situation of reduced supply, and to improve the state of government finances by decreasing evasion of the salt tax, government initiated a major reform of its salt administration. Until the war the government had controlled salt production while leaving collection, transport, and sales in private hands. Before the war, salt traders in Sichuan could purchase salt directly from the brine wells, paying a government tax at the time of purchase, and then they could distribute it freely without any government regulation.[13] In 1940, the wartime government initiated the establishment of county-level offices for wartime salt purchase and sale, attempting to gain control of collection, distribution, and sales, though by 1941 they once again handed over control of these activities to private merchants.[14]

While Bishan had had no office for dealing specifically with salt, in 1940 the Bishan County government received an instruction from the Sichuan-Xikang government Bureau for Management of Salt Affairs under the Sichuan government's Finance Department, requiring it to set up a committee to supervise purchases and sales. This was accomplished in May. In August came the order to establish a county wartime salt purchases and sales general department under the control of the county head.[15] Accordingly on September 1, 1940, the Bishan County Committee for Supervision of Salt Sales was set up, headed by a county appointee, Liu Youfu.[16]

A twenty-one-page document in the Bishan archives gives a picture of the complexity of the operation. It details forty-one issues concerning the county's handling of the purchase and sale of salt during the first year, including the types of salt bought, their sources, amounts of each and the cost, the added tax to the state, the cost of transport to Bishan (and the sizable cost of "losses" during transport), salaries, traveling fees, rent, office expenses, electricity, bonuses, and interest payments (*lixi*). The scale of the operation is shown in the figures for total purchases: 145,930 *jin* of rock salt and 258,744 *jin* of granulated salt at an average price of 1.4 yuan (which included the tax paid on it).[17]

Distribution was apparently more straightforward. The Bishan Purchase and Sales Office divided out the salt to the various sectors and merchants and set out its target prices: 1.5 yuan per *jin* for rock salt and 1.33 yuan for granulated salt. In reporting on results, the document gave a month-by-month record of sales and prices. These revealed that by the second month the county government had had to reduce its target price for rock salt to 1.4 yuan, and for granulated salt to 1.2 yuan. The final item in the document, entitled "Profits and Losses as of March 1941," remained blank.

Salt in rural markets was easily cornered by local entrepreneurs, who forced up prices, bringing hardship to the majority throughout the countryside. But by the early 1940s, the government had passed regulations to promote the establishment of salt supply co-ops in order to effect a substantial drop in prices. The government, in a recent move against speculation and hoarding, had placed restrictions on the amount of salt and certain other commodities that could be bought and held by private enterprises, while making an exception for registered cooperatives. A salt supply co-op could bring a substantial drop in prices—if it truly operated as a cooperative.

Prosperity's first venture with a salt supply cooperative was not an auspicious one. In late November 1940, a sign reading "Prosperity Salt and Sugar Cooperative" appeared over the door of one shop, forcing twelve small traders out of business. This operation was the brainchild of the ubiquitous Feng Qingyun, whose opium dealing, Paoge connections, and control of land tax collection and pig-butchering taxes have already been described. Feng formed the new salt company with capital of seven thousand yuan and registered it as a co-op. Drawing on the same group of local notables he had earlier used to form a rice tax collection company, Feng reportedly paid a bribe of one thousand yuan to a government office in Bishan to get his cooperative officially registered. His new enterprise was entitled to all the privileges promised by the state to cooperative ventures, and by January 1941 the bogus cooperative had forced the price of salt up to 1.45 yuan a *jin* in the village market, at a time when the same amount cost 1.05 yuan a *jin* in the county town of Bishan and 0.70 in Chongqing, less than half of what was charged in Prosperity.[18] Local farmers found this unbearable and were driven to walk long distances to get cheaper salt. But by April 1941, Feng's cooperative had bankrupted itself and was dissolved, with Feng personally buying up the remaining stocks of salt at a cut rate. What we had taken as a preemptive intrusion into the field may instead have been a maneuver by Feng to fleece some gullible would-be profiteers by taking them on as partners.

It was in this environment that the NCC project in Prosperity, with rural reconstruction specialists from Xiemachang, decided to launch a new salt cooperative to lighten the cost of salt for farm families. After the failure of the embroidery cooperative described in chapter 6, T. H. Sun, in search of a new idea for poverty alleviation, decided to establish a salt cooperative as the NCC's new centerpiece venture in Prosperity. Unlike the conscription and tax programs of the Nationalist government, this salt cooperative, launched in 1941 by the NCC team, was designed to bring substantial relief to farmers. T. H. Sun began to support the establishment of a salt cooperative even before Feng's bogus cooperative collapsed. His partner in this venture was Jiang Zhi'ang, who had been appointed by James Yen[19] as head of the Rural Reconstruction Institute (*Xiangcun jianshe yanjiu yuan*)[20] in the nearby village of Xiemachang. When T. H. Sun and Jiang Zhi'ang met in Chongqing, they quickly realized the potential benefit of collaboration.[21] Sun had established good relations with the community and had a functioning project that was already in place and endorsed by the county leadership. Jiang had an institute with an experienced staff who were veterans of James Yen's earlier project in Hebei, now occupied by the Japanese. The institute was in search of a suitable local project. Another factor influencing T. H. Sun's decision was that James Yen's projects in Xiemachang and in Xindu county near Chengdu enjoyed the support of Chen Kaisi, a high-ranking official in the Nationalist Party who would later assume the post of Minister of Civil Affairs. In November 1940, Sun and Jiang agreed to launch a "Prosperity Cooperative Community Experiment," in line with the long-standing goal of building cooperatives held by rural reconstructionists within missionary and NCC circles.

Under the experienced guidance of the Rural Reconstruction Institute, the preparatory steps for setting up this salt cooperative were adeptly executed. In December 1940, the three men promised by Yen's institute arrived: Yang Chenfang to prepare the community and set up the cooperative, Zhang Fumin to take charge of a training course on cooperative principles and accounting methods, and a third young man to assist them. T. H. Sun reserved for himself the role of writing up research reports on the process and impact of the salt cooperative on the community. A seven-member organizing committee that also included members from the local NCC rural reconstruction team was formed to oversee the process of establishing the cooperative. The local NCC organizers began by publicizing cooperative principles at meetings with the local authorities, teachers in both central and *bao* schools, and members of the economic division of the dormant Prosperity Community Development Association established the previous May.

The organizing committee initially sought to select a group of modern-minded young farmers for training in accounting and the principles and practices of cooperatives, but it soon decided to drop this plan because fitting the training period into seasons when farm labor could be spared from the fields or reimbursing the trainees for the time lost was unfeasible. Another difficulty was the poor educational level of such farmers. Courses to make up for these deficiencies would make the training program unacceptably long and costly. So, with regret, the idea of selecting ordinary farmers was dropped. Recruiting literate prosperous farmers or merchants, however, was not even contemplated, as they were deemed to be fierce private entrepreneurs who could not be expected to adopt the cooperative spirit.

Ultimately the organizing committee chose two candidates who were members of the local elite, the Sun cousins. Both Sun Zhonglu and Sun Zhongyao were very qualified, having gained much knowledge of the community through their respective roles as head of the township government and principal of the central elementary school. Moreover, they were both available, as they had recently lost their positions in the local government as a result of central government reforms. At least one member of the organizing committee had reservations about putting the ex-township head in charge, arguing that a person with such experience and connections would certainly not fail to profit from such a position. But those in favor pointed out that he understood the intricacies of the local scene and was widely trusted, and that furthermore, as a former township head, he had exercised restraint about seeking to profit from his position. Thus, the recommendation to select the Sun cousins was approved on the basis of their strong credentials, leadership skills, and firm support for the project and the NCC rural reconstruction team.

The three-month training course, which commenced in February 1941, had an enrollment of five trainees: the two Sun cousins for our salt supply co-op and three others, including a woman, who had been selected by Yen's institute to head up some future projects. The textbook used was an excellent simple manual of twelve lessons, already prepared by Yen's Rural Reconstruction Research Institute. For the first month, the students attended classes in the morning and afternoon, paying special attention to accounting, which was taught by Mr. Zhang. In the second month, they combined study with practical work: they had classes in the morning and in the afternoon toured the schools of the township in pairs, giving lectures to popularize the spirit and advantages of cooperatives. Ostensibly the students were the targets of this program, but in fact the organizers hoped to gain the support of the teachers—the intelligentsia of the rural community. The propagandists believed that the teachers would resent being lectured to directly but would absorb the message while it was delivered to their students. In the third month, the trainees were assigned the practical work of helping us (Isabel Brown and Yu Xiji) finish the house-to-house survey of the township. By the time the five students graduated, they had received solid training, with an especially good grounding in accounting.

At the end of May, a month after the collapse of Feng's phony cooperative, shares in the new cooperative were offered at ten yuan each. Buyers were cautious about investing until they were reassured that the venture was sound because it was backed by the local church, which had been in Prosperity for more than thirty-five years, rather than by private individuals or some recent organization such as the rural reconstruction team. Three hundred members joined in short order, buying shares to the value of ten thousand yuan. This provided the necessary capital for launching the venture. The sale set a record, according to T. H. Sun, for no other cooperative in all of China had been started without having to also borrow capital. In June, Sun Zhonglu was appointed as chief accountant and put in full charge of the operation of setting up a shop and arranging for the first purchase of salt.

An ominous sign appeared in late May with the development of tensions between T. H. Sun and the two young male organizers from Xiemachang, Zhang and Yang. This was reflected in the discourtesy Sun showed the cooperators on his occasional visits to Prosperity. The first time he treated them with open disrespect, the young men from Xiemachang were so angered that they decided to leave forthwith. But on calmer consideration, they swallowed their pride because they were bound by a formal agreement and, more compelling, they felt a strong attachment to the cooperative which had taken such effort and offered such promise. However, James Yen's institute demanded the immediate return of the three cooperative organizers. Zhang, Yang, and their young assistant departed for Xiemachang, leaving full responsibility for the church-sponsored salt supply cooperative in our hands. Even a prior arrangement for Zhang or Yang to return for periodic consultations had to be abandoned because our request for their travel expenses was turned down. At the same time, Sun Zhongyao also left to do an internship in Xiemachang. The cooperative thus lost most of its valuable expertise. Meanwhile, T. H. Sun, regarding the cooperative as successfully launched, announced in late May that he intended to devote himself to a new project reflecting his long-standing ties with the Christian Literature Society publishers: the translation of St. Augustine's *Confessions*.

An uneasy period followed as we waited for Sun Zhonglu and his supporters to get the new co-op firmly established. By this time we had a deeper understanding of the community and its leading figures and feared that the venture might end disastrously, bankrupting those who had trusted us and discrediting the church we were trying to revitalize. Gradually evidence of the struggle going on behind the scenes made itself manifest. First was the inexplicable length of time it was taking Sun to get the co-op into operation. However, by summertime he had bought stocks of salt, and Cao Yuexian, Prosperity's biggest landowner, who was a member, offered the cooperative the use of his building at No. 21 on the village street, which had been empty since the dissolving of the secret society's music club. Sun bought lime to whitewash the building and employed a carpenter to put in counters.

But then, one busy market day in July, just as this work was starting, Cao's wife arrived in the village. She stood outside the building where white-washing was just beginning and screamed at Sun Zhonglu, "What right have you to take over this building? We haven't given you permission!" And she proceeded to revile him for a good half hour. Cao's wife, a very good businesswoman who controlled the household and family finances while her husband devoted himself to leisure and high living, apparently regarded the co-op as a threat to her business interests. The co-op was forced to look for other premises. This small incident was the first indication to us that certain leading members of the community opposed the cooperative. Up to this time, no expression of hostility had come to our ears.

Throughout August the cooperative was dormant, if not dead. T. H. Sun had no time or inclination to involve himself further. In his opinion the cooperative was already a striking success: Sichuan's first cooperative with capital coming solely from its membership!

In October, at last some activity became observable, and with it a direct challenge to the cooperative began to emerge. Ordinary members in increasing numbers were coming to withdraw their names and demand their shares be repaid. Withdrawal of members could be a critical matter, for to be recognized by the government, a cooperative had to have a certain minimum membership. Later we learned that Feng Qingyun had produced this crisis: coercing his tenants, secretly getting control of the shares of some nervous investors by promising to buy their shares provided they left their names on the books, and having well-off friends buy a block of shares. Then at long last, in November 1941, came the elections for office. The man elected to leadership of the Prosperity Salt Supply Cooperative was none other than Feng Qingyun himself, chairman of the short-lived "Salt and Sugar Cooperative" set up the previous November, which had boosted salt prices to the peak of 1.45 yuan a *jin*—not to mention the fact that he was the township's biggest tax farmer, head of the office of land tax collection, and leading opium dealer.

News of this turn of events quickly reached the cooperative organizers back in Xiemachang, and they returned to Prosperity at once—and at their own expense. They called a membership meeting and announced the disbanding of the cooperative, and there, on the spot, they paid back all the share money to the individual members in whose names the shares were registered.

As groups of tenants gathered to receive their refunds, the organizers realized that their money, representing a majority block of shares, was the investment through proxies of a group of influential landlords led by Feng. In retrospect, it seems clear that none of these men was in favor of the church starting a salt cooperative and interfering with the high profits they were making through selling salt in the village at several times the Chongqing price. It was this bloc that had foiled Sun's efforts to get the cooperative going, causing the middle farmers to become apprehensive and demand their share money back, and it was this bloc that had finally elected Feng to leadership.

In dissolving the co-op, the investors did not lose any money. The Feng faction had their tenants buy shares in the cooperative for them, using their money, but in the tenants' names. When the cooperative was set up, it had a tenant as head, but after a month a new election was called and Feng, a landlord and prominent member of the Paoge, was elected. Feng was in the cooperative because of a clause in the cooperative agreement stating that no one would be barred from joining. The Feng faction then dissolved the cooperative, by election, with the agreement of all members. When the share money was returned to each member, including all of Feng's tenants, they most likely returned it to Feng.

The church organizers had not foreseen any of this; it taught them a real lesson. Their church-sponsored cooperative had become one more battlefield in the ongoing contention between rival power factions in the community, in this case the Suns versus Feng, who had the backing of Cao, indicating that the Cai lodge of the Paoge was involved. Sun—young, patriotic, openly devoted to modernizing reforms, and backed by the more independent ranks of the middle-income farmers—had been foiled by Feng. The demise of the cooperative was as unique as its establishment, for its dissolution was a public admission of failure by its promoters, and as such, it was highly unusual.

Shortly after the formal disbanding of the Salt Supply Cooperative, the Prosperity church community project that had sponsored it came to a close, unmarked by any formal announcement. The disheartened NCC rural reconstruction team was dissolved. No provision was made for Isabel Brown and Yu Xiji to prepare a report on their house-to-house economic survey of Prosperity. Staff members quietly departed for other jobs, leaving only Miss Zhu and her clinic, which the AMEM continued to finance for a period.[22] The views of the people of Prosperity on these efforts of ours were generous, but we did not learn that until many years later.

The story of this project to bring economic improvement to the rural areas throws light on this era of Guomindang rule. The NCC rural reconstruction team had paid attention primarily to the economic needs of the peasants and not to the political realities of Prosperity. They believed that they had gained the support of the Paoge for their projects. Cai, Feng, and other Paoge leaders had not given any open indication that they opposed the salt cooperative, and the reformers remained unaware of the danger the Paoge posed to their social project until the damage was done. In responding to the range of government and other reform initiatives in Prosperity during the war years, the Paoge leaders had varying interests. Cai's goal was to stop the growth of government power at the local level. Publicly he opposed certain action of township heads in the guise of protecting his constituency. Feng, in contrast, tried to gain money and power by manipulating the government's regulations, and he was willing to do the dirty work involved in bending local reform projects to his own ends. Both managed to increase their local power, in some cases by reaching out to the more educated and politically liberal elements in local society as well as more conservative forces. In political terms, the Paoge were a pervasive force without necessarily being a conservative one, as long as their direct interests were not threatened. The actions of local men of influence in defending Prosperity Market against the state and other outside interests might be more accurately characterized as measures taken to prevent, or limit, erosion of their resource base rather than as a defense of community interests.

The fate of the Prosperity salt cooperative was linked with and reflected power struggles at higher levels. While administrative changes were the first thrust of governmental reform, the second thrust was a set of measures aimed at breaking the hold of the secret society. These measures did not succeed in eliminating opium or gambling. Later, after our departure from Prosperity, the state attempted to ban the Paoge organization itself, but this had no more chance of success than the earlier measures. The petty local elite had strong links with the separatist provincial power network, a strong component of which was precisely the pervasive Paoge secret society.

The years 1940–1941 marked the peak of reform and modernization in Prosperity, and perhaps throughout Sichuan, and the beginning of the decline in such efforts. The collapse of the salt cooperative illustrates a shortcoming that has bedeviled governmental and nongovernmental rural development projects in China and elsewhere: a failure to identify the power structures and vested interests that were hostile to the reform agenda, and a corresponding failure to identify or develop allies to meet the challenge of a complex rural environment.

EPILOGUE

Piecing together what happened in Prosperity after we left, if seems that at some point Sun Zhonglu was, for a time, township head again. But he was replaced by Feng Qingyun, who became increasingly feared and hated by the local people because of his unscrupulous self-enrichment at their expense. Sun Zhongyao, Yang Huangzhang, and Wang Mingxuan collected evidence of Feng's corruption and in 1945 laid a change of corruption against him in the Bishan County court, with all three men presenting evidence. But the court rejected the charges. Sun then went to the Chongqing garrison and again pressed the charges and presented the evidence. The commander, at that time Wang Zanxiu, accepted the charges and ordered the Bishan garrison commander to arrest Feng. Feng handed himself over to the Chongqing garrison but was held for only three days. It was claimed that he paid ten million yuan in bribes for his release, at a time when this sum could have bought two hundred *dan* of rice land. In addition, he allegedly had the support of Tao Shuangxiang, reported to be a leading figure of the Shanghai Qingbang secret society, which had moved to Chongqing.

Feng continued as township head, and in the course of his six years in office he prospered sufficiently to increase his landholdings from under twenty *dan* to roughly one hundred. Much of this profiteering, by local report, came from selling military service postponements at exorbitant prices and filling the quotas through press-ganging. Then in 1945, the Farm Basics Bureau (*nongbenju*), as part of its rural reconstruction program, had provided improved corn and sweet potato seed and cotton yarn for home weaving to be lent to farmers at cost, but Feng, as township head, sold it for a profit. In this manner, Feng made himself the most hated man in Prosperity.

In the late 1940s, we were told, some people urged Feng and Sun to reconcile their differences and work together, since "Feng has money and Sun has education." But Sun refused. Then, as the People's Liberation Army (PLA) approached Sichuan and General Liu Wenhui and the Communists began negotiating a peaceful takeover of Sichuan, Feng wrote Sun, urging him to join forces against the Communists. Sun again refused. But he dared not remain in Prosperity and went to live in Bishan.

Commander Cai Xunqing also moved into Bishan, but for different reasons. Zhang Ming'an of Dingjia'ao, one of Bishan's leading secret-society chiefs and a close friend of Cai's, had apparently sworn blood brotherhood a couple of decades earlier with Liu Bocheng, who later came to be known as the victorious one-eyed Communist general. The story was that Liu had staged an uprising in the later 1920s but was defeated and escaped with his army down the Yangzi when in an encounter he was wounded in the eye. He returned to Chongqing for treatment and then to Bishan to convalesce. While there, he formed a friendship with Zhang Ming'an, and the two swore blood brotherhood. Zhang Ming'an's secretary (later his son-in-law) Ye Chunyi helped Liu Bocheng to escape. And so it happened that when the liberation of Sichuan approached, Zhang Ming'an advised Commander Cai to take no part in opposing the Communists and for the sake of his personal safety to move into town.

On December 1, shortly after Chongqing was taken over, Bishan was liberated peacefully. All three of the county's defending forces had left Bishan for the Black Forest in Yifeng Township on November 30 to enable the People's Liberation Army to enter the town unopposed. This withdrawal became known as the "Black Forest Uprising." But this did not mean peace throughout the county. Forces in Chongqing opposed to the Communist takeover fled the city through the encircling mountains and gathered in northern Bishan at the foot of the Great Mountains, where they established their headquarters in Prosperity, Danfeng, and Sanjiao townships. The leader, Zhang Xiaoliang, gathered around himself all *bao* heads, landlord forces, and scattered ex-army men that feared and opposed the Communists and grouped them as a force to oppose the PLA. Feng, the incumbent township head, joined Zhang. While there were no major engagements, innumerable small skirmishes took place and many dozens lost their lives. Among local notables killed by Feng or his men were Wang Mingxuan and Yang Huanzhang, activists in rival factions, who had remained in Prosperity. After some time the rebels were put down, and the leaders, including Feng Qingyun, were executed as political bandits (*tufei*), bringing to a close the career of Prosperity's most notorious power broker.

NOTES

1. For a discussion of Nationalist government attempts first to incorporate and then to limit Paoge and other secret society influence in Sichuan during the war, see chapter 5 of Shao Yong (2002).

2. Adshead (1992, p. 354) says that in 1909 Sichuan was "the empire's premier producer and consumer" of opium.

3. Su Shiyong (1999) writes that from 1917 to 1933, Sichuan produced the most opium, had the biggest opium market, and was home to the greatest number of smokers in China, acting also as a transshipment point for opium from Guizhou, Yunnan, Shaanxi, and Gansu.

4. Su Shiyong (1999) gives details of measures taken during the Nanjing Decade to attempt to ban opium in the province.

5. Kapp (1973), p. 122.

6. Su Shiyong (1999).

7. Zhang Lijie (2004).

8. Kapp (1973), p. 94.

9. Kapp (1973), p. 113.

10. The Nationalists were still able to retain a very small section of seawater production areas plus some of the sea salt areas in remote places, and some in the Northwest (Zhang Lijie 2004, p. 142).

11. According to Zhang Lijie's research (2004, p. 142), salt production fell by 47 percent between 1937 and 1938, and in the next several years it continued to decline.

12. Peng Hongbi (2004), p. 16.

13. Zhang Lijie (2004), p. 149.

14. For details of the attempt of the Bishan County government to expand its control over salt distribution in 1940, and its abandonment of this attempt in 1941, see Sichuan sheng Bishan xianzhi (1996, p. 245). This was part of a system in which the provincial government attempted to control salt production and distribution, allocating supplies to institutions and merchants, setting price controls and taxes, and requiring regular reports from localities to the province. For a discussion of salt taxation policy during this period, see Dong Zhenping (2004). On salt transport, government monopoly, salt administration reform, and salt production, see Dong Zhenping (2002), Jin Pushen (Jen Pu-sen) and Dong Zhenping (2001), Zhang Lijie (2004), Peng Hongbi (2004), Liu Jinghua (2005).

15. Sichuan sheng Bishan xianzhi (1996), p. 242.

16. Bishan dang'anguan (Bishan County Archives), Shehui ke 1945, chuanzong hao 1, an/zhuanhao 191, p. 161.

17. Bishan dang'anguan (Bishan County Archives), document on salt transport, no. 569, 1941.

18. The entirety of the Great Rear suffered from shortages in salt because the Japanese invasion had cut Sichuan off from the coastal salt supplies. Speculators responded by hoarding, driving the prices even higher.

19. After James Yen's Dingxian model in Hebei was overrun by the Japanese, James Yen founded the Rural Reconstruction Institute (*Xiangcun jianshe yanjiu yuan*) in Xindu near Chengdu. He also authorized Jiang Zhi'ang to establish a Dingxian model in Xiemachang. Jiang was a professor of sociology at Yenching University in Beijing. He had joined James Yen's mass education project in Dingxian County and moved with it to Sichuan in 1940. By mid-1940, Jiang had rented two tumbledown mud farmhouses and gathered an experienced staff, but he lacked a suitable project and local connections.

20. Charles Hayford (1990, p. 193) refers to this organization as the National College of Rural Reconstruction, but we prefer to call it an institute.

21. At this time, Jiang Zhi'ang was conducting a survey of two nearby townships. His report, "Wartime Local Politics in Rural Areas," was published in September 1941 by the Rural Reconstruction Research Institute Press (Jiang Zhi'ang 1941). Jiang remained for a time at Xiemachang, then went to Chengdu to teach sociology at West China Union University. He became a professor and then Dean of Studies by the age of forty. He died of natural causes during or shortly after the Cultural Revolution.

22. The details of T. H. Sun's subsequent career are unknown. Isabel Crook was told that sometime after 1949 he committed suicide.

Glossary

an yaomen	暗幺们	Secret errand boys and messengers for the Paoge
bai longmenzhen	摆龙门阵	Sichuanese term for gossip sessions
ban zhiye Paoge	半职业袍哥	Semiprofessional members of the Paoge
bang laoer	棒老二	Bandits
bao	保	Administrative unit of 10 jia, or about 100 households
baojia	保甲	Government administrative unit organized by household
Batang	八塘	Place name
bazi xiansheng	八字先生	Horoscopist
Beibei	北碚	Place name
Bishan	璧山	County in which Prosperity was located; also name of the county seat
Bishan zongshe	璧山总社	Bishan General Association of the Paoge
candou	蚕豆	Broad beans
chang	场	Market village; standard periodic market; market place in a town or city
Chengdu	成都	Place name
Chengnan	城南	Place name
chonghun	重婚	Polygamy

273

Chongqing	重庆	Place name
chuanxing dayuan	船形大院	Boat-shaped courtyard
chuxiao	初小	Lower primary school
citang	祠堂	Ancestral hall
cun	村	Village
dandao hui	单刀会	Second of two annual religious ceremonies held by Paoge to worship Guan Gong, at which organizational matters are publicized (new members, promotions, punishments, etc.)
danfang	丹方	Herbalist's special secret prescription
Danfeng	丹凤镇	Place about 6 kilometers south of Daxing
Dapeng	大鹏	Market village near Prosperity
dasheng	大圣	Shaman (female)
Daxing	大兴	New name for Prosperity township after boundary changes
dayaji	打牙祭	"Meat treat," "sacrifice to the teeth" (meal with plenty of meat)
daye	大爷	Elder Brother in Paoge lodge
Dingjia	丁家	Place name
Dingjia'ao	丁家坳	Place name
duobazi	舵把子	The top Rudder Man; high-ranking Paoge official
erba	二八	(A girl older than) sixteen
Erlang	二郎	A god local to Sichuan
erye	二爷	Second Brother
fangying	放阴	Male shaman
feilei	匪类	Bandit types
fen	分	One cent; see also "Weights and Measures"
fengshui	风水	A term used in Daoism to help people tell whether a location is suited for house building or graves by observing the environment of the location. It can also

decide the best orientation of the houses or graves.

fu	符	Inscriptions to bring good fortune in curing a disease, sold to the patient by the diviner dealing with the case
hudou	胡豆	Broad beans
Fulu	福禄	Market village near Prosperity
gao bucheng, di bujiu	高不成,低不就	To be unfit for a higher status but unwilling to accept a lower one
gaoxiao	高小	Higher primary school
Gaoyuan sijiao	高院四角	Gaoyuan Temple Corners
Gelaohui	哥老会	Brotherhood, Robed Brothers (referred to locally as Paoge)
gongqiao	拱桥	Arched Bridge
gongtou	工头	Foreman
goutian	沟田	Flood paddies
gua	卦	Diviner's instrument made of bamboo root
guahong	挂红	"Hanging up the red cloth" to ward off evil spirits
Guan Gong	关公	Folk Buddhist deity, God of War and patron god of business and the Paoge
guanggun	光棍	"Bare sticks," drifters with no ties to the community
guanhua	观花	Diviner
Guanyin	观音	Popular Buddhist diety/Goddess of Mercy
Guofei	国匪	Bandit type
Guolu	啯噜	Bandit organization
Hangkong jiuguohui	航空救国会	Salvation through Aviation Organization
hongbao	红包	Red packaging (for gifts)
huajiao	花椒	Sichuan peppercorns
Huguang tian Sichuan	湖广填四川	Hubei and Hunan (migrants) filled up Sichuan
Huifei	会匪	Brotherhoods (bandit type)
hunshui	浑水	Murky water

jia	甲	Subdivision of a bao; about 10 households
Jiang Zhi'ang	蒋旨昂	Name of a sociologist
jiangli	讲理	Mediation or arbitration, often carried out in teahouses
jiaofei	教匪	Religious sect bandit
jigu	积谷	Levy for rice storage against famine
Jixianhui	机仙会	Loom Fairy Society
junxu fei	军需费	Grain levy for army horses
kanhua	看化	Expensive consultation with diviner
kanshi	看示	Inexpensive consultation with diviner
kou	口	Opium pellet
kuli	苦力	Bitter labor
Laifeng	来凤	Place name
lajiao	辣椒	Chili pepper
lao taipo	老太婆	Elderly woman from upper-class background
laoshi ren	老实人	Simple and honest folk
lianbao	联保	Township (administrative form set up in the beginning of 1940 and repealed in July 1940)
Liang Shuming	梁漱溟	A scholar and educator
Liu Xiang	刘湘	Warlord, governor of Sichuan, 1890–1938
Liutang	六塘	Place name
lixi	利息	Interest payments
Longwang	龙王	Dragon King
maliang macao	马粮、马草	Grain levy for army horses
Maolai shan	茅莱山	Maolai Hill; landmark just outside Prosperity market village
matou	码头	Port, or meeting place for a Paoge lodge
ming yaomen	明幺们	Errand boys and messengers for the Paoge
mintuan fei	民团费	Rice levy for maintenance of the militia
minzheng ting	民政厅	Civil Affairs Bureau
Neijiang	内江	Place name

Niuwang	牛(魔)王	Cow/buffalo deity
nongbenju	农本局	Farm Basics Bureau
pai	排	Unit of ten households
paijiu	牌九	Form of gambling
pangtian	旁田	Paddies bordering flood paddies
paocai	泡菜	Pickled vegetables
Paoge	袍哥	Robed Brothers Secret Society
pengsha	硼砂	Borax; a disinfectant
bingyi shishi xiejin hui	兵役实施协进会	Compulsory Military Service Implementation Association
Puyuanzhen	蒲元镇	Place name
qing shui	清水	Clear water
Qinggang	青杠	Place name
Qingming	清明	Pure Brightness Festival (tomb-sweeping day)
qu	区	District
ren, yi, li, zhi, xin	仁义礼智信	Benevolence, righteousness, rites, wisdom, trustworthiness (names of Paoge lodges)
Renlongshe	仁龙社	Paoge lodge name
Renluoshe	仁罗社	Paoge lodge name
Renshou	仁寿	Place name
ruo guan	弱冠	A boy older than eighteen
sanhetu	三合土	A local type of cement made from lime, coal dust and dirt
Sanjiao	三教	Small market village near Prosperity
Sanmin zhuyi qingnian tuan	三民主义青年团	Three People's Principles Youth League
sao	嫂	Elder sister-in-law/wife of elder brother
shantian	山田	Hill paddies
shang yue hui	赏月会	Full Moon Committee
shengdeng	圣灯	Sacred Lamp
Shengdengsi	圣灯寺	Sacred Lamp Temple
shenjia bu ming	身价不明	"his position in society would be unclear"

shengyuan	生员	Licentiates who had passed the lowest rung of the civil service examination
shenliang	绅粮	Gentry plus grain
shenshi	绅士	Gentry
shizi	狮子	Place name
shuangbai	双柏	Double Pines
shuigou	水沟	Water Gully
Shuihu zhuan	水浒传	*Water Margin* (a novel)
shuitian	水田	Flood paddies
Sichuan sheng jin yan duli chu	四川省禁烟督理处	Sichuan Provincial Department for the Supervision of Banning Opium
siye	四爷	Fourth Brother
T.H. Sun/Sun Ensan (Sun Tianhsi)	孙恩三	National Christian Council official, director of project
tiao duangong	跳端公	Exorcism ritual
tong	桐	Tong or tung oil
tongyangxi	童养媳	Foster fiancée; girl adopted for later marriage into family
tuanjie, jinzhang, yansu, huopo	团结紧张严肃活泼	United, alert, earnest, and lively
tuanzong	团总	Local militia
tufei	土匪	Political bandits
tuhao lieshen	土豪劣绅	Bullies and evil gentry
tuzai shui	屠宰税	Pig-butchering tax
Tuzhu	土主	Earth God; local to Prosperity
Tuzhu miao	土主庙	Shrine to Earth God
Wenmiao	文庙	Confucian temple
Wumiao	武庙	Military temple
xian	县	County
xiang	乡	Rural township

Xiangcun jianshe yanjiuyuan	乡村建设研究院	Rural Reconstruction Research Institute
xiansheng	先生	Respectful form of address
Xiemachang	歇马场	Place name
Xindu	新都	Place name
Xinglong	兴隆	Prosperity (the name of a place)
Xinglong lianbao	兴隆联保	Xinglong (Prosperity) township
Xinglongchang	兴隆场	Xinglong (Prosperity) market
Xinglongxiang	兴隆乡	Xinglong (Prosperity) township
xu sui	虚岁	Nominal age
Yan Yangchu	晏阳初	Social reformer James Yen
Yangjia wan	杨家湾	Place name
Yanguang Shengmu	眼光圣母	Holy mother of eyesight
yaodian	幺店	A little trading center
yaomen	幺们	Errand boys and messengers for the Paoge
yatou	丫头	Maids
yi shi zhu xing	衣食住行	Phrase for four uses of bamboo (clothing, food, housing, transport)
yigu	义谷	Levy for rice storage against famine
yiwu jiaoyu	义务教育	Public education
yuan	元	Unit of money; one Chinese dollar
zabao	杂包	Gifts to host of parties or banquets
zhen	镇	Urban township
zhengliang	征粮	Land tax
Zhengxin	正心	Place name
zhiye Paoge	职业袍哥	Professional members of the Paoge
Zhongyang ribao	中央日报	*Central Daily* newspaper
zhongyi	中医	Practitioners of traditional Chinese medicine

zhongnian shenghui	终年盛会	Lunar New Year festival
zhuang	庄	Farming village
zhuangding liang	壮丁粮	Rice allowance for military dependents
zigong	自贡	Salt wells
ziliujing	自流井	"Self-flowing" salt wells
Zitong	梓潼	Market village near Prosperity
Zizhi cujinhui	自治促进会	Association for the Promotion of Local Autonomy

Weights and Measures

dan	石	Unit of weight (fifty kilograms); this is modern equivalent
dan	石	Unit of area required to produce one *dan* of rice; so varies in size according to productivity
dou	斗	Volume measure which varied in size as it was undergoing government reform to establish the metric system; about one liter
dou	斗	A measure of dry land according to the fixed amount of grain it is expected to yield
fen	分	Tenth of a *mu*
jin	斤	Weight measure (1.1 pounds)
kou	口	Opium pellet; size of standard dose
li	里	Distance measure; one-third of a mile or half a kilometer
mu	亩	Land measure; one-sixth of an acre
sheng	升	Volume measure; approximately one liter
shidan	市石	Land measure (twenty *shidan* = one acre or 6.44 local *dan*)
shimu	市亩	Official measure equal to .37 *dan*

Works Cited

Adshead, S. A. M. *Salt and Civilization*. London: Macmillan, 1992.

Ahern, Emily M. "Segmentation in Chinese Lineages: A View through Written Genealogies." *American Ethnologist* 3 (1976): 1–16.

Alitto, Guy S. *The Last Confucian: Liang Shu-ming and the Chinese Dilemma of Modernity*. Berkeley: University of California Press, 1979.

"Annual Report of the National Institute of Health, 1942." Rockefeller Foundation Archives, box 218, 601. Rockefeller Archive Center, Sleepy Hollow, NY.

"Bai longmenzhen shi shenme yisi?" 摆龙门阵是什么意思？ [What Is the Meaning of *bai longmenzhen*?], October 15, 2007. http://tinyurl.com/bch95ov.

"Bai longmenzhen shi shenme yisi?" 摆龙门阵是什么意思？ [What Is the Meaning of *bai longmenzhen*?], August 22, 2010. wenwen.soso.com/z/q2002434361.htm.

Balfour, Marshall C., to Wilbur A. Sawyer, December 24, 1940. Rockefeller Foundation Archives, RG 1.1, series 601, box 18, folder 161. Rockefeller Archive Center, Sleepy Hollow, NY.

Barnes, Nicole. "Protecting the National Body: Gender and Public Health in Southwest China during the War with Japan, 1937–1945." Ph.D. diss., University of California, Irvine, 2012.

Bender, D. R. "A Refinement of the Concept of Household: Families, Co-residence and Domestic Functions in Ondo." *American Anthropologist* 69 (1967): 493–504.

Bender, D. R. "De Facto Families and De Jura Households in Ondo." *American Anthropologist* 73 (1971): 223–241.

Bernhardt, Kathryn. "Women and the Law: Divorce in the Republican Period." In Kathryn Bernhardt and Philip C. C. Huang (eds.), *Civil Law in Qing and Republican China*, pp. 187–214. Stanford, CA: Stanford University Press, 1994.

Bishan dang'anguan (Bishan County Archives), Minzhengting (Office of Civil Administration), document no. 102, March 1940.

Bishan dang'anguan (Bishan County Archives), Shehui ke (Social Affairs) 1945, chuanzong hao 1, an/zhuan hao 191, p. 161.

Bishan xianzhi (Bishan Gazetteer), in *Zhongguo difang zhijicheng* 45, no. 9 (1992). Chengdu: Ba Shu shushe.

Bishan dang'anguan (Bishan County Archives), document on salt transport, no. 569, 1941.

Bishan shiyan difang fayuan (Bishan Experimental Regional Court), document no. 41–46, n.d.

Bishan shiyan difang fayuan (Bishan Experimental Regional Court), document no. 3450-447, July 12, 1941.

"Bishanxian Bihan zongshe" [The General Headquarters of Bishan County's Han Order]. File 13/1, Bishan County Archives.

Brown, Julia. Unpublished letter, February 2, 1941.

Buck, John Lossing. *Land Utilization in China: A Study of 16,786 Farms in 168 Localities, and 38,256 Farm Families in Twenty-Two Provinces in China, 1929–1933*. New York: Paragon Book Reprint Corp., 1964 (1937).

Buck, John Lossing. "Government and the Farmer." In Frank Wilson Price (ed.), *Wartime China: As Seen by Westerners*. Chungking: China Publishing Company, 1942.

Buck, John Lossing. *An Agricultural Survey of Szechwan Province, China*. Chungking: Farmers Bank of China, 1943.

Buck, Pearl S. *Tell the People: Mass Education in China*. New York: American Council Institute for the Pacific Rim, 1945.

Bulmer, R. N. H. "Leadership and Social Structure among the Kayaka People of the Western Highlands District of New Guinea." Ph.D. diss., Australian National University, Canberra, 1960.

Cai Shaoqing. "On the Origins of the Gelaohui." *Modern China* 10, no. 4 (October 1984): 481–508.

Cao Hongying. Personal interview. February 2, 2005.

Chang, Chung-li. *The Chinese Gentry: Studies on Their Role in Nineteenth-Century Chinese Society*. Seattle: University of Washington Press, 1967.

Chen, C. C. "A Short Review of Development in Maternity and Child Health Work at Chengtu" (June 1944). Rockefeller Foundation Archives, RG 1.1, series 601, box 18, folder 162. Rockefeller Archive Center, Sleepy Hollow, NY.

Chetham, Deirdre. *Before the Deluge: The Vanishing World of the Yangtze's Three Gorges*. New York: Palgrave Macmillan, 2002.

Ch'ien, Tuan-sheng. *The Government and Politics of China, 1912–1949*. Stanford, CA: Stanford University Press, 1970.

Chin, Rockwood Q. P. "Cotton Mills, Japan's Economic Spearhead in China." *Far Eastern Survey* 6, no. 23 (1937).

China Handbook, 1937–1943: A Comprehensive Survey of Major Developments in China in Six Years of War. New York: Macmillan, 1943.

"China-Szechuan Provincial Annual Report Health Administration, 1st Semi-Annual Report, 1941–1942." Rockefeller Foundation Archives, box 218, folder 2718. Rockefeller Archive Center, Sleepy Hollow, NY.

Cressey, George. "Agricultural Regions of China, Part VI." *Economic Geography* 10, no. 2 (April 1934): 109–142.

Crook, David, and Isabel Crook. *Ten Mile Inn: Mass Movement in a Chinese Village*. New York: Pantheon Books, 1979.

Crook, Isabel, with Yu Xiji. *A Community Called Prosperity*. Unpublished manuscript, 1994.

Culp, Robert. *Articulating Citizenship: Civic Education and Student Politics in Southeast China, 1912–1940*. Cambridge, MA: Harvard University Press, 2007.

Davin, Delia. "Women in the Countryside in China." In Roxane Witke and Margery Wolf (eds.), *Women in Chinese Society*, pp. 243–273. Stanford, CA: Stanford University Press, 1975.

Dennerline, Jerry. "Marriage, Adoption, and Charity in the Development of Lineages in Wu-hsi from Sung to Ch'ing." In Patricia Ebrey and James L. Watson (eds.), *Kinship Organization in Late Imperial China, 1000–1940*, pp. 186–194. Berkeley: University of California Press, 1986.

Dong Zhenping. "1937–1941 nian guomin zhengfu shiyan yunshu zhidu shu lun" [Discussion of the System of Transporting Edible Salt by the Nationalist Government in 1937–1941]. *Yan ye shi yanjiu* [Research in the History of Salt Affairs], no. 1 (2002): 18–25.

Dong Zhenping. "Lun kangzhan shiqi guomin zhengfu de ya shui zhengce" [On the Nationalist Government's Salt Tax Policy during the Resistance War]. *Kangri zhanzheng yanjiu* [Journal of Research into the War of Resistance], no. 3 (2004): 121–140.

Duara, Prasenjit. *Culture, Power, and the State: Rural North China, 1900–1942*. Stanford, CA: Stanford University Press, 1988.

Dykstra, Theodore. Papers. Yenching Library, Harvard University.

Ebrey, Patricia, and James L. Watson (eds.). *Kinship Organization in Late Imperial China, 1000–1940*. Berkeley: University of California Press, 1986.

Entenmann, Robert. *Migration of Settlement in Sichuan, 1644–1796.* Ph.D. diss., Harvard University, 1982.

Esherick, Joseph. "War and Revolution: Chinese Society during the 1940s." *Twentieth Century China* 27, no. 1 (2001): 1–38.

Eyferth, Jacob. "De-Industrialization in the Chinese Countryside: Handicrafts and Development in Jiajiang (Sichuan), 1935–1978." *China Quarterly*, no. 173 (March 2003).

Fan Shaozeng. "Huiyi wo zai Sichuan Paoge zhong de zuzhi huodong" [A Memoir of My Organizational Activities within the Sichuan Gelaohui]. *Wenshi ziliao xuanji*, no. 84 (1982).

Fei, Xiaotong. *Peasant Life in China: A Field Study of Country Life in the Yangtze Valley.* New York: Oxford University Press, 1946.

Fei, Xiaotong, and Tse-i Chang. *Earthbound China: A Study of Rural Economy in Yunnan.* Chicago: University of Chicago Press, 1945.

Feuchtwang, Stephan. "Curves and the Urbanisation of Meifa Village." In Stephan Feuchtwang (ed.), *Making Place: State Projects, Globalisation and Local Responses in China.* Portland, OR: Cavendish, 2004.

"First Report of the Szechuan Provincial Health Administration" (1941), p. 1. Rockefeller Foundation Archives, box 218, file 601. Rockefeller Archive Center, Sleepy Hollow, NY.

Gamble, Sidney. *Ting Hsien: A North China Rural Community.* Stanford, CA: Stanford University Press, 1968 (1954).

Glahn, Richard Von. *The Country of Streams and Grottoes: Expansion, Settlement, and the Civilizing of the Sichuan Frontier in Song Times.* Cambridge, MA: Harvard University Press, 1987.

Gluckman, Max. "Gossip and Scandal." *Current Anthropology* 4, no. 3 (June 1963): 307–316.

Gunde, Richard. "Land Tax and Social Change in Sichuan, 1925–1935." *Modern China* 2, no. 1 (January 1976).

Harris, Lane. "Constructing the State and Unifying the Nation: The *Baojia* in Right-Wing Guomindang Political Philosophy, 1927–1949." Unpublished paper, n.d.

Hayford, Charles W. *To the People: James Yen and Village China.* New York: Columbia University Press, 1990.

Higonnet, Margaret R., Jane Jenson, Sonya Michel, Margaret C. Weitz (eds.). *Behind the Lines: Gender and the Two World Wars.* New Haven, CT: Yale University Press, 1989.

Hinton, Carmelita. "A Mountain of Anomie: Transformations of the Soushantu Genre." Ph.D. diss., Harvard University, 2000.

Ho, Ping-ti. *Studies on the Population of China, 1368–1953.* Cambridge, MA: Harvard University Press, 1959.

Howard, Joshua H. *Workers at War: Labor in China's Arsenals, 1937–1953.* Stanford, CA: Stanford University Press, 2004.

Huang, Philip C. C. *The Peasant Economy and Social Change in North China.* Stanford, CA: Stanford University Press, 1985.

Huang Shiqian, head of the Bishan County Office. Interview. 1983.

Huang Tianhua. "Kangzhan shiqi Chuankang liangsheng de shiqing yu minqing" [Conditions and Sentiments of People in the Two Provinces of Sichuan and Xikang during the War of Resistance]. *Minguo dang'an*, no. 1 (2007): 97–103.

Hubbard, Hugh. "A Report, Visit to Sichuan, December 11–23, 1947." Excerpts in International Institute of Rural Reconstruction files.

Hume, Joy. "War Hitting American Tung-Oil Interests." *Far Eastern Survey* 8, no. 12 (June 7, 1939): 142–144.

Jacobson, Carl Whitney. "Brotherhood and Society: The Shaanxi Gelaohui 1867–1912." Ph.D. diss., University of Michigan, 1993.

"Jianchabao zaohun" [An Investigation into the Situation of Early Marriages]. Chongqing dang'anguan (Chongqing Municipal Archives), file 5, document no. 10, August 15, 1943.

Jiang Zhi'ang. *Zhanshi de xiangcun shequ zhengzhi* [Wartime Politics in Rural Communities]. Chengdu: Xiangcun jianshe yanjiusuo [Rural Reconstruction Research Institute], 1941.

Jin Pushen (Jen Pu-sen) and Dong Zhenping. "Lun kangri zhanzheng shiqi guomin zhengfu yan zhuanmai zhidu" [On the Salt Sales Monopoly of the Nationalist Government in the Anti-

Japanese War Period]. *Zhejiang daxue xuebao* [Journal of Zhejiang University] (Humanities and Social Sciences) 31, no. 4 (July 2001).

Kapp, Robert A. *Szechwan and the Chinese Republic: Provincial Militarism and Central Power, 1911–1938*. New Haven, CT: Yale University Press, 1973.

Kirby, William C. "Continuity and Change in Modern China: Economic Planning on the Mainland and on Taiwan, 1943–1958." *Australian Journal of Chinese Affairs* 24 (1990): 121–141.

Lapidus, Ira. "Hierarchies and Networks: A Comparison of Chinese and Islamic Societies." In Frederic Wakeman and Carolyn Grant (eds.), *Conflict and Control in Late Imperial China*. Berkeley: University of California Press, 1975.

Lary, Diana. *The Chinese People at War: Human Suffering and Social Transformation, 1937–1945*. New York: Cambridge University Press, 2010.

Lary, Diana, and Stephen MacKinnon (eds.). *The Scars of War: The Impact of Warfare on Modern China*. Vancouver: UBC Press, 2001.

Lattimore, Owen, and Eleanor Lattimore. *The Making of Modern China*. London: Allen and Unwin, 1945.

Lee, James. "Food Supply and Population Growth in Southwest China, 1250–1850." *Journal of Asian Studies* 41, no. 4 (August 1982): 711–746.

Lee, James. "The Legacy of Immigration in Southwest China, 1250–1850." *Annales de Demographie Historique* (1982): 279–304.

Lee, Richard. "The Pao-Chia System." *Papers on China*, no. 3 (May 1949): 193–224.

Li, Danke. *Echoes of Chongqing: Women in Wartime China*. Urbana: University of Illinois Press, 2010.

Liu, Cheng-yun. "The Ko-lao Hui in Late Imperial China." Ph.D. diss., University of Pittsburgh, 1983.

Liu Jinghua. "Kangzhan shiqi guomin zhengfu yan wu guanli tizhi de bianqian" [Variance of Salt Administrative System of the Republic of China in the Period of the Anti-Japanese War]. *Yanye shi yanjiu* [Journal of Salt History], no. 3 (2005): 3–17.

Liu Xianlan. Personal communication, 2006.

Lü Pingdeng. *Sichuan nongcun jingji* [Sichuan's Agrarian Economy]. Shanghai: Commercial Press, 1936.

Luo Minchen, practitioner of TCM [*Zhongyi*] in Daxing. Personal interviews. May 1997 and April 3, 2001.

MacKinnon, Stephen R. *Wuhan, 1938: War, Refugees, and the Making of Modern China*. Berkeley: University of California Press, 2008.

Marwick, Arthur. *The Deluge: British Society and the First World War*. London: The Bodley Head, 1965.

McIsaac, Mary Lee. "The Limits of Wartime Nationalism: Workers in Wartime Chongqing, 1937–1945." Ph.D. diss., Yale University, 1994.

Minguo zhengfu zhujichu tongjiqu [Statistical Abstracts of the Republic of China]. Shanghai, 1936.

Murray, Laura. "New World Food Crops in China: Farms, Food, and Families in the Wei River Valley, 1650–1910." Ph.D. diss., University of Pennsylvania, 1985.

Myers, Ramon H. "Cotton Textile Handicraft and the Development of the Cotton Textile Industry in Modern China." *Economic History Review* 18 (1965): 614–632.

Nadel-Klein, Jane. "Reweaving the Fringe: Localism, Tradition, and Representation in British Ethnography." *American Ethnologist* 18, no. 3 (October 2009): 500–517.

Nedostup, Rebecca. *Superstitious Regimes: Religion and Politics of Chinese Modernity*. Cambridge, MA: Harvard University Press, 2009.

Netting, Robert McC. *Smallholders, Householders: Farm Families and the Ecology of Intensive, Sustainable Agriculture*. Stanford, CA: Stanford University Press, 1993.

"The New County System in China." *Contemporary China: A Reference Digest* 1, no. 20 (February 23, 1942).

Nylan, Michael. "The Legacies of the Chengdu Plain." In Robert W. Bagley (ed.), *Ancient Sichuan: Treasures from a Lost Civilization*. Seattle and Princeton: Seattle Art Museum and Princeton University, 2001.

Peake, Cyrus. *Nationalism and Education in Modern China*. New York: Columbia University Press, 1932.

Peng Hongbi. "Lun kangzhan shiqi Zigong yan ye de fazhan" [Development of Zigong (Tsekong) Salt Affairs (yan ye) during the Anti-Japanese War]. *Kangding minzu shifan gaodeng zhuanke xuexiao xuebao* [Journal of Kangding Nationalities University] 13, no. 2 (June 2004).

"Preliminary Report of the Szechuan Provincial Health Administration, Chungking, Szechuan, China," December 25, 1942. Rockefeller Foundation Archives, RG 1.1, series 601, box 18, folder 162. Rockefeller Archive Center, Sleepy Hollow, NY.

Price, Frank, *The Rural Church in China: A Survey*. New York: Agricultural Missions, 1948.

Qin Baoqi and Meng Chao. "Gelaohui qiyuan kao" [Origins of the Gelaohui]. *Xueshu yuekan*, no. 4 (2000).

Qin Shao. "Tempest over Teapots: The Vilification of Teahouse Culture in Early Republican China." *Journal of Asian Studies* 57, no. 4 (November 1998).

Ran Mianhui. "Minguo shiqi de Sichuan baojia zhidu" [The Baojia System in Sichuan in the Republican Era]. *Wenshi zazhi* [Literature and History Journal] 5 (1999): 74–76.

Rawski, Evelyn. 1986. "The Ma Landlords of Yang-Jia-kou in Late Ch'ing and Republican China." In Patricia Buckley Ebrey and James L. Watson (eds.), *Kinship Organization in Late Imperial China, 1000–1949*, pp. 245–273. Berkeley: University of California Press.

"Report for 1922." In Official Minutes, West China [Chongqing] Conference of the Methodist Episcopal Church. Minutes of annual meetings from 1922 to 1939. Yale University Archives.

"Report of the Sichuan Provincial Health Administration, 1942." Rockefeller Foundation Archives, box 218, file 601. Rockefeller Archive Center, Sleepy Hollow, NY.

"A Review of Government Health Service in Sichuan, China for Period 1939–1945." Rockefeller Foundation Archives. Rockefeller Archive Center, Sleepy Hollow, NY.

Rowe, William T. *Crimson Rain: Seven Centuries of Violence in a Chinese County*. Stanford, CA: Stanford University Press, 2007.

Ruf, Gregory A. *Cadres and Kin: Making a Socialist Village in West China, 1921–1991*. Stanford, CA: Stanford University Press, 1998.

"Semi-Annual 1941 China-Szechuan Provincial Health Administration First Semi-Annual Report." Rockefeller Archives International Health Division, RG 5.3, series 601, box 218, folder 2718. Rockefeller Archive Center, Sleepy Hollow, NY.

Shao Yong. "Minguo banghui" [Gangs of the Republican Period]. In Tan Songling (ed.), *Zhongguo mimi shehui* [China's Secret Societies]. Fuzhou shi: Fujian renmin chubanshe, 2002.

Shaw, Earl B. "Swine Industry of China." *Economic Geography* 14, no. 4 (October 1938).

Shen Songqiao. "Cong zizhi baojia: jindai Henan difang jiceng zhengzhi de bianqian, 1908–1935" [From Self-Government to *baojia*: Local Political Change in Henan, 1908–1935]. *Zhongguo yanjiuyuan jindaishisuo jikan*, no. 18 (1989): 189–219.

Shen Zui, "Guanyu Du Yuesheng" [Concerning Du Yuesheng]. In Wu Yu, Liang Licheng, Wang Daozhi, et al., *Jindai Zhongguo banghui neimu* [Behind the Scenes with the Banghui in Modern China], vol. 1, pp. 340–387. Qunzhong chubanshe [Masses Publishing House], 1992.

Sichuan baike quanshu bian zuan weiyuan hui. *Sichuan baike quanshu* [Encyclopedia of Sichuan]. Chengdu: Sichuan cishu chubanshe, 1997.

Sichuan sheng Bishan xianzhi bian zuan weiyuan hui. *Bishan xianzhi* [Bishan Gazetteer]. Chengdu: Sichuan renmin chubanshe, 1996.

Sichuan sheng difang zhi bian zuan weiyuan hui [Sichuan Provincial Gazetteer Compilation Committee]. *Sichuan sheng zhi*: jiaoyuzhi [Annals of Sichuan Province: Education Gazetteer]. 2 vols. Chengdu: Sichuan ci shu chubanshe, 1996.

Sichuan sheng difang zhi bian zuan weiyuan hui [Sichuan Provincial Gazetteer Compilation Committee]. *Sichuan sheng zhi: nongyezhi* [Annals of Sichuan Province: Agricultural Gazetteer]. 2 vols. Chengdu: Sichuan ci shu chubanshe, 1996.

Sichuan sheng zhengfu mishuqu [Secretariat, Sichuan Provincial Government]. *Sichuan sheng xingzheng tucha zhuanyuan shizheng yanjiu hui zhilu* [Proceedings of the Conference of Sichuan Special Administrative Inspectors on Political Implementation]. Chengdu: 1935.

Skinner, G. William. *Marketing and Social Structure in Rural China.* Ann Arbor, MI: Association for Asian Studies, 2001 (reprinted from the *Journal of Asian Studies* 24, no. 1–3 [November, 1964; February and May, 1965]).

Skinner, G. William. *The City in Late Imperial China.* Stanford, CA: Stanford University Press, 1977.

Skinner, G. William. "Cities and the Hierarchy of Local Systems." In Arthur P. Wolf (ed.), *Studies in Chinese Society.* Stanford, CA: Stanford University Press, 1978.

Sommer, Matthew Harvey. *Sex, Law, and Society in Late Imperial China.* Stanford, CA: Stanford University Press, 2000.

Spence, Jonathan. "Opium Smoking in Ch'ing China." In Frederic Wakeman Jr. and Carolyn Grant (eds.), *Conflict and Control in Late Imperial China.* Berkeley: University of California Press, 1975.

Spencer, J. E. "The Szechuan Village Fair." *Economic Geography* 16 (1940): 48–58.

Spitzer, Leo. "Persistent Memory: Central European Refugees in an Andean Land." *Poetics Today* 17, no. 4 (Winter 1996): 617–638.

Stapleton, Kristin. "Urban Politics in an Age of 'Secret Societies': The Cases of Shanghai and Chengdu." *Twentieth Century China* 22, no. 1 (November 1996).

Stapleton, Kristin. "County Administration in Late-Qing Sichuan: Conflicting Models of Rural Policing." *Late Imperial China* 18 (1997): 100–132.

Strauss, Julia C. *Strong Institutions in Weak Polities: State Building in Republican China, 1927–1940.* New York: Oxford University Press, 1998.

Su Shiyong. "Minguo shiqi Sichuan sheng jinyan gaishu" [Overall Situation with Opium in Sichuan during the Republican Period]. *Wenshi zazhi* [Journal of Culture and History], no. 4 (1999).

Summerfield, Penny. *Reconstructing Women's Wartime Lives: Discourse and Subjectivity in Oral Histories of the Second World War.* Manchester: Manchester University Press, 1998.

Sun, T. H. "The Church in China's Rural Reconstruction." *Chinese Recorder*, August 1940.

Sun Zhongyao. Personal interview with Isabel Crook. 1983.

"Szechuan Provincial Health Administration, 1942," p. 2. Rockefeller Foundation Archives, box 218, file 601. Rockefeller Archive Center, Sleepy Hollow, NY.

Tang Shaowu, Li Zhusan, and Jiang Xiangchen. "Jiefangqian Chongqing de paoge" [Chongqing's Robed Brothers before Liberation]. *Chongqing wenshi ziliao*, no. 31 (1986): 119–198.

Tawney, R. H. *Land and Labor in China.* Boston: Beacon, 1966.

Thaxton, Ralph A., Jr. *Salt of the Earth.* Berkeley, CA: University of California Press, 1996.

Ts'ai, Caroline Hui-yu. "Baozheng, baojia shuji, jiezhuang yichang—koushu lishi" [Baojia Headmen, Baojia Secretaries, and Township Officials—Oral Histories]. *Shilian zazhi* [Journal of Historical Association] 23 (November 1993): 23–40.

Van Slyke, Lyman P. *Yangtze: Nature, History, and the River.* Reading, MA: Addison-Wesley, 1988.

Von Glahn, Richard. *The Country of Streams and Grottoes: Expansion, Settlement, and the Civilizing of the Sichuan Frontier in Song Times.* Cambridge, MA: Harvard University Press, 1987.

Wakeman, Frederic, and Carolyn Grant. *Conflict and Control in Late Imperial China.* Berkeley: University of California Press, 1975.

Wang Chunwu. *Paoge tanmi* [Exploring the Mysteries of the Paoge]. Ba Shu shushe chubanshe [Ba Shu Book Society Publishing House], 1993.

Watson, James L. "Chinese Kinship Reconsidered: Anthropological Perspectives on Historical Research." *China Quarterly* 92 (December 1982): 589–622.

Watson, James L. "Anthropological Overview: The Development of Chinese Descent Groups." In Patricia Ebrey and James L. Watson (eds.), *Kinship Organizations in Late Imperial China, 1000–1940*, pp. 274–292. Berkeley, CA: University of California Press, 1986.

Wei, William. *Counterrevolution in China: The Nationalists in Jiangxi during the Soviet Period*. Ann Arbor: University of Michigan Press, 1985.

Wei Zheng. "Zhang Sunping zhuan." *Suishu*, vol. 46. Beijing: Beijing tushuguan chubanshe, 2006.

West China Missionary News. Chungking, West China: West China Missions Advisory Board, 1899, 1929, 1937.

Wickam, Chris. "Gossip and Resistance among Medieval Peasantry." *Past and Present* 160, no. 1 (August 1998): 3–24.

Wigen, Karen. "Culture, Power, and Place: The New Landscapes of East Asian Regionalism." *American Historical Review*, October 1999, 1183–1203.

Wolf, Arthur P. (ed.). *Studies in Chinese Society*. Stanford, CA: Stanford University Press, 1978.

Wright, Tim. "Distant Thunder: The Regional Economies of Southwest China and the Impact of the Great Depression." *Modern Asian Studies* 34, no. 3 (July 2000): 697–738.

Wu Zhimin. Interview. Daxing. June 2007.

Wyman, Judith. "Social Change, Anti-foreignism and Revolution in China: Chongqing Prefecture, 1870s to 1911." Ph.D. diss., University of Michigan, 1993.

Wyman, Judith. "The Ambiguities of Chinese Antiforeignism: Chongqing, 1870–1900." *Late Imperial China* 18, no. 2 (1997): 86–122.

Xiao Gongquan. *Rural China: Imperial Control in the Nineteenth Century*. Seattle: University of Washington Press, 1960.

Xiong Zhaoyan. "Yijiusanliu nian 'Chengdu Daquan Fandian shijian' neimu" [The Inside Story of the 1936 "Chengdu Great Sichuan Hotel Incident"]. *Chengdu wenshi ziliao xuanji* [Selected Historical Materials on Chengdu] 7 (December 1984): 82–92.

Xiong Zhuoyun and Wu Shaobo. "Sichuan paoge zuzhi chutan" [Preliminary Research on the Sichuan Paoge Organization]. *Wenshi zazhi* (Journal of Literature and History), no. 1 (1989).

Yanagisako, Sylvia Junko. "Family and Household: The Analysis of Domestic Groups." *Annual Review of Anthropology* 8 (October 1979): 164–165.

Yang, Ching-kun (C. K.). *A North China Local Market Economy*. New York: Institute of Pacific Relations, 1944.

Yang, C. K. *Nanching: A Chinese Village and Its Early Change under Communism*. Cambridge: Massachusetts Institute of Technology, 1954.

Yang, C. K. *Religion in Chinese Society: A Study of the Contemporary Social Functions of Religion and Some of Their Historical Factors*. Berkeley: University of California Press, 1961.

Yang, Martin. *A Chinese Village: Taitou, Shantung Province*. New York: Columbia University Press, 1945.

Yen, Chiang-kwoh. "The Tung Region of China." *Economic Geography* 19, no. 4 (October 1943): 418–427.

Yi Baisha [Isabel Crook] and Yu Xiji. *Xinglong chang: kangzhan shiqi Sichuan nongmin shenghuo diaocha (1940–1942)* [Xinglong Chang: Field Notes of a Village Called Prosperity 1940–1942]. Zhonghua shuju, 2012.

You Xin. "Di sibailiushiqici de Chuan zhan" [The 467th Sichuan War]. *Dongfang zazhi* [Eastern Miscellany] 29 (November 1, 1932).

Yu, Xiji. Personal interview. June 2001.

Zang Xiaowei, "Family, Kinship, Marriage, and Sexuality." In Robert E. Gamer (ed.), *Understanding Contemporary China*, 267–292. Boulder, CO: Lynne Rienner, 1999 (1998).

Zelin, Madeleine. "The Rights of Tenants in Mid-Qing Sichuan: A Study of Land-Related Lawsuits in the Baxian Archives." *Journal of Asian Studies* 45, no. 3 (May 1986): 499–526.

Zhang Lijie. "Kangzhan houqi guotongqu de yanzheng gaizhi" [Reform of the Salt Administration during the Latter Part of the Anti-Japanese War]. *Kangri zhanzheng yanjiu* [Studies in the War of Resistance against Japan], no. 3 (2004): 141–162.

Zhang Tongxin. Personal interview. Spring 2005.

Zhang Zeheng. "Zhongguo xinan shaoshu minzu de tuzhu yanyang" [The Minorities of Southwest China and Their Belief in Tuzhu]. *Zhongnan minzu daxue xuebao, Renwen shehui kexue ban* [Journal of South-Central University for Nationalities, Humanities and Social Sciences] 26, no. 5 (2006): 60–65.

Zhao, Ma. "On the Run: Women, City, and the Law in Beijing, 1937–1949." Ph.D. diss., Johns Hopkins University, 2007.

Zhao Qing. *Paoge yu tufei* [Brotherhoods and Bandits]. Tianjin: Tianjin renmin chubanshe, 1990.

Zheng Dengyun. *Zhongguo jindai jiaoyu shi* [A History of Modern Chinese Education]. Shanghai: Huadong shifan daxue chubanshe, 1994.

Index

1911 Revolution, 13; and Paoge, 123

agriculture, 46–49; and Bishan county, 46; and water supply, 46
Alitto, Guy, 13
American Methodist Episcopal Mission (AMEM), 29, 174, 175, 176, 179, 191, 268

bamboo: uses of, 49
banditry, xvi, 29, 36–38, 54, 89–91, 153; and Liu Xiang, 125; and Nationalist government, 5; and Prosperity (Xinglong chang), 125; suppression of, 11; as survival strategy, 73, 91; victims of, 89–91
bandits: and Nationalist state-making initiatives, 154
baojia system: and conscription, 111; and Nationalist state-making initiatives, 109–112; and taxation, 110
betrothals, 205, 206; early, 214
Bishan: health clinic, 188–189
Bishan county, 9, 19; and agriculture, 21, 46; history, 20–21; and periodic markets, 11, 21–22, 24; in reform era, 14
Buck, John Lossing, 13
Buddhism: and health care, 198
buffaloes, 65–66; hiring of, 65; joint ownership of, 65

candle production, 81–82
Cao Yuexian, 27, 104, 139; and the AMEM, 109; and Commander Cai (Cai Xunqing), 128; and conflict with tenants, 108–109; conflict with Zhang-Lei shi, 106–108; and elite behavior, 109; and gambling, 93–94, 105, 143; and opium, 145, 253, 256–257; profile of, 105–109; and salt cooperative, 266; and taxation, 233; wife of, 93, 214
Chen, C. C., 186–187
Chiang Kai-shek, 57, 109–110; and opium suppression, 252
childbirth, 187, 189; and health clinic, 201–202
children: adoption of, 84, 86; taken in by relatives, 84
Chongqing, 4; and "Great Rear", 5; and Paoge, 122; Prosperity's trade links with, 22; in reform era, 14; as wartime capital, 5, 153, 205
Chongqing region: and commercialization of agriculture, 46–47; as reform laboratory, 6; and rice trade, 47
cloth: trade in, 80–81
clothing, 57–58
coal hauling, 82
Commander Cai (Cai Xunqing), 34, 104, 139, 146, 259, 260, 270; and bandits, 131; and Cao Yuexian, 128; as chief patron of Prosperity, 131; and

About the Authors and Contributors

Isabel Brown Crook was born in 1915 in Chengdu, Sichuan, into a Canadian missionary family. In 1938, she graduated from Victoria College of the University of Toronto with an M.A. in child psychology and a minor in anthropology. In 1940–1941, through an introduction by James Yen, she participated in the Xinglongchang rural reconstruction project. In 1942, she married British journalist David Crook in England and did war work in London as a member of the Canadian army. At the end of the Second World War, she began a Ph.D. program in anthropology at the London School of Economics (LSE). After undertaking a study of land reform in the liberated areas of North China, Isabel broke off her studies to engage more fully with events unfolding there. In 1948, at the invitation of the Central Foreign Affairs Working Group, she participated in the founding of the Foreign Affairs School (precursor to Beijing Foreign Studies University). Isabel went on to spend her working life as a professor at Beijing Foreign Studies University—as did her husband—retiring in 1981. David and Isabel Crook coauthored *Revolution in a Chinese Village: Ten Mile Inn*, *Ten Mile Inn: Mass Movement in a Chinese Village*, and *The First Years of Yangyi Commune*. In 2008, for her contributions as anthropologist and social activist, Isabel received an honorary LL.D. degree from Victoria University, the University of Toronto.

Christina Kelley Gilmartin (1946–2012) was born in New York and raised in Connecticut. She attended Western College for Women in Ohio and first visited China in 1974, moving to Beijing from 1978 to 1983 to work as a "foreign expert" at Foreign Languages Press. She received her Ph.D. from the University of Pennsylvania in 1986. After teaching at the University of Houston, in 1989 she took up an appointment in the History Department at

Northeastern University, where at various points she directed the Women's Studies program, the History graduate program, and the Asian Studies program. Her 1995 book, *Engendering the Chinese Revolution: Radical Women, Communist Politics and Mass Movements in the 1920s*, explored the politics of "the woman question" as it played out in Communist Party ideology and personal relationships. She was the organizer of the Gender Studies Workshop at the Fairbank Center for East Asian Research at Harvard University, an associate editor of the *Journal of Asian Studies* from 2000 to 2004, and a longtime member of the editorial board of *Twentieth-Century China*. Her coedited works include *Engendering China: Women, Culture, and the State* (1994) and *Feminist Approaches to Theory and Methodology: An Interdisciplinary Reader* (1999).

Yu Xiji (1914–2006) came from Deqing in Zhejiang Province. A famous preschool educator and a founder of the China Preschool Education Society, she graduated from the Social Work Department of Shanghai Hujiang University in 1937. She then studied and worked with Ida Pruitt, founder of the Medical Social Work Department of Peking Union Medical College (PUMC). In 1938, unable to continue her work, she fled Japanese-occupied Beijing for the Southwest, where the National Christian Council of China had offered her a position as a rural service officer in Sichuan. In this capacity, she participated in a rural reconstruction project in Xinglongchang, conducting an ethnographic survey with colleague Isabel Brown (Crook). Between 1941 and 1946, Yu Xiji worked in the Social Work Department of Cheeloo Union University in Huaxi, as well as in the Shuji Kindergarten. From 1946 to 1948 she studied preschool education at the Child Study Center of the University of Toronto and received an M.A. in psychology. In June 1948, she went to the United States for further study in child welfare at the Social Work Institute of Columbia University. Returning to China in 1949, she taught in the education departments of Huaxi University and Xi'nan (Southwest) Teachers University.

Gail Hershatter (editor and compiler) is Distinguished Professor of History at the University of California, Santa Cruz. Her books include *The Workers of Tianjin, 1900–1949* (1986), *Personal Voices: Chinese Women in the 1980s* (with Emily Honig, 1988), *Dangerous Pleasures: Prostitution and Modernity in Twentieth-Century Shanghai* (1997), *Women in China's Long Twentieth Century* (2007), and *The Gender of Memory: Rural Women and China's Collective Past* (2011). She is a former president of the Association for Asian Studies (2011–2012).

Emily Honig is a professor of history at the University of California, Santa Cruz. Her books include *Sisters and Strangers: Women in the Shanghai*

Cotton Mills, 1919–1949 (1986), *Personal Voices: Chinese Women in the 1980s* (with Gail Hershatter, 1988), and *Creating Chinese Ethnicity: Subei People in Shanghai, 1850–1980* (1992).

Made in United States
Troutdale, OR
03/28/2024

18758152R00205